Revising Women

Eighteenth-Century "Women's Fiction" and Social Engagement

Edited by Paula R. Backscheider

The Johns Hopkins University Press
Baltimore and London

© 2000 The Johns Hopkins University Press
All rights reserved. Published 2000
Printed in the United States of America on acid-free paper
9 8 7 6 5 4 3 2 1

The Johns Hopkins University Press
2715 North Charles Street
Baltimore, Maryland 21218-4363
www.press.jhu.edu

Library of Congress Cataloging-in-Publication Data will be found at the end of this book.
A catalog record for this book is available from the British Library.

ISBN 0-8018-6236-1

Contents

Preface

Sometime in the early 1970s, it became clear that in literary study "everything had to be done over." The women's movement led to personal revelations and shocking statements inside the academy as well as on the streets of Paris and in the staid courtrooms of New Hampshire and Washington, D.C. Annette Kolodny, for instance, pointed out, "Simply put, we read well, and with pleasure, what we already know how to read," and reading or teaching other kinds of texts is "tiring, demanding, uncomfortable, and sometimes wholly beyond our comprehension."[1] She went on to use that insight to begin an attack on the canon as an artificial construct that is still going on and to ask that we develop "standards for evaluating the adequacy of our critical methods." New, powerful methodologies and theoretical tools have indeed been developed, refined, and routinely used, and a new generation of critics is extending Kolodny's demand, as Toni Bowers does in the *Columbia History of the English Novel:* "Rather than denigrate (or praise) amatory fictions wholesale, critics might better ask why we define 'good' literature as we do, how our assumptions about literary value still work to valorize some voices and exclude others, and how our capacities for pleasure might be augmented by respectful engagement with works we have been trained to resist or dismiss."[2]

Those of us who joined together to produce this book represent over seventy-five years of feminist scholarship. We have seen and participated in one of the most important changes in the history of literary study. In the last quarter century, women writers' works have been recovered, completely different information about the women's lives has been discovered,[3] journals such as *Women and Literature, Signs,* and *Feminist Studies* have proliferated, sophisticated essays and books on women's texts have become routine, and, as Elaine Showalter predicted, the study of literature has been transformed and even reinvigorated. As we look around us, we see that the stories of the history of the English novel have crumbled, the "author-functions" of every major eighteenth-century woman writer have been discredited, and our conceptions of everything from the interpretations of individual texts to understanding of readers and reading have been and are still being rapidly revised. Cultural studies has accelerated these trends, and we have used and contributed to its methodologies. We share a commitment to developing "thick description," to understanding literature's crucial place in hegemonic relationships and processes, to explicating culture as a site of ongoing struggles over the norms, institutions, values, and tastes that constitute communities,[4] and to studying texts and the conditions of their creation, production, and circulation.

This collection is an example of the maturity of a discipline, one beginning to produce essays such as ours with informed historicizing, detailed textual explication, sophisticated feminist theory, and dedicated attention to the interrelationships between lives and works and between everyday existence and political processes. Although our essays are revisionary contributions to the understanding of the eighteenth-century English novel, the organizing unity is our methodology, a configuration of methods both archival and theoretical that we have learned and developed hand in hand with our feminist comrades-in-arms. There is a special joy in writing essays like these—essays that bring an entire career's worth of learning and thinking to bear on women, literature, and society. In them, we enact theories of reading that "reactivate" the texts, meaning that we demonstrate how various kinds of research produce the rich contextualization and depth of understanding that reveal the story beneath, not only of the individual but of a full cultural production that had the possibility of affecting the culture that produced it and has the potential of revealing to us why we and our society are as we are. Each essay develops different ways of doing textual analysis and of considering texts as cultural expressions and active participants in social processes. Each is alert to social change, important historical events, and enduring issues and interprets in fine detail what individuals do with them. In many cases, this method exposes the often hidden relationships between politics and literature. The contextualization and interpretation in these essays is hard won, for they represent not only intense, focused research but years of patient reading and incremental increases in understanding. Perhaps we take for granted work that is the result of a lifetime's study with Daniel Defoe, Alexander Pope, or Samuel Johnson, but for women and the novel it is relatively new and is an announcement of the future of the field.

Our essays, as is typical of our work, bring together a number of things that today are often discussed separately or are even opposed or contrasted to one another. For example, for all of our attention to the constructing power of sociohistorical forces, we give steady attention to the individual creating writer, and, in a time in which novel criticism continues to divide strongly along gender lines,[5] we attempt revisionary work on men as well as women. Mitzi Myers, for example, offers an important reinterpretation of Thomas Day along with her revisionary reading of Edgeworth and her relation to patriarchy, and the two arguments are essential to each other. Paula Backscheider's "The Rise of Gender as Political Category" offers a somewhat controversial repositioning of Richardson and Defoe as re-inscribers of the patriarchy, writers who turned the direction of the novel subtly away from the issues foregrounded in women's novels. Our essays, thus, not only interrogate what has been concluded about Edgeworth, Richardson, Austen, and others but also how we read the eighteenth-century novel and its history.

Our essays represent our commitment to parallel examinations of the subjects' interrelated lives and works. Betty Rizzo describes the use of the gothic mode (and its horrible appropriateness) in autobiographical writings by Lady Mary Wortley Montagu, Mary Delany, Elizabeth Chudleigh, and others. In passing, she points out that Horace Walpole's gothic tyrant recalls a number of things, including the usurpation of a rightful ruler's power and the mistreatment of women. Mitzi Myers's ability to use details of Maria Edgeworth's life and her early, nearly unknown writings to reinterpret *Belinda* while gracefully giving us a series of fascinating conjunctions with Wollstonecraft suggests the embeddedness of *Belinda* in its time and Edgeworth's life. One of the most exciting lines of inquiry in very recent feminist work is the exploration of how women choose genres and modes to express themselves and communicate the emotional dimensions of experiences. As Jane Miller has said, women "needed the old forms because they were the forms which had told them who they were, which they had trusted and which they now had to remake."[6] Betty Rizzo's "Renegotiating the Gothic" not only points out important moments in the novels of major women writers such as Frances Burney and Sarah Scott that depend upon the gothic but also identifies the use of (and reaction to) the gothic in the personal writings of a dazzling number of women. As Miller says is common, Rizzo finds an evolving women's tradition and can trace "its obliquities and its fluctuations in relation to that other tradition which has intended to subsume or subvert it."

Each of our essays deliberately sets out to extend understanding of how the novel participates in social processes and of the ways women perceived the public sphere and stubbornly attempted to participate in it. As Mitzi

Myers points out in her essay, print "totally changed" the situation of women, and especially in fiction women writers exhibit varying degrees of hope that the world might be changed through the writing of texts. Set deeply within personal and social contexts, many of the texts we discuss go beyond critiques of the patriarchy to reveal striking ways that women were participating in Jürgen Habermas's authentic public sphere, the arena in which social conditions are negotiated and the private assumes public significance. The texts, therefore, take on new interest and importance. In the first essay, "The Novel's Gendered Space," Paula Backscheider describes the first important decade for the novel and the excitement of the writers on whom the social and personal potentials of the new novel dawned. In a special way, she argues, the early fiction writers responded to the felt need for a space that mediates "private" concerns and "public" action. With stories of courtship, love, adultery, and marriage, they not only questioned the boundaries of the public and private but tested the theories of clergymen, philosophers, and statesmen through dramatizations. They created characters who come to know themselves, to see themselves as separate from those with whom they have relationships and from their world, but they are also depicted as sharing in common situations created by the system, the state, within which they live. In "The Rise of Gender as Political Category," she points out how many "women's issues" had become tense, public discussions and how subtly and effectively the patriarchy responded.

These early writers set the course for the work the novel would do in society, and, in the last essay, "Jane Austen and the Culture of Circulating Libraries," Barbara Benedict works on a landscape in which reading is recognized as entertainment, socialization, education, and identity display and in which women writers could refer to themselves as a "literary corporation" with considerable power. Our essays reveal the complexity of the relationships between women's writing and the culture's master narratives. In doing so, they contribute to the ongoing discovery of the reasons women's writing and especially their novels produced more anxieties than any other genre. Rizzo quotes Mary Delany's first arrival at her matrimonial home: "The day was come . . . to go to a remote country, with a man I looked upon as my tyrant—my jailor." This matrimonial despotism is as shockingly apparent in *The Wrongs of Woman*, in Rizzo's presentation of others' lives—and in Backscheider's explications of the "horrors" of marriage quietly but brutally laid out by Richardson. Over and over, these eighteenth-century authors dramatize the position of the female sex even as they write about individuals whose actions still strike the reader as springing from a personality, and our essays show the strength of women's collective voices and the moving quality of their art.

These essays cover 100 years, beginning with Backscheider's treatment of the decade of the 1720s, which was absolutely dominated by women writers but is usually treated as if it belonged to Daniel Defoe alone. She sketches how this formative decade set the stage for the social engagements characteristic of the English novel and created new spaces, including a new reader position, that continue to distinguish the form. Her second essay reconsiders the commonplace that Defoe's and Richardson's women-centered novels gave important impetus to the trend toward the novel as a site for debate over formerly private issues and feelings and that both writers advanced women's interests and were even "proto-feminists." She argues that the most revolutionary aspect of these early prose fictions, and one that Defoe and later male novelists found rather fully developed, was their exploitation of liminality. She points out that these fictions were often set in liminal spaces, such as inside coaches, and habitually brought together the public and private, mediated exchange value and use value, politicized *and* privatized their subjects, dramatized the turn from a religious to a secular world, and their authors, often in liminal positions themselves—women, Nonconformists, Catholics, and socially marginal men—entered a literary marketplace in radical transition and in a vexed relationship with established publishing practices associated with cultural capital.

Like Backscheider, Rizzo finds women's fiction a place for the imagining of the ideal man of the future and the describing of the contemporary horrors of marriage. She looks in detail at a single, major mode, the gothic, in a wide range of fictional and autobiographical writings. She points out how a familiar genre can invigorate private writings and give women an economical, moving means of expression that is both personally intense and socially interpretable. The writers, in dialogue with the fact that the gothic was associated with women, evoke it for a variety of purposes. They use it to communicate settings and experiences but often go on to use it to subvert the conventional depictions of women or to infuse incidents in realistic novels with elements that reveal women's victimization and powerlessness. In nonfiction writings, women affirmed their right to rational discourse, making it a counterpoint to the gothic tyranny of experiences they described. Through subtle comparisons of Burney and Radcliffe and Burney and Scott among others, Rizzo reinterprets the gothic and argues for a continuing tradition in which they worked over episodes and characters that illuminated common problems.

The fourth essay also begins with a text usually read as a "women's novel," a "romance of the tea-table," and, like the other essays, offers revisionary repositionings and reinterpretations that unpack political codings and narrative complexities. Mitzi Myers takes as her subject Maria Edgeworth's first feminocentric adult novel and carefully explains a central presence, Thomas Day, a pioneering author for children and writer of sternly reformist political tracts, the daughter's mentor, the father's best friend, and the patriarch who obstructed her early publishing. Because he is complexly implicated in the shifty emplotments of *Belinda,* and, because so much of this often misread (and remarkably brilliant) novel derives from real facts of Day's ideological and romantic adventures, Edgeworth's hilarious undermining of patriarchal authority has not been fully appreciated. Myers unveils the real life pre-texts that shaped *Belinda* and makes us acutely aware of the polyvalent discourse produced within texts at moments of cultural and personal crisis.

The concluding essay might be titled "The Triumph of the Novel," because it makes clear how completely the form has permeated society. Barbara Benedict richly describes that world and the anxieties, lingering and completely new, that pervade it. Many of the themes in the earlier essays, such as the novel's potential as an instrument for social control *and* an expression of social aspirations, are revisited and developed as she uses Jane Austen's life and works as an illuminating case study. She demonstrates that Austen is intensely aware of the nuanced cultural capital that reading had become and that her novels are filled with, for instance, dramatizations of the way print culture shaped middle-class female identity. She, too, writes about a form of fiction identified with women: sentimental novels. Although scholars agree that sentimental fiction dominated the late eighteenth-century literary market, they have left unexplored the way the contents, procedures and physical places of circulating libraries influenced contemporary culture. She contends that, as Austen's letters and the catalogues of these libraries demonstrate, the multivolume format increasingly favored and even commissioned by the libraries' proprietors and specific lending rules changed the eighteenth-century method of reading fiction. This in turn changed the rhetoric and structure of the English novel. Benedict argues that subscription and circulating libraries like the one that Fanny joins in *Mansfield Park* nourished the conspicuous consumption of literature, as well as other commodities, and the public display of literacy by women, thereby redefining female literacy as an arena of testing and power.

Our essays increase understanding of how women participated in the most important cultural debates and literary movements at key moments in the making of the modern world. Each explicates some of the ways that literature, society, and gender dynamically interact and illustrates how contextual richness, biographical detail, textual exegesis, and feminist theory generate new knowledge. Above all, our essays make clear how much work still lies before us—deepening our understanding of individual texts, careers, and women as well as our thinking about such large issues as the history of the English novel and how texts and some of their themes are marginalized or even obliterated.

Acknowledgments

We would like to thank Elizabeth Cater, whose research and editorial skills, dedication, and good humor contributed abundantly to this collection, and Melissa Roth and Jessica R. Smith, who helped us put the book to bed.

Revising Women

1 | The Novel's Gendered Space

Paula R. Backscheider

In 1992, William B. Warner wrote, "In the last few years the question of the novel's rise in England has felt all the shocks and complications of theoretical and political critique."[1] He concluded, however, that even the most progressive of these interpretations of the history of the English novel returns "to familiar canonical texts to stage the formation of 'the' English novel." What spawned his essay and a number of others similar to it are the work and insistence of feminist critics. Students of the eighteenth-century novel *must* now ask if the early women writers should be treated as a rival or counter tradition or, apparently most difficult of all, as an integral part of the history of the "rise" of the English novel. Warner, like most other critics, is deeply enmeshed in the Great Paradigm, a belief in the "articulatory moment" during which "Richardson and Fielding founded their [different] species of writing" (584) or, as John Richetti and I have summarized it elsewhere: "In place of the faceless, formulaic repetitions of booksellers' hacks and financially distressed female authors, [Richardson and Fielding] produced individualized masterpieces of social observation and psychological depth which point the way to the great tradition of the modern novel."[2]

Since Ian Watt's *Rise of the Novel*, Defoe has received a great deal of attention, but no one since has folded him as smoothly into a history of the novel as Watt did. Indeed, even though Defoe has become an essential part of the "Dream Team" (Defoe, Richardson, Fielding, Sterne, Smollett), he is usually treated (or not) in stories of the history of the novel as an isolated phenomenon or in the ways the women writers that have come to be called the "pre-condition" of the English novel are.[3] In this chapter, I want to revisit "his" landscape, and my intention is to bring together a number of things that today are seldom juxtaposed. These include a member of the Dream Team and a group of women writers, the popular and the canonized,[4] and the increasingly gendered novel criticism of our time. To some extent I am joining a group of feminist critics who deliberately integrate concerns with textuality and with sociohistorical processes,[5] and I am self-consciously drawing upon a configuration of theorists united by their attention to language and communication and with the part literature plays in political and social processes.

The economic and political marketplace, the print world and the social milieu, in which Daniel Defoe (and a number of important women writers) published novels has come to be well understood, but the immediate literary context, specifically that of prose fiction,[6] is still inadequately mapped. There are a number of reasons that this is so. Although the field of English literature does not suffer from the split between those who study the masses and those who study the elite to the extent that history does, this split is still common and as recently as the 1980s was pervasive. Lately, a growing divide between those producing high-order feminist work and those primarily concerned with canonical texts by men has also worked against developing good thick descriptions of an author's world.[7] This divide is painfully apparent in recent discussions of the need to revise the "story" of the history of the English novel. For example, neither Homer Brown in *Institutions of the English Novel* nor Everett Zimmerman in *The Boundaries of Fiction* (both 1996) engage fiction by women, and recent books by Jane Spencer (*The Rise of the Woman Novelist*) and Ros Ballaster (*Seductive Forms*) all but ignore fiction by men.

I intend to recall persistently that the formative decade for the English novel was the 1720s, not the era of Richardson and Fielding, and that it was dominated by Penelope Aubin, Daniel Defoe, Eliza Haywood, and a few other novelists, most of whom were women. I will argue that these 1720s writers had available a unique, relatively well-developed literary form that was already characterized—in fact, distinguished—by three kinds of spaces. This form was the creation of prose fiction writers in the generations immediately before theirs, and their generation developed it, experimented with it, and left these constituting spaces for Mary Collyer, Sarah Fielding, Samuel Richardson, Charlotte Lennox, Henry Fielding, Sarah Scott, and others to recognize as the novel.[8] The early prose fictions not only created what theorists call a space, the volume within which signification, through a joining of differences, articulates itself,[9] but created a new position for readers and also existed in a special kind of space, which they both helped define and participated in.

By calling the novel a unique form, I mean that, unlike other genres, the prose fictions that provided Aubin, Haywood, and Defoe's immediate context almost universally portrayed at least two competing perspectives, two versions of "reality" and all that that implies for the interpretation of events, actions, human nature, and likely outcomes. In other literary genres, the reader confronted the text by seeking to identify the bias; after that, at issue was *how* resolution and closure would be brought about and how satisfying and useful this text would be in, for instance, stigmatizing the opposing view (Dryden's *Absalom and Achitophel*) or reenforcing the English hegemony's ideal self-image (as Steele's *Conscious Lovers* did). In these prose fictions, *initiated* readers surely received signals that allowed them to predict a "comic" or "tragic" ending (marriage or death) and, in the process of reading, to recognize "mistakes" or "triumphs" (joining or resisting rebellion) and by them predict plot lines and resolution. What was new was the readers' expectation that they would experience *competing* viewpoints, be able to debate aspects of them, and experience the text as refracted through a prism complicating but leading to judgment rather than as seen through a magnifying glass focusing a beam of light on an ideological conclusion.[10]

I need to begin by describing the prose fiction context briefly, recalling three aspects of it and highlighting some features whose significance has gone largely unrecognized. I intend to concentrate on the years when Defoe was a serious writer of fiction, which I am considering as 1713–25,[11] although it will be necessary to glance occasionally earlier and later.

The Earliest Novels

First, prose fiction was everywhere and nowhere. By that, I mean that books categorized as novels, tales, and romances made up about .15 percent—not 15 percent but 0.15 percent—of all published works until the decade of 1720.[12] But prose fiction could be found in abundance as exempla, anecdote, illustration, joke, diversion, allegory, in French and in translation, and within sermons, periodicals, tracts, conduct books, and various kinds of "histories."[13] Second, the full-length examples could be grouped into a very few categories of fictions: amorous, travel, political, and combinations of these three. In the rapidly expanding, competitive print market, success quickly bred success and added titles in clusters to a category. For instance, nearly half the prose fictions published in 1714 and 1715 claimed kinship to Delarivière Manley's blockbuster, propagandistic, scandalous memoir, *The New Atalantis* (1709).[14] Even before *The Life and Strange Surprizing Adventures of Robinson Crusoe,* a steady stream of travel books filled with "novel" adventures existed, and after *Robinson Crusoe* "surprising" became a standard part of titles. A typical example is Ambrose

Evans's *The Adventures and surprizing Deliverances of James Dubourdieu and his Wife; who were taken by Pyrates . . . Also the Adventures of Alexander Vendchurch, whose Ship's Crew rebelled against him* (1719). Its similarities to *Robinson Crusoe* and *Farther Adventures of Robinson Crusoe* are apparent from the title alone.[15] *The Adventures of James Dubourdieu, Farther Adventures, Captain Singleton,* and many other books capitalized on the current interest in pirates and the dangerous seas.

The third element to recall in the novelistic context is that English prose fiction was dominated by women; this fact is still given recognition too infrequently and the texts seldom treated as more than a rival or counter tradition.[16] According to Judith Stanton, approximately 8 of the 201 women novelists of the century began their careers in the twelve-year period of my study.[17] Counting generously, six men, including Defoe, began careers and few published as many books as the least prolific women.[18] William Chetwood, who was primarily a playwright and prompter, wrote a collection of tales and at least two travel novels; the best known, *The Voyages, Dangerous Adventures, and Imminent Escapes of Captain Richard Falconer* (1720), seems influenced by *Robinson Crusoe*. Some of these men not only wrote the kinds of fictions associated with women but integrated women's writing into their own and were identified with what has come to be seen as the prenovel or countertradition of the women writers. Charles Gildon, for example, was a close friend of Aphra Behn, collected her novels and was her first biographer.[19] Gildon was one of the earliest examples of the original, ingenious, and rather desperate people who created and inhabited the modern literary marketplace. There were few kinds of writing that he didn't try. His prose fiction included *The Post-Boy Robb'd* (1692), *The Golden Spy* (1709), and one of the most interesting responses to the South Sea Bubble, *All for the Better* (1720). His early fictions were similar to those written and collected by Behn, Paul Chamberlen, and others.

Compared to their male contemporaries other than Defoe, the women were the best, most popular, and most influential. By the 1720s they recognized prose fiction as a potentially powerful way to inform and persuade readers. They were deeply concerned with what we know as Habermas's authentic public sphere and were determined to participate in it. In fact, some of them—notably Defoe, Haywood, and Manley—periodically worked in the political, or court, public sphere as well. Most of them published nonfiction political prose, almost all of them—including Defoe—wrote scandalous memoirs, and more than half of them were arrested for seditious libel. Lawrence Klein calls attention to the fact that Habermas is "concerned to delineate an intermediary zone" and that "communicative interactions of men and women were regarded as significant not just for the moral development of members of each sex but for the public sphere as such and its goal of advancing society."[20] Here he recalls the pressing need early modern people had to attend to their community obligations and their individual consciences. Habermas's public sphere fosters discourses "suitable as vehicle for the clarification of public morals as expressed in economic and political life, in religion and in arts and letters," and I would add in the family, including courtship and marriage (Klein, 108). In a special way the early fiction writers responded to the felt need for a space that mediates "private" concerns and "public" action.[21] With stories of courtship, love, adultery, and marriage, they not only questioned the boundaries of the public and private but tested the theories of clergymen, philosophers, and statesmen through dramatizations. Part of the sustained, lively experimentation we recognize in the novels of the 1720s can be traced to their authors' engagement with the public sphere, which naturally led to the production of texts in the zone of immediate contact with contemporary lives and issues.

At this point, I want to sketch in the landscape through representative and significant publications in four selected years:

1718:   Mary Hearne, *Lover's Week;* three translations of collections of tales; new editions of John Lyly's *Euphues* and Aphra Behn's *Histories and Novels.*[22]

1719:   *The Adventures of . . . Dubourdieu; The Secret History of the Prince of the Nazarenes and Two Turks: To which is added, The Fatal Amour between a Beautiful Lady, and a Young Nobleman;*[23] Defoe's *Robinson Crusoe, Farther Adventures,* and *Memoirs of Maj. Alexander Ramkins;* Eliza Haywood, *Love in Excess;* Sarah Butler, *Milesian Tales: or, Instructive Novels for the Happy Conduct of Life;*[24] Mary Hearne, *The Female Deserters;* Jane Barker, *Exilius* and a somewhat revised *Love Intrigues;* translation of Marie-Catherine de Barneville, Comtesse d'Aulnoy's *The Prince of Carency.*

Notable in 1719 were the supremely popular *Love in Excess*[25] and *Robinson Crusoe,* books that, perhaps, opened eyes to the enormous potential readership for prose fiction. Also notable among the collections of short stories of love, many from Spain, Italy, Portugal, and France,[26] were the books with central *individual* personalities who function throughout the books and whose internal ambivalences and uncertainties are as much the problem to be resolved as the difficulties of the external situation. In other words, their characters are subjects and often exhibit agency.

1722:   Haywood, *The British Recluse;* Penelope Aubin, *The Life and Amorous Adventures of Lucinda* and *The Noble Slaves;* Defoe, *Moll Flanders, Col. Jack,* and *A Journal of the Plague Year.*

1724:   Haywood, six novels; Defoe, *Roxana;* Mary Davys, *The Reformed Coquet.*

In the 1720s the fraction of novels more than tripled to 0.51 percent of published books, and there are even embryonic signs of a consciousness of a tradition.[27] For instance, Penelope Aubin dedicates *The Life of Charlotta du Pont* (1723) to Elizabeth Singer Rowe, who was a respected poet by then; "Madame A's" *The Prude* (1724) is dedicated to Eliza Haywood. Mary Hearne's *Lover's Week* is an epistolary novel in which Amaryllis recounts her whirlwind courtship and elopement with Philander, who has the same name as the male protagonist in Behn's *Love-Letters between a Nobleman and his Sister.* Philander has a copy of *The Histories and Novels of the Late Mrs. Behn* (1696) on the table, the novel is dedicated to Manley, and Hearne closes it with a poem Edmund Curll, her bookseller, had just published on Katherine Hyde.[28]

It is here that I want to begin to discuss the three spaces that became defining elements of the form we call novel. I do not intend to posit influence but to argue the central importance of these spaces and to point out that the women writers and Defoe were actively experimenting and moving toward actualizing the social potential of the form.

The Space That Is Woman

My argument here is straightforward. Every text has a space within it for the Other, for opposition, for obstacle, for whatever occupies the position that is not expressive of the dominant. Before and during the Renaissance, writers were at least as likely to fill that space with someone of a different class, age, ethnic origin, or religion as to use a different sex and to employ various relationships, not necessarily male-female (for instance, uncle-nephew), to portray conflicts and allegiances. The women writers of the early eighteenth century, along with groups of playwrights and poets, transformed that space by filling it with women characters who made the texts what Mikhail Bakhtin has called dialogic and with heroines who came to represent a number of things to later novelists, including especially revisionary, even revolutionary ideas—tropes of and for change.[29] Roxana, Defoe's mesmerizing heroine, is a good example. Identified with Amazons, modern individualism, female sexuality, free enterprise, and the new capitalism, described as "disorienting" the market economy, and called a "scapegoat Amazon" who "secretly serves as a proxy" imperialist, she dominates a text that has consistently been recognized as embodying threatening new structures of feeling, especially expansionist capitalism with its "cultural engagement with accumulation."[30]

Then and now, "the habit of making ordinary women of central importance" is considered the most revolutionary aspect of the early novel.[31] The heroines often stood for a self-conscious posture along a continuum ranging from dissident to alienated to rebellious, and they committed resistant even murderous acts. Charles Porée objected in 1736: "What are [women] in civil society? a part of society, but a subordinate part that must receive the law and not give it . . . . Novels reverse the natural order; they make woman independent from man."[32] Also revisionary is the way the novels figured men's treatment of women into the determination of their goodness. Thereby, the novels took steps toward the redefinition of "masculine" and of the sex-gender system.

Xavière Gauthier explains that women writers "can *make audible* that which agitates within us, suffers silently in the *holes of discourse*" and agrees with Monique Wittig that "in the *gaps*" that "your masters have not been able to *fill* with their words of proprietors and possessors" can be stories to "overthrow them" (Gauthier's emphasis).[33] In "Oscillation between Power and Denial," Julia Kristeva associates this space with the literary avant-garde and traces its history back as far as Mallarmé;[34] for her it is a "force" that has not been understood/accounted for by the linguistic or ideological system.

Woman herself is a space, and feminist theorists of all kinds have recognized and elaborated on the myriad ways this is true. Like a vessel into which any fantasy can be poured, a screen on which any image can be projected, and, in Henry James's words, "a sheet of blank paper" on which anything can be written, available as fetish, trope, trophy, and symbol, woman can stand for whatever is needed. As Hélène Cixous says, to try to speak of "woman" is to be "trapped within an ideological theater where the proliferation of representations, images, reflections, myths, identifications, transform, deform, constantly change everyone's Imaginary and invalidate in advance any conceptualization."[35] Experiencing themselves as text, artifact, and subject, early women writers filled the space with a new kind of woman character. Whether we say with American feminists that women habitually experience themselves from within and without—they watch themselves being watched even as they are subjects—or with the French feminists that woman experiences herself as a "mirror invested by the (masculine) 'subject' to reflect himself," "marked phallicly," "the locus of a more or less competitive exchange" between men and also "fragmentarily, in the little-structured margins of a dominant ideology," we are recognizing the same experience.[36] A good example is Manley's *Rivella*. Throughout the text, her body is in play. Charged with seditious libel, she is forced by the court to "expose" herself—to appear several times before the bench and "walk cross the Court . . . with her three Attendants, the *Printer* and both the *Publishers*."[37] The interrogation and appearance scenes are highly similar to earlier episodes in the narrative in which she is not believed, is inspected and treated as if on display. Manley no less than Barker exposes and satirizes society's assignment of women's relation to language. When pressed, Rivella insists that what she "said must be *Inspiration*" (113). Taking ironic refuge in lack of agency and rational control, Rivella brings the questioning to an end but is incarcerated, thus silenced.[38]

These fictions by women were filled with stories of intense personal struggles by and between the sexes and featured representations of heroines who were simultaneously object and subject. They attempted to present two (or more) compelling points of view and, even more significant, differing interpretations of events and "reality."[39] They often portrayed these as competing, irreconcilable, or even incomprehensible to the opposing view. Although the kinds of generational conflict long familiar on the stage often complicated the plot and the lovers had different interests (male freedom vs. female security, for example), strong binary opposition between young lovers animated these texts in different, more profound ways. In addition to gender, class was often a significant part of the characters' compositions, as it was not in drama. Above all, the languages operative in the culture became crucial factors. More than manners, social rituals, and a circle's mores, the prose fictions brought groups, interests, and the discourses of power into juxtapositions that exposed competition, collaboration, and other complex relationships.

These novels orchestrate genres and create what Bakhtin called "ambivalent words," words that join two sign systems creating a "hidden interior polemic."[40] In other words, as a character speaks another discourse is apprehended. This other discourse distorts and complicates the character's speech, sometimes contradicting, always relativizing it. In César du Marsais's words, ambivalent words are "louche" (cross-eyed): "for just as cross-eyed people seem to be looking in one direction while they look in another, so in cross-eyed constructions, the words seem to have a certain relation to each other, while they in fact have another."[41] When Robinson Crusoe uses "improvement," he is as likely to be speaking of his spiritual life as his material industry,[42] and the reader must sort out what is meant but soon (as numerous critics have) comes to hear both discourses in varying strengths each time. Regardless of their drastic economic necessities or the bizarre nature of their situations, Mary Davys's Merry Wanderer and Defoe's Moll Flanders and Roxana encode the platitudes and cultural judgments attached to women's conduct in speeches that reveal impossibilities and contradictions.[43] Their relationships, therefore, could be used to lay bare the sex-gender system and also the operation of class in the actions and assumed privileges of individuals. We apprehend the relational and the individual identity and understand that desire lies between, in an eloquent silence. In many cases, communication occurs between two spaces, "that of representation *by* language, and that of experience *in* language."[44] And, significantly, the authors often positioned themselves throughout the narrative to participate in the public sphere.[45]

Prose fiction, of course, was incorporating many familiar representations of the Other—Aubin's and Davys's fictions have menacing, dark-skinned, "exotic" characters, for instance—but there is a major difference: readers of prose fiction are presented with pairs of English characters of the same generation and religion in which one will be developed into a depiction of a revisionary viewpoint and, therefore, will be a threat to the dominant ideology, whether it be that of political-economic hierarchy, of the sex-gender system, or of "natural" human behavior. If the Other of the dramatic or poetic texts occupied a lead role, that character would usually be disposed of, eliminated, or revealed to be Not-Other. In the prose fictions, however, the organizing conflict was sustained by the lovers and the central point of view was frequently housed in the Other, who was not always silenced or appropriated in the resolution—if resolution was given.

This is a crucial point: The narrative point of view was that of the Other. Since the dominant social, genre-privileged point of view is indeed dominant (familiar, expected), writers had to devote a large proportion of narrative and plot space to the rival perspective if it were to be comprehended or even recognized. Even if the dominant perspective was merely alluded to or sketched in rather than fully articulated, the space in the narrative remained large because it had been so effectively transmitted and, therefore, absorbed into the consciousness of readers. In these texts, it was, however, cast into the role of competing for approval, and therefore the carriers of it, its "heroes," were tested and so was their discourse.[46] Simultaneously, this rival perspective, and its carriers and their discourse, were tested and the validity of the position in which the author of the text had cast them judged.[47] In startling moments, the hero, even an apparently admirable one, sometimes became Other. Even if the text strengthened the status quo, its tendency to give the central or sustained major voice to the non-dominant position made the novel subversive and created a space for the definition and development of a distinctively English Other;[48] indeed, this Other was often a male of the aristocracy or gentry made alien and, especially later, a father.

Thus, fiction asked those in that ruling position to accept telling or authoritative judgments about them and their ways of governing the family and society from those "below" them, those they had legislated to be silent. They insisted on the existence and importance of other subjectivities. Perhaps it should be no surprise that men and women who had grown up in a time when their religious and political groups had been officially discriminated against and silenced, as Defoe's and Rowe's had been,[49] would produce a number of writers critical of the establishment. In their hands, prose fiction took up the infrastructure of society and came to be experienced as concerned with immediate contemporary life and present issues.[50] Diverse as they were, all had grown up in a time of rapid change when the "right" religion today could make one the object of suspicion or even persecution the next.[51] By 1719, their technique of making the narrative viewpoint that of the Other was familiar, even conventional, and it provided the space that shaped what has come to be known as the mainline English novel.

Even in the earliest of these fictions, Barker's *Love Intrigues* and Manley's *Rivella*, these characteristics are apparent, especially the ability to demonstrate how things classified "private" were in fact matters of public scrutiny and concern and how absolutely fluid and porous are the boundaries between spheres. Barker's Galesia, the heroine of *Love Intrigues,* is the narrator and consistently describes her interior life and her public performances. Anxious, confused, and secretly unhappy, she displays "pretended Indifference,"[52] teasing impertinency, and even a series of costumes symbolic of marginally acceptable, mildly eccentric roles for women. She is often silent in public and keeps silence about her feelings with her family and Bosvil, the man she loves. She tries to signal her desire to marry him when given the opportunity with "broken Words" (32, 37) and body language, which she considers the appropriate feminine language of love. Thus Barker represents how social mores silence women, deny them language and, therefore, agency. At one point, Galesia says, "I kept my Words close Prisoners, till they should be set at Liberty by the Desire of his Father, or the Command of mine, or at least convey'd into the Mouth of my prudent Mother" (34). The mother, then, is given speech by the fathers, and Barker's words startlingly bring to mind Jacques Lacan's Name-of-the-Father and his theory that it reveals the structure of law, desire, gender, and difference within a specific culture.

Barker represents the space that is woman's silence and particular kind of silencing. In this text, the hero is an enigma; Bosvil's conduct, presented as contradictory and misleading by the narrator, gives us no access to his interior—the part of Galesia about which we know most. Barker has other characters quote Bosvil, but she never represents Galesia doing more than summarizing what she takes to be Bosvil's message. By excluding direct speech, she makes Bosvil unreadable, the textual Other, but the fact that *he* must declare his intentions to the fathers emphasizes his agency, his position as the carrier of the dominant, and, in turn, that Galesia is exchange value.[53] The more silent he seems, the larger his presence and power loom. Pierre Macherey notes that "We always eventually find, at the edge of the text, the language of ideology, momentarily hidden, but eloquent by its very absence" (60). As the narrative continues, Bosvil's silent eloquence, an ellipsis that creates unusual semantic fullness,[54] pushes Galesia into the margins, into bizarre behavior, and into a greater discrepancy between her exterior and interior life. Barker forces the reader to notice, to investigate the silence, for "it is the silence that is doing the speaking," exercising power and revealing the limits of Galesia's possibilities (Macherey, 86).

These early fictions often manage to charge the space that is woman and the space that is opposition in literary texts with political meanings. On the simplest level, they tend to position themselves on an already politicized field, thereby turning apparently innocuous episodes into socially symbolic novelistic discourse. Many locate themselves with political publication as early as the title pages. In *The Female Deserters*, Mary Hearne narrates the story of Isabella, whose family has been ruined by supporting King James II. Barker sets her fiction in St. Germain's Garden, which every reader would associate with James II's French refuge. Manley places her narrative in the Somerset-House Garden, the garden of the ancient palace where Cromwell's body lay in state and, more pertinently, where Queens Henrietta Maria and Catherine of Braganza lived, and promises "Secret Memoirs and Characters of several considerable Persons." The acerbic Manley writes that "the better Part of the Estate [of Rivella's father] was ruin'd in the Civil War by adhering to the *Royal Family*, without ever being repair'd, or scarce taken Notice of, at the Restoration" (14), and Barker's characters discuss "what they had to hope or fear from the Success, or Overthrow of either or both Parties."[55]

On another level, what we might call today the personal is politicized. At issue in all three Galesia texts is whether it is, as her mother says, Galesia's duty and "business" to marry.[56] If she does not carry out her social, community function, her life must be justified on other grounds, and that appears a more difficult question for her than for Manley, who opens her narrative by positioning Rivella between the poles of Madame Dacier and the Duchess of Mazarine. Galesia's fantasies in the periods when her hopes of marriage to Bosvil wane are of roles accepted as useful in her culture: morally and aesthetically pleasing poet with Katherine Phillips, "the Matchless Orinda," as the model; a Lady Bountiful with knowledge of healthful remedies;[57] and household manager.[58]

Manley's allusions are more provocative. Anne LeFèvre Dacier, whose *Les Poésies d'Anacréon et de Sapho* (1681) and the recently published *Iliad* (1711; English translation 1712) had made her one of the most respected Hellenists of her time, was one of the women discussed for membership in the Académie Française. A country girl who had left her first, much older husband, returned home, and then moved to Paris with a few of her father's books, became the editor of five volumes of the prestigious Delphin classics series, married the classicist André Dacier, and was granted an annual stipend from the king; she was occasionally satirized for her learning and for her tenacious if tactful requests for payment owed her for contracted work.[59] She, like Manley, was a thoroughly professional woman writer in the public sphere. Hortense de Mancini, duchess of Mazarine, came from an illustrious French family, one in which the ceiling painting in the central gallery of her father's palace portrayed Apollo surrounded by French intellectual women depicted as the muses.[60] She had run away from her allegedly abusive husband, become the mistress of King Charles II, and until her death in 1699 presided over a notoriously fashionable combination salon and gambling house.[61] In a forthcoming book, Frances Harris argues that women of this class and generation were reared for and took for granted the possibility that they could have a political career, employment, in the inner circles of the court.[62] Manley, as personal attendant for about eighteen months beginning in 1693 to Barbara Villiers, the duchess of Cleveland and another of Charles II's mistresses, was part of this mind set (in fact, she claimed that she had expected to be one of Queen Mary of Modena's Maids of Honor). Several incidents in *Rivella* depict the clandestine influence such women wield and how they use friends and male relations and their friends.[63] In giving these two women as those most appropriate to whom to compare Rivella and most useful in helping the reader "see" Rivella, Manley conjures up intelligence, education, the power to fascinate without great physical beauty, mysterious allure, presence, and influence in a glittering public sphere.

Through the Somerset House garden Manley's text invokes a woman's tradition rich in cultural and political capital. Anne of Denmark had commissioned spectacular masques by Inigo Jones and Ben Jonson at Somerset House in the early seventeenth century; Charles I gave it to Henrietta Maria, patroness of Walter Montagu and Edward Sackville, earl of Dorset, and she lived there before and after the Civil War; after Charles II's death, Queen Catherine of Braganza made it her home, and the first Italian opera performed in England was staged there. Thus, Manley allies herself with cultured queens and uses the artistic association of Somerset House to make the kinds of statements about herself in English letters that Behn had made in *Oroonoko*. *Rivella* suggests how self-conscious Manley was and underrated she is as a writer.

References to Galesia's loyalty to King Charles II and to the government become part of an ideological framework that helps Barker construct a character who exists in both the public and private spheres. In the revenge fantasy filled with "ambivalent words" at the center of *Love Intrigues*, Galesia imagines killing Bosvil with a rapier, delighted "to see the Blood pour out of his false Heart," and is confident that "our Sex will . . . keep an Annual Festival, on which a Criminal like him is executed: the Example perhaps will deter others, and secure many [women from harm]" (43–44). This passage repeats the culture's belief about public executions and again, this time in a negative example, Galesia casts herself in a role beneficial to her community. In contrast, Manley's text represents and re-interprets very public, historical actions. Among many other examples Rivella is described as saying that she was performing a patriotic action with pride in attempting to discredit "a *Faction* who were busy to enslave their Sovereign, and overturn the Constitution" when she published the *New Atalantis* (109).

Earlier, Manley had cast herself as Delia in the *New Atalantis* and produced another autobiographical narrative. Barker's and Manley's fictions (and Behn's before them) occasionally jolt modern readers, because their authors strikingly and in a variety of ways insert themselves in their texts. Rather than an autobiographical or an inartistic slip, I see this characteristic as a deliberate strategy and an important, evolutionary step in the history of the English novel.[64] Although these texts put into public discussion a range of women's experiences not previously represented, the effect was to present women as vitally concerned with the public sphere and also to heighten awareness of women's shared, general condition.[65] They also exploit the feeling that women are outside of history, outside and yet permeating sites of hegemonic negotiation (influencing in the bedroom and at the dinner table, for instance). When Defoe uses Moll Flanders and Roxana and deliberately and painstakingly makes Captain Singleton and Colonel Jack men without countries, he gains the same advantages.

With Nancy Miller I would argue that women's texts reveal the "sometimes brutal traces of the culture of gender; the inscriptions of its political structures."[66] These early fictions do this cultural work, and they bring together not only the interpenetrations of the public and private spheres but often demonstrate the influence each domain has on the other.[67] Manley's fictions, for instance, were effective in discrediting the Marlborough circle because they evoked an image of the kinds of incestuous, closed power peddling and decision making that Jürgen Habermas has described as the *ancien régime* court public sphere. Her power was in the ability to make persuasive a government in which influence and advancement come from private interests, even sexual ones, rather than from alliances based on respect and concern for the commonweal.

Defoe shared this ability to make vivid the inscriptions of gender, power, and political structure. Moll Flanders's first romance is a detailed example of the courtship stories told in the early English novel by women. The older brother is speaking the languages of his position and the social order, and he expects her to understand, or at least to conform when initiated.[68] Much of their conversation comes to be about interpretation; she, for instance, insists they are married, and he says he will "be as good as a Husband to you." They often ask each other what the other means, surprise each other, and describe some statements as "mysteries."[69] Moll's reality is not his, and that hers is about such concrete facts as their physical intercourse, her pregnancy, his vows, and the intractability of her feelings for him as a whole person whose conversation, company, and body she enjoys does not matter.

Social class is all that matters, and relational identity is presented by Defoe here and elsewhere as a crippling obstacle to individual identity and aspirations.[70] Indeed, Defoe seems to suggest that it is an obstacle to what might be called entitlement. Unlike Smollett's "Miss Hatchway" in *Peregrine Pickle*, Moll's (and Roxana's) conduct reveals no "irrepressible class signature."[71] Middle-class girls and heiresses as well as poor girls are seduced, and Moll is not presented as the ungrammatical, babbling, basically crude character of later novels or as the lusty, lascivious servant girl of low comedy. By natural capacity and cultivated talent, Moll has proven herself equal or superior to the older brother's sisters, and her later career confirms the pattern of impersonating the middle class, achieving all its tokens and marks but papers, and then being ejected. In a shrewd observation, David Oakleaf points out that "Defoe's heroines are no more predatory than, say, the schemers in Congreve's *Way of the World,* but Congreve's plotters . . . are fixed by the genealogical and financial certainties symbolized by the black box containing the definitive contracts."[72]

In this socially symbolic episode, the older brother treats the younger almost as ruthlessly as he does Moll. Robin's feelings and future simply do not matter, and he can be deceived and exploited without guilt or repercussions. The sustained attack in the literature of the period on the aristocratic male is extended to those in other classes, specifically the gentry and successful commercial men, who adopt the attitude that family and prosperity put them above the law. In *Love-Letters between a Nobleman and his Sister,* Behn had written that the world of love mattered more than politics. Although she comes closer to offering a competing ideology to the dominant patriarchal one than most of the next generation of novelists including Barker, she initiates an important strain in the novel that the others follow by exposing the contradictions and hypocrisies in society or by suggesting the need for a competing ideology in the space which is gendered female. Manley, Defoe, Haywood, and a few other writers, however, spin out a competing domain in great detail, and, in doing so, markedly reveal the power structures and their implications in the dominant.

The Reader's Space

My second observation is equally straightforward: The prose fictions of this period created a new space for the reader and cast that reader as judge of characters and plot structures in a revolutionary way. Behn, Manley, Aubin, Haywood, and Davys were all playwrights and understood the role of consumer as judge. But judge of a work as *parole* in a genre and of its performance, as dramatic prologues and epilogues conventionally invited, is quite different from the demands put on readers who were charged with recognizing characters and plots as socially symbolic acts.[73] In other words, more than for most plays, the text is apprehended as a quite direct enactment of the social that simultaneously makes visual historical formations, articulates contradictions and unresolved problems in a community, gives access to the secret dreams, shames, and hatreds alive in the class and sex-gender systems, and encourages the reader to interrogate the culture.[74]

Because novels more often leave texts open and even invite the reader to judge the narrator as well as the episodes and characters, both reader position and author stance become socially symbolic acts.

Aphra Behn's *Oroonoko* is a familiar example of an engagement of the reader, who is asked not only to share the narrator's judgments but to hear the narrator's case for her own helplessness and judge her actions. Barker's fiction ends with Galesia turning to Lucasia, her auditor and "reader," with the statement, "how far I stand justify'd or condemn'd in your Thoughts, I know not" (70). Lucasia gives a reflective answer. Haywood's *City Jilt* (1726) says that "the *untempted* Fair, are little capable of judging her Distress"[75] but weaves the story so that all can judge. The French romances were full of contests in which a group of friends decided, for instance, who in a narrated tale was the most miserable, most virtuous, or most wronged, and surviving letters of the period record that English readers engaged in consideration of such points in conversations and letters.[76] It became a convention in the novel to turn to the reader and invite such evaluative discussions. Frances Brooke, one of the best-educated women writers, begins the preface to the second edition of *The Excursion* (1785) with an appeal to her readers, whom she calls an "unprejudiced bar": "'I APPEAL TO THE PEOPLE,' was the celebrated form in which a citizen of ancient Rome refused his acquiescence in any sentence of which he felt the injustice. . . . I find myself irresistibly impelled to use the same form . . ." Richardson laboriously revised *Clarissa* repeatedly in efforts to shape the judgments of his readers, and Fielding teased and competed with his as he gradually revealed, for instance, Allworthy's limitations and Blifil's perfidy.

The more dialogic the text, the more the reader is cast in the space of the judge and feels in the presence of a trial. Bakhtin notes that in the baroque novel, "The idea of trial organizes the material throughout, at a deep and sustained level."[77] He speaks of the hero and the hero's discourse, and these elements are indeed made inseparable and are tested in these texts. The statement, however, could be made of Restoration drama as well, and the proviso scene and expanded parts for women in a variety of kinds of plays had added the testing of the heroine and her discourse. The statement, too, could be used to describe most of the major, late poems of Alexander Pope, in which he pits his poetic voice and persona against the satiric worlds he creates, worlds overpopulated by the papers and printed pages (not words) of Grub Street hacks and political hirelings.

These fictional texts put a great deal more than the hero and heroine and their discourses on trial, however, and, generally, the texts do not become monoglossic as does, for instance, Part I of Aphra Behn's *Love Letters between a Nobleman and His Sister.* Behn's novel, in fact, provides an arche-typal scene. Sylvia writes to Philander, "all that I feared . . . is fallen upon me: I have been arraigned, and convicted, three judges, severe as the three infernal ones, sat in condemnation on me, a father, a mother, and a sis-ter."[78] Defoe's characters repeatedly call on readers to make judgments.[79] After Moll discovers that she is married to her brother, she pleads, "I leave it to any Man to judge what Difficulties presented to my view," and after her conviction, she says, "It must be the Work of every sober Reader to make just Reflections . . . as their own Circumstances may direct."[80] Richardson's great scene with Clarissa ringed by her angry family is very much in the tradition, and Joseph Highmore selected it to paint as one of the illustrations of key scenes.[81] In order to make them artistically satisfy-ing, their authors had to organize the diverse voices and heteroglossia into a structured, satisfying system, and the reader position is factored into key scenes.[82]

In fact, the establishment of the experience that the narrative is speaking directly to the reader, who knows more than any character, contributes to the experience of interiority and intimacy that characterizes so many nov-els and is one of the form's distinguishing, persuasive possibilities. Because texts have been left open and resolutions indeterminate, generations of readers can reaccentuate the texts, thereby foregrounding those parts that speak to their age, and are forced to judge stories by ethical and political standards and then to evaluate those standards anew. It is bad history, or at least ahistorical, to treat *Oroonoko* as a slave narrative,[83] and yet Southerne's dramatic adaptation of it caused riots in the slaving city of Liverpool years after its publication and performances were prohibited,[84] and, in the wake of the American Civil Rights movement, the book has found new readers and a place in the classroom on this basis.

Readers are always to some extent unpredictable free agents, and au-thors, by demanding that readers be the bridge between text and life, thereby move the text into an authentic public sphere; thus historical reaccentuations are inevitable. Women protagonists intensify this effect because they have what Catherine Clément has called "dangerous sym-bolic mobility,"[85] and these texts, mostly by women and filled with women as speaking subjects, exhibit the potential for subversive symbolic tex-tuality. Plato observed that Woman "provides a ground for all that can come into being . . . precisely that which makes us dream."[86] In the cultural contradictions that women's stories reveal, language sometimes fails but the author creates a gap that forces judgment even as it resists interpreta-tion.[87] When a space is most apparent and seems an abyss (or "excess"), as it is between the two women's stories in *The British Recluse* or between the two parts of Elizabeth Inchbald's *Simple Story,* the way the space in the novel and the reader's novelistic space work together becomes clear. The reader of *Moll Flanders* experiences just such an abyss upon reflecting on the "transition" to Moll's criminal career,[88] and the results are unsettling as questions arise about human nature and the roots of evil and as suspicions grow about the similarities among marriage, crime, and trade. What we do not understand about Moll's psyche constitutes us as participants in the text; in other words, the gap in the text must be filled by reflection or even engagement. Such spaces invite readers to go beyond discussion of alternatives and contests to test themselves. Moll Flanders, for instance, frequently invites the reader to confess to similar criminal inclinations,[89] and the later novel of sensibility overtly invited the reader to measure personal responses.

The Liminal Space

The most revolutionary aspect of these early prose fictions, and one that Defoe and later male novelists found rather fully developed, was their exploitation of liminality. These fictions were bringing together the public and private, mediating exchange value and use value,[90] politicizing *and* privatizing their subjects, dramatizing the turn from a religious to a secular world,[91] and their authors—women, Nonconformists, Catholics, and socially marginal men—entered a literary marketplace in radical transition and in a vexed relationship with established publishing practices associated with cultural capital.[92] They and their texts occupied a liminal space. By liminal space, I mean one on the boundary between two states of consciousness that partakes of both realms in a binary system, one in which new knowledge is produced and "forms of symbolic action . . . in which all previous standards and models are subjected to criticism, and fresh new ways of . . . interpreting experience are formulated."[93] Liminal spaces conform to the rules, assumptions, and practices of neither sphere and are places of discovery and change.

Often associated with maturity and initiation rites in anthropological literature, liminal spaces in the best novels go beyond that to form a special province of world discovering and problem solving and are not usually created to bring about a familiar, determinate, socially sanctioned state of being. Already open to political allusions, positioning, and even purpose, these fictions became increasingly permeated with morality. Any historian would say that in that time the religious was the political, and theorists as different as Christopher Hill and Fredric Jameson have pointed out that the controlling, organizing trope of the era was religion.[94] "Morality," in fact, poured into the vessel that was the novel from two sources. One was religion, and the most published form of writing was religious material. The other was the long tradition of civic humanism and the active discussion of the relationship between public and private conduct and "virtue." Both used the metaphor of the family as microcosm endlessly.

The foundation, therefore, was firmly laid for the novel to move into a liminal space, one permeated through and through by religious, political, social, and personal concerns. This fact also laid the groundwork for the novel to become one of the constitutive elements in Jürgen Habermas's authentic public sphere with its critical dependence upon a literary public sphere.[95] Habermas himself remarks that "the two forms of public sphere [political and authentic] blended with each other in a peculiar fashion" and that the family, "the intimate sphere," "was profoundly caught up in the requirements of the market," which "we call 'private.' "[96] No wonder his authentic public sphere is often described as "unstable," "fictitious," and "ambiguous," and scholars have labored to make this positive. These early fictions, including the less overtly political ones, took advantage of this major, unrecognized constituting characteristic of Habermas's authentic public sphere: of necessity it includes a liminal space. Liminal space provides exactly what Dena Goodman recognizes, "It was the ambiguity of this new sphere of activity that gave it the kind of discursive freedom it had."[97] This discursive freedom is the novel form's great strength and explains, among other things, how a "domestic novel" such as *Clarissa* can be permeated with the social and political.

It is important to remember that the authentic public sphere arises from the private, not the public, sphere, from the realm of production and reproduction.[98] In this new space, public opinion was formed, not only by Habermas's coffeehouse *habitués* but also by newly deliberative groups. Among these new groups were women, who, during and immediately after the Civil War, had gained access to the public sphere and become increasingly adept at using many of the printed forms believed to shape public opinion.[99] The generation of men and women who had seen or experienced the personal consequences of public actions, the loss of employment, estates, opportunities, and legal rights including inheritance in the aftermath of the Civil War, the Restoration, and the so-called Glorious Revolution, were unlikely to think in terms of older conceptions of separate private and public spheres.[100] For them, the personal was the political, and many of them draw upon and self-consciously operate in the public and private spheres simultaneously.

The more we work with the prose fictions of these decades, the more conscious we are of the tensile strength of the union of public and private and the novel's liminal position. Elizabeth Singer Rowe's *Friendship in Death: Letters from the Dead to the Living* (1728) surely confounds the modern reader, and yet these qualities are present in her "pious" work.[101] In Letter 3, she colors the mother's grief for her son with lamentations for the loss of an entailed estate and in other places condemns the values of the aristocratic Church of England characters.[102] Her text, not just located between public and private, property law and maternal loss, but between Heaven and earth, is taking part in the active experimentation of the ways the novel could be moral propaganda, access to the hearts and minds of the culture, and, therefore, an instrument of change.[103] Penelope Aubin had celebrated Defoe's work on just these grounds; in the preface to *The Strange Adventures of the Count de Vinevil,* she remarked that he had discovered a new way to teach morality at a time when "Religious Treatises grow mouldy on the Booksellers Shelves in the Back-Shops."

By recognizing the novel as liminal space, we can understand the form and its "work" in society better, open new lines of critical exploration, and even refine Habermas's explanation of the significance of print to the formation of the authentic public sphere. Habermas describes a felt need for a space that mediates "private" concern and "public" action,[104] and the novel both models it and provides it. The dialogic nature of the novel and the particular position of the reader release the potential of literature to be a site for the clarification of identity and of public morals as expressed in economic, legal, medical, political, and religious life. As readers move into the text, they experience the liminality of an initiation—where identity and public morals are the heart of the ritual.

Characters and readers are shown to be *both* individual and part of groups. The main characters come to know themselves, to see themselves as separate from those with whom they have relationships and from their world, but they are also depicted as sharing in common situations created by the system, the state, within which they live. As Lincoln Faller points out, the proliferation of points of view is typical of all of Defoe's novels and, in *Col. Jack,* where it is especially prominent, Jack "becomes all the more substantial, complex, and interesting because of the 'otherness' readers are led to sense around him. The more alert one grows to Jack's particular subjectivity, the more aware one becomes that the world . . . is composed of subjectivities."[105] And yet, Jack believes the plantation master is speaking of his individual crimes, and he is certainly depicted as being the product and victim of common situations.

To a large extent, the development of the English novel is the history of the development of the psychological novel and, as John Richetti has pointed out, of the means of constructing social commentary driven by moral judgment, and even in these early fictions this gravitation and that toward the novel's function in identity clarification are obvious. The commonality of the situation of deliberative groups, especially women, are reinforced at the same time that characters gradually discover how individual they are, how their perceptions, sensibilities, and interests are painfully different from the people they love and even identify with. In the detailed descriptions of the lovers' emotions, the subtle changes and the movement from one shade of feeling to the next, the subject comes to know herself and to see herself as separate from the beloved and, often, her community or "the world." The differences are emphasized. As Moll Flanders discovers that the older brother does not want what she thought they both wanted, does not feel what she thought they felt, she experiences both her lonely individualism and her sex's and class's collective situation.

Part of the establishment of novelistic space as a liminal space can be traced to early writers' obsessions with courtship and with referential detail. Courtship is a liminal space—it is between childhood and adulthood, between dependency and responsibility, between autonomy and relationship, and invested with private and public concerns. Intimacy and personal happiness are no less issues than economics and the families' symbolic capital. Everyone is making judgments, and the discourses and realities of the major characters are being tested. By seeing courtship as a socially symbolic space, we are reminded that a plurality of authentic public spaces exist at any time, emerging around contested issues or configurations of issues. Drawn to questions of authority, property, and a new sense of public investment in private economic interests as well as to new concerns about the nature and rights of women, readers could find immediate social commentary as well as the "warm writing" of Richetti's fantasy machines.[106]

The time of courtship could be made into a subversive space. Women writers throughout the century remarked that it was the single moment in a woman's life when she had power, and it was also the time in which identities were clarified and hopes for the future formulated. As Joan DeJean has pointed out, early French fiction was often controversial because women rejected marriage or accepted it only on their own terms. In this fictional space, women characters (and occasionally men) often had a speech or two that DeJean calls "*prise de parole*" and in the theatre would be called "points," moments of holding center stage and "exploding" into a special vitality and power; at these times they often announce themselves in "'radical upheavals' economically and politically," even metaphysically. Here, in Ellen Donkin's words, they "created a space in which women, not Woman, could be heard." These speeches often laid out the condition of women's lives or envisioned a new situation for women.[107] Roxana's "feminist" speeches to the Dutch merchant and to Robert Clayton are examples. Her speeches bring together her experiences as a wife, mistress, and wanderer, a series of adventures that portray her as perpetually forced to define herself against others and, significantly, socially named positions. She sees her in-laws' stable homes as though through a window—in fact, she is often portrayed as looking through windows—and moves into and out of roles and situations without ever belonging to them. The landlord calls her wife, and she is wife and not wife to him until he is killed; Jack joins various communities of thieves but returns loot—thief and not thief, part of an underworld and yet an individual sensibility. "Defoe's criminals never quite get absorbed into the social; but then neither do they ever seem so incoherent and strange as to stand insolubly beyond it. Such an odd and shifting liminality makes them both fascinating and provoking, almost scandalous in their anomaly," Lincoln Faller muses.[108]

The often lampooned particularity of the novel began in this period, too: "How to escape from the besotting particularity of fiction?" Robert Louis Stevenson asked, "'Roland approached the house; it has a green door and window-blinds; and there was a scraper on the upper step.' To hell with Roland and the scraper." These early writers, however, were linking the details and manners of everyday life to the systems of power operative in the culture as a self-conscious strategy. They made clear that they understood that detail is capital and cultural capital. Thus, their fictions become both world discovering and problem solving. Fiction presented itself as both a production of reality and as a reproduction of reality, the object of the writer's orientation and oriented toward its object,[109] and, therefore, it occupied both a liminal and a mediational space. It may be true that people in marginal positions, as these authors were, are fascinated by the details of the lives of the more fortunate and of the conduct and processes that lead to political, economic and cultural power. By extension, these texts would attract an audience of marginal and socially mobile people who, like the authors, are mastering details and systems. Defoe has been recognized as understanding and commodifying contemporary "interest in how to achieve a practical mastery of a specific ensemble of ethical techniques—a particular 'practice of the self'—and to make the conduct of the self into an object of ethical attention and work."[110]

Certainly these novels record these things, but they also use the same details to reveal how arbitrary and artificial social hierarchy is. Impersonation and disguise, cross-sex "passing,"[111] manipulation of social and moral identity are everywhere in these fictions: Fantomina, Moll, Roxana, Sylvia in *Luck at Last,* Amoranda in *The Reformed Coquet,* and even Robinson Crusoe as he assumes titles, voices, and physical positions with each new arrival on his island. Sex, gender, class, authority, ethnicity prove not to be natural or inevitable. The prevalent use of clothing and disguise by all the writers, including Defoe, suggests what a preoccupation the instability of categories often treated as natural was. Fantomina is but an extreme example of Haywood's protean characters, and even Mary Davys's characters defy sex and age with their disguises. In *The Reformed Coquet,* Berinthus disguises himself as a woman in order to kidnap Amoranda, and the young and vigorous Alanthus passes through most of the novel as the elderly, somewhat meddling Formator. The disguises double and triple. At one point Amoranda plans to thwart the plans of her foppish suitors Callid and Froth by dressing her footmen as herself and her maid; the already-camouflaged Alanthus talks Amoranda into allowing him to impersonate her and enjoys beating the fops. Arentia, a childhood friend, brings Berinthus disguised as Berintha to visit and they trick Amoranda into a barge outing. He throws off his disguise and abducts her, but Alanthus disguised as a "gentle Stranger" appears. "I presume, Madam, you are some self-willed, head-strong Lady, who, resolved to follow your own Inventions, have left the Care of a tender Father to ramble with you know not who," he chides, and increases the comic suspense by continuing, "I am sorry for you, but I am no Knight-Errant . . . I wish you a good Deliverance." Moll Flanders tells us that she "generally" "took up new Figures, and contriv'd to appear in new Shapes every time I went abroad" (262), and several of her escapes depend upon the perception of her class. Descriptions of Defoe's characters' clothes, as of Haywood's, are filled with class markers, and the authors take obvious pleasure in exploiting their symbolic value. Haywood has characters adapt their language to class: Beauplaisir "perceiving she had a Turn of Wit, and a genteel Manner . . . chang'd the Form of his Conversation."[112] Haywood puts a rake in the now-trendy horse broker's coat and has the lascivious Fantomina wear a stylish jockey's coat; Defoe locates Roxana in a moment in fashion: "more shap'd to the Body, than we wear them since, showing the Body in its true Shape . . . the stuff a *French Damask,* very rich."[113]

Defoe's novels, like those of the women writers, are filled with initiation episodes that lay bare the deep structures and power relationships within Western culture. When Moll enters Mother Midnight's community and Roxana enters the Quakers', they leave the familiar social order and enter into new systems. Every contact that Moll Flanders has with the law reinforces the sense that it is the possession of the rich and reveals contradictions within it. The more details we know, the more carnivalesque the *enforcement and administration* of the law is. When Moll enters the Mint,[114] the contradictory attitudes toward debt as crime and the debtor as fugitive except on Sunday and criminal/not-criminal prefigure the contravention of the transported criminal with enough money to buy freedom upon arrival in the colonies. Newgate, thus, becomes the symbol of the larger, structural disorder in the legal system, the next to last stage in a progressively carnivalesque sequence that concludes with transportation, not Newgate.

It is the detail, too, that often pushes the reader into the space of judge. Defoe does not flinch from depicting the sentimental value of the bundle of baby things taken in Moll's first theft even as he portrays Moll's desperate need and then horrified guilt. He lingers over Moll's impulse to kill the child whose necklace she takes; in the physicality of Moll's handling the necklace, its identification with the child's soft, smooth neck, there is the glimpse of the evil in her heart and, we are forced to entertain, in the human heart. We "draw back and demur," Faller points out.[115]

Conclusion

As a final argument for the inseparability of male and female novelists of the period, the essentiality of writing both sexes into the history of the English novel, I will set Defoe beside Eliza Haywood, the other novelist who dominated the 1720s. The work of both looks different.[116] In many ways, she is his soul mate. Inscribed in their fiction is the pervasive rise of capitalism, the triumph of secularism, an address to a very wide range of readers, and an image of the modern woman. Time is the fourth dimension of space, and Defoe and Haywood experience London as chronotope, thereby assimilating history and hegemonic processes into their fiction far more completely than any of their contemporaries. Marginal, resilient people, they and their fictions were repeatedly stigmatized as scandalous. They were also the most sustained and ruthless critics of society, especially class relations, and blended gritty realism with various kinds of initiations, fantasies, and older, recognizable genres.

Many of the same criticisms are made of their "primitive," "sloppy," "incredible," rushed publications with characters lacking "sophistication" and "complexity."[117] In fictions that do what theirs do and that are as intensely engaged with the subject matter characteristic of their work, it might be expected that meaning may be elusive or partial, because it is *in media res*.[118] They operate in the zone of contact with *incomplete* events in the public sphere. What, in the larger sense, do Moll Flanders and Glicera (heroine of *The City Jilt*) mean? Both can be read as monstrous women. Moll becomes part of a predatory underworld, contemplates murder, and has none of Col. Jack's scruples. Glicera devastatingly bilks and humiliates an Alderman and ruins Melladore, whose death she greets with "happy Indifference" (59). Rationalizations for Moll's and Glicera's conduct and hardheartedness are easy to find. Moll is for all practical purposes a penniless orphan, is seduced and forced into what she regards as incest, and consistently preyed upon. Glicera is orphaned, impoverished, seduced and left pregnant, and then courted by lascivious suitors with dishonorable intentions. Readers often experience Moll as attractively resilient and ingenious;[119] they remember comic moments with pleasure. Haywood paints Glicera's hopes of happiness and dependence on Melladore after her father's death, then makes her the victim of his heartless seduction and cold letters, and seals her fate: "The Affair between her and *Melladore* being blaz'd abroad, was of too much Disadvantage to her Reputation, to suffer her to imagine she should be able to make her Fortune by Marriage" (20).

Moll Flanders's position in the Colchester family and the underworld in which she moves, Roxana's life as the Prince's mistress and her descent into the hidden culture of early eighteenth-century Quakers, and Col. Jack's and Moll's time in the colonies—a land between wilderness and commercial England, between sweating slaves in rags and pampered women in silk—allow the same juxtapositioning of attitudes, practices, and social rituals and reveal hypocrisy, contradiction, and ethical issues with great power. Similarly Glicera's state between father and fiancé and then in the world of the unmarriageable, always between exploited and exploiting, is one of process and liminality that underscores relativity. These texts often reveal the dark questions within the sleek answers: what is to happen to the pregnant Glicera when Melladore writes, "I thought you Mistress of a better Understanding than to imagine an Amour of the nature our's was, should last for ever" (16)? The people who cheat the British Recluse and the men who seduce Moll and Glicera go free. In text after text, Defoe and to a lesser degree Haywood leave us to contemplate the causes of evil, unable to satisfy ourselves about whether its sources are in the human heart or brought about by social pressures. They tease us into confronting why the "evils" in society, such as ignorance and want, result in moral evil for the naive and wanting. Are we to admire or loathe Moll and Glicera?

Moll Flanders and Glicera are revisionary and shocking in the ways that many of these fictions' female protagonists are—they are economically independent women whose behavior and, perhaps, nature devitates from the known or expected. They have the power to retaliate.[120] Unlike many of the heroines, however, they are part of the modern city of London and its new underworlds. Bakhtin has extended the idea of the chronotope in "The *Bildungsroman* and Its Significance in the History of Realism" to a searching study of the assimilation of time in novels by a special use of setting and kind of character creation. For both writers, London is Bakhtin's chronotope; places named and described are what Defoe called in *A Journal of the Plague Year* "speaking pictures," for they bear not just "the *visible* coexistence of various epochs"[121] but traces of the laws and social practices that shape relationships within modern England.

The dialogue of the characters is filled with "ambivalent words" and impresses the reader with the coexistence of codes of feminine behavior and of capitalistic philosophy. The commercial ending of Glicera's "make her fortune by marriage" jars, but when she or Moll forgets that they are commodities that must have exchange value, they lose. As a character speaks, another discourse—often one from a residual structure of feeling or hinting at an emergent one—is apprehended. The other discourse distorts and complicates the character's speech and the interpretation of the text. It may be contradictory but it is always relativizing. Glicera frequently refers to a providential world, one in which order and justice are meted out by God; indeed, she often presents herself as God's instrument or even partner: "The utmost malice of the wrong'd *Glicera* was not fully satiated; ample was the Recompence which Heaven allowed her Injuries" (58), we are told at the moment he is bankrupt and Glicera in possession of the mortgage to everything he has left. Yet in these lines, we hear the pure malicious revenge of the wronged woman, the older phrases of the romantic seduction tale, and the money-economy of the City and its new gaming women. Glicera's motive and "character" are, therefore, complicated and made ambiguous. Similarly, Moll Flanders is perpetually in dialogue with the operative social codes, secular and Christian, and all are operative in her speech at various times. Prohibitions and justified transgressions repeatedly coexist. Depending on the genre voice (criminal life, spiritual autobiography, formal realism) the reader hears,[122] Moll's "repentance" is variously interpreted.

Many of Haywood's lines, like Defoe's, juxtapose idealistic common-places and the realities of, for instance, the marriage *market*. In the contra-dictions surrounding women in the period and the felt space between discourses, the reader apprehends the character as space permeated by time. Bakhtin posits that in some texts the protagonist "is forced to be-come a new, unprecedented type of human being," an individual who "emerges *along with the world*," an "image of *man growing in national historical time*."[123] Moll Flanders has long been recognized as such a char-acter, and Glicera and Helena, Melladore's wife, are in some ways more sobering prophetic images of the modern woman because they represent the underworld of the fashionable woman, one people could imagine mid-dle- and upper-class women joining. Helena, who ruins Melladore by shopping, is completely beyond his control, and the law makes him re-sponsible for her debts. Glicera becomes the society woman who supports herself by accepting gifts and playing cards, always promising more than she intends to give or pay. Like Moll and Roxana, she has a confederate who schemes with her and advances her tricks. By the time this novel appeared, cards were already seen as a dangerous, corrupting, even addic-tive pastime for women. Both Defoe and Haywood take advantage of the fear that card playing had dangerous sexual possibilities; as Moll heaps the coins in her lap, she is not far from masturbation, and the bodies of Glicera and the Alderman are the real stakes in their game, as Lady Townley had been in *The Provoked Husband*. Women like Glicera would be depicted and condemned more strongly in later decades.[124]

These novels, then, gave readers characters that seemed to prefigure the kind of person that was emerging along with the modern world, a person both identical with and symbolic of it. Their "ambivalent words" often established a polyvocal narrative expressing the individual and the tradi-tional simultaneously.[125] Spheres of life usually "controlled by tradition, custom, rigid role expectations and outright inegalitarian exploitation of women," many categories of men, and their work were giving way to radical new demands and practices.[126] The liminality of the texts becomes complete here, as the authors, characters, underworld settings, and even historical process—"history half-made because it is in the process of being made"—are on the boundaries of states of being.

Julia Kristeva asks in "Women's Time" if "women's desire for affirma-tion now manifests itself" in literary creation "because, faced with social norms, literature reveals a certain knowledge and sometimes the truth itself about an otherwise repressed, nocturnal, secret, and unconscious universe," because it exposes the "unsaid" in the social contract, and because it makes "a space of fantasy and pleasure out of the abstract and frustrating order of social signs."[127] The question might be asked of the novel form and addressed through the work of Defoe and the other writers who laid the foundation for the special power and usefulness of the novel. The three spaces discussed in my essay interact dynamically to put in sharp contact the public and private, public interests and private desires, community norms and personal values, news and fable, history and story, reportage and fantasy, observed fact and aberrant perception, belles lettres and popular culture, "art" and polemic, social "truth" and utopia or nightmare, macabre naturalism and phantasmagoria.

Readers experience the novel as between genres, continue to pick out the orchestration of genres and modes, and test the experience delivered by the text, regardless of its mode, and assent, deny, or integrate it into the totality of their experience. Tellingly, Michael Boardman argues that Defoe "discovered a new form in the blank spaces of his earlier works, principally in the gap between the pseudofactual" forms and what I would call his novelistic purposes.[128] Readers *use* the novel in the ways they develop psychological understandings of human nature and conceptions and interpretations of reality. In the space Julia Kristeva and Luce Irigaray flesh out as the Imaginary, readers and the novel often contribute to an interplay that is dialogic with their culture and with history. They are in a liminal sphere, on the borders of the binaries listed above and at their junctures, points of intersection, and articulations (where jointing together occurs).

As Seyla Benhabib says, "The public sphere came into existence whenever and wherever all affected by general social and political norms of action engage in a practical discourse, evaluating their validity."[129] The literary public sphere had become a place where people could "have a say" in the formulation, stipulation, adoption, and enforcement of these norms,[130] and the novel attracted writers (and readers) with limited access to poetry, drama, and even history. In fact, John Guillory has called them "between literate and illiterate."[131] Novels endlessly create these little public spheres. Consider, for instance, coach travel, certainly one of the dominant plot devices and thematic tropes. In a private, even intimate, enclosed space, characters are also in a public conveyance in the public sphere and also moving from one symbolic place and condition to another. Charles Gildon sets his novel about the South Sea Bubble in a coach in order to make clear personal and governmental blame and results. In this space, his characters and others create an ephemeral authentic public sphere, come to understand their social contexts better, and to separate their interests and personalities from the other travelers. The travelers in *All for the Better* are a "jolly Parson," a middle-aged lady "too Old to be impertinently Gay and Talkative; and too young to be Sour and Moross [*sic*]," a French gentleman, "young pert Fellow . . . of a voluable Tongue, malicious Wit, and . . . no manner of regard to Truth," "a grave Gentleman," and the narrator. The young man tells the first story, which is an attack on the South Sea directors, and the narrator corrects all of his details, exonerates the directors, and blames the investors: "Avarice did for them all that the extravagant Vices and Follies of Youth us'd to do, for the uncautious Spenders of Estates; they hoped to gain Wealth, by the mad Humour of the People, they laid out their Money in Humour, and are ruin'd by Humour" (59–60). As the coach rolls along, each traveler tells a tale about money and money-making in the early eighteenth-century. Individually, they reveal their relationships to the economy and the possibilities their sex, class, age, and national origin allowed them. Collectively, they give a broad picture of contemporary economics, which Gildon makes moral as well as social and political. One character says, "I'll venture no more on the Rocks of *Exchange-Alley*, [an] *East-India* Voyage is not half so Dangerous" (42), and each tale leads someone to observe, "This indeed . . . is a remarkable Punishment for Avarice" (39). The characters who have tried the riskiest investments have repented, learned to practice charity, and are most loved and appreciated.

Born at a time when the culture had used the family as metaphor to discuss its greatest political and religious questions and when it was deeply engaged with renegotiating the nature, rights, and abilities of women, the novel used woman as its master signifier. As one of a plurality of public spaces, it joined and initiated numerous practical discourses evaluating the validity of social and political norms.[132] Whether writers attempted to communicate women's experiences and situations or used Woman or a woman character as trope, they took advantage of the fact that women's identity and class were not fixed as men's were. Simultaneously creatures with "dangerous symbolic mobility" and prisoners of social restraints, they had the potential for subversive revelation and utopian glimmers.

These texts *force* interpretation by creating idiopathic characters and plots, by stretching readers' sense of what was socially and politically possible, by multiplying subjectivities, by creating myths of human adaptability, endurance, or intelligence rather than of quest and resolution, by creating plots that resist familiar paradigms and expected logic of plot, by employing nonrealist, "lyric" prose.[133] Kristeva extends Mikhail Bakhtin's argument that narratives with carnival, "dream logic," and other modes often associated with women's texts have the power to release transgressive, revisionary scenarios and possible relationships as well as to lay bare the real configurations and pressures of systems of power.[134] Novelistic discourse "is not characterised by its realism, then, but . . . by its capacity to reabsorb the real into the flux of the possible."[135]

I suggest that, rather than struggle with the form's "ambiguity" and lack of satisfactory definition, we embrace its liminality, explore it, and revel in it. Small and large lines of inquiry open. Certainly a great deal of the abiding hold of the novel is its boundary-penetrating, liminal existence.

2 | The Rise of Gender as Political Category

Paula R. Backscheider

The great subject of the early English novel was courtship, and some of the best recent criticism of Samuel Richardson's *Clarissa* examines the drastic things he did with it. It is now well established that the writing of his text coincided with a period of enormous insecurity over the ideal definitions of "masculine," "feminine," and "happy marriage." Two generations of writers, most of them women, had made prose fiction a major vehicle for bringing debate on formerly private issues into public discourse, and many writers were overtly exploring the form's potential for moral instruction.[1] Although other discourses were and had been discussing contemporary family relationships, prose fiction was notable for its attention and suitability to that discussion. Much of Restoration and early eighteenth-century prose fiction took as its subject the relationships between parents and children and between the sexes during courtship. Dozens of novels by women had taken the imposition of a husband on a woman as a theme, and many included detailed, scathing critiques of contemporary attitudes and practices. Jane Barker, for instance, dramatizes the ambiguities forced on young couples in *Love Intrigues* and satirizes her parents' choices of suitors in later volumes of the Galesia trilogy. Significantly, these fictions were written in a culture that had long relied upon marriage metaphors to explain the relationship between monarchs and their subjects and had paralleled health and order in the state with that of its microcosm, the family. The landscape, thus, of even "amatory fiction" was deeply politicized, fraught with questions of hierarchy, order, and "rightness."

This essay, substantially revised here, was first published as " 'The Woman's Part': Richardson, Defoe, and the Horrors of Marriage," The Past as Prologue, ed. Carla Hay with Syndy Conger (New York: AMS Press, 1995), 205–31. I am grateful to the American Society for Eighteenth-Century Studies for permission to include it.

It is a commonplace that Richardson brought together, laid bare, and extended discussions of these key processes and analogies, which were already obsessions in the culture. Tassie Gwilliam, for instance, in a discussion of Richardson's major characters summarizes the anxious atmosphere in which Richardson's contemporaries generated "discussion of the sexes, admonitions against crossing gender boundaries, intense scrutiny of the behavior proper to each sex."[2] Her conclusion, that "the barrage of models and concepts that Lovelace deploys to understand, shape, and conquer the idea of woman through Clarissa fails to create a definitive interpretation of femininity" (109), is a good example of the contribution *Clarissa* continues to make to our understanding of the construction of gender. Terry Eagleton in *The Rape of Clarissa* sets Richardson within Antonio Gramsci's explanation of the way a rising class "must secure *cultural* hegemony over its opponents" and argues that *Clarissa* is "an agent" of the bourgeoisie's "attempt to wrest a degree of ideological hegemony from the aristocracy."[3] He and others have seen Clarissa's death as "an absolute refusal of political society: sexual oppression, bourgeois patriarchy and libertine aristocracy together" (76). Such readings have helped create a Richardson who is a Friend to Women, an encourager surrounded by women correspondents, a father of respectable women writers, and something of a hero to many late twentieth-century feminist critics.

It is my contention, however, that Richardson inscribed the patriarchy approvingly on Clarissa's death, raised the stakes for women in these debates, and left a dangerously mixed legacy for his so-called female imitators. He did extend the discussions of issues of crucial importance to women and the way the novel form could be used to participate in them, but his more important achievement was to modify them. By giving powerful definition, endorsement, and impetus to two hegemonic redefinitions of masculine and feminine, he assured that the novel would become a crucial site, battleground even, for ongoing discussions of cultural issues affecting marriage, the family, and the "woman question." Because Richardson denied knowledge of women's fiction, I will use an influential text of the 1720s written by Daniel Defoe as a bridge to earlier treatments of his themes and foreground two ideas of sex and gender common to them all, one concentrated on the "domesticated man" and the other on the heroine.

An enraged father tells his daughter that she "can have no Reasons, that are sufficient" to refuse marriage to the man of *his* choice. When she persists, he pronounces, "From this time forward you are no Relation of mine, any more than my Cook-maid." He forbids his other children to "relieve her, nor own her, nor call her Sister." Defoe's heroine asserts, "No Father can command counter to God's Commands." This story of a "stubborn" daughter caught between biblical injunctions is the 181-page first part of Daniel Defoe's three-part *Religious Courtship: Being Historical Discourses, on the Necessity of Marrying Religious Husbands and Wives Only,* which he published in 1722—the amazing year that produced *A Journal of the Plague Year* and two novels, *Moll Flanders* and *Col. Jack,* which are at least partly about marriage and marital relations.

Samuel Richardson had printed this first section of *Religious Courtship* in 1729, and there are many similarities between *Clarissa* and Defoe's *Religious Courtship.*[4] The conflict between the authoritarian male and the individual woman allows these writers to capture important currents of opinion alive in the culture. Both Richardson's and Defoe's fathers are outraged that the commandment, "Honour thy father," is not sufficient in itself to assure their daughters' compliance. Defoe, the more subtle textuary, has the father ask belligerently, "has it not been always the Right of Fathers to give their Daughters in Marriage? nay, to bargain for them even without their Knowledge; Did not *Caleb* promise his Daughter *Achsah?*"[5] The resistance of the daughters, based explicitly in Defoe's text on "be not unequally yoked" (2 Corinthians 6:14) and in both on the Judeo-Christian conception of marriage as a sacred covenant mystically determining that "the twain shall be one flesh" (Mark 10:8), clearly has the sympathy of both writers.[6] Richardson, for instance, has Clarissa conclude, "My soul is above thee" (2:382). The daughters are torn, grief-stricken, loving but utterly firm, and the fathers surprised, furious, and impassioned. Both fathers, as Defoe's text says, do little but "make Work for Repentance."

Even small touches show Richardson's close reading of Defoe's text, and many of Defoe's ideas receive extended treatment in *Clarissa.*[7] For example, the aunt in *Religious Courtship* contrasts negative and positive authority, a theme that Richardson develops artfully and in great detail; also both daughters have sympathetic aunts and irreligious uncles. Defoe makes the differences in religious piety the reason the daughter cannot accept her suitor, while Richardson takes a broader interpretation of Defoe's "difference in principles" and makes Lovelace guilty of active evil. One of Clarissa's rejected suitors is more like Defoe's gentleman than Lovelace is. Clarissa explains that "poor Mr. Wyerley" was a "jester upon sacred things . . . who seemed to think that there was wit in saying bold things which would shock a serious mind" (1:269).

In both texts the fathers receive chastening educations. Defoe constructs

Religious Courtship so that the father learns that his duty goes beyond allowing his daughter to refuse a suitor; in the second part of the book, another daughter, for whom her father has made too few inquiries, marries a Catholic and, again out of harmony with the man's principles, is miserable until his death. This one and Defoe's other conduct books sometimes illustrate not only the misfortunes and even tragedies brought about by fathers who, like Clarissa's, are tyrannical and passionate, but also those caused by fathers who give up their rightful authority (another failing of Clarissa's father). Richardson dwells on the father's resulting suffering and regret and certainly makes the proper responsibilities of fathers as explicit as Defoe does.[8]

As Mark Kinkead-Weekes and others have observed, these texts were "in the direct tradition of puritan instructive writing,"[9] but both writers chose "histories" as appropriate modes of presentation. This term implied for them life stories with a beginning, middle, and end, and, as Defoe and the writer of its preface explained in *A Family Instructor,* although no actual individual was the subject, personalities, opinions, and events were such that "the Substance of each Narrative is *Real.* And there are some whole Dialogues to which, with very little Alteration, I my self could put *Names* and *Families.*"[10] Both Defoe and Richardson were aware that they were lengthening familiar prose forms, many by women,[11] and both respond to critics. In the Notes on the Third Dialogue in the first edition of *The Family Instructor,* Defoe explained, "There seems to be more Circumlocutions in this Dialogue . . . and some may suppose them unnecessary, but if they strictly examine them, they will find them not useful only, but necessary; the last to preserve the Cadence of things, and introduce the Substance of the real Story by necessary Gradations" (Appendix, 273). Richardson echoes, "The Letters and Conversations, where the Story makes the slowest progress, are presumed to be characteristic. They give occasion likewise to suggest many interesting *Personalities.* . . . To all which we may add, that there was frequently a necessity to be very circumstantial and minute, in order to preserve and maintain that Air of Probability." (8:297). As early as the second edition of *Biographia Britannia* (1793), Richardson was seen as imitating Defoe's "dramatic form":

> Richardson seems to have learned from [Defoe] that mode of delineating characters, and carrying on dialogues, and that minute discrimination of the circumstances of events, in which De Foe so eminently excelled. If, in certain respects, the disciple rose above his master, as he undoubtedly did, in others he was inferior to him; for his conversations are sometimes more tedious and

diffuse; and his works, though beautiful in their kind, are not by any means so various. Both of these writers had a wonderful ability in drawing pictures of human nature and human life. ("Daniel De Foe," 5:75)

Although Defoe wrote no epistolary novels, his conduct books, and especially *The Family Instructor,* had included letters between family members and situations and subjects similar to some in Richardson's *Familiar Letters on Important Occasions.*[12] In contrast to Richardson, Defoe rapidly turns his story away from the heroine to the religious education and serious conversion of the gentleman suitor, and he provides a happy ending for the young people. Now harmonious in principles, they "lived afterwards the happiest Couple that can be imagin'd; having a sober, regular, well-govern'd Family" (181). In *Clarissa,* Belford may be considered a similar character and might have supplied the same kind of happy ending, and I shall begin by tracing his conversion story.

Lovelace designates Belford, a young man with £1000 a year, his likely successor as leader of the rakes' fraternity, and it is Belford who joins Lovelace at the White Hart in the days before Clarissa is lured away.[13] In fact, Lovelace once jokes that Belford may be worse than he and at another time that Belford's plan to make restitution to those he has harmed will bankrupt him, and Clarissa concludes sternly, "I find . . . that [Lovelace] had always designs against me; and that you all along *knew* that he had: would to Heaven you had had the goodness to have contrived some way, that might not have endangered your own safety, to give me notice of his baseness. . . . But you gentlemen . . . had rather see an innocent fellow-creature ruined, than be thought capable of an action which, however generous, might be likely to loosen the bands of a wicked friendship" (6:297–98). Furthermore, she doubts the "earnestness" of his remonstrances with Lovelace. Lovelace's letters are full of dramatizations of Belford's voice; he imagines, for instance, how "thou wilt rejoice with me at my conquest over such a watchful and open-eyed charmer." His letters make vivid their society: a true fraternity of competitive, adventure-seeking young men who hardly see their victims, let alone have the ability to imagine the distress they cause. Much like the heartless seducers of Eliza Haywood's fiction, their only society is a masculine one, and they perform for each other. And they are, as Rita Goldberg wrote over a decade ago, criminal, and the male world, just as it is in Haywood's and Aubin's fictions, is seen to create powerful institutions and, therefore "not to be trusted by their victims, who are usually women." "Rapists and the rapacious alike go free."[14] Haywood repeatedly demonstrates that the law and the church, for instance, have little to offer women as she does with Alinda in *The Invisible Spy* (1755), but Richardson goes beyond anything she wrote in having Lovelace imagine himself acquitted of the rape of Anna Howe and her mother: "the whole crowded bench, will acquit us in their hearts; and every single man wish he had been me!" When Belford says he now hates him, Lovelace chides Belford, "Have I been guilty of any offence thou knewest not before?" (6:359).

Yet Lovelace knows another side of Belford. He characterizes Belford as clever and a man of sense, and he obviously expects Belford to protest his extravagant immoralities even as Belford appreciates and abets them. Belford does do both, and the length and detail of *Clarissa* allow Richardson to effect some subtle shifts in Belford's character. At first Belford's protests are just as Lovelace predicts, and his aid is rather active and his appreciation obvious. It is he who deliberately, and at Lovelace's instigation, embarrasses Clarissa at the dinner by trapping her into pretending to be already married. Partly because of his necessary absence from London and partly out of conviction, his aid becomes silence—conspiring by inaction, guilty by silence. He comes to call Lovelace a "panther" but still wants to hear "what gradations, arts, and contrivances" Lovelace uses (4:25). As audience and voyeur, Belford deserves the disapproval Clarissa expresses toward his actions. As the narrative continues, however, Belford's protests are wholehearted, his appreciation becomes clear-sighted perception of awesome evil, he refuses Lovelace's instructions,[15] and he comes to aid Clarissa more actively than we ever know he did Lovelace.

Embedded in *Clarissa,* thus, is a conversion story somewhat similar to and no less didactic than Defoe's.[16] Like Defoe's young man, Belford's sense and latent morality are obvious. He acts as a true friend to Lovelace, attempting to keep Lovelace's best feelings alive, pleading "*thy own sake and thy family's*" (3:242), and repeatedly reminding Lovelace that such another woman and such a chance for happiness cannot be expected again. He, like Lovelace's family, sees the prosperity and national influence within Lovelace's reach. From the beginning, too, he acknowledges that they believe in "a future state of rewards and punishments" and intend to repent in the convenient future.

Belford's story illustrates how deeply read Richardson was in the pious literature of the period and how artfully he could draw upon different narrative and thematic elements.[17] First Belford rather unobtrusively goes through the six-step repentance process familiar to all Protestants of his time: an awareness of sin, a sense of both divine wrath and of obligation to God, humiliation before God, confession, hatred of sin, and "accepting, receiving, and resting upon Christ alone for justification, sanctification, and eternal life, *by virtue of the covenant of grace.*"[18] By volume seven, Belford has progressed to the point of feeling shame and loathing for his sins and of dedicating himself to the Christian life. He exclaims to Lovelace, who has become the personification of evil and the evil life they have shared, "I hate thee heartily!" "Every hour I hate thee more!" (6:358). In the face of skepticism and ridicule he writes, "Thou tellest me that thou seest reformation is coming swiftly upon me. I hope it is" (6:390). He announces firmly, "I will endeavour to begin to repent of my follies while my health is sound, my intellects untouched, and while it is in my power to make some atonement, as near to restitution or reparation as is possible, to those I have wronged or misled" (7:194). The rest of *Clarissa* shows that he fulfills this vow.

The experienced reader of religious literature would have recognized early in Belford one of the literary signs of a person blessed with God's grace and, perhaps, predestined for salvation: Belford finds "speaking pictures" all around him and has the gift of productive reflection on them and on his experiences. The series of deathbed scenes that Belford witnesses can be read as a dramatic presentation of the history of the progress of his conversion as well as an important means of his spiritual enlightenment. Forced to attend his dying uncle early on and even read prayers to him, Belford witnesses the slow, painful death of a rake. That this man is his older mirror image is made clear, as is the fact that "poor Belton" is also a version of himself. Unlike Lovelace, Belford has the gift—some would say grace—to recognize the pertinence of others' experiences and to "give due weight to the reflections that arise from [them]."[19] His letters come increasingly to sound like the period's sermons and spiritual autobiographies.[20] During this time, Belford becomes both example and voice for traditional conduct-book moral sentiments. In near-set pieces, he praises the Bible over pagan authors, for example, and "corrects" a number of "worldly" opinions and definitions, as he and Clarissa do "friendship."[21] He finds the amusements and acquaintances of his past both reprehensible and boring; of Mowbray, for instance, he says, "I was surfeited with Mowbray's frothy insensibility" (7:161).

Second, and perhaps more interesting, is the way Belford's story can be related to Defoe's and other marriage manual's major argument. One of the basic tenets of the Pauline philosophy of marriage is stated in 1 Corinthians 13–16, which includes the idea that "the unbelieving husband is sanctified by the wife, and the unbelieving wife is sanctified by the husband. . . . For what knowest thou, O wife, whether thou shalt save *thy* husband?" Belford writes that he has begged Clarissa's influence "to draw me after you, to the world you are aspiring to!" (6:350). English literature, rather than transmitting this theme consistently, often mingled the construction of the unbelieving lover with the injunction to avoid bad company; this tendency was especially pronounced where the "weaker" and allegedly more easily influenced sex, the woman, was the believer. In *Religious Courtship*, the younger daughter says, "for my part, I need no wicked Discouragements to pull me back in my Duty, no ill Examples to allure me to Folly, I want all the Assistance possible the other Way" (33). Clarissa exclaims of Lovelace: "My soul disdains communion with him" (6:376). In contrast, *The Family Instructor* includes a marriage between a gentle, religious man and a rebellious woman; she becomes a good Christian.

In the ensuing scenes between Belford and Clarissa, Richardson mingles the illustrations of the redeemed person's pleasure in the means of grace, which are common in manuals of piety, with representations of improving conversations, which are common in conservative marriage manuals. Not only does Belford discover pleasure in the Bible and in going to church, but he enjoys conversations with Clarissa on such topics as "the vanity and brevity of life," "the happiness of timely preparation" for death, and on the pleasures of virtuous actions. They are "very attentive" to each other and mutually pleased with the "fine observations" they make on each other's discourses. Sometimes they take notes or ask for written records in order to continue their reflections. Such conversations with the built-in insistence upon the satisfaction and even joy the participants felt in them take place between Defoe's characters as well, perhaps most notably in *The New Family Instructor* (1727), another of Defoe's books printed by Richardson.

There are, in fact, a number of similarities between Richardson's representation of Belford's and Clarissa's relationship and those in courtship novels as well as in pious marriage manuals. Belford's devotion to Clarissa is often expressed in the terms of romantic love. He says, for instance, "My life and my fortune . . . are devoted to your service"; "All I beg is that you will not suffer any future candidate or event to displace me"; and "I expressed some jealousy . . . ." When she dies, he laments the loss of her "delightful and improving conversation" more than anything else, as do survivors of good spouses in pious books. It is significant that Belford recognizes Clarissa's worth at once upon meeting her and, in the phrases of puritan literature, "yearns toward the good" she actualizes.[22] Lovelace teases him for saying he would give £1000 for her good opinion, and he says unselfconsciously that he is "proud" of her conversation and condescension.

In fact, it is Belford's view of Clarissa that Richardson increasingly imposes on the reader. By 2 May, Belford describes her as "the virtues and graces all drawn in one piece" and is "ready to regret such an angel of a woman should ever marry" (4:11). Later he says that even were she restored to the full-bloom of health and beauty, he could not "have the least thought of Sex" with her (7:299). Belford, thus, gives some of Anna Howe's more mundane observations about Clarissa's being suited for the next world eloquent, even poetic, expression and helps set in motion the rhetorical process by which she will become "all soul."[23] To a large extent Belford's record of Clarissa's appearance, conversation, and effect on people brings about the transformation that readers like Ian Watt have recorded.[24]

As the narrative concludes, these statements multiply. Belford says in August, for instance, "every time I saw her I more and more considered her as a beatified spirit; and as one sent from Heaven to draw me after her out of the miry gulf in which I had been so long immersed" (7:253). He sees her as participating in a "companionship with saints and angels" and, as others have noted, Clarissa's white garments, which Belford describes as "virgin white," shine as though bathed in supernatural light. Belford's conception of her is endorsed by other characters and, therefore, reinforced and established as the correct interpretation. When Wyerley's letter demonstrates Clarissa's saving influence on him, he says that virtue is "your essence." Anna Howe describes how she and three other women rejoice that they know a woman who has done so much honor to their sex. Finally, Clarissa's coffin is carried by six "maidens"; thus Richardson inscribes yet another image of her sainthood and her celibacy.

The sketch of Defoe's life in Laetitia Barbauld's *British Novelists* (1820) mentions *The Family Instructor* and *Religious Courtship* among "those works by which [Defoe's] name has been best known to posterity." She continues, "their dramatic form of dialogue, supported with much nature and feeling . . . has thrown into the familiar stories and incidents of domestic and common life, have made these publications . . . exceedingly popular to this day" (17:iv). Nancy Armstrong and others have persuasively demonstrated how important these texts were in the social and domestic changes that took place in the era, and Belford is a significant example of the characters created at the time when modern opinions about marriage and the family were being consolidated and when the stage was

being set for the flowering of the domestic novel of the second half of the
century.

Between Defoe's and Richardson's texts a considerable number of novels
about courtship and family relationships had been published. In fact, many
of them were by women. In these early fictions, the sex that invented and
perpetrated the unsatisfactory courtship rituals was often presented as
enigmatic, insensitive, or even stupid. Jane Barker's Galesia stories begin
with the inexplicable behavior of Bosvil and include near-marriages to a
man who committed highway robbery "out of a Frolick" and to a suicide.[25]
Eliza Haywood's fictions are full of libertines, shallow seducers, and liars.
Some of them, like Beauplaisir in *Fantomina*, do not even recognize former lovers in different dresses. Mary Davys's heroines are often coerced
into marriage or raped and then married; one of her heroines describes her
honeymoon: "I embraced him with the same desire, I shou'd have done a
Serpent, and went to his Bed with more loathing, than I shou'd have gone
to a stinking Dungeon."[26]

Within these early novels are embryonic expressions of longing for the
utopian husband. Eliza Haywood creates Worthly in *The British Recluse*
(1722) and expands him into Charles Trueworth in *The History of Miss
Betsy Thoughtless* (1751). Penelope Aubin creates Belanger (*The Life of
Charlotta Du Pont*, 1723), de Feuillade (*The Strange Adventures of the
Count de Vinevil*, 1721), and others. In these few good men and in the men
for which characters such as Galesia hope, the desire for men who will
listen to, take seriously, and esteem women is clear. Most of their statements recite the conventional list of desires; here is a typical one:

> beloved and respected by all that knew him, for his discreet behaviour, hu-
> manity, and affability; he went afterwards on his travels . . . ; he has a much
> larger estate than your fortune could expect, unincumbered with debts,
> mortgages, or poor relations; his family is ancient, and by the mother's side,
> honourable; but, above all, he has sense, honour, and good-nature.[27]

Defoe's gentleman who takes someone's words seriously and seeks his own
salvation appears to be the familiar hero of pious works such as Bunyan's
Pilgrim's Progress and Defoe's three *Family Instructors*. However, the fact
that he takes a young woman's objections very seriously, treats her re-
spectfully and faithfully, and returns reformed and hopeful to marry her is
unusual and places him in the company of these women's creations.

Claudine Herrmann in *Les Voleuses de langue* has pointed out the fact
that women's fiction often attempts "to invent the man of the future."[28]
Belford, like the reformed gentleman in *Religious Courtship*, shares many

characteristics with the man of the future, "the domesticated man" being created in other contemporary texts. This man has often been a rake, a dissolute profligate, or a passionate hothead; sometimes he has been the unappreciated, moderate individual, but he is unlike Richardson's Hickman in that he has traveled and is a powerful, mature, effective participant in the public sphere. In Defoe's texts he is as likely to be a father as a young man and has often been a merchant in a foreign country. Accustomed to independence, to assuming authority, and to a lack of family intimacy, he needs adapting to life in a household and perhaps calming and taming as well. In the texts by Defoe and in *Clarissa*'s Belford we see the process, for the domesticated man comes to be self-controlled and a "man of feeling" who can say, "I am convinced that a capacity of being moved by the distresses of our fellow-creatures is far from being disgraceful to a manly heart."[29] Completely without avarice or even much interest in money, Belford is a good manager, knowledgeable about the law, a reliable man of business; the fact that he is the chosen comforter and estate administrator for a widely diverse group of characters attests to his good nature, good sense, and honesty.

Unlike many of the male characters in fictions such as Frances Burney's novels,[30] Belford is a man upon whom women can depend for humane and competent fiscal management. He takes the words and example of a young woman seriously and changes; he learns to choose right action and friendship with a woman over the traditional loyalties and clichés associated with male friendships. Finally he longs for a good marriage in which he can "live a life of reason" and hopes for a woman "whom I could love and honour, and whose worthy example might confirm my morals." The rules he lists for his household's government could have come from Defoe's conduct books—there will be "good order" because he is a "good example," he will be visited and respected by the best and worthiest people, there will be no swearing, and improving books and conversations will abound (8:139–40). As Defoe's suitor says, a man "should never be a complete Gentleman, till he became a religious Man; and that the more of a Christian he was, the fitter he should be for the Conversation of the best and greatest Men in the Kingdom" (58). Unlike Soames or even Lovelace, Belford effortlessly imagines proposing "handsome settlements." Comfortable with women's intellectual capacities and moral character, he feels no fear at the idea of their having some independence from him.[31] Such characters and Belford gave powerful "permission" for the hope that this domesticated man would become the "ideal husband and father."

It has become a commonplace that the eighteenth century created a feminized man. As early as 1792, Robert Bage wrote in *Man As He Is:* "The manly manners of our more immediate ancestors we have exchanged for the manners of women. We have gained in gentleness and humanity; we have lost in firmness of nerve and strength of constitution" (1:272). Like so many commonplaces, this one is only partially accurate and, when applied to the novel before 1745, more misleading than helpful. The women writers before Richardson may have been domesticating the ideal husband, but they were not feminizing him. They gave him experiences and characteristics not available to women and demanded of him abilities and behaviors that they did not valorize in female characters. Their heroes had traveled, had liberal educations that had cultivated their tastes and sensibilities, had managerial and often legal experience, and were bold men able to take initiative and think on their feet. The reasons for this outline of their utopian man are obvious—not only did women need economic security but men opened the world to them. Conversations, libraries, and shared cultural artifacts educated them, and women's hopes and expectations for their educations were rising with their hopes for improved marriages.

Upon analysis, it is clear that this commonplace obscures Richardson's work as much as it distorts that of the early women writers. Although Richardson has been seen as creating a "feminized man" in Lovelace, Hickman, Grandison, and other characters and been, in Tassie Gwilliam's words, "deeply implicated in Lovelace's identification with femininity,"[32] Belford is not feminized and by the end of the novel Belford has shed these characteristics that he shared with Lovelace. Belford, confident, efficient, and cultured, may have "gained in gentleness and humanity," but the "bear" of a man has not lost the "firmness of nerve" and other "masculine" traits. Like the "man of the future" that women's treasured hopes were creating, he is the figure of consolidated wealth, authority, and respect.

Belford is, however, jealous, but because he fears that Clarissa will appoint another executor for her will not because he fears a romantic rival. He does not coax her into health and marry her. In the final part of this chapter, I would like to suggest that Richardson provided, indeed imposed, a resolution on problems and contradictions that women's fiction had made apparent and that he did so in ways that deflected novelistic discussion away from feminist concerns.[33] I shall begin with a comparison between Clarissa and a singularly exemplary female character created by a woman and move to a brief discussion of some of the patriarchal interventions in Richardson's text.

Clarissa, Richardson says, was created "as an Exemplar to her Sex" (Preface, 1:vi), although he insisted: "we know there are *some,* and we *hope* there are *many,* in the British dominions . . . who . . . have reached the perfections of a Clarissa" (Postscript, 8:298). By making her a ruined woman in the world's eyes, redeeming her reputation, and "consecrating" her, Richardson accomplished something daring and original. Clarissa is not primarily the penitent fallen woman[34] or the seduced woman, nor is she the disaffected revenger. At a time when love was almost invariably depicted in popular literature as an irresistible inclination and women as prone to being "swept away" or overcome by their tenderheartedness and trust, Richardson created female characters who, in Anna Howe's words, were "able to turn that lion, Love, at her own pleasure, into a lap-dog."[35]

Before Clarissa, the most notable such character is Marie-Madeleine de Lafayette's Princess de Clèves.[36] Like Clarissa, the Princess is not simply exemplary but proposed by her creator as having taken an action "no other woman would be capable of" (147). Lovelace has defended himself successfully before his angry family by saying that Clarissa "was the only woman in the world 'who would have made such a rout about a case that is uncommon only from the circumstances that attend it.'"[37] One of the most significant aspects of these characters and of Defoe's heroines is, in the words of Claudine Herrmann regarding the princess, that each "took her education too seriously; she did not observe the conventions but attempted to go deeper in the only domain where a woman was permitted to act, that of virtue" (19). This statement is equally true of Clarissa. As her will makes clear, her education, primarily carried out by her mother, by Mrs. Norton, and by a series of admirable clergymen, laid the groundwork for the inflexible standard of behavior she set for herself. Both the princess and Clarissa pushed the moral statements of their culture to the point that their contradiction of social codes and behavior became undeniable and, indeed, intolerable, because they put these codes and behaviors on trial and thereby called everyone's principles and conduct into question.[38]

In their ruthless honesty, their naked demand that people live up to their avowed ethical codes, they set up situations from which they and their positions had to be exiled. The princess is struck by her husband's glorification of sincerity,[39] and in a moment of desperate optimism asks for his protection—but protection from her own feelings. He is, finally, driven to confess, "What you expected from me was as impossible as what I expected from you." He goes on to admit feelings every bit as contradictory and passionate as Lovelace's and with the same ultimate conclusion: "I have violent and wavering emotions which I cannot control. . . . I adore and hate you; I offend you and ask your forgiveness; I admire you and am ashamed to do so. There is no peace in me nor any reason either. . . . I only ask you to bear in mind that you have made me the unhappiest man in the world" (163).

Both women are completely unsuited for the societies in which they live, and both reject a series of compromises available in their societies. Everyone expects Clarissa to relent and marry, and the princess could be expected to have a discreet affair with de Nemours and, after her husband's death, marry him. These compromises were also resolutions to less-than-ideal but accepted social problems, such as loveless arranged marriages and the lack of satisfactory divorce procedures. Story after story in *La Princesse de Clèves* makes the point that adultery was acceptable, in fact more likely than fidelity, and that spouses, even royal ones, learned to accommodate themselves to it. Similarly, a number of stories and the urgings of the most admirable characters in *Clarissa* demonstrate, in Lovelace's crude, blunt words, "MARRIAGE . . . thou seest, Jack, is an Atonement for all we can do to them. A true Dramatic Recompence!" (6:227). What these writers, and Defoe as well, do is push the culture's statements about ideal virtue to the point that they deconstruct themselves and render the heroines strange. Although Defoe spares his heroine the test of her resistance by the rather rapid reform of the hero, his text labels her singular, quixotic, and even extravagant, and in the rest of the text neither of her sisters imitates her. At one point, Anna calls Clarissa "an alien." These writers are conscious of the matrix of social forces that determine that immoderate virtue will unleash a chain of inexorable consequences that, destructive as they are, still expose and punish a hypocritical society.

The heroines can be the means of this exposure because of their second exceptional characteristic: as was noted throughout the century, these heroines in Erasmus Darwin's words, "retain a more considerable degree of command over their affections than those of apparently less exceptionable romances."[40] At the heart of Defoe's and Richardson's cases are the self-control combined with the "prudence and fine understanding" of their heroines. Both writers present their heroines as exceptional human beings. With female characters, they can intensify the perception of the moralists' position. Without authority or any of the recognized kinds of power,[41] vulnerable and conspicuous, they pit their perception of right action against other codes of conduct, many invested with the values of communal good and of long tradition. Judgment for the eighteenth century was an intellectual act, a faculty of the mind. As for a poorly or differently educated man, but to an even greater degree because of questions about her different "nature," a woman setting her judgment against the experienced, university educated man's judgment could be expected to raise skepticism, questioning and easy rejection.

Such women were not new in prose fiction. It was, however, far more common for this woman to appear cold and even manipulating. Characters like Mary Davys's Amoranda in *The Reform'd Coquet,* even if they consistently exhibit self-control and probity, often begin as thoughtless coquettes in need of reform, and Haywood's characters like Glicera, who when seduced and abandoned becomes a scheming harpy, are more common (*The City Jilt*). What was often presented as problematic was not the intelligence of the woman but her "heart," her ability to love. It is notable that in Darwin's next sentence, he criticizes another novel, *Plain Sense,* for going too far in its representation of a woman in control of her heart. Readers of *Clarissa* since the date of its publication have debated whether or not she ever felt love for Lovelace. The Princess de Clèves's dilemma is caused by the fact that she does not know what love feels like, and Clarissa is as unmoved by the men she meets as the young princess. Like the princess, she is made to feel that she should come to feel "love" toward a man, and many of her early letters explore with Anna Howe what love feels like and if she feels it. These characters, in sharp contrast to such fictional heroines of the late seventeenth century as the Portuguese nun, are able—and determined to remain able—to control their behavior.

Here the contrasts in these novels are more significant for my purposes than their similarities, and it seems that Richardson intended them. The princess learns what love and physical desire are. She is drawn to de Nemours's perceptiveness, urbanity, and sensibility—his intelligence and personality—and feels physical desire. Madame de Lafayette traces the princess's discovery of love in her novel and makes it explicit. By the end of the novel, the princess can discriminate among fine shades of feeling and compare de Clèves's and de Nemours's love, both as directed toward her and as experienced by her. In contrast Richardson leaves Clarissa to conclude that she never felt more than "a conditional kind of liking." In one short, highly compressed conversation, de Lafayette captures the subjects of numerous novels by Restoration and early eighteenth-century women. M. de Nemours asks, "what is this phantom of duty which you are placing between me and my happiness?" (188). The choice of pronouns—"me," "my"—shows the masculine egotism, the assumption of prerogative. *Clarissa* startlingly echoes the princess's description of de Nemours's character; Belford writes, "What is the love of a rakish heart? There cannot be *peculiarity* in it" (3:245). The princess tells de Nemours, "it is not my duty to risk" "the misery of seeing your present love grow cold" (189). She goes on to compare the two men's love and chooses "my own peace of mind." This choice is, of course, Clarissa's, too, though Clarissa's is mingled with the narrative of religious salvation.

Madame de Lafayette dares to evoke the conventions of passionate love and to have the princess read de Nemours's character in the most pragmatic, pessimistic way, and, in turn, rejecting both optimistic, fanciful faith in her charms and short-term happiness and renouncing the life of admiration and public amusement that was her destiny. Like the characters of most novels by women, the princess experiences such strong sensations that thoughts of Heaven are temporarily pushed aside. Clarissa, in contrast, surrenders her dreams of earthly happiness. Her sainthood, her fitness for the next world are confirmed, and the fact that she suffers seems of a piece with the pattern of the saint's life.

As I have argued elsewhere, many of the novels written before 1740 were powerful, explicit critiques of English courtship rituals. They illustrated the difficulties of getting to know the intended, the problems inherent in sanctioned social discourses, and the conflicts bred in different objectives and expectations. Some gave some space to depicting marriages, but most focused almost exclusively on the unfolding (and often unraveling) courtship. Women writers were struggling to bring into public discussion subjects and experiences previously excluded. They were exposing, even ridiculing the contradictions, hypocrisies, and ruptures in the public discourses and social codes that defined courtship rituals, the ideal man, and the good marriage. Although early women's novels may appear to conform to the traditional courtship plot of love and marriage and do give lip-service to marriage and motherhood as woman's purpose in life and duty (cf., even Barker's *Patch-Work Screen*, 79), their texts offer alternative patterns for women's lives. They do not invariably conclude with marriage, and sometimes they go so far as to suggest with Mary Astell that the single life can be preferable.[42] The princess goes into solitary retirement; Jane Barker's Galesia celebrates the single life, some of Haywood's heroines retire with a female friend, and, although widowed mothers abound, few seem interested in remarriage. The widowed heroine of Haywood's *Fruitless Inquiry* (1727), for instance, does not believe any man can manage her son's inheritance as well as she can.

Richardson, as Defoe had, joins in this enterprise of critiquing courtship and went on to depict marriage powerfully as the inevitable continuation of courtship. Few sections of the early volumes of *Clarissa* are as intense as Clarissa's meditations on marriage:

To be given up to a strange man; To be engrafted into a strange family; To give up her very Name, as a mark of her becoming his absolute and dependent property; To be obliged to prefer this strange man to Father, Mother,—to every body:—And his humours to all her own. . . . To go no-whither: To make acquaintance: to give up acquaintance: To renounce even the strictest friendships perhaps; all at his pleasure, whether she think it reasonable to do so or not. . . . A thousand things may happen to make that state but barely tolerable, where it is entered into with *mutual affection:* What must it then be. . . . (1:207)

Especially as she describes her mother, who has "on all occasions, sacrificed her own inward satisfaction to outward peace," Clarissa is explicit about the potential horrors of marriage. "Has she," she asks, "by her sacrifices always found the peace she has deserved to find?"[43]

Like a sounding bell, she has consistently paid tribute to her mother's "prudence and fine understanding," but finally she concludes these qualities wasted when accompanied by too much submissiveness. Poignancy colors the majority of statements about Clarissa's mother: Anna, for instance, writes, "Your Mother, when a maiden, had . . . a good share of those lively spirits which she liked in your Father. She has none of them now. How came they to be dissipated?" (2:16) In fact, Clarissa has seen few happy marriages, and the novel is full of negative statements about marriage. Anna Howe writes to Belford, "When I look round upon all the married people of my acquaintance, and see how *they* live, and what *they* bear who live *best,* I am confirmed in my dislike to the State. Well do your Sex contrive to bring us up fools and idiots, in order to make us bear the yoke."[44]

Both writers emphasize that "Marriage is a Case for Life, and must be well consider'd; and the young Ladies are to bear it, fall it how it will" (*Religious Courtship,* 139). As Defoe said, "The hazard is chiefly on the Woman's side." Equally emphatic in their work is the idea that all future happiness—in this world and most probably the next—is at stake. In one of many similar passages, Col. Morden writes solemnly to Clarissa, "Your duty, your interest, your temporal and your eternal welfare, do, and may all, depend upon this single point, *the morality of a husband*" (letter 2:lxxiv). Rhetorical strategies repeatedly show the woman's "happiness of my future life" cast in the balance with "my brother's ambition," "what fine settlements," and other unworthy weights.

These ideas were, of course, familiar to all readers of conduct books. What Defoe and especially Richardson were doing was giving new dimensions, new significance to these principles. By moving them into the novel's more dialogic form they more fully reflect the culture's increasing interest in the family and in woman's nature, especially her intellectual capacities. Their firm opinions and detailed portrayals of family members in traditional roles and as individuals with continuous reference to the larger society assured that their texts would participate actively in the changes occurring in the culture. They joined in the critique of the amassing of wealth at the cost of discounting as a worthy goal happiness and developed the point in precedent setting ways. They also acknowledged women's actual circumstances. Over and over, Richardson makes clear that women of many classes have money—Sally Martin's mother brings "a handsome fortune" to her husband; Clarissa's mother has brought her husband a larger fortune than Clarissa "will carry to Mr. Solmes," and even Lovelace is surprised at the size of Clarissa's fortune. When Anthony Harlowe proposes to Mrs. Howe, he makes it clear that he will control her fortune "because, you know, Madam, it is as creditable to the wife, as to the husband, that it should be so," and only if he dies first will she be £10,000 "the better" (4:158–59). Clarissa's prudent economy, laid out at the time she and Lovelace are corresponding about settlements and her charities and in her will, is based on insight into such things as what she needs and enjoys, what is befitting to her station, and what can be appropriately done for others.

Consistently, however, Richardson provides resolutions that served to obscure temporarily problems raised in women's texts about definitions of ideal men and of good marriages and that acted to redirect discussion toward different aspects of recognized problems, aspects that were in general less revolutionary and threatening to the patriarchy. Texts such as *La Princesse de Clèves* had repeatedly revealed, as Herrmann says, "There is absolutely no degree of grandeur that protects against woman's frightful condition" (32). And it is almost impossible to find a woman whose condition is happy in pre-Richardsonian fiction by women. In fact, like runs of musical scales, texts throughout the century include women characters in each life stage and of various social degrees and repeat that the *condition* of women prevents fulfillment, security, and happiness. The heroine in Haywood's *Fruitless Inquiry* (1727) is on a quest to find one completely contented and happy woman, and the effect of the doubled and tripled life stories that are told by characters in her fictions, Aubin's, and Davys's is to reinforce a line from Haywood's *A Wife to Be Lett* (1724): "To what Fate are wretched Women born!" Those who are happy have made themselves so, usually by creating unconventional social positions or by acts of will nearly heroic. Some are even mutilated, symbolic representations of what experience has done to them, as Penelope Aubin's Maria in *The Noble Slaves* (1722) and Arbriseaux in *The Life of Charlotta Du Pont* are.

Many of the earlier novels by women have seemed to have ambiguous or unsatisfactory conclusions.[45] Even eighteenth-century women writers complained about the number of books by women about love, but as Herrmann observes, "If women did not generally experience the love they yearn for as a repeated impossibility, they would dream about it less" (63). This statement, with its insistence upon "impossibility" and "dream" does much to explain these texts' lack of resolution and closure. The glimmers of longing for "the domesticated man" and the marriage that could come from union with him accumulate from text to text. Over and over these authors conjure up a blending of companionship, mental stimulation, and sexual attraction. Mary Chudleigh writes of the man who would want "a Companion, a Person in whom a Man can confide, to whom he can communicate his very Soul."[46] Even Penelope Aubin, one of the writers whom John Richetti classifies as writing "pious polemics," was setting up contrasts between the man who gave her heroine "a noble Fortune, lovely Children, and a Husband who lov'd her beyond expression and deny'd her nothing" and the man who could give her the greatest "Satisfaction . . . mortals attain in this Life," possession of the person she "ardently loved."[47]

Defoe and Richardson tap into this longing, and Defoe comes quite close to creating such characters. Against a backdrop of tortured consciences that always interrupt happiness, in Moll and Jemmy, Roxana and the landlord, and Roxana and the prince, we see men and women enjoying each other fully. They converse, their hours together speed away, they understand each other. And they feel strong sexual attraction. Defoe, however, reduces Jemmy, the prince-of-the-road highwayman whom people come to see in Newgate, to a mannikin to be dressed up with a gun for hunting in Moll's retirement, has the Prince repent, and leaves Roxana with the Dutch merchant, a steady man who can make her a countess but has never been able to fire her imagination. Carol Flynn has observed that "it cannot be accidental that while [Defoe's] men more often than not flee desire, his women embrace it,"[48] and this fact and the marriages in Defoe's novels suggest, perhaps, his perception that men and women are quite different. Col. Jack and Capt. Singleton marry matronly women broken by poverty and hardship; in spite of their adventurous, seeking, public lives they lack the private desires of Moll and Roxana. That Defoe admits the sexual, however, cannot be denied. In his most extended discussion of religion, society and marriage, *Conjugal Lewdness*, he always includes "mutual Delights" as a foundation for happiness (see 113).

Richardson makes references to Clarissa's body prurient and palpably products of the imperialistic male gaze. James Harlowe, described in this scene as "the unnatural brother," gazes at Clarissa "from head to foot," and says to Soames, "Look at her person!" Lovelace often describes her shape, her "bosom swelling," "more charmingly protuberant for the erectness of her mien." During the carriage ride, he surreptitiously watches the movement of her "inimitable beauties." In a reversal of phallus worship, he worships the breast, "the beauty of beauties," her "dazzling beauties," and, as Jocelyn Harris, notes, evokes the imagery of Robert Herrick (71). Richardson empties Clarissa's body of desire and then corporeality. In the second edition Richardson removed the most material and physiological description of Clarissa, Lovelace's fantasy of her with the twins at her breast, "pressing . . . the generous flood into the purple mouths" (4:260). Not only are such references rebuked by Belford and set in contrast to his own chaste admiration of Clarissa's appearance, but Clarissa seems more and more to be an aerophyte.[49] Thus Richardson's text redirects attention from the man that the women were creating and the sexuality that they were learning to express to the construction of the domestic woman with moderated, communal desires.

Similarly Richardson removes the shine from male characters who might have fleshed out the dreams of the domesticated man. Like the ideal man described in Haywood's texts, Belford has a university education, has gained ideas and perspective from it, has traveled in Europe and England, and had had varied and interesting experiences. He can talk about them entertainingly and draw inferences and analogies from them. Among the qualities frequently ascribed to Belford are learned, humane, calm, brave— even fearless, resolute, and clever. He has "honour" and stands by "points of honour"; he can speak with the assurance that fortune and birth give him: "As to the legacy to myself, I assure you, sir, that neither my circumstances nor my temper will put me upon being a gainer by the executorship" (8:94). Clarissa notices his "appearance and air of a gentleman" and even at the first meeting finds him good-natured, obliging, and "complaisant" with "a polite and easy manner of expressing his sentiments" and "a logical way of argumentation" (3:335). His wit and perceptiveness reveal themselves increasingly frequently.[50]

Richardson, however, disqualifies him from being a romantic hero by making him a burly, heavy-featured man.[51] Lovelace compares him to a bear and refers to his "clumsy sides," "fat head," "porterly shoulders," "strong-muscled bony face," and awkwardness. Some of these phrases, such as "porterly shoulders," partake of class prejudices and deny Belford aristocratic status as surely as Richardson does Hickman. That Belford is also described in middle-class occupational poses has the same effect.[52] Belford does, of course, marry the heiress Charlotte Montague, the cleverest of the women on Lovelace's side of the family. This marriage is exemplary but also stripped of mutual fascination and of the sexual element. In *Sir Charles Grandison* Richardson creates a hero much like Belford, yet another "domesticated man," who provides a powerful cultural model.[53]

The second marriage with which Richardson leaves his readers is Anna Howe's to Hickman.[54] It is not surprising that the characteristics of woman about which Richardson writes powerfully in his conclusion are not spirit, liveliness, or even steady principles but "*humble* and *modest,* yet *steady* and *useful,* virtues" that the domestic woman and the angel in the house would exemplify. He has, after all, endorsed Anna's lukewarm feelings for Hickman, a man used for a messenger and ridiculed through most of the novel.[55] In his belated defense of Hickman, Richardson points out that he added two letters to enliven his character, and he also assembles the most favorable statements about him but inadvertently calls to mind the choice the princess refused to make: "Ladies . . . should rather prefer the honest heart of a Hickman, which would be all their own, than to risque the chance of sharing . . . the volatile mischievous one of a Lovelace" (8:294). As late as 2 October, Anna writes, "were I to have chosen a Brother, Mr. Hickman should have been the man; virtuous, sober, sincere, friendly, as he is" (8:179).

Carol Flynn has pointed out the irreconcilable desires in Defoe's fiction and conduct books, and the final descriptions of the marriage between Howe and Hickman make these same conditions obvious and also point out the inadequacies of mid-eighteenth-century language. Flynn demonstrates the contradictory desires for freedom and limitation, individualism and subjection, justice and hierarchy and specifically notes the strains upon fiction that tries to contain both demands for equality and justice within marriage even as domestic harmony depends upon the subordination of the wife.[56] In the "Conclusion Supposed to be written by Mr. Belford," conventional gender characteristics are reversed, for Howe is given "fine sense and understanding" and Hickman "virtue and good nature." His degree of happiness, but not hers, is asserted.[57]

The next few paragraphs struggle to present an example of the way their egalitarian marriage works.[58] The subject is the administration of Clarissa's poor fund. Anna "has allotted" a part of the management to Hickman (reserving to herself Thursday mornings for "her part of the management") and she allows him to choose four objects of charity. That she has so small a part of the week as her share could suggest a subordinate status, or it could indicate that she is the true overseer, like a good steward checking her bookkeeper's work. A more likely interpretation, perhaps one implied by the line, "she assumes the whole prerogative of dispensing this charity," is that he manages the money and she, like a Lady Bountiful, gracefully gives it and receives the recipients' grateful admiration and praise. "In every other case," we are told, there is "one will" between them, although she sometimes demands the tolerant and ingratiating treatment he gave "Miss Howe" even as she simultaneously acknowledges that "she owes him" for his patient courtship and his "generous" behavior in marriage. Thus, Hickman's "right" to be authoritarian and perhaps even tyrannical is acknowledged, and the new kind of marriage the Hickmans seem to represent appears to include play-acting within the normative ideology of the patriarchal marriage. Certainly Alexander Pettit is correct to say that Richardson renders Anna impractical, foolish, and ineffectual.[59]

In *Sir Charles Grandison*, Mrs. Shirley describes her reluctance to marry a man she did not love and the episode in which a friend brought her to her senses. In fact, she summarizes the story line of *La Princesse de Clèves* as her adolescent fantasy: "Suppose, after I have vowed Love to a man quite indifferent to me, I should meet with the very one, the kindred soul, who must irresistibly claim my whole heart? I will not suspect myself of any possibility of misconduct . . . but must I not, in such a case, be for ever miserable?" She even tells her husband of the conversation.[60] The climax of the story is that her friend Mrs. Eggleton notices a book on Mrs. Shirley's table—*La Princesse de Clèves*. She calls the princess "a silly woman" who "was mistaking mere *Liking* for Love." Mrs. Shirley went on to marry and share a happy life with the man. Richardson's critique implies that "mere *Liking*" is mere physical attraction, "a *tindery* fit," fascination with a man "agreeable at a Ball," and the time period to which Clarissa's words about "a kind of Liking" refer (and Richardson's Postscript in which he says she was "*in Liking* only") also suggest an attraction to the appearance and cultivated charm of the man. Since its publication, readers and critics have attempted to discredit the princess's "refusal of love," and many have done it by attacking the representation of the awakening of the heroine to what love is.[61] Richardson is part of this group, and one of his characters says that Mrs. Eggleton "argued poor Love out of doors" (3:400), and even the answers to her invoke duty.

Madame de Lafayette seems to have recognized the skepticism her book would raise. M. de Nemours asks, "Do you think that a woman who was really in love would ever have told her husband? It must be somebody who does not know about love" (145). Although he is attempting to mislead another character and his frame of reference is the highly specific, elaborate code of conduct practiced at that court, he introduces the doubt that can be then addressed almost as directly as if the rhetorical objection/counter-argument structure were being used. His words remind the reader of the code of conduct and simultaneously of the fact that the princess's code of ethics locates her outside of them. His words are also part of the masculine code that associates love with possession and penetration; the princess's actions obviate or at least make less likely and more difficult an adulterous affair. Later the princess says to de Nemours, "I cannot help knowing that you are a born lover. . . . Every woman alive, whether from love or vanity, longs to make a conquest of you" (190). The princess is different; she can control her passions and is therefore immune from acting on the desire motivated by "love," and she lacks the masculine competitive desire motivated by "vanity" of conquest.

In this text we can see the interplay of the three modes of desire in the sexual and textual economy described by Nancy Miller in "Writing from the Pavilion." She points out that the "masculinist discourse" "prizes the time of possession," as de Nemours does, the feminizing "seeks a loving negotiation with the feminine," as the Prince de Clèves does, and the feminist "valorizes the hour that precedes and essentially *precludes* possession." This definition, written to describe other phenomena, is inadequate to describe the feminist resolutions available in women's texts of the period.[62] Although love in *La Princesse de Clèves* is the fated, usually irresistible "inclination" familiar to French romances and platonic plays (for instance, 98, 137, 179), it cannot be denied that the princess has been in de Nemours's company often enough to be drawn to his companionship as well as to his "person." This text and others seem to play literary patterns and expectations against their own fictions, to incorporate a strong sense of women having the capacity for individualistic actions derived from unique personal pasts, and to admit possibilities for happiness independent of heterosexual experience. Most of these texts did present courtship, a variety of Miller's "hour" preceding possession, as almost uniquely a time when women had power, but some of them also valorize a time after the mating dance when women reach self-possession, usefulness, and happiness.

Richardson's novel is not part of this enterprise. Clarissa has, in a sense, handed Anna to Hickman. Her will, which functions as the first of two conclusions, or resolutions, to the novel, is an example of the way Richardson inserts patriarchal interventions into social discourse. Clarissa gives Hickman her miniature of Anna and her words make clear that Hickman is to replace her as Anna's closest friend and confidante. She urges, "let it not be long before you permit his claims to [your hand]."[63] Clarissa uses the word "claim," which suggests possession, if not a pre-existing right earned by his devotion. In contrast to Clarissa, the princess, and Haywood's Fantomina, Anna can be "claimed," and her vestiges of independent free will become indulgences. Moreover, this marriage is self-consciously positioned beside the women's friendship. Richardson has elevated Clarissa's and Anna's friendship, significantly casting it in the language of female friendship associated with the poetry of Katherine Phillips, the "Matchless Orinda." This kind of friendship had been praised but was also vaguely threatening. Not only is there evidence in the literature of the period that men feared friendships between women that became too close, for they were suspected as sites for scheming and for sharing unauthorized knowledge, but also that Orinda's friendship carried from the beginning subtle overtones of lesbianism.[64] Clarissa writes to Anna with the heightened emotionalism of Orinda: "How much more biding and tender are ties of pure friendship, and the union of like minds, than the ties of nature! Well might the sweet singer of Israel . . . say that the love of Jonathan to him was wonderful; that it surpassed the *love of women!*" (6:372). Anna has insisted that she "heartily despise[s] that sex"; "How charmingly might you and I live together, and despise them all!" she writes (1:178).

Another set of problems increasingly evident in the texts of the period concerned the transfer of economic assets to children,[65] and sibling rivalry was a means of representing them. *Clarissa* makes clear that even in a family with a single son contention and issues of the deepest social significance can break out. Again, Clarissa's will imposes a resolution by returning almost all of her property to her father for redistribution. In fact, Clarissa's will is highly gendered. Except for Mrs. Norton, an object of charity, the women receive art objects, clothing, books, hand-made items, lace, and devotional aids, and the men symbols of patrimony: "the" family portraits, inherited plate, jewelry with strong family significance, and property or money. Dolly, for instance, receives the books and music instruments common to women's social education but not the means to protect herself from a bad or failed marriage. She will be spared the envy that destroyed Clarissa's life, but she will not have the chance to use her independent means better.

Both Defoe and Richardson redirect attention from the troublesome common practices of English families to the stories of fathers, and these stories are about control and order more than about revising values and aspirations. As Anna Howe says, "Is true happiness any part of your family view?" This question might have been asked during many contemporary discussions of marriage. Susan Staves has pointed out that later literature about ruined maidens often focused at least as much on the suffering of fathers as on that of the young women and shrewdly locates much of the elegiac tone in these texts in "the death of an idealized older form of the family undisturbed by the free exercise of the wills of the inferior members."[66] Although Defoe and Richardson foreground the experiences and consequences for women, this residual structure of feeling is present as it is not in the novels of Aphra Behn and Eliza Haywood. Lovelace, for instance, sexualizes the hierarchy and concomitant submission to the father in terms of mourning for the orderly family: "I would have the woman whom I honour with my name . . . forego even her *superior duties* for me. . . . Be *a Lady Easy* to all my pleasures, and valuing those most who most contributed to them. . . . Thus of old did the . . . wives of the honest patriarchs; each recommending her handmaid to her lord, as she thought it would oblige him."[67]

Women's texts were making the problems of courtship and of the construction of the ideal man troubling; Defoe and Richardson shifted the focus to marriage, a setting with great appeal to women but one that distracted attention from men and focused it on "woman." More than any other male writers of the eighteenth-century, they saw women's situation clearly and managed to comprehend many of its causes and implications. They helped teach us to look for suffering, strife, and even tragedy in ordinary people's family lives. As Richardson says in his preface, the correspondence between Clarissa and Anna Howe is "upon the most *interesting* subjects; in which every private family, more or less, may find itself concerned" (1:v). Defoe, father of five living daughters, and Richardson of four had in their own lives the conflicting experiences of the patriarchal father produced by their culture and of the parents confronting the beloved individual.

Reared in a church tradition that used marriage metaphors to explain the relationship between God and his people and in a nation that used metaphors of the family to articulate relationships within the state and often saw the health and order of the family as a microcosm of the health and order of the state, they could not avoid conceiving the sexes in binary political terms. As the discussion of marriage and the relationship between the sexes developed in the novel form, the political nature of family and courtship conflicts became increasingly obvious. Novels are full of metaphors, analogies, and allusions that draw attention to the parallel ideological strains in the family and in the larger society. Robinson Crusoe sets himself up as king and enslaves his subjects and kills his pets. Lovelace gloats and remarks, "What a poor thing is a monarch to me!"[68] Questions of authority are writ large, and the inseparable nature of the private body and the public stakes emerge frequently. Nancy Armstrong, in a rather offhand remark, says that the novels that best exemplify "novel" for us are "those which translated the social contract into a sexual exchange." Gwilliam points out how frequently Lovelace compares himself to an *Eastern* monarch, a more despotic and solitary ruler than a Western one, and he fears Clarissa most when she seems like these "exotic tyrants" to him.[69] Even as this comparison emphasizes the extent to which the other sex is Other, alien, hypnotic, it also explicates the ways state power is generated. Both women and men write obsessively about power, about restraint and resistance, oppression and self-respect.

Both Defoe and Richardson perceived some of the implications of the marginality of women and recognized them as symbolic of their own authorial and social marginality. Their texts, then, are among the first that self-consciously present the rise of gender as political categories and the poignancy of the invasion of public opinion into private spaces. They began to question how one can be a male authority without being a tyrant, how enough space can be created for male and female discourse.[70] Yet Roxana is destroyed, and Clarissa and Anna act out the two common resolutions for the courtship plot: death and marriage. It should not be forgotten that Richardson wrote Lady Bradshaigh that men had a responsibility to assert their power and command obedience in marriage and, after several serious letters from her, concluded: "I am sorry to say it, but I have too often observed, that fear, as well as love, is necessary, on the lady's part, to make wedlock happy; and it will generally do it, if the man sets out with asserting his power and her dependence."[71] The beautiful, dead, chaste saint becomes spectacle and exemplar, not solution and model. In fact, unlike Defoe's women, *Clarissa* begins to reveal the reasons that woman cannot be the trope for an emergent form of power. Lovelace knows himself as no literary character ever has before, Belford emerges with a plan for his spiritual and material life, and Clarissa is returned to a plot that man, not woman, drew from the political unconscious.

Thus Richardson deflected attention from the problem of how women might achieve happiness and what they might demand of men and marriage to a resolution that calls for female virtue, exemplary forbearance and sacrifice, and literary closure. As I have argued elsewhere, closure almost always tends to protect existing power structures, and so it does here.[72]

If Clarissa's death is "a political gesture, a shocking, surreal act of resignation from a society whose power system she has seen in part for what it is," it is primarily a resignation, the obscuring of the individual who would not "cede the smallest outpost—not a breast, not a lip" and the creating of the exemplary woman.[73] This exemplary woman is not Haywood's or even Aubin's; rather it is the disciplined woman whose "charms of mind and soul are to displace those of the body,"[74] a conduct book woman with virtues and even a nature with clear gender borders and margins. One of Barker's, Haywood's, and de Lafayette's triumphs was creating women characters who were both dramatizations of the position of their sex and also individuals whose actions still strike the reader as springing from a personality. Richardson does that with Clarissa and Anna Howe, but then contains and erases the possibility by giving us patriarchal closure. As Gordon Fulton says, Belford's Clarissa is no longer "actively producing meaning, assessing, judging, assigning significance"; rather, all of the characters (and most readers) *project* onto her dead body the customary definitions of woman: erotic object, object of sentimental pathos (29).

On balance, Defoe and Richardson did further women's cause. Using the family as political microcosm, as site for dialogic conflict, and as the space in which the coming divide between public and private was prefigured and negotiated, they expanded the subject matter and significance of the form exponentially. It cannot be denied, however, that Richardson diverted the river of novelistic discourse in ways that muted some of the revisionary, even revolutionary inquiries of the early novel and made conservative sources of social order seem at stake. His contribution is, therefore, a quite mixed contribution to fiction presenting women's greater demands on marriage and on authority figures within the family. Studies of mid-century courtship and marriage novels show that Richardson's chaste, disciplined heroines become something of a norm, women who have learned what qualities win admiration and which determine alienation and death.[75] It is my belief, however, that Richardson's novel spawned as many revisionary texts as imitative ones by women, and a detailed study of the resistances and rewritings within them is overdue. Richardson deflected attention from many of their concerns and aspirations, but he could not kill them; we owe it to women's history to reinscribe them.

3 | Renegotiating the Gothic

Betty Rizzo

Much has been made of the gothic mode in the hands of eighteenth-century women, most of it assuming that the gothic was a particularly compatible form to women in their capacities both as readers and as writers. In fact, hysteria and depression might popularly be identified as the emotional correlatives of the gothic. And the suitability for women of the gothic, as both controlling genre and occasional mode, was first of all authorized not by the women, but by the establishment, which did not consider hysteria and irrational emotional excess emanating from male homosexuals displeasing either. From one point of view the argument can be advanced that the gothic in all its altitudes was certainly encouraged and sanctioned and possibly elicited by the establishment from its female and homosexual authors to demonstrate the rational superiority of middle and upper-class male heterosexuals. But to this essential point women writers, both encouraged to write the gothic and rewarded and published for writing it, devised a number of reactive, defensive responses, responses that ranged from demonstrations of the extreme abuse required (and mounted) to deprive women of reason, to boycott or refusal to show women departing from rational self-control, to encoded messages of female rationality and refusal to impose closure until both males and females acquired *both* reason and sensibility.

Satire is the intellectual method, the gothic the emotional method of dealing with the threat of evil. Satire can be generic, like Juvenal's satires, Swift's *Tale of a Tub,* or Voltaire's *Candide*—that is, an actual genre arguably distinguishable from a poem or a novel; or it can be modal—as in sections of Sterne's *Tristram Shandy,* Fielding's *Tom Jones* or Burney's *Evelina*—that is, a satiric voice *within* a work of another genre. Whether generic or modal, satire was largely forbidden eighteenth-century women because it was judgmental of men, thus exercising the rational faculties and encouraging attitudes of moral superiority. The best-known generic satire written in the eighteenth century by a woman is Jane Collier's *An Essay on The Art of Ingeniously Tormenting* (1753), in which she was assisted by her friend Sarah Fielding, though, not surprisingly perhaps, assistance has been attributed to both Samuel Richardson and James Harris.[1]

The gothic as a literary mode was suitable to the inferior author because it involved the emotional response to evil of the impotent—discomfort, fright, terror, or horror. The rational were not considered properly to enter these states, let alone to write about them; acquired philosophical habits, available only through the education given privileged males, were supposed to enable those males to respond with equanimity to any blow. These states are, of course, unfamiliar to no one. But at mid-eighteenth century (and before that and after) to discover a man in a state of fright was comic; as rational control was the male prerogative, the frightened male became instantly demasculinized. The man who slunk pusillanimously away from a challenge was permanently dishonored and risible; the man who like Lord George Germain or Admiral Byng was judged guilty of cowardice on the field of battle was humiliated, ostracized, in Byng's case shot, and in Germain's case unmasked as homosexual. Partridge, in *Tom Jones,* his hair standing on end at the rising of the ghost in *Hamlet,* is ridiculous, *unmanned.* Men—save for the lower orders, of course—were assumed to have their passions firmly in submission to reason at all times, and moreover, to have their view of the world in submission to reason as well—the universe a fine-tuned and in process of becoming a fully comprehensible machine. Women, on the other hand, were *not* in control and were intentionally humored and cosseted when demonstrating their irrationality to the satisfaction of their superiors. Their little terrors, their shrieks, their fainting fits were indulgently approved and encouraged; their romantic (dependent) friendships were sanctioned; it was actually all a demonstration of inadequacy and was rewarded with condescending approbation that, of course, elicited further performance. Moral strength from women, though of course often enough demonstrated, was not officially sanctioned. For male onlookers the display of women in prolonged states of disorientation and fright may have satisfied sadistic longings but, even more importantly, ratified theories of gender difference. Theories of gender difference resulted in theories of the gendering of genre, and the gothic became officially the medium of the irrational and hysterical, women and homosexual males.

The condition of fright may result from a variety of both internal and external causes. Freud considered that contact with the uncanny—that is, an apparent encounter with some idea once long ago familiar but now rejected as untrue—is frightening, ego-disturbing, because it stimulates a regression to a time when the ego had not yet marked itself off distinctly from the external world and other people. Thus the appearance of ghosts in the gothic novel might, by threatening his sense of autonomy, vicariously chill even a male reader in the privacy of his closet, but the utilization of the supernatural must indict both author and responsive reader for irrationality, for rationality depends upon a conviction of autonomy. By its very nature the gothic is uncanny, reviving buried unconscious notions, an action also symbolized in its plots of ancient times, edifices, and religion. Shari Benstock, relating Lacan's schema of the "mirror state" of psychic development to autobiographical writing, notes that the child is served up a false image of a unified "self," that the "mirror stage" is "a metaphor for the vision of harmony of a subject essentially in discord." The unconscious is the seam between the inside and outside, the space of difference, the gap that a drive toward unity of self can never close—and the space of writing.[2] This must particularly be true of writing—and reading—the gothic. Any writing, but especially the gothic, may therefore involve visitations of discomfort and even fright. Powerlessness must trigger in anyone a disturbing image of a not fully unified or autonomous self and therefore frighten. Such theoretical explanations may underpin the fright experienced by victims of abuse, violence, and other instigators of feelings of powerlessness, real or fictitious.

Yet these were the conditions in which many men and most women in the eighteenth-century habitually existed. To express insecurity, fear, and a sense that this was not after all a world ruled by rationality was arguably more realistic than to use one's immense privilege to demonstrate that it was. To show a general aristocratic insouciance was, therefore, to demonstrate one's superiority, safety, seamless harmony, privileged exemption from horrors, and fit citizenship in the newly comprehensible and controllable universe. It would seem, then, that those who experienced and confessed to fright may well have had a clearer view of the actual universe in which they lived than those who purportedly did not. But those who did not were the ones empowered to define, and because they were endorsing an ideology with specific limits, they defined the gothic as an excessive and overemotional form.

In support of this conclusion, Paula Backscheider notes that modern theorists of the novel are suggesting that the gothic form is "now widely accepted as an expression of dissatisfaction with the possibilities of conventional literary realism" and quotes Pierre Mabille, "The real goal of the marvelous journey is the total exploration of universal reality." "This sense of the unknown, of the unpredictable," she goes on, "the essentially threatening nature of the world, and especially of the possibility for familiar limits to collapse underlies the gothic experience. . . . It is the fear of what might happen, of what human beings, even a friend or relative, might suddenly do."[3] The authors of gothic literature were indeed deconstructing the touted well-ordered intelligible world of their masters who were as busily constructing that world as an exhibition of their (sole) dominion.

The single most important identifying feature of the gothic, as I want to show here, is that it accomplishes, though usually in symbolic terms, the exposure of the usurping patriarch, an impostor who is willing to use his power in the most brutal ways in order to perpetuate it, but who in order to perpetuate it must keep his inferiors in darkness as to his unjust tenure and his nefarious means. In the end his ejection from power usually follows his victims' illumination. In this fashion the gothic is essentially a politicized genre. The template perfectly conformed to the English idea of the Roman Catholic church, but it conformed to the situation in England as well, where everyone, whether they approved in a political sense or not, knew that a usurping family was in possession of the throne and that a group of powerful aristocrats ran affairs for their own advantage. This perception undoubtedly contributed to the dissemination of power down the pyramid so characteristic of the period, even privately to the occasional restiveness of more disempowered family members to whom it might appear that the patriarch had also usurped his power and privilege. It was not surprising that those most threatened by the establishment, women and male homosexuals, should ruminate on these conditions through gothic imaginings.

But if the spectacle of women's succumbing to gothic imaginings, thus "proving" their pusillanimity and unfitness, was not displeasing to the patriarchal establishment, the form itself was so rich that it provided multiple means of compensation to the women themselves, and multiple means of deconstructing the message of women's inferiority. Exposing the patriarch and then disposing of him in fictions and reapportioning the power must have provided considerable satisfaction. Ellen Moers pointed out that the gothic, by providing "a device to send maidens on distant and exciting journeys without offending the proprieties," allowed heroines the unusual freedom to move about inside and outside of castles.[4] This is true: gothic heroines when they go adventuring very refreshingly violate many of the feminine proprieties. But sometimes even more important if less obvious than their unusual amount of movement is their ratiocinative activity and exploration: cast upon their own resources with no paternal or uxorial guide, they express curiosity and investigate; they speculate on their discoveries; they theorize; they act without consultation rather than plunge for protection into a man's arms. For the gothic heroine, getting out of danger hinges on understanding herself, her situation, and the nature of her adversary. Hers is not a hubristic sense that through understanding she will be equipped to run or interpret the universe; but through understanding, through knowing what he knows, a heroine could face her antagonist on more equal terms. Symbolically, her education at last is equal to his and so she is equally equipped to understand and to act. If maturity for a man meant the pretense, at least, of a seamless self, these heroines appear to mature by the male prescription. All this is heady business and is one important source of satisfaction for female readers of the gothic (as it was for female writers) that is the obverse of the sexual and the *frisson*. The standard plot of the female gothic at its best—as in Ann Radcliffe— provided an allegorical road map showing women their dilemma and the way out—through education. If the readers, unlike the heroines, had no excuse for violating the feminine proprieties, they still might conclude that by keeping their heads, exerting fortitude or internal resistance, and using their minds to understand their situations, they might find a way out themselves.

Much has been written on the gothic as the figurative expression of women's position. The gothic vocabulary is often as applicable to the life of the female reader as to the heroine: both reader and heroine experienced what Eve Sedgwick has noted to be defining conditions of the gothic: enclosure and deprivation—which might include incarceration, live or symbolic burial, coercion, isolation, the absence of light, the absence of information, the loss of autonomy, the threat of incest or rape: no permission to penetrate, great danger of being penetrated.[5] It is an all but general assumption now that women, if unconsciously, read the plight of the gothic heroine as a symbolic expression of their own.[6] This is also true. But it should be emphasized that the darkness, often expressed as the sudden extinction of a lamp by a gust of wind (or patriarchal breath?) or as a state caused by the patriarchal denial of the means of penetrating light, figures the important denial to women of the information so formally denied women in their separation from the masculine texts and seats of learning where they would have acquired the male postures of rationality that would illuminate their plight and thereby help them escape it. They are required to subdue their terrors, to solve the mystery, to understand their situation. That light denied also symbolizes the interdiction of reasoning for themselves. But because the heroines in their lonely darkness do treasure the little they can learn and continually add to it, do theorize about it and test their theories, *do* reason, the gothic mode sometimes provided another means of vicarious satisfaction to women. At the end of Radcliffe's novels the mysteries are cleared away, and the heroine, who has stubbornly clung to her powers of reason despite all temptations to give way to self-directed sensibility, understands almost everything. In the general satisfaction that all has been explained to the reader, the fact that the heroine has emerged from mental darkness into a power-bestowing light that the patriarchy might consider a little excessive for a woman is fortuitously overlooked.

The consideration of the gothic mode as the mode assigned to women writers because most compatible with the female gift of sensibility thus becomes complicated and problematized; the response of women writers to that assignment begs analysis. Perhaps a reminder here that conventionally the separate assignment of reason and sensibility to the two separate sexes resulted in the confinement of reason to the masculine gender will be useful. Mary Astell was an early counter-claimant of the equality of woman's reason to man's. She ingeniously considered that one proof of woman's great mental and moral strength was her ability to defer to man because of social necessity, for the purpose of social order. It took great wisdom and goodness, she said, "to give up the Cause when she is in the right and to submit her enlightened Reason, to imperious Dictates of a blind Will, and wild Imagination, even when she clearly perceives the ill Consequences of it, the Imprudence, nay Folly and Madness of such a Conduct."[7] But during the eighteenth century, the convenient stereotype of woman as the emotive counterpart to rational man increasingly dominated.

Janet Todd notes that women were more and more encouraged to live up to the new concept of sensibility and therefore not to use calm reason. Alice Browne notes that women were considered to be less rational or at least "expressed their rationality in ways that had more to do with taste and intuition, and less with logic and abstract thought." Elizabeth Bergen Brophy notes that "Weakness of intellect, 'natural imbecility,' especially in the faculty of reason, coupled with an inherent tendency to the uncontrolled, the passionate and the impetuous meant that women should be under the care and guidance of the superior creature who was gifted with wisdom, rationality, and strength."[8]

At the start of the century woman was seen as too passionate emotionally and (especially) sexually to behave rationally (as men of course did). At the end of the century decent women, now endowed with obligatory sexual passivity, were too regulated by feeling and sensibility to behave rationally. Women's sexual nature had been in theory anesthetized but if her sexual nature had been radically retheorized, her emotional nature had not, and man remained the only proper, rational master. And if with her ascribed emotional and intuitive nature she might have understood more of the limitations, negative aspects, and implications of the dominant ideology than her rational superiors did, they never suspected it and certainly never detected it in the gothic.

By mid-century for women writers the directions were clear. Women were not to write rational discourse; their provinces were the sentimental novel or drama or moral treatises designed to instruct women and children about their proper spheres. Or novels, that new form apparently without classical pedigree. The novel of sensibility was a particularly proper female domain. Elizabeth Griffith could produce—aware that it would sell—a much-approved success, *The Delicate Distress* (1769), in which a healthy young married woman resists the comfort offered her by a sincere and deserving lover and nearly dies of the distress deriving from a husband in the grips of an unlucky passion for an unworthy but fascinating siren. Both her refusal to listen to another attractive man and her decline were precisely on target at the time, as Griffith, who had to support a family by writing, well knew. This novel is modally gothic, its sentimental frame story redolent of gothicism because of the seeming immobilization and helplessness to fight back of the heroine paralyzed by the contemporary form for good women, and is inset with a variety of tales in the romantic or gothic mode. The innocent heroine, unaware that she does not possess her husband's full love and of his prior affair with an artful and experienced woman he cannot forget, herself completely *encased* within her marriage and home, can only react to events without influencing them, finally succumbs emotionally and physically to her misery, and revives only because of the fortuitous return of her husband's affections and regard.

How can the quietly virtuous domestic woman of sensibility compete with the exuberantly sexual and plotting dragon lady? Ignorance is, as always, her enemy; when she and her husband are in the presence of his former mistress, she is the one who is out of the secret and so she behaves with inappropriate kindness and consideration, which only makes her look, to the others, like a fool. Even when she understands the situation, her hands are tied: by 1769 good women did not contrive plots; nor did they complain to their husbands because a complaint would suggest he was less than perfect. By sheer good fortune—and the opportune misbehavior of her rival—she is left in the end a far safer and more mature woman, accepting of the postulate of the novel that no one is responsible for the passions which assail as irresistible impulse. Knowledge once again has been won, if hard bought, and she is equipped to continue in her station as lady of the manor.

The gothic mode as utilized by Griffith was clearly a compatible form for women. Men had no objection whatsoever to women's acknowledging their situation and their helplessness to remedy it or to their decline into the sickbed or hysteria. In the gothic world the characters succumb to known or unknown terrors, suffer from incapacities forced on them, or, naturally inadequate to the challenges they face, give way to imagined evils and suffer a variety of emotions unacceptable for the privileged male, such as terror and despair. In particular it would seem their reasoning powers are inadequate for solving their problems, which require the penetration of ancient secrets and modern plots to unmask and defeat the powerful usurper—in this particular case, as in many others, simply a husband. Meanwhile their autonomy is stolen from them. And all the dismay engendered certified the form as very proper to the female author of the gothic who, while privately indicting contemporary society, as Griffith certainly was, was conceived of as in fact validating current ideology of woman's place in the world.

Women writers did not, however, easily or quickly adapt to the gothic pattern of cruelly aggressive males and victimized women. The romances of the women writers of the early eighteenth-century often minimized gender differentiation, writing plots in which both men and women were equally libidinous and, sometimes, destructive. Both men and women in the novels of Behn, Manley, and the early Haywood are ingenious plotters, whereas one finds that, gradually, decent eighteenth-century women like Griffith's heroine become incapable of contriving plots or counterplots even when their preservation is at stake and even when they are the victims of other ingenious plotters. Others less virtuous or Providence itself must intervene to save them.

By contrast, in Manley's *The Power of Love in Seven Novels* (1720), women are quite equal to men as ingenious, impassioned, and vengeful predators, and there are both women and men of scrupulous delicacy. In this volume of one long novella and six short tales (1) The beautiful young wife of the elderly Duke of Savoy falls in love with the portrait of a handsome Spanish nobleman and feigns an illness so as to pledge a pilgrimage to Campostella and thus meet him; she succeeds, the couple meet and fall in love, but virtue preserves their chastity. A duke at her own court, passionately in love with her and rebuffed, manages to counterfeit a scene of illicit love between her and his own nephew, kills the nephew to suppress his explanation, and sees her condemned to die. Her Spanish lover in disguise fights her accuser and wins her freedom and then her hand. It is the virtue of the couple (despite the Spanish plot of the "fair hypocrite") that ensures their eventual happiness. Obviously at this date the ability to plot is a positive not a negative characteristic even in a woman, and mental ingenuity is applauded. (2) A physician plots to drug and impregnate a young noblewoman with the aid of her companion, then offers to marry her to cover her shame, later boasts of his deception and is killed in a duel by her former lover whom, however, she cannot now marry as he has killed the father of her children. She ends her life in a convent. (3) Violenta, a woman of inferior estate, is privately married by a nobleman who then marries a woman of his own class. Violenta entices him to her bed and dissects his perfidious parts into gobbets, which she throws from her window, is thus, because of her undisguised crime, detected and subsequently beheaded. (4) A marquis who has married beneath him discovers his wife has taken an inferior lover, forces her and her maid to hang the lover, and then secretly immures them with the body. He is apparently undiscovered and unpunished. (5) Another husband detecting his ungrateful wife in adultery treats her and her lover with great apparent courtesy and then feeds her a poisoned salad. Having acted the devoted husband, he is undetected. (6) The daughter of King Otho of Germany and a valiant cousin of hers, like most protagonists in the book passionately in love, elope in the dress of pilgrims; they are robbed, made destitute, befriended by a forest hermit, and assume a humble country life in his cave. Their son feeling his nobility, proves his heredity in the army through heroic action and is discovered by his grandfather, who forgives his daughter and restores the family to his court. (7) A young man and a beautiful nun fall in love and elope, unaware that they are half-brother and sister. Discovered, he is hanged, she burnt alive.

Manley's standards for women, whether virtuous in passion or passionately destructive, are the same as her standards for men. Both genders are equally mastered by the passion of love, and self-control, including the imposition of chastity, is exhibited by the best of both. At one critical point the heroine of the first tale is enjoined by her maid, "Be not so far mastered by your Passions, as to fall into a Womanish Weakness, unworthy your Rank or Understanding." The princess of the sixth tale is stronger and braver than her lover, whom she has to shore up against adversity; it is she, not he, who delivers a funeral oration over the grave of their hermit benefactor. And the book is dedicated to Lady Lansdowne, who left her home and family to share her lord's fortunes, praising "Your Fortitude, Heroick

Vertue, and Conjugal Love, which chearfully carried You to support a voluntary Eighteen Months Imprisonment with your Lord." It is doubtful that the ideology of 1720 so equated the attributes of both sexes, but Manley struggled to do so as Eliza Haywood did in the contemporaneous *Love in Excess* (1719–20), in which both men and women suffer uncontrollable passion, contrive vicious plots, or demonstrate virtue. And though some of Manley's tales can be identified as modally gothic, only the unworthy characters ever succumb to dissolution in emotion. In fact, Manley adopts classist rather than sexist attitudes. The encroaching physician, his companion accessory, and the ungrateful wife of the fourth tale are motivated by a moral incapacity apparently owing to inferior class, while the seeming peasant son of the sixth tale becomes a valiant warrior because it is in the blood. In particular Violenta's lack of control of her passion, which results in her own death—the aristocratic avenging husbands are clever enough to get away with their murders—is attributable to her inferior heredity. Conversely, the nobly born women are equal in ability and resourcefulness to the men. This ideal of men and women equal in the attributes of reason and passion is thus a familiar one at the start of the eighteenth century, a point important to remember when women at the end attempt to restate and reintroduce it.

But conventions change, and after mid-century virtuous women in fiction slowly grew unimpassioned and passive. Lady Mary Wortley Montagu's court tales, which may date from as late as 1746–56,[9] were written abroad where their author had been living since 1739, a fact that may account for their anachronistic portrayal of Mademoiselle de Condé and the philosopher Fontenelle as both equally impassioned to the point of madness; that the male lover brought to an excess of emotion is a revered philosopher is also a telling point. In "Louisa," the Duke D'Enguien loves to the point of contracting *hereos,* the medievally diagnosed (and most unfortunate) disease of impassioned love that renders the victim unrecognizable. The submission of the reason to the passions is not gendered by Montagu despite the late date, and the ideology of her tales, certainly not formed by developments at home, is in curious contrast to Sarah Fielding's *The Adventures of David Simple* (1744), in which both males and females, still construed, if now defiantly, as similar in both reason and sensibility, are all uniformly sexually repressed and despite all disillusionment and persecution remain firmly rational and unimpassioned.

It has been noted that Sarah Scott contrived the romantic adventures of her heroine in *The History of Cornelia* (1750) as genuine gothic trials. The novel has everything a gothic needs except emotional affect, for the heroine refuses to suffer and rigorously retains her rational outlook. Cornelia is a wanderer figure—a figure very much present in the imaginations of women at the time, a woman without shelter, connections, or wherewithal, cut off from the patriarchy, intoxicatingly but frighteningly free. Scott's response to this fantasy is to paint her heroine as unrealistically resourceful, brave, self-controlled, and successful. The victim of the irrational passions of many, she retains her own rationality. Her uncle-guardian represents the ubiquitous usurping tyrant of the gothic, the powerful patriarch whose unjust control must be combated, exposed, and bested by the youthful hero or heroine. His incestuous designs force Cornelia to flee and to hide her identity. She is abducted twice and escapes from both rape and a brothel. She is imprisoned in a castle's secret room and in the Bastille. She will not marry an unworthy man and when the man she loves is traduced as a libertine, she renounces him—the ultimate test of the rationality and strength of a heroine, proving her independent moral standards and self-reliance. Already well-educated, Cornelia supports herself as a governess. When at last her lover is proved worthy, she marries him and together they establish a utopian neighborhood. The heroine's trials are pure gothic but she never wavers or despairs. Scott's position is prototypical, but later women would learn from Horace Walpole to utilize gothic emotions of bewilderment, terror, even despair, to enhance the attractions of their books.

When Scott reworked her theme in *A Journey through Every Stage of Life* (1754), her heroine Leonora, still more triumphant, takes a small company with her and supports them by masquerading as a man and using her talents as teacher, tutor, preacher, portrait painter—all talents, incidentally, which Scott possessed but by which she could not earn money. Leonora thus demonstrates that society refuses permission to women to use their talents to support themselves and that it is much simpler for a man to roam the world. Dedicated to showing women as at least the equals of men, Scott would have scorned to depict them as frightened or inadequate. Working against mid-century stereotypes of gender, she managed, by presenting her fictions as romances, to get away with her audacious plots.

She would, however, use the gothic mode again. In *A Description of Millenium Hall* (1762), a number of women in a number of short narratives are wickedly mistreated by men. The beautiful little Miss Mancel has been adopted by her guardian solely for his subsequent sexual usage and escapes only through his unexpected death. Miss Melvyn is forced into a miserable match by a designing stepmother abetted by a father who too carelessly submits to his wife; her husband forbids her to see her friend and virtually immures her and she is released from durance only by his eventual death. Lady Mary Jones is narrowly saved from an elopement with an already married man. Harriot Trentham, whose "reason governed her thoughts and actions," is jilted by her lover for a silly flirt whom she herself cannot teach to think. While men might with impunity own their natural children, Miss Selvyn learns of her errant mother's identity only on that mother's deathbed. These women, all eventually saved through the kindness of Providence alone, end their stories in the serenity of the Hall where plots end and community is born.[10] Other communities too are released from sometimes near-gothic torments. The handicapped community of the physically abnormal is saved from being put on display and mocked. Unmarried women are saved from the humiliation of becoming paid companions. The animal creation is preserved from unnecessary torture. Even the environment is lovingly maintained. Tess Cosslet has described "a separate female world from where they make subversive criticisms of the world that is run by men" as a world achieved in Charlotte Brontë's *Shirley*.[11] That separate female world is often achieved by the female writers of the gothic.

The condition of the Jamaican slaves revealed by Scott in *The History of Sir George Ellison* (1766) is pure gothic, as in fact the condition, faithfully related, of any slaves must be, deprived as they are of liberty, free choice, knowledge, and wages, beaten and treated like animals. Scott is fully aware of this fact, even as the white Jamaicans are not; but again, characteristically of Scott, the inner feelings of the slaves are not exploited; the tone of the book is consistently one of cheerful reason. When Ellison is thwarted in love, his task is to subdue his disappointment and to make possible the marriage of the woman he loves with the man she prefers. Scott takes a position different from that of Griffith, who followed the earlier tradition proclaimed by such writers as Eliza Haywood in *Love in Excess* that the passion of love could not be gainsaid or countermanded, that the lover was not to blame. Ellison's love came not as a *coup de foudre* but as the result of observation of merit and the mistaken notion that his object was still free to choose. He was unable to free himself from it—when he learns that his rival is likely to die, he cannot resist a stirring of happiness—but he was able rigidly to control it. Scott was temperamentally incapable of exploiting emotion.

Richardson's *Clarissa*, if it were not so many other things, might be classified as a demystified gothic, that is a gothic removed from antique times and foreign spaces to the eighteenth-century English world. Certainly if not generically gothic it is modally so. It features the abuse of patriarchal privilege, its usurpation by brother James, its exploitation by Lovelace, and the eventual exposure of the unworthiness of all the assuming patriarchs, while Clarissa is serially deprived of liberty, autonomy, estate, the right to communicate, her control of her own body, and at last her life, and at various times expresses sufficient terror and disorientation to qualify as a gothic heroine. It is no accident that the tradesman Richardson interested himself in indicting the male privilege from which he himself was largely excluded.

But it is generally accepted that Horace Walpole with *The Castle of Otranto* (1764) produced the first generic gothic novel, and one significant distinction between his plot and Richardson's is his long ago and far away setting while the distinction between his plot and that of Scott's *Cornelia* is that his characters respond emotionally in realistic terror to the natural and supernatural assaults on them. The plot that took possession of him derived from a dream of a giant hand in mail on a banister. Walpole, almost certainly homosexual, and thus like Richardson and Scott an outsider, conceived his marvelous tale, in which both young men and young women are tyrannized by the usurping tyrant, as a romance. That usurping tyrant must in this case have derived in significant part from Walpole's father Sir Robert Walpole, the super-powerful prime minister who had usurped the power of a usurping king, George II. Walpole, of course, is the prototypical patriarch whose powers in the gothic are always misappropriated and bolstered by secret machinations that necessitate ever-increasing oppression of the ignorant. In this respect Sir Robert Walpole, as imagined by his son, inspires all the gothic villains to follow.

Walpole's dream and the narrative he subsequently wrote at white heat in a burst of atypical male hysteria might indeed derive from both a terror of paternal punishment for unorthodox sexual behavior and a compensating perception of the gap between his father's acclaimed achievement of a great stable period in English history and the truth, which he must have seen at first hand, about his father's corrupt means of maintaining control through massive bribery, and a close and dreary second-hand view of the true character of George II and his consort. Thus, in the cases of both his father and the king, he was apparently conscious of the spuriousness of the tyrant's claims of the right to rule either through birth or through virtue. The ubiquitous theme of the impatience of the young to supplant the established elders (and change the rules), the elders' determination to maintain their power, without which the comedy of the period, let alone the tragedy, could scarcely have thrived, is also often adapted to the gothic in the theme of the pure and as-yet-uncorrupted youth in brave conflict with corrupt authority. It is a gothic theme accentuated beyond the comic into the realm of the perilous where the young must, in order to survive and vanquish, master the secrets of the elders and then, as rightful heirs, supplant them.

Beyond his exaggeration of that perpetually relevant and interesting theme, Walpole's great contributions to the romance of the ancient castle were first the addition of characters, if not realistic at least fully recognizable, from contemporary drama and then, most important, their consistent experience of terror and horror communicable to the reader, this last a dominant identifying characteristic of the gothic second only to the theme of the usurping patriarch. Through the steady fortitude of the hero or heroine the reader may pursue vicarious adventure, but through the extremes of emotion experienced by the fictitious protagonists as they combat the powerful father, the reader does not *observe* but *feel* their plight; and as we know from the prevalence of horror movies in our time, many people are addicted to vicarious terror. Vicarious disposal of the frightening father was equally gratifying at the period, as one can see from the disposal of the domineering Stuart kings and the transformation of the vengeful Jehovah into the predictable deistic machine. So Partridge's ridiculed response to the appearance of Hamlet's father's ghost is actually precisely what the readers of the gothic longed to experience.

In order to produce this effect, Walpole had first to provide characters with whom the reader might empathize, and then to subject them to every kind of terror—threats of death or rape by the tyrant Manfred, threats of retribution by supernatural powers. Manfred himself—carefully characterized as having good qualities as well as the bad ones caused by his entrapment in unmerited, stolen empowerment—is frantic at the first supernatural event and moves on to anxiety and horror at the next, but is never rendered incapable of outrageous action. But his daughter Matilda is trembling and terrified before him and faints when he orders the peasant Theodore beheaded, and his ward Isabella trembles throughout the tale, is half dead with fright and horror at his marriage proposal, is in agonies of despair when the gust of wind extinguishes her lamp. The servants, distinguished by their superstitions and volubility (class distinctions are commonly upheld in the gothic), are terrified by the genuine apparitions. Despite the general panic, however, Theodore, the hero and rightful heir, is cool as is the long-suffering wife Hippolita, and, apart from two brief episodes, the daughter Matilda. Isabella, threatened by Manfred with a forced and bigamous marriage and the obligation to produce many heirs, is most consistently reduced to a state of trepidation. And faithful to mid-century ideology, unlike the heroines of several decades earlier, these women are no longer motivated to action by libidinous passions or vengeful fury; the discarded wife, Hippolita is compliant rather than vengeful, and as the pursued, Isabella can only flee but cannot plot or retaliate. The novel thus sets up a paradigm of cool controlling men and sexually threatened, abused, and disintegrating, or at least disempowered, women, leaving some reparative work for women writers.

And despite some risible improbabilities (such as the giant sword and helmet), the book had an enormous success and influence. The reader's opportunity to experience a *frisson* elicited both emotional and sado-masochistic satisfaction, and the gendered difference of response to stress and terror increased the éclat. The implication that the imaginary ordered political world of the 1730s and 1740s might in reality have been a world in which a tyrant impostor or two resorted to any crime necessary to preserve power may or may not have reached the author's consciousness or that of his readers. What the book did do was to encourage the expression of what now appears to be excess emotionality in the confrontation of situations that were essentially political. This was therefore not a new phenomenon in the 1790s. There was apparently something extremely seductive about deposing illegitimate tyrants but at the same time something terrifying about it. A great deal of the emotionality of daughters toward their fathers in the second half of the century may owe something to the same terrifying but seductive impulse toward deposition.

Walpole's formula, conceived at one blow, did not immediately triumph. In 1777, Clara Reeve set out to imitate but also to refine Walpole's invention, and her refinements suggest her unwillingness to subject her heroines to terror. She noted in the preface to *The Old English Baron* that though we can allow for the appearance of a ghost, Walpole's book was made risible by its "violent machinery." She eschewed violence, and her softly haunted suite of shut-up rooms and her gentle ghosts appearing particularly in dreams are never comic.

Less obvious is her omission of terror, particularly of terrified women. Only in the secret past had the baroness been threatened with marriage to her husband's murderer (a favorite theme), fled the castle, given birth in the fields, and drowned while seeking protection for her child. But there is no indication that she was ever emotionally overwhelmed by her trials, and we meet her only as a calm and loving spectral presence. The young woman Emma, who is to marry the rediscovered heir, is scarcely characterized at all and rarely ruffled. The peasant-heir is invariably noble and collected.

Though recognized as a generic gothic novel, the book has been almost universally judged disappointing and dull and is usually out of print. For one thing, the castle is inhabited only by a blamelessly virtuous brother-in-law of the murdering usurper, who himself remains for a long time offstage and fails to threaten the discoverers of his misdeeds; his sins are in the past, and unlike a proper tyrant he is unwilling to abduct and kill in order to prevent their discovery. It is the absence of terror emanating from this limpid villain that renders the book tame and—even on the symbolic level, because the villain does not faithfully represent the presence of the power of the patriarchy—untruthful. Politics may underlie this difference, for Walpole was always a republican, while Reeve, well read politically, was a conservative and a believer in the old hierarchical values. Her message in 1777 may well have been that tyrannical outrages were confined to the past, and though past misdeeds might be discovered and rectified, present power was in the hands of the well-intentioned. Such an interpretation was not, however, general.

Women writers throughout the century continued to support the principle of women's ratiocinative powers and their equality to those of men even as they learned to manipulate the popular gothic mode. One important locus of this manipulation is in their autobiographical writings and their letters. Women in their private or semiprivate writings were generally reluctant to admit to terror or loss of self-control. A woman like Lady Mary Wortley Montagu can describe a gothic situation in which she found herself entrapped for ten years while scarcely admitting to discomposure. While she was living in Brescia, she was exploited by the Palazzi family who, as Isobel Grundy writes, "evidently assume that an elderly foreign woman (all alone and presumed to be wealthy) can have no right to any cash, jewels, or land to which the head of a noble family in the prime of life does not have a better claim."[12] She is isolated in a ruinous house, lured away so her jewels can be stolen, cheated into buying properties to which the titles are not genuine, relieved of various sums of money. A growing sense of the perfidy of Count Palazzi, a growing terror at the realization of the lengths to which he will go, fail to afflict her; she remains peculiarly passive. Finally when she seems to be about to escape Palazzi's control, she recognizes that she is a prisoner, her very life threatened. Every gothic theme is exploited *except* that of terror in the victim, who the "Memoir" presents as "a woman who not only allows herself to be milked by Palazzi year after year, but who seems almost complicitous in her own exploitation, too apathetic to exert control, willing to excuse rather than accuse her oppressor, tacitly accepting the victim-role which she does not recognize or name."[13] Grundy avoids speculation as to whether Palazzi, almost thirty years her junior, was Lady Mary's lover (as was rumored) and was exacting his fees, and such a relationship might well have interfered with a gothic interpretation of her exploitation by Lady Mary. At any rate Lady Mary's philosophical complaisance precluded, as Grundy remarks, the use of gothic convention.

> She can afford no build-up of suspense, no steadily increasing conviction of something rotten somewhere, if she wants to make her own continuing acceptance appear sane. As well as youth, beauty, energy, naivete, and un-committed future, she lacks a heroine's willingness to perceive transcendent evil and to go in terror of her life. In her account the elements of com-monplace and of grotesque comedy (which novels found permissible in ser-vants but not in a villain) stifle the emerging gothic mood. That strategy for combining the roles of victim and heroine is closed to her. (343)

That is, she refuses to relinquish the role so dear to her of thinking subject to admit for one moment that she has lost autonomy. So dear is that image to her that throughout the ten-year ordeal she writes to her daugh-ter in quite another mode, as a cheerful expatriate, never mentioning her problems with Palazzi. In the "Memoir," in apparent control of herself to the end, she outwits her captors and escapes to Venice, where, though she finds Palazzi ensconced in her house as a part of her ménage, she manages at last to rid herself of him. She was sixty-seven when the ten-year episode concluded and might easily have died, almost literally in his hands, during that period.

Here is a refusal, in an account probably recorded for use in a lawsuit should one ensue, in which the victim of genuine gothic terrors refuses to acknowledge or yield to them. Though she must have experienced mo-ments of terror or despair, in her writing Montagu simply repudiates the gothic mode in order to claim her rationality and her control of circum-stance at all times and all costs.

Mary Delany (probably the original of Scott's Mrs. Morgan in *Millen-ium Hall*), on the other hand, briefly interprets her experience through the gothic mode when long years after she writes about the miseries of her first marriage and of her emotional breakdown on entering for the first time her husband's Cornish seat. The inability to remove oneself from painful circumstances or to assert one's autonomy, to deny one's company to those who denigrate and abuse one, is precisely the kind of condition that may elicit the gothic sensibility—a sense of rising terror of worse evils to come expressed in images of deprivation and incarceration. Delany was many years removed from the date of her first marriage when she wrote her recollections of it, and she had experienced since that time a second happy marriage and a tranquil widowhood, but clearly she wanted to evoke the horrors of the situation in which she had been sold into marriage by her uncle to a man she thoroughly disliked and whom she had informed she never could love. "The day was come," she wrote in recollection of this period, "when I was to leave all I loved and valued, to go to a remote country, with a man I looked upon as my tyrant—my jailor; one that I was determined to obey and oblige, but found it impossible to love."[14] In this fragment of autobiography she renames her husband Gromio and his Cornish seat Averno, the entrance to the underworld; indeed, the quality of life there during the seven years of her marriage suggests Persephone's season in hell. Even looking back upon this period of her life, Delany was incapable of treating it without a trembling sensibility. She uses the gothic to convey in economic fashion the horror of the situation into which she had been forced.

> When we arrived at Averno, the name of his seat, I was indeed shocked. The castle is guarded with high walls that entirely hide it from your view. When the gate of the court was opened and we walked in, the front of the castle terrified me. It is built of ugly coarse stone, old and mossy, and propt with two great stone buttresses, and so it had been for threescore years. I was led into an old hall that had scarce any light belonging to it; on the left hand of which was a parlor, the floor of which was rotten in places, and part of the ceiling broken down; and the windows were placed so high that my head did not come to the bottom of them.
>
> Here my courage forsook me at once, and I fell into a violent passion of crying and was forced to sit down some minutes to recover myself. My behavior to be sure shocked Mr. Pendarves, and I was sorry I had not a greater command of myself; but my prison appeared so dismal, I could not bear the surprise, not expecting to see so ruinous a place. (1:35–37)

Delany is confessing not to a present weakness but to one that was long past and deliberately summons up the gothic to convey not only her distress but the injustice of what had been done to her.

A similar moment is recorded in Elizabeth Chudleigh's autobiography. The putative duchess of Kingston was much given to romanticizing her life and aggrandizing her power, but would never, one would imagine, choose to picture herself as a gothic, victimized heroine. She was manly in her sang-froid during the events of her life and in her account of them and boasted of her male prerogatives in a way that once paints the duke as her own particular gothic victim:

The first fervour of his passion cooled, the duke began to perceive the faults of his wife, and to grieve extremely at her extravagance and carelessness; he expostulated with her, but it was useless. Elizabeth acknowledged no law but her own capriciousness and arrogant will, and made her husband feel the full weight of the chain he had assumed. He was gentle and yielding, and quite unequal to a contest with his lady; he sank into a state of perfect submission, but became fretful and delicate; and after some years of patient suffering, he died of consumption in 1773, leaving the duchess sole heiress of his fortune, on condition that she not marry again. Elizabeth was affected by her husband's death, for, though imperious, she was not hard-hearted.[15]

The duke's might have been the sorry story of many a wife. Chudleigh paints herself as the perfect tyrant, consciously glowing in the reversal of roles. But there must have been some faltering of her confidence during the dark days before and during her trial for bigamy in 1776, after Kingston's relations had (falsely) determined that to disprove her marriage would be to revoke his bequest, and accordingly attempted to prove the legality of her previous marriage to Augustus Hervey, now Earl of Bristol. When she was summoned from Rome to appear before a court of her peers at Westminster, her failure to have done so would have resulted in a sentence of outlawry. She was not apprised that on her return bail could be posted, and she anticipated immediate imprisonment. She suspected her Rome banker of collusion with the Kingston heirs and had to force travel money from him at pistol point. She set out bravely but broke down in health on the journey, developed an abscess and a fever and became critically ill. Carried in a litter to Calais, she was taken to a hotel unconscious and delirious. Here she lay for some weeks in a state which she sums up in a sentence: "She fancied herself in prison, abandaned [*sic*] by the world, and given up a powerless victim to her enemies." In those weeks, then, she apparently suffered the agonies of the persecuted and the powerless, the deprived and incarcerated; but as she herself remarks, these were *fancies*, the effect of fever and delirium. The agonies were prolonged during the trial but never publicly revealed or admitted. On her arrival in London and after confabulation with her lawyers, the trial was delayed for a year while her physicians claimed at one point that she had fallen mad, at another that a paralytic attack had destroyed her memory.[16] The trial finally occurred in April 1776, when Chudleigh was confirmed in her inheritance but also convicted of bigamy and would have been burned in the hand had not her legal husband's elevation as Earl of Bristol exempted her as a peeress. A decree of *ne exeat regno* (confinement to England) was issued; Chudleigh invited friends to dine, had her coach driven conspicuously about the streets, and set off in disguise for Dover, sailing at night in an open boat covered by a borrowed cloak. Still in possession of Kingston's wealth, she was now an exile abroad.

There is material ripe for gothic treatment here, but save for the sentence revealing a period when her imagination put her into a state of terror, Chudleigh imperiously ignores the invitation. Her courage and her triumphs were her theme of choice. Her description of the trial is delivered in measured language and demonstrates inward terror but outward unremitting self-control. She retained counsel but claims to have conducted her own defense and to have preserved an outward calm throughout the trial though "her mind was distracted with a thousand anxieties and fears, and no tongue could describe the torture she endured" (1:230). Her friends had asked her during the period of her trial to abate two practices that were attracting unfavorable notice: she refused to observe the Sabbath "with all the strictness required by her fellow-countrymen," and "her neck and arms being very handsome [she was now fifty-six], she very naturally wished to display them" (1:229). But "this imperious lady had been too long accustomed to consider her slightest caprice as a law to which all should bow, she unhesitatingly refused to do that which she considered would reduce her to the level of ordinary mortals."

To depict oneself as a gothic heroine is, like Delany, to confess to one's powerlessness, one's victimization at the hands of the patriarchy. It was, however, Chudleigh who had made a bigamous marriage, who had managed to divert her duke's wealth from its proper patriarchal disposition, and who here plays the gothic tyrant. Though there are moments when Chudleigh doubts her own powers, she always triumphs over her enemies and her depiction of further distresses is romantic but not gothic, for she never succumbs, is always a heroine, and maintains her right to enjoy passion where she finds it. In Rome in 1775 she had fallen in love with "Prince Warta," an adventurer, son of an ass-driver at Trebizond. His charms were his assured princely manner, the handsomest person "that nature ever produced," and magnificent clothing aglitter with jewels, "which sparkled on every part of his dress, from the waving plume of his hat, to the brilliant hilt of his sword" (1:237). He was precisely what Kingston had feared when he abjured Chudleigh not to marry again. Like hers, Warta's conversation was brilliant and she was in love with him "with that excess of passion that is felt by some as they decline in years, when they seem to gather all the energies of their being into one last effort of tenderness. This strange passion conquered all the lesser feelings of her soul" (1:237).

While Chudleigh was in England awaiting trial, Warta was unmasked by the Turkish ambassador as "a Greek Adventurer of the worst character." He was arrested and imprisoned in Holland, where he drank poison from a ring and died, leaving a sentimental letter for Chudleigh (she claimed) that confessed his imposition and reaffirmed his love: "Farewell again, but not for ever—yet we shall meet in the home of souls like ours, where, stripped of earthly prejudices, each shall be judged upon his individual merits. Until this happy day, farewell, farewell, beloved" (1:242). Her first response to the blow of loss was conceivably to write his letter. But she was determined to rise above pain, injury, and despair, all of which were beneath her state.

> This unfortunate event nearly overwhelmed the duchess; her crushed affec-
> tions and her wounded pride waged fearful warfare in her breast; but she was
> obliged to meet society, to cloak her agony in smiles, and hide from a cen-
> sorious and ill-judging world the struggle that rent her soul. In public she
> was calm and cheerful, but within the sacred precincts of her own chamber,
> where no unsympathising eye was by to mock her grief, she poured forth the
> anguish of her heart in tears and sighs. (1:242)

This is romantic suffering and posturing without terror, princely self-control, the loss of a lover but no loss of autonomy. Her lover Warta had died rather than submit to that loss.

Delany's recollection, written to her niece but understood to be potentially more widely circulable, is an attempt to use the gothic in order economically to direct her readers to an interpretation of her situation: powerless, in despair, imprisoned by an unfeeling patriarch, a warning not to sell young women into marriage in that manner.

Gothic terror could also be simulated for selfish purposes. Elizabeth Foster, bosom friend of Georgiana, duchess of Devonshire, and mistress of her friend's husband the duke, was abroad in 1785 to conceal the birth of her child by the duke and kept private journals still extant intended for the eyes of the Devonshires, to both of whom she played romantic friend. As a separated wife without sufficient money, she had played on the sympathies of the duchess from the start as "poor little Bess." Apparently for years both husband and wife contributed to her support.

During Foster's first obligatory trip abroad in Naples in 1785 she was concealing her seven-months' pregnancy and boasting a conquest: "My God, my God assist me—help me to hide my shame and sorrow from the friends it would afflict—I must undeceive the D. of Dorset in his opinion of me—it is too good a one—yet how to do it, and not endanger my secret?

I hate to deceive—yet here it is virtue. What can be greater misery to a feeling and delicate mind than to lose the Virtue it cannot cease to love?"[17]

However histrionic her plaints, she is in a genuine panic about the possibility of (deservedly) losing her reputation and her place in society: "Perhaps in two months, friends, fame, life and all future peace may be destroyed and lost for ever to me. If so, my proud soul will never, never return to England—Cruel friend—when I could not stay to be supported and comforted by you, should you have plunged me in such misery? But it was not his fault. Oh no—his nature is noble, kind, tender, honourable, and affectionate. Passion has led us both away—" (26). Bess's biographer notes rather cynically that she was a student of *La Nouvelle Heloise*, "to say nothing of *Les Liaisons dangereuses*" (23). Proliferating dashes signal an increasing loss of control. "I can no longer calm the agitation of my mind—dangers seem to multiply around me—my shape increases every day—my health grows weaker—I know not what will become of me—" (27).

She loves to paint her torments because she knows they will stimulate sympathy. During a dinner party the conversation turns on the misfortunes of Lady Ossory, separated from her husband and pregnant by her lover,

> with a thousand observations and remarks on such a situation as hers was, the cleverness of some women in concealing their being with child, with all that she went thro', and that she said herself that she scarcely knew how to support her misery—that she read without understanding what she read, and that she had lost all repose—and all this I was obliged to listen to with an appearance of tranquillity and with a distracted mind—what will become of me? I do not, cannot guess—but all must end soon—to be away too from him, for whom I suffer—Oh heavens, have pity on me—(27)

And later "Perhaps the Almighty will protect and save me from disgrace and infamy—I can bear all but that—and the loss of his love for whom I have sacrificed myself" (28). Three days later, "Oh, how full of fears I feel—."

Foster had in truth become a wanderer, unaware as yet that the duchess's love for her would incorporate her safely into the Devonshire ménage. If her claims of a violated conscience ring hollow, her gothic extravagances recording her fears of permanent exile from society and public humiliation are justified. Though she was to be saved by the license allowed great dukes, there was always her equivocal position to be explained away, though everyone really understood her situation. Years later she would describe herself after her marriage to John Thomas Foster disintegrated in

1781 as "without a guide; a wife, and no husband, a mother, and no children . . . by myself alone to steer through every peril that surrounds a young woman so situated" (5). The duke and his complaisant wife were the providential answer. Essentially the production of the journals from abroad was for them, as excerpts dating from her second departure to the continent in 1787 make clear. "Oh, it was bitterness of grief to lose her—but him—his last embrace—his last look drew my soul after him—I remained motionless—even now, it is present to me. I see him—he is fixed in my heart—this guilty—heart—Oh, why could I not love him without crime. Why cannot I be his without sin?" (41). And again, a passage that could not fail to affix the duke more firmly:

> I deserve to suffer, and will not complain—Oh, may I see my beloved friends again, for they are dearer still to me than all else in the world!—She is the kindest, dearest, best most beloved of friends—and he is and must be ever the very soul of my existence—I will cease to live in error with him, tho' with shame and blushes I confess it, one moment passed in his arms, one instant pressed to his heart, effaces every sorrow, every fear, every thought but of him—but this must not be, shall not be—no, I'll live for him, but as his friend; still will I share, if he will let me, his every thought, his cares, and his anxieties, or his happiness, still will he find my heart adopt and make its own whatever can interest him, still will his pursuits be mine, whatever he likes or dislikes, will be pleasing or otherwise to me, for not only are my natural inclinations like his, but the instant his are known they become mine without a thought to make them so. (43)

This is an evocation of the gothic terrors of separation, isolation, penury, and deprivation of passion (which it is unlikely anyone ever felt for the lethargic duke), but though Foster may indeed and legitimately have suffered such terrors, her writings of them are intended to fix her friends and their admiration of her heroism more firmly. Finally, the preservation of her outpourings for production to her saviors is manipulative. Incredibly she managed to maintain her love affair with the duke and her romantic friendship with his wife at the same time, to live with them both in harmony, to raise her children in their nursery, and on the death of the duchess, to marry the widower.

Elizabeth Steele, the biographer of the actress-singer Sophia Baddeley, is another writer, this time for publication, who exploits the gothic to arouse sympathy for her subject and for herself. From 1769 to 1773 Steele managed Baddeley during her career as performer and, more lucratively, as courtesan. In her biography Steele paints a green world inhabited by the two women, where, however, they are savaged by male incursors.[18]

When Baddeley's favorite lover John Hanger, Lord Coleraine, lures her away and then locks her up, she escapes "black from her shoulders to her wrists, with the blows Lord Coleraine had given her; he having beat her unmercifully; and she was once afraid he would have murdered her."[19] Hanger, who had deserted Baddeley but enjoyed showing his lasting power over London's most desirable courtesan, always did his worst when the two women were separated. Steele describes these episodes as filled with false promises and betrayal, physical abuse, abduction, and murderous intent. But most of the men they know are profuse in promise but violent and faithless: Mr. P. tricks the two women into signing a note and then arrests them; Lord Melbourne promises to be Baddeley's friend for life, then without notice ceases paying her (incredibly exorbitant) bills; the actor William Brereton gives her a venereal disease; Stephen Sayre threatens her life. In the hands of the American republican Sayre, Baddeley is reduced to the worst of states: Steele discovers her in bed in advanced pregnancy in a fireless room, ill, deranged by her addiction to laudanum, unable to bear light, to eat or to drink. "At intervals she would talk, but it was only of me, and the love she bore me; that she fancied herself a supernatural being, and sometimes a China jar" (6:146). In the hands of men, Steele charges, Baddeley habitually suffers such disasters.

The recourse to gothic themes in the discourse of all these women appears either to represent frankly an atypical period of real terror now (importantly) long subdued or to be employed to attract sympathy. It is far more usual for a woman writer of discursive prose to maintain a rational mode, as Steele normally does, most typically celebrating her manly exploits, the tricks played on the pair's clients, their escapades, and adventures.

And of course, even as Chudleigh, Delany, or Steele wrote of these frightening events, they, rationally analytical, recollected them in full emotional control. Only Foster, writing like Pamela or Clarissa to the moment, appears to record her terror as it occurs. Circumstanced as she was, the guardian of important secrets, she would have been foolish indeed to harbor such a revealing record—had it not been even more important to keep the sympathies of both duke and duchess—perhaps even to suggest to them the horrors of the exposure of all three if they failed to support her.

Sarah Fielding, in *The Adventures of David Simple* (1744) and its sequel, *Volume the Last* (1751), composes a quasi-gothic demystified (or set in contemporary life) tale typical of the mid-century attitude of women writers to the mode. As in Scott's *Cornelia*, the gothic world, so discernible to women, surrounds the virtuous enclave in *David Simple*, cheating, betraying, robbing, taking all they have, even their children. Fielding is more realistic than Scott. But even as they lose everything including their lives, they preserve their Christian dignity; it remained for Walpole to add the entrancing terrors of his victims. Scott's *A Description of Millenium Hall* and *The History of Sir George Ellison* are both in a sense anti-gothics. *Millenium Hall* resolutely opposes the rational altruistic standards of the Hall's women managers to the tyrannies of the patriarchal structure, and the women prevail. The life of the Hall encapsulates and isolates the former gothic victimization of its inmates. In *The History of Sir George Ellison* again tales of the distresses undergone in the world by women of Millenium Hall end in the stasis of community through the efforts of the protagonists, efforts mirrored in his own community by George Ellison. Moreover, Scott's superior women refuse to exploit sentiment and emotionalism or to leave reason to the men. Instead Scott humiliates Lamont, the younger of the two male visitors to Millenium Hall, with his realization "that the persons who so much excelled him in reason as well as virtue, were women, were of that weak sex, which he had hitherto considered only as play-things for men; a race somewhat superior to monkeys; formed to amuse the other sex during the continuance of youth and beauty, and after the bloom was past, to be useful drudges for their convenience. To be disabused of so favourite an error, galled him intolerably."[20] What Scott was emphasizing in *Millenium Hall* was that in order to prevail, a virtuous community must have an unassailable financial foundation; her Hall is far better endowed than the community of David Simple. One conclusion to be drawn may well be that ordinarily women were deliberately kept unfunded and therefore unempowered to work change or to undertake reform.

Another conclusion is that both Fielding and Scott, following the implications of earlier writers like Manley and Haywood (but not their analysis of woman's natural attributes), insisted on the equal distribution of reason and sensibility to both genders, insisted that superior women and men were those endowed with both, but with the reason always in control. The communities of David Simple and Millenium Hall both depend on the structure and organization imposed by their members, and their administration requires in addition to reason the most perfect consideration of all others. Those who attack them, in the case of David Simple disastrously, are invariably lacking in empathy for others, or sensibility.

For Frances Burney the exertion of reason, as for Scott, is necessary to women, but her heroines present the problem of the young woman of full sensibility who has been deprived of the education and experience necessary for the training of the reason she needs to protect herself. Burney is most impressed by the manner in which the cards are stacked against women by providing them no chance of managing alone. She makes her point by totting up the forces that oppress women. This is the theme of all her novels, and all her heroines are powerless against the powers of a number of incapable and occasionally malevolent males. She is markedly the most pessimistic of women writers about the prospects of a woman surviving by use of her reason alone, but she indicates how very heavy the attack on a lone heroine must be before she breaks, and her intentions might be claimed as the most proto-feminist of all the women writers. More pessimistically than Scott but more realistically, she considers that *as things were,* any woman requires a measure of patriarchal protection in order to survive. And for Burney, as for many women, the tyrannous patriarchal world is best represented by the gothic.

There are already gothic elements in *Evelina* (1778), the first and lightest of her works, but they tend to be comic, as, for instance, in that bad fairy godmother Madame Duval. Evelina, unsure of her proper identity, is sometimes frighteningly threatened by misidentification, as when she is briefly abducted by two prostitutes in Marybone Gardens, pinioned between them, and momentarily indistinguishable from them, or as when she is abducted by Sir Clement Willoughby and threatened with rape because she is not clearly a marriage prospect. With all the sensibility in the world, Evelina sets out with no experience and little ability to judge. She is explicitly instructed by her guardian-mentor to judge for herself and to act on her judgment. And in the first book of the novel she can be said to acquire judgment, in the second to acquire the ability to act on it. There have been and are wicked schemers in her life who attempt to ruin her: the nurse who changed her at birth; Sir Clement, the lover who tries to take illegal possession; her grandmother, who would marry her to a boorish dolt. She skirts or outdoes these threats by remaining rational while undergoing much disquietude and at last acquires the insight and maturity to assume the true identity vouchsafed her as her father's daughter and her suitor's wife.

But in *Cecilia* (1783) and *Camilla* (1794) disaster really threatens and we realize that for Burney uninformed sensibility can result even in death and destruction. Both novels commence almost sunnily in an ordered patriarchal world, then pitch the heroine slowly downward into gothic isolation, deprivation, and loss of control. Through little fault of their own— through seemingly only minor mistakes, what a man might easily get away with—the heroines are isolated from their true friends, victimized by false ones. Burney uses gothic themes to express her sense of lone women's victimization and powerlessness. She anatomizes the reasons why she believes a woman cannot stand alone in her society. Scott's narratives, compared to Burney's, seem like fairy tales.

Cecilia tries to oppose her reason to the trials she encounters, but though she might have had the resources to survive alone, she is not allowed to try and is laid under an impossible burden of restrictions.

She begins an apparently lucky and autonomous life in a seemingly orderly social environment. But the uncle who dying has left her rich has stipulated that her husband must adopt his name: she is a conduit for perpetuating himself. Moreover, only eighteen, she must live until of age with one of three guardians, none of whom is fit to advise her. These conditions and her lack of experience as an almoner doom her to victimization. The real world is inhabited by apparent friends plotting to get her money. Her first guardian will strip her to pay his debts and will attempt to sell her to a friend in marriage. Even her most trusted friend, Monckton, is plotting to rid himself of his rich old wife and marry her. She should at all costs have guarded her power—her money—but Cecilia's kindness and her lack of penetration are played upon until she has lost the resources of her minority. Then she falls in love, not with a complaisant second son, but with the only son of a proud family. After she has married him, she loses the rest of her wealth because he cannot change his name to hers.

Both Cecilia and Burney were victims of a greedy world, Burney because George Cambridge, the man she loved, would not marry a portionless novelist of no proud heredity, Cecilia because apparently she could not be loved for herself. Both Burney and Cecilia were saddled with patriarchal sanctions, then left to work out their own salvations. Burney's writing career at the time was closely guided by her two fathers, Charles Burney and "Daddy" Crisp; Cecilia too has to obey multiple guardians with their own agendas. Cecilia, wanting to do right, isn't always certain what is right to do and makes near-fatal errors. Her only security lies in never descending to the level of the manipulation of Miss Bennet, the meanness of Lady Margaret Monckton, or the shallow and silly selfishness of her friend Mrs. Harrel. She has no real positive female model. Burney had no recourse except to write; Cecilia could only be steadfast of character and develop her understanding, the only resource of many a gothic heroine. But in Burney's world, because of the empowerment of men, this resource is not sufficient.

Moreover, the control that Scott's heroines do gain over their lives through reason and moral judgment is precisely what Cecilia slowly yields up. She begins a gothic descent in which even reason is slowly overwhelmed. Ann Radcliffe was subsequently to draw a clear distinction between terror and horror as opposites: "The first expands the soul and awakens the faculties . . . the other contracts, freezes, and nearly annihilates them." The first, accompanied by uncertainty and obscurity, is an important source of the sublime; the second is not.[21] Burney also draws an important distinction between terror and horror, but her definition makes a moral distinction similar to Johnson's, for whom (in his *Dictionary*) terror is fear and horror is terror mixed with detestation, "a passion compounded of fear and hate, both strong." The distinction is helpful toward an understanding of the frequent use of the two words in Burney's last three novels, which anatomize the double motivation for her heroines' descent into madness, first the cruelty of others, but then, more tellingly, the errors of the heroines themselves. The distinction was very important to Burney, who incorporated the emotions of her heroines into her novels in the most detailed (and gothic) fashion.

Cecilia is a strong woman driven to desperation by the gothic punishments of the establishment, to which she will not give in. She is not easily frightened. Her temperament is basically happy and sanguine. Her first distresses are characteristically felt for the unjust treatment by her guardian Harrel of his creditors; she as yet fears nothing for herself.[22] She is first actually frightened by an impending duel of which she is the unwitting cause (138). She is frightened again by Mrs. Harrel's distresses over her husband's impending ruin (263). When the ruined Harrel blackmails her by threatening to cut his throat on the instant if she does not disburse and save him, she vacillates between indignation and terror that she may become responsible for his death. She is frightened, compassionate, recollected, indignant, terrified, recollected again, repulsed, then stripped by the moneylender for whom she signs a bond for £7500. Thus, at first her reason prevails with only occasional episodes of fear and terror, both of which are excited by the misfortunes not of herself but of others. Her one moment of *horror* (or fear mingled with detestation) occurs at Harrel's suicide threat, which results in her agreement with the money lender (271).

Thereafter the terror accelerates slowly with her enmeshment in the impossible demands of the patriarchal establishment. When the Harrels try to force Cecilia to marry Sir Robert Floyer, purportedly to provide a home for Mrs. Harrel but actually to appropriate her fortune, she is momentarily petrified but soon coolly extricates herself from the arrangement. She is indignant when the Harrels try to frighten her with Mrs. Harrel's fears (386). But new threats of suicide from Harrel once again rouse terror (289); this situation is quite beyond her capacities to handle. When Harrel has taken virtually all the £10,000 at her disposal and has shot himself at Vauxhall, her response is, naturally, horror, implying her moral detestation of his action (414, 416). But her reason soon reasserts itself and it is she who procures a doctor and makes all the subsequent arrangements.

Cecilia has experienced distresses in plenty when two-thirds through the book Burney reminds us, "Compared with the general lot of human misery Cecilia had suffered nothing; but compared with the exaltation of ideal happiness she had suffered much." But when Cecilia agrees to marry Delvile secretly, she suffers for the first time in her life "the new-born and intolerable terror of conscientious reproaches" (576). The horror now begins in earnest: fear mixed with detestation of her own actions.

Cecilia's ruminations on her approaching marriage tell her that while she has "hitherto invariably possessed the consolation of self-approving reflections," she has lost that consolation by agreeing to a clandestine ceremony without the sanction of Delvile's parents. These feelings provoke her horror when the ceremony is interrupted. The clergyman inquires if anyone knows of impediments and a concealed Miss Bennet, the agent of Monckton, appropriates Cecilia's undelivered vow in her cry, "I do" (626). Cecilia, imagining there may indeed be an impediment on Delvile's part, is shocked speechless, amazed, terrified. Delvile asks her to trust his honor; and she replies that she must trust her own reason. So far so good: but her own reason is once again insufficient. She is stupefied by sorrow, left "quite without motion, and almost without sensibility" by Mrs. Delvile's determined opposition to the match (684), but feels terror when Mrs. Delvile's life is suddenly endangered, and, as at the scene of Harrel's suicide, knows better than to "indulge in selfish grief, where occasion called her to action for the benefit of others" (685). She undergoes terrors at Mrs. Belfield's insinuations to Delvile's father of her attachment to Belfield (788), but her terrors are less for herself than for the happiness of her lover, and in fact the misunderstanding leads to Delvile's second duel. Her response, predictably, is horror when she learns that it was her supposed protector Monckton who had sent Miss Bennet to stop her wedding (835), and she feels horror again at the (premature) announcement of his death.

Her reason is threatened at the realization that Delvile has fought a duel with Monckton and she feels terror (847–48), but when an attempt is made by a strange caller to terrify her into parting with money, she is firm. She cannot remain calm, however, when she knows that Delvile is to fight again, this time with her protégé Belfield. She is now overcome with the utmost terror and misery, and at last her reason, instead of asserting itself, snaps. "She was wholly overpowered; terror for Delvile, horror for herself, hurry, confusion, heat and fatigue, all assailing her at once, while all means of repelling them were denied her, the attack was too strong for her fears, feelings, and faculties, and her reason suddenly, yet totally failing her, she madly called out, 'He will be gone! he will be gone! and I must follow him to Nice!'" (896).

Terror for Delvile; *horror* for herself. Detestation of her own behavior leading to her lover's endangerment is too much to bear. Cecilia runs madly through the streets until, exhausted, she ends up on the floor of a shop. Responding to her frenzy, the people there shut her up in a room alone where, raving, she passes the night. Darkness, isolation, terror, incarceration, madness. This is the end result of a young woman's attempt to manage on her own. And who is to say that Burney is not more realistic than Scott? It is not that in every exigency Cecilia does not try to make reason prevail; it is only that without the support of any of her three guardians she is powerless.

The end of *Camilla* would be very similar. In both novels the heroine is tested by her continuing efforts to handle her own problems; and in both novels she mismanages so tragically that those she loves best are implicated in her fall—her literal fall into illness and delirium. What follows in both novels is the symbolic death of the girl who mistakenly thought she could cope alone, and then the resurrection of the girl by the man she loves to a quite different life, one in which she yields her autonomy to her husband who will direct and protect her. The efforts toward independence have been disastrous and the death of the independent girl is genuine enough. These denouements indicate that Burney agreed with her predecessors that sensibility without reason was dangerous but doubted that women even adequately prepared to balance sensibility with reason could prevail alone within the patriarchal structure. In *Camilla* Burney proffered Mr. Tyrold's beneficently tendered letter in an ironic spirit: he explains why girls should not be reared to practice reason and virtually recommends that they be brought up as unformed as possible so as to make it easier for them to conform to their husbands.[23] Burney's novels consistently warn women of their ill preparation for autonomy, warn them also of the traps put in their way. If her view is pessimistic, it also exposes the way in which women were kept imprisoned, unenlightened, deprived, powerless, and, potentially, finally maddened.

Burney's next novel, *Camilla*, called attention to the poor education women were given in the right use of reason. Camilla's father delivers the meretricious sermon as to the advisability of forming young women as little as possible; and the foolish, selfish, totally unqualified governess Miss Margland executes the program. Dr. Orkborne, the self-centered tutor of the worthless Clermont Lymere, has been equally deficient. The novel is marked by the schematic of characters with sensibility but no reason (Sir Hugh), characters with reason but without sensibility (Marchmont), characters with neither (Miss Margland, Clermont, Orkborne). It is not Burney's fault if we do not grasp what is needed for an exemplary human being.

Before Burney returned to the novel with *Camilla*, however, the dark court years, during which the queen reportedly ordered her to write no more novels, intervened. The tragedies she wrote instead allowed Burney to express her own plight in plots in which she could figure as a tragic heroine.[24] Once again the tyrannic patriarchal structure is imaged in gothic devices. In *Edwy and Elgiva* begun in April 1790, Edwy, a tenth-century Saxon king, has married but cannot acknowledge Elgiva; in the end both die. The blameless Elgiva is incarcerated, forced to join her husband only through secret passages, never acknowledged as queen, reviled, abducted, and finally murdered. An obstacle to the dynastic plans of leaders of church and state, she is repudiated as a worthless courtesan, but her death destroys the king who has been sustained by her love. Not coincidentally, by 1790 Burney had suffered the rejection of two men who had courted and appeared to love her, George Owen Cambridge in 1783–85 and Colonel Stephen Digby in 1788–89. Both found her fascinating and engaged too far with her but neither proposed; neither her fortune nor her background and bloodlines were suitable. Elgiva's rejection may echo Burney's by Cambridge because Cambridge's father, though always her gallant friend, played a role in his retreat. The play deals with the unfair rejection of a blameless heroine who both loves and is beloved but who has no dynastic backing. Unfriended, Elgiva cannot survive alone. In such circumstances, reason avails a woman nothing. The security of the king's love is delusory. A young woman requires the support of the patriarchal structure to survive and cannot win in combat with it. This is Burney's emendation to Scott's overoptimistic prescription. Her use of the gothic does indeed severely indict the establishment.

In *Hubert de Vere, a Pastoral Tragedy,* written later the same year, Geralda has ruined her own life and driven her lover to madness by marrying Glanville as the price he exacts for sparing her uncle-guardian. Having lost Geralda, Hubert commits himself to Carulia, a maiden dying for love of him. Despite the lovers' many self-abnegating scruples, the fates eventually free them to marry. Here the recurrent theme of the maiden immolating herself in an unwanted marriage to save a father-figure expresses Burney's image of court life as a loveless marriage and of herself as sacrificed to that marriage to aid her father, who required royal support for both himself and his sons. Burney had needed strong patriarchal support to succeed in life but instead had a father so powerless that she was forced to sacrifice herself to save him and her brothers.

In *The Siege of Pevensey*, Adela proves her filial piety by refusing to extricate herself from the most excruciating dangers at the cost of marrying her lover without her father's consent. Later, to save her father, she is willing either to marry her persecutor or to enter a convent. In the end she is rewarded with her lover, but the theme of the heroine's willingness to sacrifice herself for her father in marriage or a convent—both fair images of the court—is again present.

These tragedies are tragedies because the patriarchal world is filled with vicious, selfish, tyrannical people who have power and care nothing for others. The plot of the final tragedy, *Elberta*, written out on 303 scraps of paper, has been reconstructed by Margaret Doody and Stewart J. Cooke.[25] Fragment 265 presents an image of the heroine as wanderer: "A Female is mentioned, who wild & unknown is seen roaming about—no one is informed whence she comes—woe is in her voice, terror in her aspect;—she never weeps, yet frequently wails, tho' in terms unintelligible from their wildness—." Here is the wanderer figure, bereft of all patriarchal support, that is at the center of Burney's imaginative experience, as it was of Scott's, that expresses her deepest fears of what might ensue for women freed from or ejected from patriarchal supervision. For Burney this figure cannot stand alone and maintain her reason. Burney either believes women are inferior in emotional strength or she believes that the world is particularly hard on women ensuring that indeed they cannot function alone—surely the latter. And although she demonstrates female weakness, which must have been pleasing to the patriarchy, she also emphasizes the particular cruelties practiced on women. Moreover, her parables are probably the most realistic of all, far more so than those of Scott or even Radcliffe. *Cecilia* and *Camilla* could be defended not simply as modal but as generic gothics for the torments and deprivations visited on their heroines and the analysis of their tortured emotions, which the reader is invited to share.

After Burney's escape from court and her felicitous but financially insecure marriage, she returned to novel writing because the tragedies had provided no money. Notes toward her next novel made during the court years substantiate her concern for the undeveloped reason of the young: "It is a mistake to suppose the intellect weak in youth, because the judgment is erroneous. Precaution is not natural to youth, whose greatest [danger] because greatest weakness is confidence in its first impulse, which is commonly pleasant because kind. To be just requires more reflexion; to have foresight demands more experience."[26]

Camilla may at first seem lighter in spirit than *Cecilia,* in part because patriarchal power here resides in the hands not of a tyrant but of a well-meaning and affectionate fool. Sir Hugh, the disposing elder, lacks judgment and reason as much as do the proposing young. (That is, patriarchal power is disposed of inappropriately.) Soon Camilla's sister Eugenia is reduced by the unthinking *bêtiseries* of Sir Hugh to a pock-marked cripple and in compensation he bestows upon her the inheritance designed for Camilla. No longer a designated heiress, Camilla is disempowered.

As her troubles deepen while her small debts grow large, it is as though she has fallen through the trap door never sprung by Evelina and even more dangerously than Cecilia, into the world where evil operates. Her father is imprisoned, her lover turns away, her reckless brother is deservedly disinherited by his rich uncle, and she ends at last isolated, resourceless, and on the point of death in an inn, scarcely able to procure a clergyman. Like Cecilia she dies figuratively and is reborn as a wife, owing everything to the man who at length decides to save her. The reprieves of Cecilia and Camilla may represent the failure of the heroines' own efforts, the benignity of Providence, but even more represent the power of the patriarchal world, which can brutally banish but when properly mollified may consent to intervene.

Burney, like Camilla, had a father and brothers who could not protect her, who needed help themselves. She had trusted friends like Cambridge's father and Stephen Digby who refused to incorporate her into their safe worlds. For a young woman in such a precarious position, small failures of judgment—in Camilla's case a spirited inattention to the opinions of others, a carelessness about indebtedness—produce great woes; fools can do real harm; lovers are not dependable. Camilla herself has invited the loss of her lover, her parents, all sympathy; she ends alone, hungry for food and love, enclosed in a strange room in an inn, deprived of all but life itself.

The structure of the novel, like that of *Cecilia,* owes much to the alternation of the heroine's intellectual illusion that she controls her own life with her not always controllable emotions; she sways between apparent reason and a sensibility sometimes out of control. She is perfectly capable of obeying her father's injunction not to reveal her love for Edgar until he has revealed his for her, despite the torment of his continuing nondeclaration (the result of Dr. Marchmont's unreasonable insistence that *she* must first make known her real preference). Her emotions at first are not so terrible: apart from being in love, she is occasionally distressed, ashamed, confounded, unhappy, consternated, dismayed, mortified, saddened, and so on, sometimes by the problems of others but often because of her own too-spontaneous behavior. After the initial dark shades that lead to Camilla's disinheritance, the increasing darkness is gradual. But then harm comes from every direction: from the mismanagement of lovable fools like Sir Hugh; from the interference of the misogynistic and controlling Dr. Marchmont; from the pretended kind ministrations of the nest-feathering Mrs. Mittin; from the selfish extravagance of the favorite brother Lionel; and from the quiet schemes of the seemingly submissive Miss Margland.

Camilla's more negative emotions, strong because she is an emotional person, but not overly strong for the situations that evoke them, include both terror and deep grief over her misdeeds. She is not so beset by terror as Cecilia, but she is considerably more afflicted by miserable guilt. She is brave, not easily frightened, and quite unselfish and empathic to others. Thus, she feels no great emotion either on being named Sir Hugh's heiress or on being deprived of that title, but she *is* terrified after she has begged that Lionel be allowed to ride a horse when he rides it too recklessly (22).

Frantic grief and overpowering dread enter the adult world early with Eugenia's illness and accident, but Camilla remains a sunny intrepid child. When Lionel for a jest announces the presence of a mad bull while the family is out walking, Camilla is the least frightened of all (132); when Lionel traps her with Eugenia and the vulgar Dubster at the top of an unfinished building and they are taunted rather than assisted by passing market people, she is frightened only by the unfamiliar abuse (285). The foolish Miss Dennel, who feigns agonies of terror at imagined ills, is twice a contrast to Camilla's calm self-control (388, 423). Burney writes that her heroine "possessed that fine internal power of the thinking and feeling mind to adopt courage for terror, where any eminent service may be the result of immediate exertion" (388), such as Cecilia demonstrated when Mrs. Delvile's life was endangered. At Tunbridge, when Mrs. Arlbery's horses threaten to bolt down Mt. Ephraim, Camilla remains firmly holding the reins, then takes her opportunity to throw herself from the carriage, remaining collected all the time (403). All this control legitimates the emotions of terror that do eventually beset Camilla by distinguishing them from the silly trepidations of the unthinking and unfeeling Miss Dennel. Because Camilla is so feeling, she is susceptible to genuine terror when those she loves are endangered. She is terrified by news that her uncle is dying (324), that Edgar has been kicked by a horse (345) or menaced by a dog (539). Some of her terrors are more ideologically stirred: she is terrified, since Edgar is not designed for her, that her parents may conjecture her feelings for him (220).

Mingled with the terrors she must increasingly undergo is the misery she feels at the blows to which she herself has not contributed—Lionel's dreadful downward course, Eugenia's relationship with the wicked Bellamy, the claims of the partisans of the silly beauty Indiana to Edgar. But worse is the misery she feels about the misfortunes for which she *is* partially responsible. Although Sir Hugh, Lionel, and Clermont have each done more to injure the family finances than she, Camilla bears the heavy responsibility of having provided the precipitating factor leading to her father's imprisonment for debt. Though nothing could have been a more appropriate punishment for her father, who had effectually imprisoned Camilla in an imposed passivity and hypocrisy that prevented her finding happiness with Edgar, she can, of course, derive no comfort from his humiliation.

Terror does accelerate. Camilla and Mrs. Mittin are pursued as suspected shoplifters (614, 624), appropriately because Mrs. Mittin is indeed not overly scrupulous as to how she acquires goods and because Camilla is ordering goods from shops for which she cannot pay. She responds with terror to Lionel's announcement that his debts must now end either in his father's ruin or his own exile and imprisonment (504). She is terrified when she discovers that a duel may be fought on her behalf (638–39) and terrified when she discovers the body of the scheming Bellamy at a halfway house (871, 873). Finally she suffers the terror that her mother will never forgive her for her father's imprisonment (883). The worst terror is at her separation from everyone who loves her, a terror emphasized by Bellamy's cruel refusal to take her in when she is without shelter or protection and her discovery that her uncle's house is deserted. Here she is so overcome that she sinks to the floor.

Greater than her terror at repeated assaults from without, however, is the horror of her remorse, which overcomes her in the last volume. Remorse for her past conduct, which had led to Sir Sedley Clarendel's gift to Lionel of £200, provokes the horror she feels when Eugenia suggests that she is now constrained to marry Sir Sedley. She will not, however, immolate herself as the heroines of the tragedies and later Juliet in *The Wanderer* will do, perhaps because a brother does not merit the same sacrifice that a father does. She is horrified (616) as well as terrified at being taken for a shoplifter, which suggests that she recognizes the implicit justice of the charge, and she knows that Mrs. Mittin is in actuality her accomplice. She is petrified as well as horrified when she learns how much Mrs. Mittin has spent on her behalf (692, 741). She feels horror when her parents, devastated by Lionel's misconduct, take comfort in their erroneous belief that she is engaged to Edgar (752); and she is horrified rather than terrified at her father's distresses (766).

Burney has carefully traced Camilla's descent into the gothic, her education in evil. Two-thirds through the book, the horror of being pursued as a shoplifter seems to Camilla the most terrible event of her life (616). When Bellamy abducts Eugenia, Camilla is overcome with detestation of the man and faints with horror; once again this is the most deadly woe she has ever undergone (804). Soon she will undergo woes more deadly when she learns that her father has been imprisoned for debt.

In *Camilla*, Burney explores far more deeply than in *Cecilia* the implication of the victim in her own debacle, and gothic terrors are more painful when mixed with self-recrimination: horror is worse than terror. But Burney never suggests that either terror or horror could be reduced through a reduction of sensibility. Sensibility, no matter how dangerous when uncontrolled by reason, is a good not to be discarded. Neither does Burney, however, educate her heroines into discretion and suggest that thereafter, like Tom Jones or Haywood's Betsy Thoughtless, they can live self-directed useful lives. She pretends to no such sanguine view of woman's place in the real world. Her point about Camilla like her point about Cecilia is that once safely married to a man of combined reason and sensibility and thus vicariously entrenched and empowered in the patriarchal structure, she will have nothing further to fear.

Burney knew Scott's works, but she takes the dark and more realistic view of woman's capacity to win autonomy through an exertion of combined sensibility and reason, both of which her heroines have but which never prove enough. Her reworking of Scott's wanderer in her own last novel *The Wanderer; or, Female Difficulties* (1814) emphasizes this point. Cecilia and Camilla became wanderers, but the figure of the woman wanderer provides the dominating image for Burney's last work. The second part of her title indicates that she was still interested in the obstacles to female autonomy. Her wanderer, Juliet, is considerably more mature and resourceful than either Cecilia or Camilla, but in the end she, too, must be saved by masculine intervention. Burney believed that the obstacles put in women's way were formidable. And to the end she expressed the obstacles through the use of the gothic mode.

The enemies that Juliet must withstand include both the French disciple of Robespierre, who has forced her to marry him in order to save her guardian the bishop, and the cupiditous English brother of her father's second wife, who does not want her legitimacy recognized in England—enemies on both sides of the Channel. Burney does not want to suggest that female difficulties—or the difficulties a woman faces in making her way alone in the world—are insuperable. In fact they "are not insurmountable, where mental courage, operating through patience, prudence, and principle, supply physical force, combat disappointment, and keep the untamed spirits superiour to failure, and ever alive to hope."[27] But Burney's purpose now is patently to shame the world into allowing women better work opportunities and conditions. Conservative though Burney has always been considered, she had now to an extent been encouraged by the spirit of Revolution. The flawed Elinor Joddrel, an unrestrained Revolutionary, a figure, perhaps, of Wollstonecraft, has a firm sense of the wrongs of women and is in many ways, in addition to her making it possible for Burney to express radical ideas, quite attractive; it must be remembered that she has the good sense and taste to be in love with Harleigh. Burney's objection to her method is that by denying the conventions that hamper her, by putting on man's dress and men's prerogatives, Elinor cannot win, having "strayed from the beaten road, only to discover that all others are pathless" (836). But Burney uses Elinor's voice to speak truths despite her opinion that Elinor's method cannot succeed. One has only to think of Elinor's explanation of the indulgences allowed her soon-to-be-married sister: "it is a rule, you know, to deny nothing to a bride-elect; probably, poor wretch, because everyone knows what a fair way she is in to be soon denied every thing!" (44)

But there are other ways of making her points. Burney is exploring and pleading for the expansion of the means by which an unmarried woman can earn a livelihood. The virtuous Gabriella, a shopkeeper, says, "The French Revolution has opened our eyes to a species of equality more rational, because more feasible, than that of lands or of rank; an equality not alone of mental sufferings, but of manual exertions" (612). Juliet only seeks a way to survive by means of manual exertions. Having lost her money in her escape from France and unable to reveal herself or to appeal to her English relatives, she must fend for herself. She is a wanderer, and, "Alas! she cried, is it only under the domestic roof,—that roof to me denied!—that woman can know safety, respect, and honour?" (638).

Juliet's laments are meant to notify the world of its patriarchal unfairness, not of her capitulation, for she never capitulates. She carries with her a letter from the bishop with advice, which she reads and rereads. It is like the advice of Villars to Evelina. "Where occasion calls for female exertion, mental strength must combat bodily weakness; and intellectual vigour must supply the inherent deficiencies of personal courage; those, only, are fitted for the vicissitudes of human fortune, who, whether male or female, learn to suffice to themselves. Be this the motto of your story" (204). It *is* the motto of her story; Juliet will not, like Cecilia or Camilla, be crushed by her opponents, even if Burney *does* allow her under her own efforts only to survive and to endure while prosperity must await the arrival of male reinforcements.

Juliet's adversities are far greater than the adversities faced by a man in similar straits. As a woman she is constantly blamed and rejected simply for being alone and unprotected. "How insufficient . . . is a FEMALE to herself! How utterly dependent upon situations—connexions—circumstance! How nameless, how for ever fresh-springing are her DIFFICULTIES, when she would owe her existence to her own exertions! Her conduct is criticized, not scrutinized; her character is censured, not examined; her labours are unhonoured, and her qualifications are but lures to ill will!" (257). Moreover, her work opportunities are limited. Juliet teaches music, works as a seamstress and in a millinery shop, is a companion and a shopkeeper, moving beyond the range of the jobs available to other middle-class women who might not have had adequate musical or sewing skills. In all employments she is barely recompensed if even that. In most employments she is reviled and despised.

Juliet is unlike Cecilia and Camilla in several ways. She has elected to undergo heroic testing before the novel begins and she withstands it throughout the course of the book. She has elected her trial knowingly; it does not descend on her unexpectedly. Another great difference is that she never incurs her own reproaches. Terror she may feel (though not so often as her predecessors) but horror at her own shame, so debilitating to Cecilia and Camilla, she does not. Cecilia and Camilla both become wanderers briefly at the climax of their adventures and cannot stand up to the trauma. Juliet is a wanderer from the start and never succumbs. She is the figure of Burney's mature experience, of her own accomplished survival.

For two-thirds of the book Juliet is a wanderer in a world indifferent to her; then at the point at which in all three novels the heroines become dreadfully beset, Juliet is discovered and the pursuit begins. She is hunted by her husband's agents from cottage to cottage, into the New Forest and out again. But she keeps her head, disguises herself, wards off dogs, rapists, and smugglers fearful of detection. Providence may finally send the solution to her problems (in the form of last-minute patriarchal assistance), but she has survived on her own to benefit from the assistance. Burney's message is that of the bishop and, further, that women must have more favorable circumstances in which to strive. "A dearth of useful resources, was a principal cause, in adversity, of FEMALE DIFFICULTIES" (664). The book is a brave resolution of Burney's earlier fears for a woman beset and alone. She may have flinched at the plight of an ingenue alone in the world, but from the outset with *Evelina* she had recommended that women must be capable of brave exertion, must become sufficient to themselves. In her last book she protested against the injustices practiced against women. Moreover, though she suffers repeatedly, Juliet is not driven to the verge of madness by these injustices, reduced to crumbling, ill or mad, to the floor. Opposing recourse to overt rebellion, Burney believes that women must remain decorous without, like Elinor Joddrel, seizing rights that admittedly they ought to have. She is therefore confined to reasoning with the establishment about its unfairness to women who ought to be given every chance to support themselves respectably and to enjoy alternatives to marriage: not coincidentally, there are no happy marriages in this long book. *The Wanderer* is not modal but generic and demystified gothic, and Burney uses the gothic to indicate the depth of tyranny and victimization that women faced. To demonstrate to the privileged their duty to divest themselves of privilege and to their victims the extent of their victimization was a worthy if not a very hopeful task, but at least in her final novel Burney's points are more overtly stated, less encoded, than they were formerly.

Charlotte Smith's *The Old Manor House* (1793) is often characterized as a gothic, and certainly all three women of the Manor House are hard beset. Smith takes something like Burney's view that women unsheltered by the patriarchy will be victimized. Mrs. Rayland is a rich old woman of basic good sense and a large estate, but she cannot really protect herself. Lennard, her companion, rules her through manipulation and manufactures a false will to make herself her mistress's heir; her butler uses the house for smuggling activity; she cannot prevent the neighborhood gentlemen from poaching her game; and eventually she becomes a virtual prisoner of Lennard and her co-conspirators, who isolate her and prevent her making peace with her family. Then the apparently self-sufficient Lennard, who has easily mastered Rayland, marries foolishly and is imprisoned by her husband who only wants her inheritance. Monimia, Lennard's grandniece, is a prisoner in a tower, frozen both mentally and emotionally until Rayland's heir Orlando offers a course of reading and love; and when she is turned away by Lennard, she becomes a wanderer. So it is Orlando who, though poor, must save both Lennard and Monimia, Orlando who squares off with the butler, the poachers, and Lennard's unworthy husband to set all right. Orlando is also a gothic victim, but it is the three women who suffer isolation, incarceration, and the deprivation of love, which amounts to a claim that these deprivations are a female fate.

Both Orlando and Monimia, however, are reduced to become wanderers—a fate more extreme in the gothic than incarceration. The wanderer may be experiencing a condition essential to the movement from patriarchal incarceration to autonomy but is at once both completely free and completely unprotected, and the lack of restraint in itself can be terrifying to the person used only to restraint, while the lack of protection is even more terrible. Throughout the book there is a failure of domestic welcome for most characters most of the time. Rayland Hall is almost totally inhospitable; Orlando, the presumptive heir, is received there on sufferance and Monimia has the most tenuous of rights to its shelter where she is confined to a tower. Orlando's home is warm and friendly to its own, but poor, and Monimia as his wife is received there grudgingly. The home of Orlando's uncle in London is cold and forbidding and the general who wants to elope with Orlando's sister will not invite him in even for a moment. At least Orlando's wanderings as a soldier in America provide (admittedly minimal) protection, but he finds himself in a hostile countryside at war. Protagonists who endure homelessness are familiar enough in the romance or gothic—they have included Scott's Cornelia, Leonora, several of the women in *Millenium Hall,* and all of Burney's heroines. This pervasive theme of homelessness, or of not belonging, is at sharp odds, meant to contrast, with the patriarchal ideal of the hospitality of Old England, which obviously was to be extended only to complaisant allies and properly submissive subordinates. The establishment was supposed to be generous and hospitable, its doors open to the needy and the traveler. The experiences of the victims of the system suggest that for those who were neither useful nor amenable there awaited a cold reception. Lennard, a sycophantic flatterer could always have found a home; Monimia could not.

Smith takes a view of woman's ability to manage alone that is perhaps the most pessimistic of those considered here. She does not take advantage of the separation of her lovers to follow the adventures of Monimia and develop her resourcefulness. Instead Orlando returns from abroad, discovers his forlorn family, finds a method of supplying their needs, recovers Monimia, and investigates the mystery of Rayland's will. Then he rescues Lennard from her evil husband, now about to incarcerate her as a lunatic, and in return she relinquishes Rayland's true will so that he is at last acknowledged her heir. Monimia has been tutored—educated—by Orlando, but is no equal in ratiocinative power. Smith is here a consistent (realistic) relier upon patriarchal powers, and Monimia's happiness must depend on Orlando's having at last taken his rightful place among the patriarchs. Orlando has a splendid understanding and his sensibility, as it often does with heroes and heroines, takes the form of a fine moral sense of the decisions on which he then acts.

But Monimia's adventure, as she tells it to Orlando, shows that she has profited from the limited education he has afforded her through books and conversation. She has avoided despair and even suicide: "nor could I . . . have lived, if some of those books you taught me to read, and to understand, had not instructed me, that it was impious to murmur, or resist the dispensation of Providence. . . . Perhaps too, the hope . . . of living in your affection, and of being beloved by you . . . lent me a portion of fortitude."[28]

In the course of her life without protection she is "sold" to a lascivious baronet who is patient enough to delay her ruin, then hunted, humiliated, insulted; "terror" is the word she repeatedly uses to describe her responses. She does a great deal of trembling even as she relates her adventures. It is plainly Providence that has at last brought her to the friendly shelter where Orlando discovers her. Providence is, of course, the machinery of the gothic.

On the other hand, Smith indicates a degree of fortitude in Monimia that might perhaps be proportional to her degree of education and reason. She has been separated from Orlando, her only friend, and has lost neither her head nor her principles nor her virtue, has persisted and endured, and despite ample provocation has not allowed her great sensibility to lead her either into despair or into infidelity. Though she has been saved by the intervention of Providence and by Orlando's resourcefulness, neither of these could have helped her had she not exhibited such fortitude. Smith, like other women authors, has used the gothic miseries of the world to express its corruption and like them she has opposed to corruption her protagonists' reason and fortitude. It is not Monimia's sensibility that has saved her so much as that portion of reason tutored in her by Orlando. But safety is not achieved by either Monimia or Orlando until he recovers his proper inheritance. A patriarch must be male but must also be financially independent. And apparently no woman writer could honestly propose a safe harbor for her heroine other than marriage to a hero of combined reason and sensibility.

Claudia Johnson has suggested that the gradual male adoption of sensibility may by the 1790s have left many women, to whom sensibility had been prescribed, without a specific gender site, forcing them to choose as roles either mannishness or hyper-femininity.[29] Women writers, however, could make another choice—a determination that both genders must combine reason and sensibility to form complete rather than half beings. Though there were male fictive characters like Mackenzie's Man of Feeling and Goethe's Werther whose reason seems to have been suppressed by feeling, ordinarily the man with sensibility had it well under control so that Tom Jones (in the end at least) and Matthew Bramble had it all, as did Camilla's Edgar and Juliet's Harleigh. If the reasoning male could also acquire sensibility, that might indeed pose a threat to the woman of sensibility but it might also suggest that she too could enjoy a similar combination of attributes—and that was the solution championed by women writers until Austen could present Elizabeth Bennet as endowed with both attributes—and wit as well!—without explanation or apology.

This prescription of a husband with both reason and sensibility, a man kind, just, and discerning of merit even in women, is the prescription responsible for the invention of such unlikely paragons as Scott's, Burney's and Smith's heroes. The very fact that these heroes must combine both attributes in actuality rather than in pretence only suggests that to preserve a balance their wives must do the same. The invention of men as women would have them but as they are not constitutes another point where women may stand and "make subversive criticism of the world that is run by men." These heroes are fictitious creations only, and no one knew that better than the women who created them. They represent rather a prescription for men as they *ought to be*, with combined sensibility and reason, and that reason not at the service of the usual tyrannical impulses but at the service of empathic, altruistic, benevolence.

Ann Radcliffe's novels *The Mysteries of Udolpho* (1794) and *The Italian* (1797) follow Burney's design, further exaggerate the gothic, intimate the same messages, and help to inspire the creation of the more robust heroine Juliet in *The Wanderer*. An analysis of *The Italian* will illustrate this point. Like Emily St. Aubert in *Udolpho*, Ellena Rosalba is a beautiful young woman of fine character and perfect sensibility but insufficiently educated in the ways of the world and not yet dreaming of using her reason to learn to understand how those ways inflect her own life. Writers like Radcliffe and Wollstonecraft, who sometimes may be seen as suspicious of sensibility in women, are, in fact, only suspicious of sensibility unregulated by reason, and rightfully so. Ellena is, of course, to keep her sensibility; she has only to learn to understand her position in society and what has happened to her and why, an understanding that any woman needs in order to control her own life. Ellena, even more than Emily, also has perfect taste, is an artist, and understands how to look at landscape, abilities that may not seem all that unusual to us, but that in fact enlightenment ideology accredited only to traveled gentlemen of education and leisure.[30] Obviously, too, Radcliffe, whose landscape descriptions are an important characteristic of her novels, also claimed a refined taste.

Shaftesbury, Hume, Hutcheson, and Hartley all considered that a sense of beauty and a moral sensibility were related. Moreover, Ellena, who does fine embroidery and painting to support herself and her aunt, has that most important of female virtues, fortitude to endure and withstand. But at the start of her adventures "her mind was not yet strong enough, or her views sufficiently enlarged, to teach her a contempt of the sneer of vicious folly, and to glory in the dignity of virtuous independence."[31] Her travels through the mountains, which incidentally provide her the broadening experience gentlemen craved, are aesthetically educational. But she cannot reach emotional or intellectual maturity until she has learned the answer to the mysteries: who is she, (what knowledge did her aunt fail to convey on her deathbed?); who precisely are the others she encounters (the villainous Schedoni, the nun Olivia?); who can she trust? This is the kind of puzzle we must all work out when we leave adolescence, and like Ellena we will not reach maturity until we at least approximate the answers.

After the noble Vivaldi has fallen in love with Ellena and his proud mother has had her abducted, what follows for her is a long series of tests which she meets with judgment and—an additional problem for a young and friendless woman—decorum. She must use her mind: after Vivaldi has discovered her immured in a convent, ought she to let him remove her or not (122)? Seeming helpers, like Brother Jeronimo, may actually be traitors, and she has to doubt and discern. Correctly, though drawn by the call of the blood to her lost mother, the nun Olivia, she doubts her too. She and Vivaldi note that "we have been too ready to believe what we wish" (162). Interpreting observed phenomena must be done as carefully as interpreting human behavior. At the climax of her trial, when she is incarcerated in the lonely house by the sea where Schedoni is to murder her (until his erroneous conclusion that she is his daughter), her observations have become more acute and accurate (211, 250), she acquires additional fortitude under stress (165), and she begins to theorize on the evidence she has: as the arrest made just as she and Vivaldi were at the altar about to marry was in fact not, as the arresters claimed, made by the Holy Office, since she has not been taken to the Inquisition at Rome, they must have come from Vivaldi's mother, the contessa, and he must be safe (213). In fact, throughout this ordeal she makes a series of good guesses and conclusions (210–13), most importantly avoiding the poisoned food given her (216). Subsequently she listens and observes, working out the puzzle bit by bit (271). Her kindness helps to save her. By preventing the murder of the guide leading her with Schedoni from the seaside house, she provides for his confession at Rome that will lead to Schedoni's exposure as both the murderer of his brother, Ellena's father, and the enforced husband of Ellena's mother, Olivia.

In terms of gender Radcliffe has balanced *The Italian* by providing her hero Vivaldi with a parallel progress toward integration. His own ordeal consists of the abduction of Ellena and thereafter his imprisonment and interrogation by the Inquisition. Toward the end Schedoni explains to Vivaldi that his prevailing weakness is "a susceptibility which renders you especially liable to superstition" (397). But by that time Vivaldi has already corrected his habit of leaping to conclusions, of crediting appearances, of believing in insincere performances. Instead of providing a hero with reason who must acquire sensibility, Radcliffe has equalized her young people as both needing to acquire judgment and penetration. The past that must be understood is represented by the buried secret, which also encodes the problem of the identity of Ellena, but also by the secret of Vivaldi's mother's plots, of Schedoni's enmity. The mysteries of individual natures must be unraveled before one can grasp how and why the individuals will act and have acted.

As in *Cecilia* (and as in *Jane Eyre*), there is an interrupted marriage in the middle of the book: in all cases at the moment of interruption the lovers have not yet completed their progress toward maturity, or integration of the faculties of reason and sensibility, and are not yet ready for marriage.

Radcliffe's determination, after she has skillfully milked her apparent supernatural phenomena for maximum effect, to explain them away again by recourse to natural laws, has often been noted. Here is another claim by a woman author to enlightenment reason; Radcliffe, unlike the servants in her tales, rejects superstition in an effort to demonstrate her own superior reason.

The demystified gothics of Mary Wollstonecraft and William Godwin, like that of Richardson and (it might be argued) Austen in *Northanger Abbey*, of course, make the same point about the establishment's corruption in the service of the preservation of privilege. In *Maria; or, The Wrongs of Women* (1798), Wollstonecraft stands, arguably, for the integration of reason and sensibility, indicting the lover who uses a false sensibility to seduce, and strengthening both Maria and Jemima by, as Janet Todd has suggested, allowing each to teach the other her single attribute, Maria's sensibility, Jemima's reasoning power.[32] In the public sphere the male establishment, in the private one the husband and the lover prove equally corrupted by privilege, and Maria suffers all the torments of the gothic heroine. Those who emphasize Wollstonecraft's dislike of sensibility in women mistake her fear and contempt of sensibility *alone* in women for a proscription against it. Without empathy and consideration for others, all humankind would be in the kind of sad straits in which Maria finds herself simply because she has possessions—money, a child—over which she has no legal claim. But women must learn to reason. Godwin's Caleb Williams is, of course, beset by the powerful Falkland because he has learned his secret, the secret that proves his unworthiness to hold his position. Though Caleb possesses both attributes, he is hounded almost to death for having broken the code. At the period of the French Revolution, when class issues had been thoroughly outed, it was appropriate that these radical writers outed the subject of the gothic, patriarchal imposition, and postulated as a corrective against the suppression of women the nurturing of both reason and feeling in both genders. And the rise in consciousness of the criminality of the establishment was liberating and releasing an uprising of feeling—anger and terror—at this realization before the 1790s.

Thus, although the literary establishment rather liked women authors to employ themselves in writing gothics, always thought of as novels of excessive sensibility, the women authors were actually employed in using either the gothic mode or genre to achieve something in addition quite different from what it was thought they were doing. Rather than aligning their heroines with an irrational and tremulous sensibility, they were insisting that both hero and heroine combine sensibility and reason—a combination that rendered them more complete persons than the tyrants who, they were more and more openly charging, oppressed them. Nor, apparently, had their real-life tyrants the intellectual powers to read what in sober reason the women were writing.

Women who in their public or published writings employed the gothic as genre or mode often used it precisely as a separate female world from where they made subversive criticism of the world that is run by men, and more than that as a place from which to reaffirm their right to rational discourse. They made use of gothic elements to sketch palimpsestically the adverse background with which their protagonists must contend. And while the establishment assigned the gothic to women writers as one of their appropriate provinces, women writers in their private writings determinedly used rational discourse, except at the crucially distressing episodes where they wanted to signify their distress under obvious tyranny. What appeared to be, then, an acquiescence in the patriarchal assignment of reason to men and sensibility to women was in actuality the sturdy rebuttal, in which men often concurred, that both genders should strive to develop and express *both* intellect and the passions. If Lacan is right, if we are all in fact subjects essentially in discord, we all equally desire concord.

4 | My Art Belongs to Daddy?
Thomas Day, Maria Edgeworth, and
the Pre-Texts of *Belinda*:
Women Writers and Patriarchal Authority

Mitzi Myers

> *Death of the Father would deprive literature of many of its pleasures.*
> *If there is no longer a Father, why tell stories? Doesn't every narra-*
> *tive lead back to Oedipus? Isn't storytelling always a way of search-*
> *ing for one's origin, speaking one's conflicts with the Law, entering*
> *into the dialectic of tenderness and hatred?*
>
> *Roland Barthes,* The Pleasure of the Text *(1973; trans.*
> *Richard Miller, 1975; New York: Hill & Wang, 1986), 47.*

Maria Edgeworth's *Belinda* (1801) is usually labeled a romance of the tea table, a novel of manners, a young lady's entrance-into-the-world courtship fiction in the Frances Burney tradition, a tame precursor that Jane Austen inexplicably lauds to the skies in *Northanger Abbey*. When *Belinda* is positioned within the ideological war of ideas that shaped fiction in the 1790s, it is most often read as coercively domestic because of its satiric portrait of the mannish dasher Harriot Freke and its conversion of the dissipated Lady Delacour to model wife and mother: yet another victim of the "woman's private sphere" explanatory paradigm that still underpins most thinking about late Enlightenment female literary production.[1] Most recently, postcolonial readings discover plantocratic leanings on Edgeworth's part because of the tale's West Indian characters, and gay-oriented critics propose Freke as protolesbian because she loves to take the breeches part. In whatever sense we may define her as queer, she is certainly not the satiric portrait of Mary Wollstonecraft some have suggested, and her blatant advocacy and practice of sleeping with men other than her husband query any simple sexual explanation of her frolics (the literal meaning of "freke"), as do the strangely shifty gender and generational locations of virtually every character.

For example, the two young heroes are notably effeminized, adepts in emotive and actual crossdressing (Augustus Vincent indulges in gushy language and volatile mood swings; Clarence Hervey sways a mean hoop). The women are powerful for good or for bad, and the men often weak and boorish—fops mockingly defined by their omnipresent "little sticks," near illiterates, gamesters, and sots. Even the model representatives of the older generation commit spectacular gaffes in judgment, whereas the seventeen-year-old titular heroine is suprarational, the mentoria of her elders, and the numerous even younger children shrewdly assess adults and notably intervene in the action. (The focality and vocality of the children who migrate from Edgeworth's juvenile tales to her work for grownups is politically resonant in no simple way.) Ignoring the intricacies of Edgeworth's bizarre plot and sparkling dialogue, the rather spotty (and sometimes dotty) criticism is much more concerned to cite *Belinda* as an exemplary case of ruinous patriarchal intervention than to explore what genius Austen found in it or to unpack its political codings, its allusive narrative complexities, or its remarkable crosshatchings of the wildly romantic with the solidly referential, the visual with the verbal—the multiple prints, paintings, miniatures, inserted letters, and reported scandals that proliferate through its pages. The reductive mythology of Maria Edgeworth as daddy's good little girl, docilely ventriloquizing paternal ideas, joyfully complicitous in the patriarchal ideology that oppresses her, needs examination at every level, for Richard Lovell Edgeworth's influence over his daughter still thematizes discussion.[2] That the father's maladroit tamperings skew this novel even worse than his other interventions remains a staple in Edgeworth criticism, although the paternal critics do not always concur on his literary crimes.

In the case of Maria Edgeworth's first feminocentric adult novel, the genetic father's authority is doubled, because Clarence Hervey, Lady Delacour's platonic gallant and Belinda's first love, the hero of one plot and the antihero of the mystery subplot concerning "Virginia St. Pierre" (a parodic recycling of French forefathers such as Jean-Jacques Rousseau and Bernardin de Saint-Pierre), owes much to Thomas Day, as does Belinda's second love, the Jamaican Mr. Vincent, who is indebted to Day's terrible little Tommy Merton, the West Indian bad boy that Mr. Barlow, the tutor of Day's series, *The History of Sandford and Merton: A Work Intended for the Use of Children* (1783, 1786, 1789), takes three volumes to shape up.[3] Day, pioneering juvenile author, writer of sternly reformist political tracts, and antislavery propagandist, was the daughter's mentor, the father's best friend, and the patriarch who stopped the young woman's career cold—until his 1789 fall from a barely broken horse freed Maria Edgeworth to be what Day deplored, a published authoress.[4] Thomas Day was thus instrumental in Edgeworth's temporary blockage as a professional writer, and she never forgot it. But he was also an inspiration, a muse whom she played with, satirized, subverted, appropriated, impersonated, punished, and reformed. Indeed, her first published work for adults, *Letters for Literary Ladies* (1795; rev. ed., 1799), a most useful gloss for *Belinda*'s gender bending and female intellectuality, still dazzles with its virtuoso crossdressing. Masquerading as both Day and her genetic father, Edgeworth provides her own version of Mary Wollstonecraft's *A Vindication of the Rights of Woman* (1792), which had appeared during the Edgeworths' two-year stay in Bristol in the early nineties. (Wollstonecraft and Edgeworth, like many other innovative thinkers female and male, shared the same publisher, the radical Joseph Johnson.)

In *Forester* (written earlier, but also published in 1801), a Day turned idealistic and grotesque adolescent stars in one of Edgeworth's best young adult tales, wherein he is slapped down for silliness, credited for genius, and obliged to mend his eccentric ways and acknowledge the claims of sociality and smart women. Day-cum-Forester, along with the other quixotic teenagers who people the groundbreaking *Moral Tales for Young People*, thus opens up a new literary genre for a newly targeted literary market, a "young adult literature" category and readership still undervalued today and widely thought to have no history.[5] (It should go without saying that "moral tale," used by Edgeworth for adult as well as juvenile fictions, does not signal the didactic story reducible to a simplistic "moral" tag that some critics expect; allusive, like most everything in Edgeworth, the term requires contextual elucidation as French and *philosophe*.) Day echoes through other early work as well, but he is perhaps most complexly implicated in the shifty emplotments and characterizations of *Belinda*. Because so many authorial attitudes and narrative incidents in this underinterpreted tale are layered over Day's ideological and romantic adventures, Edgeworth's comic undermining of patriarchal authority cannot be fully appreciated until we know the real life pre-texts and literary precedents that shaped *Belinda*. More important than Edgeworth's own father to this tale is Day, the bad surrogate dad.

In *Belinda* (where Day figures in even more guises than noted here), the narrative recreation of his plot to pygmalionize the orphan he christened "Sabrina Sidney" explodes from a comedy of intellectual incest into a global critique of patriarchal romances of femininity—a critique both ideological and structural. Day's mentorial scripting of his orphan as the properly feminine character for the marital romance he wanted to tell about his life terminated with the girl's peremptory dismissal for violating an arbitrary rule of dress. But real life left Day's authority unquestioned and Sabrina a marginalized dependent, a boardinghouse resident with an allowance contingent on good behavior. In Edgeworth's novel, however, print and female storytelling confer a public power that private fact denied. *Belinda*'s plot abounds in fathers fictional and factual, even the most exemplary of whom are wanting: Edgeworth's is, ultimately, a tale of child power, of smart, resistant youngsters who shape up their elders. My study of *Belinda*'s pre-texts—including the gendered retellings of "Thomas Day" in the letters, memoirs, and narratives of other contemporaries as well as in Edgeworth's own *Letters for Literary Ladies* and (very briefly) *Forester*— helps modern readers decode Edgeworth's novel for what it is: not a tame recycling of daddy's ideas, but a remarkably sophisticated takeoff and parodic revisioning of multiple fathers (and mothers). Only when we too recognize Maria Edgeworth's tales as problematic palimpsests can we fully appreciate the "good" daughter's wicked pen. Making "Thomas Day" available for scrutiny unweaves but one strand in an extraordinarily allusive fiction that not only takes storytelling as its subject and form, but also offers us a way to reread and perhaps to recategorize women's storytelling as constitutive of the public sphere.

Thus this study is not the full-scale reconceptualization demanded by so complex a tale as *Belinda,* my candidate for at once the best and most misread (or underread) woman's fiction of the Revolutionary decade. These years, we need to remember, included for Edgeworth not just a French Revolution read about from afar, but the 1798 Irish Rebellion that ended literally next door to Edgeworthstown little more than a year before she planned *Belinda:* a war that above all dramatized the interpenetration of "public" and "private," the inseparability of words and actions, the insufficiencies and vulnerabilities of patriarchal authority. Instead, my essay provides some of the pre-texts that make such a rethinking possible. In situating Edgeworth's tale at a highly politicized historical crossroads as well as within domestic psychobiography and conventional "feminine" genres, it also makes a brief for reading women's fictions against the fullest possible sense of the past. In exploring the backgrounds of one woman writer's coming to writing, it more globally addresses issues of gender and authoriality, of text and context.

That "the master's tools will never dismantle the master's house" has become a feminist critical commonplace, for Audre Lorde's warning to modern white middle-class feminists has a larger resonance.[6] Lorde's words vividly, physically, image the theoretic attention to the experience of constraint, of woman's estrangement from language, that shapes so many current critical models of the house of literature. However costumed, the ticket-taker's always at the door, female objects only! No speaking subjects allowed! Historically, of course, we all know what theory daily problematizes: that the big event of the middle-class woman's beginning to write—greater than the Crusades or the War of the Roses, Virginia Woolf asserts—not only really happened despite woman's variously theorized aphasia but did so even earlier than Woolf thought.[7] But do these women just expropriate the male writer's speech, beset by "anxiety of authorship," uncomfortably handling tools not shaped for their hands? Have they ever had, do they need, a special language of their own, as Woolf and contemporary French feminist thinkers contend? Is the staple palimpsest of acceptable surface and subversive subtext—the "madwoman in the attic," the bedroom, the cellar, ripping apart the master's house—a paradigm answerable to all historical women writers?[8] Is the female author who did not growl or go mad just another victim of patriarchal complicity, a docile child expert at the game of "Daddy Says"? Joking about his unusually short daughter's debt to Dr. Erasmus Darwin's medical treatise *Zoonomia* (1794–96) in writing *Practical Education* (1798), Richard Lovell Edgeworth amusingly literalizes this view of woman's relation to the dominant discourse: "Maria recurs frequently to your authority . . . and has, I think, pardon my paternal partiality, managed your gigantic weapons with as much adroitness, as could be expected from a dwarf."[9]

Indeed, Maria Edgeworth's notorious father fixation enrolls her among literary history's least likely candidates for rebel daughter. Filial feeling touches numberless letters, and its nexus with authorial gratitude generates the extended account of literary partnership that is the ultimate source for critics' standard account of patriarchal politics; whether they replicate or interrogate the daughter's depiction, they perforce rely on her own narrativization. She is the literary fairy godmother who dramatizes her younger self as inarticulate Cinderella or Sleeping Beauty rescued by her father's nurture.[10] The sixteenth chapter of Edgeworth's continuation of her father's life is the locus classicus for the paternal preceptor's facilitating his daughter's entrance into literature, freeing her from "vacillation and anxiety," at once inspiring muse and stylistic critic: "I am sure I should not have written or finished any thing without his support. . . . Such, happily for me, was his power over my mind, that no one thing I ever began to write was ever left unfinished. . . . Few female authors, perhaps none, have ever enjoyed such advantages, in a critic, friend, and father, united. Few have ever been blessed in their own family with such able assistance, such powerful motive, such constant sympathy" (*Memoirs of RLE*, 2: 333–52).

She recurrently images her involvement with writing and her father as collaboration, an enabling interdependence, a mutuality of give and take. If the uncharacteristically awkward sentence struggles to obfuscate who actually holds the pen, Edgeworth's description of how the *Essay on Irish Bulls* (1802) took shape nicely typifies this motif: "Working zealously upon the ideas which he suggested, sometimes, what was spoken by him, was afterwards written by me; or when I wrote my first thoughts, they were corrected and improved by him; so that no book was ever written more completely in partnership. . . . it would now be difficult, almost impossible, to recollect, which thoughts originally were his, and which were mine." Destabilizing the opposition between spontaneous feminine orality and ordered masculine discourse built into much modern theory, Edgeworth authorizes herself as transcriber, amanuensis, her father verbally supplying notes, ideas, or materials. The virtuoso performances of Irish idiom in *Bulls,* for example, she characterizes as "unembellished fact," repeated and acted by the father, which she "instantly wrote word for word, and the whole was described exactly from the life of his representation" (*Memoirs of RLE,* 2: 346, 352, 336–38).

But if Maria Edgeworth's official conceptualization of herself as female writing subject seems at first take another exemplary instance of the father tongue's dominance, the dissonance between her tale of textual production and the polyvocal praxis of her fictions reveals her account's insufficiency, its genesis in psychological need. However valuable as a record of her art's emotional grounds, Edgeworth's sketch of her entry into literature occludes the constitutive role of writing itself, the specific discursive tactics that construct subjectivities and stories. Detailing Edgeworth's actual language games suggests an alternative mythology of female literary practice: not an intellectual incest unproblematically reproducing the father tongue, but a playfully emancipatory recycling, challenging, and reinvention of patriarchal narrative. I scrutinize some of Edgeworth's sources and their relation to her life and fiction not to confirm the common view of her art as a literalizing of the "real" but to query it, to argue for a subtler relation between the master's tools and texts and the daughter's literary habitation. In lieu of an explanatory model totalizing benign or malignant patriarchal influence, I trace Edgeworth's engagement with hegemonic masculine plotters like Day, Rousseau, and Saint-Pierre as a more capacious and elastic dialogue between woman writer and father tongue: a daughter's aesthetics of play that demystifies paternal authority.

Privileging the sign of the child, Maria's parodic *écriture juvénile* thus helps us renegotiate literary history's stereotype of Edgeworth as author via her own renegotiations of masculine fictions of woman. A critical feminist reading of *Belinda* and some of its pre-texts that argues for Edgeworth's tale as a critical feminist reading of multiple androcentric texts, a ludic revision of hegemonic male plots, helps us in turn to revise the hegemonic masterplots of literary history and theory. Altering and enriching our sense of how women's texts work, Edgeworth's multilayered allusions and patriarchal recyclings offer a heuristic for how gender is formalized in narrative structures themselves. Although strands in *Belinda* seemingly align with two quite different notions of fiction—a prosaic, world-reflecting realism and an extravagant, self-reflexive romanticism—I argue that both narrative impulses coexist in Edgeworth's work, that both are central to her ambitious novels, that her interplay of transparency and theatricality interrogates issues of gender and representation substantive not only to the development of the period's fiction but to its cultural politics as well. Rather than simply rehearsing patriarchy in Maria Edgeworth's life, I want to tie lived experiences to their literary embodiments, to look at how patriarchal master narratives assume textual specificity, and to read narrative structures as themselves gendered. Edgeworth's subversion of Day's and recent history's patriarchal plots must be read in her work, where masculinized narrative constructions unravel through both the intellectual address of female conversation and contrivance and the untutored recalcitrance of the female body and gaze, where male romantic fictions are outflanked by both woman's realism and alternative feminine constructions of romance. The shape of Edgeworth's early career and the structure of her texts are imbricated in familial and cultural patriarchal politics, but despite her recurrent equation of authorship and childship, she is never simply the guileless filial conduit for a didactic father tongue.

Belinda's patriarchal recyclings and gendered emplotments emerge most problematically in the enigma that veils Clarence Hervey's renaming and romanticizing of the supposed orphan Rachel Hartley, who is to play Sophy to his Emile, Virginia to his Paul. The riddle appears early in the book and informs the plot to the very end, rendering Hervey's changeable conduct inexplicable to Belinda and thus allowing her other key suitor, Mr. Percival's West Indian ward Augustus Vincent, room to maneuver. But the puzzle was not just clumsily tacked on to eke out the novel when Lady

Delacour's melodramatic death was decided against, nor is it a paternal interpolation in a didactic vein, as Emily Lawless and others obsessed with patriarchal emendation have suggested. Anyone who thinks so might note how early and elaborately the clues that ultimately coalesce to demystify the mystery are embedded and how vitally the abortive wife-training thematizes Edgeworth's ideological critique of contemporary masculine fabrications of the feminine. Tightly inwoven with *Belinda's* multiple fables of identity, the sequence has no readily extractable univocal "moral."[11] The Clarence-Virginia relationship is a sexual tease as well as a textual mystery, for Virginia is at once Hervey's daughter, pupil, wife-to-be, and reputed mistress. Ultimately she is revealed as the abandoned child of a now repentant West Indian planter; having lost his son and the wife he married after deserting Virginia's mother, he obsessively searches foundling hospitals for the teenage daughter he knows only from a miniature painted in childhood, a deathbed token from the dead wife he had not publicly acknowledged.[12]

Hervey's secret quest for Virginia's now emotionally disturbed father attempts to displace the daughter's fettering gratitude onto the rightful progenitor, but it makes his vacillation with Belinda still more illegible. Initially as adolescent as he is charming, he is a far cry from the lover-cum-father of *Evelina* or *Emma*. (It is a rare Georgian novel in which the smart women test the lover-heroes and find them in need of the surveillance and shaping up typically meted out to heroines like Camilla.) Moreover, Edgeworth's recycling of patriarchal master narratives simultaneously reproduces their figuration—woman as sentimental heroine and passive object of the male voyeur's desire—and subverts it. Virginia almost ruins several lives by persistently enacting the "grateful" feminine role she has been taught, and she further confuses fictions and reality by her addiction to the romances which supply her only reading. Like her dead mother earlier seduced by novels into a runaway secret marriage, Virginia looks at first like a sentimental stereotype. But she is not simply the deluded daughter as satiric object, for Clarence as mentor-hero is equally quixotic and deserves a comeuppance most leading men escape. Parodically, Virginia turns out to have a gaze and a fantasy of her own, although Hervey is emphatically not the visionary hero who haunts her sleep and is ever before her waking eye. She is, it turns out, wildly in love with a picture of a man she has never seen because she imagines him as Paul in Saint-Pierre's romance.[13]

If Clarence merely fancied that he wanted a Virginia, his Rachel turned Virginia really does desire Paul. She may not know who he is, but she cannot keep her thoughts off his "figure."[14] Despite her penchant for nurturing roses and nestling pet bullfinches in her bosom, despite her blushes, fainting, and intellectual indolence, Virginia is not merely a docile body. With surprising self-command, she hugs her fancy to herself. When she learns that her returning father will make her an heiress, she rejoices only because she thinks perhaps she can buy off the protector she does not want (the virgin's version of the roué's dismissing the mistress he tires of). Only because she thinks Clarence expects it does she agree to marry him and certify her gratitude; only because he thinks she is hopelessly in love with him and her reputation compromised does Clarence, despite his genuine love for Belinda, manfully plan to wed his dream turned nightmare. Virginia's heroic determination to immolate herself on the altar of gratitude grotesquely exaggerates and thus calls into question that culturally ubiquitous "feminine" virtue (an ironic twist the more arresting because Edgeworth herself so highly values it). Clarence is a comic Frankenstein, condemned to marry the creature whose very conformity to what society supposedly expects of mindless woman critiques good little passive girls. Only because of female curiosity, gossip, and fondness for macaws and finches do Clarence and "Paul" each wind up with the right "bird." Paul demystified, it turns out, is just like Jane Austen's real sailor brothers and fictional Wentworth or Edgeworth's Walsingham in *Manœuvering* (1809), an entrepreneurial sea captain in the Revolutionary wars. Saving the day with inspired detective work and storytelling skills, Lady Delacour (the Scheherazade–Blue Beard's wife doubling for the author) delivers Clarence and Virginia from their gendered entrapments: her dazzlingly orchestrated denouement metafictionally reveals cultural norms as, well, fictions, useful social glue, perhaps, but always open to renegotiation.[15] Her allusive parting couplet tweaks the audience with the tale's purported moral, "no doubt / You all have *wit* enough to find it out," but only a rash critic would dare serve up just one (434).

Unlike the novel's other semiorphan heroines, Belinda and Lady Delacour's neglected daughter Helena, each a wise child and exemplary teacher of her elders who thinks for herself and demonstrates presence of mind in every emergency, irrational Virginia is as disturbing as comic in her suturing of performed femininity and naked emotional need. Her filial fantasies stirred by romance reading, Virginia had "secretly nourished the hope that she should not for ever be a *deserted child*. . . . the belief in what the French call *la force du sang* was suited to her affectionate temper and ardent imagination, and it had taken full possession of her mind. . . . 'My *father!*—How delightful that word *father* sounds! . . . Oh, how I shall love him! I will make it the whole business of my life to please him!'" (372).

Virginia may be a heroine whose literary genealogy goes beyond Rousseau and Saint-Pierre to Greek romance cliché—the first editions even include a mole, the bodily mark that certifies paternal property—but her story is psychically resonant too. No one familiar with Edgeworth's life can help recalling the little girl's dazzled response to the return of her long-lost father: the "gentleman in black" who "instantly struck" the abandoned daughter's imagination with "the idea of his being sublimely superior to all she saw before."[16] And no one familiar with Edgeworth's comments on her own work—she has no tougher critic—can forget her impatient slander of her nominal heroine as too much of a prudent "stick," even after authorial revision to make evident Belinda's feelings as well as her rationality.

Virginia's relations with bogus and real fathers are thus charged textual sites conflating romance and realism, nature and nurture, cultural critique and feminine subjectivity. Complicating the narrative affiliations and disaffections of this multilayered fictionality is the Virginia sequence's derivation from real life, from Maria Edgeworth's own family history, for it is based on Thomas Day's appropriation of a foundling to train according to the fantasies of femininity he had imbibed from Rousseau, the same constructions of woman that had delayed Edgeworth's public debut for a decade. Day's epistolary diatribe against writing women was rebutted by Richard Lovell privately, but the family respected Day's anathemas against female authorship publicly. He was her father's best friend for twenty-three years and a paternal figure Maria was taught to revere in childhood. However vehemently her father disagreed with Day about the female right to literature, family deference kept Maria out of print during the 1780s, although she continued to write for household consumption. Concluding her father's memoirs after Richard Lovell's death in 1817, Maria recalls that although she only heard those letters read once (they were apparently burned by her father), they remained vividly alive in her mind. Ever discreet and urbane, she says little more, but Day is crucial in the genesis and gendering of Edgeworth's early career. He is a surrogate father whose word is not law, whose attributes can be split off, questioned, and laughed at; his life and works are old texts she can quote, revise, and enter into dialogue with. A refraction and transformation of the voices that women writers inherit from tradition, Virginia's genealogy also emblematizes Maria Edgeworth's lived and literary lineage.

Materializing the ambivalence of patriarchy's cultural legacy, the complex and contradictory circulation of Day through Edgeworth's texts enacts both the woman writer's problematic relation to that legacy and the entanglement of liberatory and oppressive strategies in enlightened eighteenth-century masculine culture. Day's patriarchal romance of the mythic creator who yearns to construct and to own the girl that he imagines exemplifies the revisability of hegemonic male plots. Whether Day comes across as a civic humanist hero or a harebrained humbug depends on how the educational plan that *Belinda* addresses has been read (or erased). Perenially susceptible to prurient curiosity (Virginia's fate), Day's experiment in social engineering also demonstrates the period's diversity of gendered emplotments. Kaleidoscopically suppressed or foregrounded by Day's first published biographers, reticent James Keir and outspoken Anna Seward; told and retold in multiple accounts by Richard Lovell as well as by Maria; available to women writers as liberatory Spartan heroism in Mary Wollstonecraft's educational writing and young Mary Anne (Galton) Schimmelpenninck's saucy reenactments, as inept masculinist child-rearing in Elizabeth Gaskell's account of Charlotte Brontë, or as sentimental fantasy in Frances Burney's French exercise books, Day's tutorship is simultaneously the most widely known "fact" about him and what can never be known as fact because it began as an imagined story and can only be read through variant narrative structures: an amusing reminder that history is fictions, that fictions constitute history.[17] Appropriately, *Secrecy* (1795) is Eliza Fenwick's title for her epistolary version of the sequestered woman who embodies gendered lessons about "Nature" versus "Art."[18]

Like the man himself, Day's place in cultural studies is at once eccentric and exemplary. One Victorian biographer claims his primary motive is "to shew that the world has made no mistake in affixing the word 'eccentric'" to Day's name and memory.[19] Historian Paul Langford has more recently made Day's politics the subject of detailed study as a case history of the "unresolved contradictions within sentimental politics," a record of high-minded abstraction withdrawing before balky fact. In a judgment that surely would have enraged a man who prided himself on his originality and gritty individualism, even when his virtues soured into misanthropic isolation, Langford finds Day valuable for what he represented rather than what he did, for the "contemporary attitudes which he embodied."[20] No doubt the dour late Day, whose idealisms and philanthropies produced little practical change and who increasingly felt himself beset by ingratitude and misunderstanding, preferred his continuing identification with Rousseau, the outcast genius of the *Solitary Walker* rather than the buoyant mentor of *Émile*.[21] Although he was a founding member of the Society for Constitutional Information (to which Thomas Holcroft and other noteworthy political figures belonged), played a part in the reformist extra-parliamentary Association movement of the 1780s, and even considered becoming an M.P., Day (like his idol Rousseau) never thought of himself as a practical politician, but as an unimpeachable censor of Fashion and Custom.[22] Had he gone in for political rough-and-tumble, what Dickens calls his "adamantine inadaptibility" might have eventuated in another rigidly moral Incorruptible, an English Robespierre.[23] Ironically, Day is certainly remembered not for the pamphlets he prided himself on, but for his private life, his shadowy presence in Edgeworth criticism, and above all, for the remarkable popularity and longevity of his works for little boys.[24] Indeed, Gerald Newman characterizes *Sandford and Merton* as a paradigmatic work in the formation of English national identity, a telling indicator of the "coherence and maturity" of emergent nationalism in the eighties, an "archetypal story of alien pollution told by the English story-teller to the English about themselves."[25]

Day's seemingly wild schemes are the logical product of his Enlighten-ment systematizing, at once embodying and debunking the philosophical fantasy of rational transcendence and the masculinist hubris of the mag-isterial knower. He epitomizes the contradictions and the absences that ground the period's totalizing universalism.[26] But Day also demonstrates male hegemony's ambidextrous cooptation of feminine feeling: its simul-taneous effacement of female subjectivity as the irrational Other and its appropriative masculinizing of sensibility. Day's self-representation as so-ber reasoner masks a visionary romantic—strikingly captured by Joseph Wright of Derby in the tall thick body echoing a phallic antique column behind, the otherworldly gaze just raised from a dropped book.[27] Day is that oddly hermaphroditic late-eighteenth-century figure, the man of rea-son who is also the man of feeling. Day's first memorialist finds his "re-markable degree" of sensibility and stoic fortitude determinative and elab-orately explains how feminine sympathy and manly firmness only *seem* contradictory.[28] Later literary historians entitle their studies "An English Disciple of Rousseau," "The Child of Nature," "A Philosopher in Search of the Life of Virtue and of a Paragon among Women," or "The Crank."[29] Friends describe the "character he aspired at" as that "of defending the rights of mankind," and chroniclers of antislavery writing and agitation give Day high marks for his poem *The Dying Negro* and his tract on slavery (Keir 38). Because the initial version of the poem (cowritten with Day's friend John Bicknell) appeared in 1773 and the tract (written in 1776) in 1784, Day has strong claims as a pioneer voice against black slavery as well as that of the working poor, the marginalized groups whose cause he embraces in the loftiest of civic humanist rhetoric.[30] Mary Wollstonecraft, who was judging from an episode in "one of the most instructive books, that our country has produced for children," enlists Day as Rousseau's antitype, an ally in her cause of strengthening female education, and others too have thought feminists owed him a debt.[31]

But in *Sandford and Merton*, as in Day's own life, a brief for more rational female education is subsumed within a masculinist republican ideology constructed from Stoics and Spartans, Romans and Rousseau. Like Richard Lovell, Day was heavily influenced by a strong-minded mother; she exemplified "the magnanimity of Roman and Spartan matrons" that her son conflated with Rousseau's Sophy.[32] As a teenager she checked a charging bull's career by fixing him with her eyes so a terrified friend could scramble over a stile—an anecdote used in John Aikin's famous children's tale "Presence of Mind" in *Evenings at Home*.[33] To share the ideal of rigorous retirement that thematized his life, Day wanted a woman who united the "purity of female virtue with the fortitude and hardiness of constitution of a Spartan virgin, and with a simplicity of taste" that spurned the luxurious manners he deplored (Keir 16–18). Yet, records Maria Edgeworth, he was so prejudiced against female literature and wit that "he was nearly of Sir Anthony Absolute's opinion" and thought simple letters enough without their mischievous combinations (*Memoirs of RLE*, 2: 342). A supporter of American independence who damned colonial slaveholders because "universal morality" and rights allow no property in another, Day himself personifies the imperialist fantasies of the dominant white male ruling class.[34] Appropriating the stance of Enlightenment philosophy's transcendental rational subject, the all-wise knower who underwrites western culture's metanarratives of domination and subjugation, Day purchased two illegitimate foundlings to indoctrinate: devalued and marginal Others for his own private colonialist project.

The extraordinary self-consciousness with which Day set about embodying an idealized masculine ideology and the vivid anecdotes of his earliest biographers make the details of his life (often garbled) better known than his work.[35] Problematizing the relation between the written and the "real," competing constructions of "Thomas Day" illuminate his generative function in Maria Edgeworth's art. (They pose questions about the role of her art in subsequent literary history's reconstructions, too, for *Belinda*'s 1801 rendition of Day's experiments precedes most biographies and is quoted as fact in George Warren Gignilliat's authoritative 1932 study.) Accounts of Day rely on the first official biography by James Keir (1791), a reincarnation of the subject as Stoic hero, and (more heavily) on the vividly idiosyncratic accounts of Anna Seward in her life of Erasmus Darwin (1804) and Richard Lovell Edgeworth in his *Memoirs*, written in 1808–9 and published in 1820, Keir as entirely occluding Day's misadventures with women and education as Seward and Richard Lovell dramatize them.[36] Shortly after Day's death, Maria apparently wrote a full-fledged life of Day; her continuation of her father's memoirs speaks of taking down the start of a biography that Richard Lovell never published, but Lady Dorothea Charnwood discovered that "a little manuscript life of Mr. Day in my hand" was actually completed by Maria from her father's reminiscences.[37] Maria states in the *Memoirs* that she had not read her father's own autobiographical manuscript until after his death, but she knew Day intimately from personal experience and Richard Lovell's words before she used him as literary springboard and dialogic other in the first decade of her career. After her father's death, Maria tried to get back her biography of Day from Sabrina Bicknell to whom it had been given when the Edgeworths' project was forestalled by Keir's study, but whatever Maria wrote immediately following Day's demise has apparently disappeared; it is not among the family papers.[38]

In contexts involving her father, Maria likes to invoke notions of writing as a transparent linguistic medium and herself as unmediating conduit, as she does with the first manuscript life of Day—a mythology of literary origins that obscures the constitutive nature of her writing itself. Moreover, Richard Lovell's final account comes *after* his daughter's multiple recyclings of Day's life and works. Maria Edgeworth's Thomas Day circulates back through the father's representation. Richard Lovell's repudiation of his friend's follies is also in part a judgment against his own former self, a rejection of the disembodied reason and totalizing masculine theory with which Day so strongly identified. "I feel almost as if I had done an injury, as if I had betrayed some confidence," Richard Lovell writes uneasily. He claims he did not mean to ridicule a friend, but just to show "that there may be too strong an adherence even to reason" (*Memoirs of RLE*, 1: 350–51), a criticism applicable to himself that his daughter had already implicitly made and would make explicit in her continuation of her father's memoirs after his death. In rewriting Rousseau's, Saint-Pierre's, and Day's patriarchal narratives from a woman's perspective, Maria Edgeworth undoes the commodification and objectification of Day's two foundling pupils and gives her fictional girl a voice denied her prototypes: a legitimation of abandoned daughters within the text that simultaneously legitimates the female narrative project that contains them. In re-presenting and specularizing Day's life and works, she brings up questions about the construction of femininity, masculinity, and her own authorship, even questions about representation itself. In reimagining Day's textualizations of self and Other, she is also enacting parables about her own writing's founding referential premise and its transgressive antimimetic impulse, its filial piety and its filial impiety.

Richard Lovell Edgeworth and Thomas Day became close friends before Maria was born. They had attended the same college, but Edgeworth was four years older, already a married man and the father of a young son when they met in 1766. His teenage union with Maria's mother was the only unhappy marriage of his four, so Edgeworth was often away to escape a depressed wife who "lamented about trifles"; when he was home, he busied himself experimenting with machines and educating little Dick according to Rousseau's system, which he followed for five years.[39] Day and Edgeworth were mutually "dazzled by the eloquence of Rousseau" and moral philosophy, but Day was as morose, uncouth, and asocial as Edgeworth was vivacious, witty, and gregarious (*Memoirs of RLE*, 1: 181–84, 274). Richard Lovell loved women and displayed a remarkable gift for winning and wedding them, but Day was suspicious of the female sex and all social forms as currently constituted like his mentor Rousseau, though much less appreciative of woman's erotic power. Boasting his insensibility to beauty and accomplishments, Day bluntly entertained mixed company with harangues on the evils let loose on mankind by love, and his stout body, stoop-shouldered, pockmarked, his unpowdered hair curled "Adam-like" about his brows, testified to his beliefs as forcibly as his tongue. Anna Seward, who met him a few years after Edgeworth and was the recipient of confessional letters she was supposed to burn but did not, thought his tall, full form "looked the philosopher . . . in his meditative and melancholy air a degree of awkwardness and dignity were blended." She found him less amusing, graceful, and brilliant than the agile Edgeworth, but "more highly imaginative, more classical, and a deeper reasoner." Day's integrity, friendship, and charity countered the "tincture of misanthropic gloom and proud contempt of common-life society" that marked his "peculiar character." Still, Seward felt obliged to correct the press's saintly obituaries when Day died in 1789. "With very first-rate abilities," he was "a splenetic, capricious, yet bountiful misanthropist" who gave most of his fortune to the poor, though convinced they would just as soon cut his throat, and who chose to live in a lonely and unpleasant situation "to be out of the stink of human society": "He took pride in avowing his abhorrence of the luxuries, and disdain of even the decencies of life; and in his person, he was generally slovenly, even to squalidness" (Seward, *Memoirs*, 18–19; *Letters of AS*, 2: 330).

As her early works and her continuation of her father's *Memoirs* testify, young Maria's sharp eyes registered all Day's foibles during the family intimacy and several childhood visits on her own. Traveling over England in 1818 to collect opinions on the manuscript, she wryly records Lady Lansdowne's love and admiration of Day as depicted by her father: "Had she seen him she would not have endured his manners however 24 hours." The rest of her comment has been discreetly scissored out.[40] Despite Day's uncombed, unpowdered hair and ablutions confined to "washing in the stream," Edgeworth's *Memoirs* mark this acquaintance as "a new era" in his life. He was impressed by Day's "highmindedness" and "true patriotism," thought nobody else "reasoned so profoundly and so logically," and pronounced him "the most virtuous human being whom I have ever known," the "man of the most perfect morality." Maria's mother, however, detested Day, though she had never complained about her husband's London frolics with the wild Sir Francis Delaval, whose fashionable dissipation *Belinda* plays off against Day's philosophic retirement—laughing allusively at contemporary culture's contradictory masculinist representations, as in the quasi-hero Clarence Hervey, against which the tale constructs its feminized alternative.[41] His wife's jealousy of his new confidant worried Edgeworth, but this "most intimate and unvarying friendship" long outlasted her life. A few months after Maria's birth in 1768, Day, Edgeworth, and little Dick left Mrs. Edgeworth and her "infant daughter" in England and went for a long visit to Edgeworth's paternal estate in Ireland, where Day's quest for the perfectly prepared wife commenced (*Memoirs of RLE*, 1: 180–84, 336, 193).[42]

Belinda's fictionalizing of Day's life and its cross-referencing of Clarence Hervey, Rousseau, Saint-Pierre, and the phallocentric culture of the western intellectual tradition satirize Day's own literalizations. Day took *Émile* as his script and awkwardly alternated—as does Hervey—between playing the marriageable youth and recreating the tutor's educational scenario. Book V proclaims that it is not good for man to be alone and fantasizes the masculinist philosopher's ideal helpmeet, "Sophy, or Woman": "Where is her dwelling-place, where shall she be found?"[43] Day thought rustic Ireland afforded prospects and professed himself the admirer of Edgeworth's sister Margaret, the woman who became Maria's beloved surrogate mother, Aunt Ruxton. Day wanted to marry more out of duty than love so he could retire to a hideaway with a perfectly virtuous woman in a perfect marriage and raise perfect children. He craved a congenial, obedient wife who disdained luxury and subordinated all her tastes to his. She needed enough intelligence to debate everything from high ideals to the most trivial matters of daily life with logical accuracy, yet Day simultaneously feared a learned lady who would speak her own subjectivity instead of mirroring his. Like that of his mentor Rousseau, Day's position on the role and education of woman is a rhetoric of contradiction, important not just for its specific psychobiographic impact on Maria Edgeworth but also as a symptomatology of the ambiguous literary and cultural traditions the late-eighteenth-century woman writer's art had to negotiate. Day kept approaching attractive women, well-bred, well-read, and fond of enlightened social pleasures—the fashionable ladies his theories deplored: Margaret Edgeworth, Honora and Elizabeth Sneyd, and the bluestocking beauty Madame Suard, among others.[44] Even after his educational project was under way, he made tentative matrimonial forays for years, but he was as notoriously unsuccessful as Richard Lovell—whose second and third wives (the Sneyd sisters) both rejected Day first—was the reverse. Edgeworth's father was repelled by Day's table habits, but Margaret put him on probation; like Émile, he was sent into the world to mend his manners. Day later remained on good terms with the Sneyd sisters, but he detested Margaret's taste for politesse and polished conversation as much as Maria relished it. Several rejections later he wrote an unpublished letter to Anna Seward that would have horrified his sometime pupil Maria, recollecting "Miss Edge" with "contempt" and "Detestation": "I see her as I should a Toad, which I would not injure, but I cannot help beholding with abhorrence."[45]

When Day came of age in June 1769, he determined to carry out the Rousseauistic scheme he had long dreamed of. If politeness and genteel education had corrupted every likely matrimonial candidate, Pygmalion would have to construct his Sophy from childhood's more malleable material. Reenacting the archetypal myth of the male artist-creator who makes the feminine subjectivity he seeks, Day's "design more romantic than any which we find in novels" is more than just an odd source for one section of *Belinda* (*Memoirs of RLE,* 1: 214). Day's literalization of *Émile* is irresistible to any writer interested in sexual politics or drawn to the dialogue between historical fact and the fictions by which it creates itself. Because Day's experiment so strikingly foregrounds gender (and class) difference, it is always inevitably gendered in the telling. Outspoken Anna Seward is often said to have savaged Day, but she is mainly concerned to balance James Keir's magisterial Stoic and universal knower—Day as a Cincinnatus who stuck to his plow—with the juicy domestic details the official memorialist occludes. In her 1804 memoirs of Dr. Erasmus Darwin (the notable scientific precursor of his famous grandson Charles and a celebrated poet in his own day), Seward dilates on the "singular instances of philosophical love" in Day's domestic history, telling Walter Scott not to expect a biography of a learned scientist from her "feminine Darwiniana": "If not the widow's, it is the woman's mite in biography" (*Letters of AS*, 6: 94, 125). Since she came to loathe Richard Lovell (and vice versa), what is surprising is not that their accounts differ but that their scenarios so largely agree. Like *Belinda*'s recyclings, their variants participate in the period's discourses of gender difference, clarifying Maria Edgeworth's choices in transposing "fact" to fiction. Despite "a person neither formed by nature, nor cultivated by art, to please," as the attractive and flirtatious Richard Lovell diplomatically puts it, Day nevertheless expected to "win some female wiser than the rest of her sex, who should feel for him the most romantic and everlasting attachment—a paragon, who should forget the follies and vanities of her sex for him." Edgeworth's experimental subjects were home grown, but a bachelor who "nursed systematic ideas of the force of philosophic tuition to produce future virtue, and loved to mould the infant and youthful mind" had to look abroad. To "assist him in forming the minds of his children to stubborn virtue and high exertion," Day resolved that his wife-to-be "should be simple as a mountain girl, in her dress, her diet, and her manners; fearless and intrepid as the Spartan wives and Roman heroines.—There was no finding such a creature ready made; philosophical romance could not hope it. He must mould some infant into the being his fancy had imaged" (*Memoirs of RLE*, 1: 181–82; Seward, *Memoirs*, 34–35).

Since Day despised distinctions derived from birth, wealth, culture, and leisure, illegitimate or immoral origins did not worry him; he would be substituting apprenticeship in wifehood for the training foundlings could normally expect. Young Day and John Bicknell, an older but still unmarried London barrister friend, went first to the Shrewsbury branch of the London Foundling Hospital. Seward and Edgeworth both became good friends of the pupil Day kept longest, but they differ on how the bachelors appropriated two girls of eleven and twelve. Seward protectively provides written certificates of moral probity and a detailed contract of upright intentions; Day fulfilled most of the conditions she names, but he was bound by his own puritan virtue rather than laws. The rules did require that a child be bound apprentice to a married man, so Edgeworth, who was not even present, later discovered that he had the renamed Sabrina Sidney under his official protection. Bicknell chose her for her fine auburn curls, her long eyelashes, and her melodious voice; Day defined her source by a first name for the river near the orphanage and her destiny by the last name of a favorite hero, Algernon Sidney, the theoretical republican executed for alleged conspiracy against Charles II. (No doubt he also recalled the "Virgin pure" of Milton's *Comus*, ll. 824–26.) In case the first child did not fulfill Day's marital expectations, he wanted another in reserve, so he and Bicknell found a pretty blonde at the main London institution. Since it apparently never occurred to anyone to wonder what would happen if Day did not fulfill the pupils' marital hopes, it is noteworthy that Edgeworth's Virginia *does* have desires of her own—and they do not focus on marrying her benefactor. Oblivious to irony, Day called the second candidate Lucretia, the associations with classical republican courage outweighing rape and suicide. Although a nineteenth-century writer found that a T. Day gave fifty pounds toward the London Foundling Hospital's funds in 1769, the year the little girls were selected, Day acted in no official capacity because he was not elected as a governor until 27 December 1770.[46] Day's writings may critique the racial and class privileges he enjoyed, but property, status, and leisure enabled his gendered fantasy.

Conferring identity and connoting property, the power to name belongs to a patriarchal discourse of power. Like the classical names given eighteenth-century blacks in Britain, "Sabrina" and "Lucretia" objectify human subjects and cast their bearers as characters whose bodies and minds act out their owners' fictions. Hervey's Virginia St. Pierre and Vincent's Juba the man and Juba the dog underline and ironize this commodification (though *Belinda* shows further reasons for these choices too). Hervey appropriates a seeming orphan, renames her, has her painted portraying the character he has chosen for her, and publicly exhibits as his property the framed and labeled "fancy piece."[47] Identical titles signify Vincent's affection for man and dog—each the best of its kind because it is his—and their equivalent status as belongings, Addison's famous black warrior against imperial empire no longer connoting freedom but colonial possession. Foundlings (like racial Others) are marginal, socially invisible beings whose status signifies vulnerability, passivity, sexual availability, powerlessness. They have no official voice except through compliance and complicity. Female foundlings, sin's produce, are multiply identified with the order of nature, of matter to be molded—the perfect site for educational intervention and inscription. With exemplary clarity, the unfamilied girl also calls attention to the cultural production of gender itself, to the formation of subjectivity as a social construct rather than a phenomenon of nature. (Eighteenth-century educators would surely be amused at postmodernism's arrogation of their insight.)

Day's educational scenario is a masculine cultural fantasy of subordination, a set of disciplinary practices for mastering the girls mentally and physically. Their bodies were in no danger of sexual violation, thanks to

Day's Stoic disdain for passion and pleasure rather than to institutional precaution. Officials could not have known about his schoolboy challenge to a profligate nobleman, and the London neighbors, where he first took the girls, were understandably curious about the strange ménage. Day then carried his charges abroad despite the French decadence he condemned so that, Seward and Richard Lovell concur, "they might receive no ideas, except those which himself might choose to impart." Since they knew no French and he took no English servant, their minds were "open to such ideas and sentiments, and such only, as he desired to implant." All the values encoded in "fashion" horrified Day. With *Émile* as his guidebook, he slowly taught the girls to read and write, and ridiculed and reasoned them into hating dress, luxury, fine people, and titles. His chief qualifications for a wife were simplicity, perfect innocence, and attachment to himself. He was not, Richard Lovell drily remarks, "sufficiently aware, that ignorance is not necessary to preserve innocence" (Seward, *Memoirs* 37; *Memoirs of RLE,* 1: 216–17). However laudable, the father's sentiment does not tidily sum up what goes amiss in the Virginia sequence or in Day's enactment of *Émile* either, as it is often said to do.

Sugared with a romantic sensibility that allured female readers into foregoing claims to reason and public life, Rousseau's misogynous sequestration of woman paradoxically flatters her by promising national moral regeneration through private domesticity.[48] *Belinda's* revisionary alternative to masculine representations of women's subjectivity, education, and cultural contribution emerges not in polemic but in play, in its allusive rereadings of Day's and others' readings of the masculine literary tradition. For Day's friend Keir, society is natural and necessary to human formation, so the official biography works hard to attribute Day's "Quixotism of virtue" to romantic youth and Rousseau's seductions—what Day himself calls "the extravagancies of a warm heart, and of a strong imagination"—but Keir also admits that Day's characteristic feature was his unequaled "consistency of principle with conduct" (20, 9, 29, 90). Very serious and very worthy, Day never outgrew his stiff-necked adolescent idealism or accommodated himself to social practices, as does Maria Edgeworth's fictional counterpart *Forester,* a teenage Diogenes who fancies himself Cato the Censor. With delicate malice, Day's onetime pupil transmutes her reclusive fictional misfit from grotesque body—an elephant, a mad dog, a scabrous hand, a pair of filthy thumbs—to a reformist political writer active in the print world and welcomed back into social harmony, mocked, matured, and forgiven. But the obsession with improvement and retirement that Day's early educational project memorializes was lifelong, and Edgeworth's continuing dialogue with those themes shapes much of her work in turn: the rational domesticity and enlightened thinking for oneself thematized in her fiction and educational tracts respond to the authoritarianism and antifeminism that transgress Day's (and Rousseau's) reformist rhetoric.

Day self-consciously identified himself with Rousseau as tutor and cultural critic, roles that continued to shape his work and self-concept long after he dismissed Lucretia and Sabrina. Day's (and Bicknell's) poem *The Dying Negro* plays a complex part in *Belinda;* here I want only to note Day's continuing preoccupation with Rousseau in the poem's reprintings. The second edition of 1774 added a six-page dedication (by Day alone), praising Rousseau as the one modern philosopher uncorrupted by modern manners, whose life and writings alike are noble patterns for imitation (his abandoned children go unmentioned). Assimilating himself to his dedicatee, Day illuminates the political implications implicit in his wife-hunt, his opposition to Maria Edgeworth's public career, and his ongoing educational agenda. Contrasting modern refinement with the "rugged virtues of antiquity," Day lashes an effeminized world, where women frequent "assemblies of nocturnal riot" and overly civilized men are emasculated by softness and sensuality: "Let eunuchs . . . insult the memory of Lycurgus. . . . But [i]f our boasted improvements, and frivolous politeness, be well acquired by the loss of manly firmness and independence; if in order to feel as men it be necessary to adopt the manners of women," at least we should be consistent and not mix the barbarities of slavery with effete civility.[49] In 1793, Day's publisher Stockdale posthumously issued an expanded and revised dedication and poem set from papers left with him by Day; the first edition to appear with the authors' names, it also includes an antislavery tract by Day and correspondence with Bicknell over whether they should accept a premium for the poem. Disinterestedness, says Day, is "the first duty of every man who professes the difficult and the glorious task of enlightening his fellow creatures": "I could not easily reconcile my mind, after having talked of stoicism and J. J. Rousseau . . . to thank any set of persons for presenting truth, virtue, and J. J. Rousseau, with an hundred guineas" (*DN* 1793 xi).

The third volume of *Sandford and Merton,* published in 1789, the year of Day's death, similarly appropriates Rousseau's mantle. It concludes with a prophetic denunciation of "the ruin of all the nation"; England's downfall is sure to result from idleness, effeminacy, and modern female education (3: 299). Day's progressive book for juveniles typifies the gender politics of masculine bourgeois reformism with which so many women's works of the

Revolutionary years are in contestatory or conversational dialogue. Since women's and men's writings are marked by gender, class, and race as well as politics, there can be no monovocal liberal or reactionary position, though the man of reason can claim authoritative insight into the nature of reality as he endlessly reduplicates himself. Wise old Sophron and Chares and sturdy little Harry Sandford are the most explicit self-portraits in Day's three volumes; but Greek, Spartan, Roman, Scythian, Arab, Highlander, American Indian, African black, the Reverend Mr. Barlow, or Farmer Sandford, all Day's exemplary teachers speak with one voice, that of the transcendental rational subject, the universal masculinist knower. (It is easy to see why one little nineteenth-century reader thought God and Day were the same.)[50]

Day's ability to transform his materials into the image of his own subjectivity still makes for compelling reading. Every country, every point of view is assimilated to Day's, just as all the interpolations and digressions make up one grand legitimating narrative of a utopia where men are men, women women, and England free from "sickly delicacy" and "foreign graces." Her men should emulate the "severe and rugged virtues" that elevated Rome above all other peoples; her women need their minds and bodies hardened, as in the account of Selene that Mary Wollstonecraft quotes approvingly in the *Rights of Woman.* "We seem to forget," Day laments, "that it is upon the qualities of the female sex that our own domestic comforts and the education of our children must depend": women's polite accomplishments are the "polluted sources" from which "private misery and public servitude" originate. The disembodied reason and emergent bourgeois public sphere Day would align with men depend on women's bodies and the virtues "learned and practised at home." Day's reformist book for British boyhood mostly inculcates survival skills for beleaguered masculinity. The two brief histories of Sukey Simmons's and Selene's "robust and hardy education" allow girls "parts of knowledge which rarely fall to the lot of ladies" (the laws of nature and a little geometry), while scanting languages and ornamental arts like music. Above all, "domestic oeconomy is a point of the utmost consequence to every woman that intends to be a wife or mother," yet Day's hardy girls, unlike Wollstonecraft's new women, are reared by men, not mothers (2: 226–29; 3: 275, 206–7). Aside from the cautionary example of Mrs. Merton, whose sentimental spoiling encourages Tommy's aristocratic, West Indian faults, the maternal role is as occluded in *Sandford and Merton* as it is in *Émile.* Because, like Wollstonecraft's, Maria Edgeworth's enlightened domesticity shares tropes with masculine thinkers, it is important not to elide

late-eighteenth-century women's differences from reformist-minded men
or from their more conservative sisters.[51] Edgeworth grants woman reason, wit, worldly wisdom, command of language and conversational skills,
sociability, and the power to change herself and others; there is no Maginot
Line between the attributes of the sexes, nor is the private sphere imper-
meable to the public world. Like Rousseau, Day needs woman most as
the domesticated Other against whom the male citizen defines himself
(though the dauntless Spartan mothers of *Émile*'s Book I are much more
to his taste than Rousseau's erotic maneuvers with Sophy's sensibility); the
universal rights of nature turn out to be masculine.[52]

Taking his cues from Rousseau, Day spent some months in Avignon
living out his educational dream of enclosure and perfect control. In his
1769 letters to Richard Lovell (and later to Anna Seward from Lyons),
Day enjoyed vituperating the "universal infidelity" of the French, "all the
sweet connexions of domestic life unknown," but with a misogynist under-
tone that might have made Wollstonecraft think twice about citing him
against Rousseau: "the most disgusting sight of all is to see that sex, whose
weakness of body, and imbecility of mind, can only entitle them to our
compassion and indulgence, assuming an unnatural dominion," regulating
men's lives by "caprices, weakness, and ignorance."[53] He had "allotted
myself a kind of task in life" and fervently attributed his missionary zeal to
Rousseau, "first of humankind!" If he could save only two books from
destruction, they would be the Bible and *Émile:* "a most extraordinary
work—the more I read, the more I admire . . . a perspicuity more than
mortal. . . . Every page is big with important truth." Day's image is revealing, himself and his works engendered by *Émile*, the pregnant book.[54] The
letters to Edgeworth printed in the *Memoirs* record unqualified mentorial
triumph and pupil malleability. Perfectly convinced of his principles, Day
gloried in his charges' unequalled good temper and his role as creator and
cynosure of a mini-harem: the girls "have never given me a moment's
trouble, are always contented, and think nothing so agreeable as waiting
upon me." Enabled by Lady Delacour as authorial surrogate and maternal
novelist, the fictive girl-pupil in *Belinda* gets to tell her story too, but only
twice in the printed "factual" accounts does Day's adoptive orphan speak—
within the enclosure of others' letters, of Day's in 1769, of Maria Edgeworth's in 1818. "Perhaps it may divert you to see an original letter from
Miss Sabrina Sydney, word for word dictated by herself: —'Dear Mr.
Edgeworth . . . I love Mr. Day dearly, and Lucretia. . . . I hope I shall have
more sense *against* I come to England. . . . I love Mr. Day best in the world,
Mr. Bicknell next, and you next.'—All this is . . . a faithful display of her

heart and head" (*Memoirs of RLE*, 1: 224–26).[55] Day's letter is at least a key source for the sentimentalizing of Sabrina's supposedly unrequited affection for Day in Richard Lovell's *Memoirs*.

Anna Seward, who met Day and Sabrina when they returned from France and took up residence in Lichfield in 1770, tells a different story about feminine resistance. The girls had "teized and perplexed him; they quarrelled, and fought incessantly." They had to be rescued from drowning and tended during smallpox. They screamed if left with anyone who did not speak English, so Day was tied to their bedside playing nursemaid. "Heartily glad to separate the little squabblers," Day parted with Lucretia when he reached England, portioning her off so that she wound up a shopkeeper's wife. Having found Lucretia "invincibly stupid, or at the best not disposed to follow his regimen," as even Richard Lovell remarks, Day redoubled his efforts to implant the "characteristic virtues of Arria, Portia, and Cornelia" in thirteen-year-old Sabrina and moved into a house at Lichfield with his remaining pupil (Seward, *Memoirs*, 37–39; *Memoirs of RLE*, 1: 217). Sabrina's unprotected situation stirred no scandal in the cathedral town, unlike the fictional world of *Belinda* where gossip's omnipresence and Virginia's tainted reputation become thematic. Sabrina seems to have pleased almost everyone she ever met but Day; she was especially befriended by Canon Seward and his family, and Anna kept in touch with her after Day abandoned his project. Seward's hilarious account of Day's discomfiture is sometimes read as pure invention, but the hardy female education recommended in *Sandford and Merton* is just a less stringent version of his earlier experiment, again derived from *Émile*.

Like Sophy, Day's pupil symbolized a male tutor's anxiety, fear, and redemptive dream, but Day textualized the properly female that would enable the properly male in flesh rather than fiction. Just as his philosophic principles could be read in his own unpowdered hair and seedy clothes, Day sought to imprint his rules on Sabrina's body. Rousseau argues that children can be taught to master pain and to fear nothing; from a gun's flash, Émile will learn that "even pain has a charm of its own" (30–31, 95). When Day burned Sabrina's arms and shot at her petticoats, Seward claims she flunked the heroism test, but young Mary Anne Schimmelpenninck thrilled to hear how Sabrina "stood unmoved when, every morning, he fired a pistol close to her ear, and how she bore melted sealing-wax being dropped on her back and arms; and we were told of her throwing a box of finery into the fire at his request."[56] Sabrina's mind was apparently less docile than her body. Averse to books and science, how could she educate youth, "who were to emulate the Gracchi"? Seward explains Day's

failure as a motivational problem; his rigidities cut off all Sabrina's induce-
ments except "the desire of pleasing her protector, though she knew not
how, or why he became such. In that desire, *fear* had greatly the ascendant
of *affection,* and fear is a cold and indolent feeling." (Interestingly, fright
has no place in the surviving Richard Lovell Edgeworth account of 1808–
9, but Virginia's fear of offending Hervey in *Belinda* antedates Seward by
several years.) Seward claims that after a year's fruitless trial, Day "re-
nounced all hope of moulding Sabrina into the being his imagination had
formed," packed her off to a nearby boarding school, and began pursuing
Honora Sneyd, who had been reared by the Seward family after her
mother's death (Seward, *Memoirs,* 39–41). In Richard Lovell's differently
gendered story of the waiting pupil's love, Day later resumed his project
more seriously than ever.

Anna Seward passionately adored Honora Sneyd, whose multiple perfections punctuate Seward's letters and verse for a quarter century after the
younger woman's early death.[57] Major John André, one of several rejected
suitors, reportedly faced his execution as a spy cheerfully because he had
preserved Honora's miniature.[58] Visiting Day, the unhappily wedded
Richard Lovell fell wildly in love for the first time in his life. While still a
flirtatious adolescent student, Maria's father had dutifully married her
mother when he realized her affections were too far engaged for him to
back out, a fact curiously echoed in the fictional Clarence Hervey's honor-
able resolution to marry Virginia because he thinks she loves him. What
only death could do in real life, the omnipotent female storyteller manages
in *Belinda,* when her proxy Lady Delacour unravels the mystery of Virginia's actual love object, thus freeing Hervey from his Day-dream and
permitting him to address the exemplary heroine Belinda (another of
Maria Edgeworth's many versions of Honora, the cool stepmother she
officially admired but had not much liked as a little girl). Although the real
Honora Sneyd possessed neither the Spartan education nor the "white and
large" arms Day fetishized, he nevertheless resolved to pygmalionize her
personality into his retirement ideal and wrote to ask his friend if Edgeworth could conquer his illicit passion.[59] As a test, Richard Lovell brought
his wife and children for an extended stay with Day at Lichfield and even
delivered Day's written proposal to the "dangerous object." (What the first
Mrs. Edgeworth may have surmised about this experiment to validate
masculine rationality and friendship remains unrecorded.) Honora, who
eventually became the first of Maria's three stepmothers and a prototype
for the rational mother in her children's stories as well as the thinking
heroine in her adult novels, answered Day's "arguments in favour of the

rights of men" with a "clear, dispassionate view of the rights of women." Husbands should not have unqualified control over a wife's actions, seclusion from society was not necessary to preserve female virtue, and "reasonable equality" was the basis of mutual confidence. She had no intention of retiring from the world for "any dark and untried system." Day sickened with a fever and had to be bled (*Memoirs of RLE,* 1: 245–50).

Even though he still had Sabrina in reserve, Day was soon in pursuit of Honora's sister, Elizabeth, brought up in another family and just arrived in Lichfield where their widowed father reassembled his grownup daughters. More conventionally pretty and more fashionable than Honora, she reasoned less and thought Day "the most extraordinary and romantic person in the world." But if she stayed home and took to serious reading, Day had to earn the right to abuse fashionable accomplishments by acquiring them. Taking little Dick (Maria's older brother was to turn out another failed experiment in applied Rousseau), Richard Lovell and Day sailed to Lyons in 1771, one fleeing a dangerous passion, the other pursuing modish manners. "All my intellectual faculties . . . are melted down," Day exclaimed in disgust: "I am a lac'd coat, a bag, a sword, and nothing else. I am become a Type, a parable, a Symbol."[60] Meanwhile, Edgeworth toiled at complex engineering projects and introduced his model pupil to Rousseau; the philosopher was impressed, but thought (rightly) that a real little boy might prove less tractable to his tutor than the subservient Émile.[61] Mrs. Edgeworth went over briefly, staying just long enough to return pregnant; despite her dislike for Day, she was escorted by him, coming to claim the expected reward of slaving eight hours a day at riding, dancing, and fencing. But Elizabeth Sneyd found Thomas Day, fine gentleman, more ridiculous than Thomas Day, blackguard, as Day jestingly styled himself. Richard Lovell did not return until Maria's mother died in 1773 following the birth of her third daughter; he married Honora within four months and took her to Ireland (*Memoirs of RLE,* 1: 237–61, 341; Seward, *Memoirs,* 43–44).

After Day's rejection by Elizabeth Sneyd in 1773, his English friends remained on the lookout for a suitable wife and proposed the rich Esther Milnes of Yorkshire, romantic, philosophic, with a superior understanding certified by schoolgirl essays and poetry. Day, still seeking "a picture that exists in [my] imagination," wanted to know if she wore long petticoats and had big white arms, but finally concluded a cautious courtship by marrying her in 1778.[62] In Richard Lovell's account of Sabrina's fate, Day continued to mold his pupil's "mind and disposition to his own views and pursuits" and "certainly was never more loved by any woman, than he was by Sabrina," nor was any woman "to him ever personally more agree-able"—not much of a compliment to Esther Day, who totally subordinated her tastes to her husband's and grieved herself to death less than three years after him.[63] Day's fetishizing of the unfashionable female body was Sabrina's downfall; she was too artless to pass a lover-mentor's test. "She did, or she did not, wear certain long sleeves, and some handkerchief, which had been the subject of his dislike, or of his liking; and he, considering this circumstance as a proof of her want of strength of mind, quitted her for ever! . . . I could not have acted as he had done." When Étienne Dumont read Richard Lovell's account in 1818, Maria records that he "hates Mr. Day in spite of all his good qualities" for being the kind of man who "'raises a great theory of morals upon an amour propre blessé'": "'he is one who if he should take it into his head a woman should not wear powder in her hair would raise a great discourse to prove that the woman who should be *capàble* to wear powder should be *capàble* to commit murder'" (*Memoirs of RLE*, 1: 337–46; *ME: Letters from England*, 91).

Belinda is a reparative mythology romancing the abandonment of daughters and making their fate come out right; the real-life resolution of Sabrina's story resists fairy tale. By the suspicious terms of Day's will, she was to receive £50 a year until she married and then £500, on the condition that "she relinquish every promise, engagement, or contract, which I have made with her."[64] No longer under Day's care, she lived on her annuity in provincial boarding houses, carefully maintaining her respectability and sometimes visiting friends in Lichfield. When she was close to thirty, Day's old friend John Bicknell decided to get married. He had selected Sabrina for her beauty as a child, but "thought so little of her" as the project progressed that he rejoiced in Day's escape from such a més-alliance. Having preferred wit, writing, and dissipation to briefs, he had never much prospered; now he was sickly and sought "a friend, perhaps a nurse, for his declining years." He looked up Sabrina, "fell desperately in love," proposed, and was conditionally accepted—a sudden passion iron-ized by Maria's juxtaposition of convenience and fine feeling in the second volume that completes her father's life (*Memoirs of RLE*, 2: 111–14). Sabrina asked Day's consent to this prudential escape from spinsterhood; he warned her against it because of Bicknell's health, but he paid the promised sum. Whether Sabrina profited from Day's training or, as Seward would have it, her boarding school years, Day's textualization of the feminine escaped the tragic sexual fall Rousseau imposed on her fictional prototype: the author's admission that even the most meticulous senti-mental wife-rearing will not work.[65] Sabrina made a model wife and brought her husband two boys, John Laurens and Henry Edgeworth, curiously memorializing the three men Day had claimed she loved best as a child: John Laurens, son of Henry Laurens of South Carolina, and enlightened on slavery, had been a surrogate son for Day, who deeply mourned his early death. Sabrina's marriage lasted only from 1784 to 1787; Bicknell died from a paralytic stroke and left his wife and infants unprovided for. His brothers refused to help and Day allowed her £30 a year so that she would have to exert herself. She did. She applied to Charles Burney Jr. and soon became housekeeper and general manageress of his schools at Chiswick, Hammersmith, and finally at Greenwich, where her sons were educated; the eldest was admitted to the bar and became a Fellow of the Royal Society in 1821.[66]

The wife of the man whose satire blaming foreign music for English degeneration so enraged the elder Charles Burney that he tried to buy up all the copies wound up faithfully serving two generations of younger Burneys until her death.[67] The friend who had vouched for the wife-trainer's moral probity so that Day could secure two orphans was discovered after his death to have been a notorious roué, unknown to Day: "Lord! what a pale, maidenish-looking animal for a voluptuary!" exclaimed Anna Seward, who heard about Bicknell's reputation when she set afoot a subscription for the widow.[68] Seward cleaned up the father's past in her *Memoirs* for Sabrina's sake, only to be furiously attacked by Bicknell's son for exposing his mother's illegitimacy.[69] Perhaps the working woman Sabrina Bicknell resented being cast once more in the role of sentimental heroine, a now faded beauty fallen on hard times: "the amiable, unfortunate Mrs. B." (*Letters of AS*, 2: 245). Surprised as a biographer by what she had implied as a storyteller, the novelist whose work persistently engages the relationship between fact and fiction, romance and realism, discovered in 1818 that, like the abandoned daughters of her own much earlier *Belinda,* Sabrina had a voice of her own. When Maria Edgeworth showed Richard Lovell's manuscript autobiography to Day's former protégée, she was disconcerted to discover attitudes very different from her father's recollections of Sabrina's unrequited love. Since Mrs. Bicknell's abscessed back and school duties prevented her from traveling, Maria took her father's and her own sections about Day's project to Greenwich, where she had to read them aloud because Sabrina's eyes were bad: "It was disagreeable to me as you may guess—especially to read about the *foundling hospital.* . . . I was struck with a great change in Mrs. Bicknell's manner and mind. Instead of being as Mr. Day thought her helpless and indolent she is more like a stirring housekeeper—all softness and timidity gone! She spoke of Mr. and Mrs. Keir with great resentment and of Mr. Day as having made her miserable—*a slave* &c! It was a very painful visit to me" (*ME: Letters from England*, 121–22).[70] Just as Sabrina's bodily activity signals the insufficiency of masculine explanatory narratives, her outburst against the perspective of disembodied reason claims her own subjectivity and history, her refusal to remain the static and devalued Other. Thomas Day's burial site was obliterated when the church burned in the suffrage protests of 1914.[71] Sabrina might have been amused could she have known that the preacher of female retirement would be erased by public woman.

But the choicest intertextual irony in this marriage of familial and literary history is the debt Edgeworth's early writings owe to the man who tried his best to stop them. The family memoir's language for Thomas Day's influence on the young Maria is coded much like that for her first stepmother, Honora Edgeworth. Both adults are official objects of veneration, philosophical and almost inhumanly virtuous figures who stirred Maria to salutary emulation. Soon after her father's third marriage (to Honora's sister Elizabeth), Maria, still a boarding school pupil, was afflicted with an eye ailment that threatened her sight—and earned her a little of the family sympathy she so desperately craved. She always remembered her Aunt Ruxton's kindness to "a child with inflamed eyes and swelled features for whom nobody else cared" (*ME: Letters from England*, 15). She spent her 1781 holidays, as she had others, with the Days: "the lofty nature of his mind, his romantic character, his metaphysical inquiries, and eloquent discussions took her into another world. The icy strength of his system came at the right moment for annealing her principles." Day dosed her with kindness and nauseous tumblers of Bishop Berkeley's tar water, gave her the run of his library, and directed her studies. "His severe reasoning . . . awakened all her powers, and the questions he put to her, and the working out of the answers, the necessity of perfect accuracy in all her words, suited the natural truth of her mind, and though such strictness was not always agreeable, she even then perceived its advantage, and in after life was grateful for it."[72] James Keir concludes his hagiography of the childless Day by urging "some ingenuous youth" to "catch the generous enthusiasm" and devote himself to the "service of mankind" (100–101). He got his wish—but Maria's homage is spiced with ironic critique. As in the story-dialogues between the autobiographical Rosamond and her impeccably rational mother in Edgeworth's juvenile series, the impetuous, witty daughter always wins the literary laurels.

Day's close questioning and his penchant for argument anticipate the conversation with his life and works that marks Maria Edgeworth's early writings. If an author's models of cultural identity and personal subjectivity emerge through confrontation with an Other, Day's construction of the world and the woman author played a provocative role in Edgeworth's coming to writing. Because his personal intervention had stopped her fledgling literary career, he was not just another misogynist. But Day in turn enables her intervention in patriarchal attitudes, her feminocentric recuperation of reformist ideology. When the Edgeworths settled in Ireland in June 1782, Maria almost immediately embarked on a literary career of sorts. As her adolescent letters to her former schoolmate Fanny Robinson indicate, she was reading widely and excited about the prospect of authorship. By December, her translation of Madame de Genlis's epistolary educational manual for parents was already being corrected by her second stepmother (Elizabeth Sneyd) and her father. Translating Genlis's several correspondents entailed multiple impersonations; interestingly, Richard Lovell thought that unlike "most misses," she did the male voice best (*Memoirs of RLE*, 2: 72). Although she had worked quickly, publication was forestalled by Thomas Holcroft's version, and Day, who had been shocked even at this oblique approach to authorship, congratulated Richard Lovell on his narrow escape. Maria was 21 when the Edgeworths were stunned by Day's death in 1789; she claims that she never forgot the "change in my father's countenance" when he got the news that his best friend was gone at 41 (*Memoirs of RLE*, 2: 103). He named the son who had just been born Thomas Day Edgeworth, but the infant, left in Ireland during the family's two-year residence at Clifton, died in 1792; so did Mrs. Day, who had just paid them a visit. With tidy symbolism, the last of the Days passed from life to literary history the same year that the *Vindication of the Rights of Woman* appeared. Several of Edgeworth's early children's and adolescent tales have a Clifton-Bristol setting; she did much other writing there, too, including work on the material that became *Letters for Literary Ladies*. Like *Belinda*, this 1795 first publication belongs to the feminist interrogation of patriarchal attitudes initiated by Wollstonecraft's 1792 manifesto for rational woman.

Significantly, Edgeworth launched her public literary career as a male impersonator, indeed in double drag, as *two* gentlemen writing about female education and woman's place in society, dominant concerns in her life and much of her fiction, including *Belinda*. Rather than a premier example of the repressed daughter "writing as if she were her father's pen" that Sandra M. Gilbert and Susan Gubar identify in the *Letters* ("it can hardly be viewed as an act of literary assertion"), Edgeworth's recycling of Day must be read as predictive and paradigmatic, a comic mimicry that makes a mockery of the misogyny it reproduces.[73] Some accounts of the book read as if the *Letter from a Gentleman to His Friend upon the Birth of a Daughter, with the Answer,* that opens the volume were a naive recapitulation of Day's and Richard Lovell's extant letters. Others depict it as a novice's unknowing stumble onto a mined ideological terrain. It is neither. Written a decade after the original correspondence, the *Letter*—along with the *Letters of Julia and Caroline* and *An Essay on the Noble Science of Self-Justification* that round out the volume—marks the birth not of a daughter, but of a writing woman. Reinventing the exchange that aborted her initial literary venture, Edgeworth appropriates Day's voice to, quite literally, authorize herself. Reduced to male midwives assisting female literary nativity, both masculine voices invite a parodic reading, the rational utilitarian parent as well as the comically irrational masculinist "Day." Edgeworth knew the faults of the father she adores. Via her portrayals of would-be male rationalists in the *Letters* and the novelette *Forester,* she anticipates her later critiques of his valorization of reason and the proud self-sufficiency that isolated him from the larger human community (and almost got him murdered during the 1798 Irish Rebellion). The dialogic opening text of the two gentlemen's letters is an expository trial run for the later fiction, a toying with the old texts, old voices, and old attitudes that must be destabilized so that women writers and women characters can talk in their own tones and have their own say on society's doings. It is not the work of a parrot, but of a savvy parodist.[74]

Jane Austen and most of the period's other female writers may shirk man-to-man converse, but it is an Edgeworth specialty. It is noteworthy that when the family went abroad just after *Belinda*'s publication, an amateur handwriting expert was positive Maria's "could not be that of a woman and then he came off by saying it was only the writing of a manly character—further still from the truth."[75] They are both right. Vestimentary impersonation, it has been suggested, may be read as either a simple denial of feminine identity or as a double denial that reasserts the female subject.[76] Edgeworth's psychic crossdressing is a testamentary legacy assumed not to evade but precisely in order to skirt the issue. Edgeworth's bilinguality—or, to borrow the title of an unpublished adolescent play, her "double disguise"—is not the textual sign of timidity or patriarchal complicity. Rather, like the warrior women who donned manly attire to gain access to forms of agency, experience, and achievement otherwise available only to men, the authorial impersonator unsettles the status of behaviorally encoded sexual difference. Like the numerous female fighters whose stories Dianne Dugaw chronicles and shrewdly explicates, Edgeworth can write just like a man and even be mistaken for the distinguished Dr. John Aikin, Mrs. Barbauld's brother, by the *Critical Review*.[77] Her masquerade is revealed only because she chose to put her name on the revised second edition of 1799, not because she failed to wield a male pen. Arguing that eighteenth-century Female Warrior ballads interrogate the significance of gender, Dugaw concludes that such literary masquerades do not privilege the masculine at all: "at a deeper level they actually subvert not only the privilege of one gender over the other, but the very category of gender itself," disclosing an implicit cultural conception of gender as "a shifting, histrionic, and potentially deceptive code system."[78] Revealing the plasticity and theatrics of conventional gender markers, rational women and sensitive nurturing men who cross customary gender boundaries scramble the system's bipolar codes, but they do not necessarily confound sexual identity when they challenge culturally assigned gender traits. To identify Edgeworth's fondness for breeches parts as the mark of "lesbian panic" (as do some recent commentators) is to decontextualize literary strategies.[79]

As a female work by two "gentlemen," Edgeworth's letter and its answer further problematize the gendered identities, at once newly labile (for men) and newly prescriptive (for women), that such writers as Rousseau and Day had propagandized. Their late-eighteenth-century hegemonic patriarchy evaded stereotypical masculinity by coopting feminine sensibility, yet simultaneously disallowing female rationality. Having incorporated culturally female power, the man of reason cum man of sensibility suffers from an effeminophobia that domesticates, privatizes, and silences woman.[80] Mr. Barlow of *Sandford and Merton* expresses Day's deep suspicion of women as genteel temptresses who brainwash men "that the great object of human life is to please the fair" (1: 34). Fashionable female education inevitably produces Miss Matildas who speak French better than English, play the harpsichord "divinely," and excel in drawing the "figure of the naked gladiator" (2: 225). Naturally, orates Farmer Sandford at the book's close, they cannot "milk a cow, or churn, or bake, or do any one thing that is necessary in a family," for "once gentility begins, there is an end of industry." Unless the government ships boarding-school girls to the colonies and imports "a cargo of plain, honest housewives," where is the sturdy English yeoman to find a mate? (3: 301–3). Keir aptly describes *Sandford and Merton*'s moral mission in images of disease, war, and sexual threat: the "infection" to be "guarded against" is "ostentatious luxury and effeminacy" and the worst because "most predominant, is effeminacy of manners," obsessively associated, as in Day's letters from France, in his Appendix to Bicknell's satire against the elder Dr. Burney, and in his posthumously published miscellaneous pieces, with woman, France, fashion, and literary and artistic culture.[81] Female authorship symptomatizes the degeneracy of English society as a whole. Day's cure for the threatened emasculation of English virtue is masculinist moral rearmament against, in Sarah Maza's phrase, "what might variously be termed the feminization, eroticization, or privatization of the public sphere under Louis XV."[82] Enlightened men of feeling like Rousseau, Day, and Saint-Pierre could challenge the current social definitions of manhood and power and still remain real men only by positing the enlightened woman as emasculating public Amazon, the obverse of Rousseau's Sophy, Saint-Pierre's Virginia, and the "gentle Lady of the West" Day apostrophizes in a poem written during his juvenile rambles over Dorsetshire.[83]

Like Clarence Hervey, Day kept a journal, but his vision of domesticity was not what Edgeworth renders reformist in *Belinda*. "Sequestered in some secret glade," uneducated ("by native sense alone refin'd"), and apparently aphasic ("Eyes that with artless lustre roll, More eloquent than words to speak"), Day's retired heroine lives only for him; she has no public contribution to make and nothing to say.[84] Nor do the well-trained daughters in a posthumously published satire that parallels *Sandford and Merton*, "The Trial of A.B. in the High Court of Fashion": Day's notion of civic life, at once classical and primitivistic, invests A.B.'s sons with the "sacred ardor" of the Greek and Roman republics, but the ideally educated girls "have learned that the greatest ornaments to a woman are simplicity, modesty, and obedience." They have no accomplishments, do not go out, and see little even of other women, "lest like their own sex they should acquire a taste for trifles and dissipation." In place of Fashion, the plaintiff A.B. explains, he has taken Reason as his guide, "fixed and unchangeable in its own nature, never fluctuating with external accidents, nor governed by the opinion of others."[85] Fashion and Reason are loaded terms in Edgeworth's lexicon, too, and *Belinda* needs to be read as the great precursor of her brilliant analyses of fashionable life a decade later, but her domestic community imagined within a Revolutionary public sphere and Day's masculinist and asocial primitivism are very different reformist inflections.

What Day's destroyed reprimand to Maria's authorship may have looked like and why the crossdressing of subjectivities and bodies achieves metaphoric status in Edgeworth's early work is more precisely deducible from another of Day's occasional pieces. An essay originally meant for the *Public Advertiser* exemplifies the contemptuous satire of female intelligence and learning that Maria Edgeworth could not forget and kept refuting.[86] The demonic opposite of Day's gentle Lady is the Amazon, the *salonnière* whose publicly circulating wit and writings make her meta-phorically a slut, who can only emancipate herself by unmanning men. Writing in the 1780s, Day's persona "Clerimont" uncannily presages the sarcasm and sexism of Richard Polwhele's notorious poem, *The Unsex'd Females* (1798). The best-known combatant in the anti-Jacobin propaganda wars fueled by William Godwin's revelations of Mary Wollstone-craft's extramarital indiscretions, Polwhele's diatribe is exemplary in its linkage between woman's writing for her rights and her riding for a fall; the intellectual warrior woman risks alignment with the whore. (Masculine paranoia in the Revolutionary years seems unable to distinguish intellec-tually inspired writing from nymphomaniac writhing or to read Godwin's paean to his dead wife as more than pornography.)[87] Exemplary, too, is Polwhele's polarization of the Amazon and the domestic woman. Because Day died before the feminist and political controversies of the 1790s, it is hard to pinpoint what menacing works "asserting the rights of the sex" he is faulting for corrupting women over the "last twenty years," but his grievances against French sociality and feminized salon culture are not just the spleen of the bumpkin who failed to master savoir-faire.[88] Rather, they testify to what literary critics sometimes forget: the sense of cultural crisis that marks the decades between the American and French Revolutions—worries over luxury, corruption, fashion, improvement, politeness, ex-panding print culture, and especially women's felt presence in the public sphere.[89]

Late-eighteenth-century female education is always Day's chief culprit, at once indicator and instigator of broader cultural change. What is at issue is not a petty quarrel over female accomplishments, but a struggle over access to and definition of the social sphere. Emancipated from their for-mer restraints, Day's enlightened "fair adventurers" turn to the "career of literature," so that there is "scarcely a private family without its authoress." Print culture and the woman writer will infect every personal relationship, as lovers and mothers abandon the domestic province for public exposure: "A polite education may be considered as a species of inoculation, which effectually prevents the fair patient from feeling any subsequent attack of shame or timidity during the rest of her life." For Day, any authorship is equated with scandalous exhibition, but he seems especially sardonic about female fiction. A woman who presumes to amuse or instruct the world inevitably loses "that interesting delicacy, that amiable tenderness, that irresistible softness," which used to "constitute so essential a part of the female character"; having unsexed her mind, she takes to dressing like a man and "strutting about as an Amazon." Thus no enlightened heroine has anything but "a most supreme contempt for retired domestic life," but while women approach the "licentiousness of manhood," men appropriate the "distinguishing characteristics of the other sex": a love of trifles, adornment, garrulity, and coquetry, an "aversion to every manly employment." Day's satiric solution is to recognize custom's "gross mistake in casting the parts of the two sexes." In future, ladies can "spend their lives in public . . . be jockies, libertines, or authors," while boys learn modesty, blushing, and a love of retirement: above all, they will "be debarred from pen and ink, and convinced that it is totally inconsistent with male softness and delicacy, to emerge from virtuous obscurity . . . and become either the wonder or ridicule of the town." Mere man is helpless against "chains which Venus and Minerva both conspire to weave."[90] Day's caustic response to the ambiguities in the contemporary construction of gendered subjectivity that perturb him reinscribes the desired polarity by a simple reversal. His androcentric politics cannot recognize that sexual identity is not synonymous with gender-coded behavior, though sexual roles may be socially functional. Nor can he entertain the possibility that the Amazon and the domestic woman need not be binary opposites.

Edgeworth's second gentleman's rhetorical strategy, most fully elaborated in the expanded second edition, is to interrogate Day's polarization of the writer and the good woman, to demonstrate that the career of literature also includes the profession of maternal education. Like Wollstonecraft's *Rights of Woman*, which Edgeworth had obviously absorbed, this argument is a self-conscious rehabilitation of woman's rationality and her rights to education and literature. And like Wollstonecraft's reproduction of Rousseau in order to refute him, Edgeworth's dialogic form incorporates the misogynist within her own text where she can overwrite his outbursts and have the last word. It is appropriate that the misogyny that reduces women's historical agency and power to boudoir politics is itself reduced to materiality, a body of text that can be quoted, manipulated, exposed. Far from being aphasic or linguistically disadvantaged, Edgeworth shows herself the mistress of the master discourse, rationally emasculating masculinist argument just by representing its platitudes and representing them within a pro-woman environment. The first gentleman who would speak for manly reason comes off as sadly illogical, bested by Edgeworth's intellectual transvestitism; she can play the part better than "Day" can. Her recreation of Day's "eloquent philippic against female authorship" begins with the classic chauvinist rejection of woman's wit, that most dangerous gift for a daughter, familiar from generations of conduct books: "a female wit," Rousseau remarks, "is a scourge to her husband," anticipating Lord Delacour, who fears his wife's wit as a weapon (*Memoirs of RLE*, 2: 342; *Émile*, 371; *Belinda* 138). Maybe so, but a talent for wit and ridicule was recognized as Maria's forte from her school days on, wit is the autobiographical Rosamond's distinguishing characteristic, and the "perfume of wit" (in Sydney Smith's phrase) enabled the brilliant reputation as a conversationalist that Edgeworth enjoyed in maturity. If *Letters for Literary Ladies* makes a case against antiquated notions of female authorship, it also presages *Belinda*'s self-conscious brief for a female fiction as witty as Lady Delacour's discourse, as rational as Belinda Portman's behavior, at once "so clever and sensible!"[91] Nature, custom, and education unite to unfit women for any civic or cultural contribution, the first gentleman pronounces. "In the course of my life it has never been my good fortune to meet with a female whose mind, in strength, just proportion, and activity, I could compare to that of a sensible man."[92] The exceptional woman is *ipso facto* deformed: "female prodigies . . . are scarcely less offensive to my taste than monsters" (1795, 5, 3). Like Polwhele, whose compromised conservative masculinity hystericizes female rationality and literary agency into a predatory "Amazonian band—the female Quixotes of the new philosophy," Edgeworth's first gentleman allies militancy and monstrosity.[93] When woman's education has been attempted, she turns exhibitionist yet produces no socially useful work. She only estranges herself from her less literate sisters and repels possible suitors: "our sex usually consider a certain degree of weakness, both of mind and body, as friendly to female grace." The learned especially do not want *femmes savantes*: why should "two books" wed? Because no man wants to marry "Hercules-Spinster," "Day" falls back on Burkean salutary prejudices (a nice jab at the politically revisionist real-life Day whose agenda was the ideological deconstruction of "prejudices" by Reason).[94] His comparison of cultivated women with the Swiss proud of their goiters better describes the masculine complacency that closes his epistle: "if not *just*," his opinions "are at least *common* in our sex" (1795, 34, 32, 4, 42).

"Day" himself in the guise of the first gentleman thus exposes the gendered contradictions in his thinking that *Sandford and Merton* papers over: the hardy Spartan girls that Wollstonecraft and little Mary Anne Galton admired versus the Amazonian authoresses who terrify Day's newspaper persona "Clerimont." If educated women are monsters of difference, the first gentleman's rhetorical commonplaces divulge the deformity of chauvinist typicality. As an all-embracing moral view unconstrained by political compromise, custom, or precedents, Day's Reason supposedly mandates the transcendence of the partial: because "there can be no prescription pleaded against truth and justice," the American colonists must necessarily "admit the whole human species to a participation of your inalienable rights."[95] But the disinterested thinker who thus sternly rebukes his American correspondents for enslaving blacks while insisting on white colonial freedom cannot see past his own goiter. Day, always self-consciously representing upright Reason, is here revealed as himself the intellectual hunchback he assumes any female intellectual must be. The second gentleman's 1795 response has its moments. "Day" has set himself up in pontificating that "projects in education are of all others the most hazardous" (and who should know better), but the father's concession that "we have no right to try new experiments . . . at the expense of our fellow-creatures, especially on those who are helpless," tells against his own younger self as Dick's Rousseau-intoxicated tutor, too (1795, 21, 44).[96] Edgeworth as her own father comically aligns "Day" with Anthony Absolute's endorsement of female illiteracy, as she does again in completing the paternal biography, and, in contrast to Day's insistently virile faculty, she slyly genders Reason itself as female (1795, 67–69, 45, 58; *Memoirs of RLE*, 2: 342). The original version of the answer counters animosity toward female intellectuals mostly by arguing that the cultivated woman does not turn into a man, but a wife: Absolute's helpmate would need more than "her simple letters, without their mischievous combinations" and the "ability to count as far as twenty."[97]

Edgeworth was not satisfied with this anonymously published refutation of "Day," however, so a thoroughly revised edition appeared in 1799 under her own name: "the *Second Letter* upon the advantages of cultivating the female understanding . . . . has been written over again; no pains have been spared to improve it, and to assert more distinctly the female right to literature" (1799, iv–v; 1993 [xxvii]).[98] *Letters for Literary Ladies* consists of three assorted pieces given a publisher's title that Edgeworth was stuck with, but the revision specifically develops the implications of the two gentlemen's correspondence as letters on female literature and hence female access to public discourse. The second gentleman's rewritten prowoman statement anticipates *Belinda*'s "Rights of Woman" chapter much more clearly than did the 1795 version. Moreover, further complexifying her transfers between texts and between lived and literary experience, Edgeworth not only signs herself a woman writing as two men but also adds a new and significant epigraph that the recent Everyman reprint unaccountably fails to include: "A Wit, that temperately bright, / With inoffensive light, / All pleasing shone; nor ever past / The decent bounds that Wisdom's sober hand, / And sweet Benevolence's mild command, /

And bashful Modesty before it cast."[99] Perhaps the most popular poem by one of the later eighteenth century's most popular poets, Lord Lyttelton's monody for his much loved first wife is innocuous itself but contextually striking, for not only do both Day and the enlightened father express fear of female wit but so does Lyttelton himself in another poem that plays an important part in both the *Letters* and the paternal *Memoirs* (it turns up again early in *Belinda* as well): the one work of Lyttelton's that Samuel Johnson celebrated for "much truth and much prudence," the 1731 "Advice to a Lady."[100]

Day as first gentleman warns that "the intoxicating effect of wit upon the brain, has been well remarked by a poet, who was a friend to the fair sex," erroneously glossed in the 1993 reprint's editorial notes as Pope's rousing Belinda to anger by having Spleen visit her in *The Rape of the Lock* (1993, 8, 81 n. 9). But Edgeworth could expect her audience to recognize the allusion and to recall its context, Lyttelton's blunt advice to another Belinda on how to get and keep a man: please, defer, do not be witty, remember that retreat is "a woman's noblest station" and that love is the "important business of your life."[101] Edgeworth's 1820 remembrance of Day's horrified attack on her authorship conjoins Day as Anthony Absolute with his frequent repetition of the Lyttelton lines that she also notes Dr. Johnson was said to have quoted to another female authoress: "Nor make to dangerous wit a vain pretence, / But wisely rest content with modest Sense; / For wit, like wine, intoxicates the brain, / Too strong for feeble woman to sustain; / Of those who claim it, more than half have none, / And half of those who have it, are undone."[102] Yet Lyttelton is also cited in both versions of the father's reply as exemplary of the new model marriage between equals and friends that he advocates, and the lines on female wit from the "Monody" in the revised edition of *Letters for Literary Ladies* belong to this different conception of woman: learned, rational, strong of mind, manly in sense, and, yes, witty (1795, 72; 1993, 37). Adding the epigraph endorsing wit for women not only questions both gentlemen's worries about that proverbially dangerous quality but shows Lyttelton contradicting Lyttelton—the hard-nosed advice to Belinda versus the paean to wife Lucy's union of feminine tenderness and masculine reason. Twitted by Day with Lyttelton, Edgeworth uses Lyttelton to twit back, not only here but in her 1801 tale, whose eponymous heroine, a teenager wise enough to counsel the grownups, doubly alludes to and playfully refutes Pope's and Lyttelton's Belindas by emulating Lyttelton's wife Lucy, whose lofty prudence scorned suspicion and "without weakness knew to be sincere."[103]

In demanding "solid proofs of utility" and claiming that women do not traffic in "useful literature," the 1795 first gentleman is a sitting duck for the elaborated argument of social utility that the 1799 second gentleman provides, the demonstration that it is precisely women's contributions that are most functional in reforming the public sphere (1795, 8–9). Just as the revision seeks to suture Day's radical disjuncture between prudence and understanding, Minerva and mothers, it cleverly glides from cultural literacy to authorship. The period's broad definition of "literature" as humane learning enables interlinked arguments for improving female education and for recognizing women's importance in an expanding print culture.[104] For the first gentleman's nightmare scenario of intellectual degeneracy and social isolation, Edgeworth counterposes an alternative narrative of female development and civic contribution. For the mentor-lover model of cultural and literary transmission conventional in fictional texts and masculine lives, Edgeworth as the second gentleman substitutes a maternal educational mission aligning mind and mothering, a utopian vision elaborated in other educational works and embedded in *Belinda* too. For Day's and Rousseau's equation of women's textuality with self-exhibiting theatricality, she substitutes the scene of their reading and writing as a site of maternal instruction that occupies social as well as domestic space. Writing as her own father, Edgeworth invests the writing mother, and the woman who writes for mothers, with socially transformative power, a textual reproduction of feminized and domesticated values as potent and more radical than the sexual reproduction of their bodies.

Day's *Public Advertiser* essay sneers at mothers who have produced works their children can read. Rousseau, who "hate[s] books" (*Robinson Crusoe* excepted) and pronounces reading the "curse of childhood," stigmatizes female textuality in particular. Since they "make a bad use of this fatal knowledge," why should little girls even learn to read and write? He describes a child who finds the mirrored image of herself in the act of writing so ugly that she flings away her pen, and he invites his readers to specularize a woman's room similarly: "what makes you think more highly of her . . . to see her busy with feminine occupations . . . her children's clothes about her, or to find her writing verses. . . . If there were none but wise men upon earth such a woman would die an old maid" (*Émile* 147, 80, 332, 372). The imaginary male femininity of Romantic educators like Rousseau and Day blames maternal neglect for social depravity, gestures to mothers' power in childhood, and tutorially occupies the maternal educative site. The good mother is born from the tutor's head—as in Day's and many fictional heroes' playing the mentor-lover—or from her textualization of his teaching: the mothers who will learn not to be Mrs. Merton by copying what Mr. Barlow does, the mothers who will be sufficiently flattered by *Émile*'s brief initial salute to collude in their own reduction to Sophy, as smitten with Rousseau's portrayal as she is with Fénelon's picture of Telemachus. "Would you restore all men to their primal duties, begin with the mothers. . . . when mothers deign to nurse their own children, then will be a reform in morals," *Émile* opens flatteringly, only to substitute textual for sexual power: "the real nurse is the mother and the real teacher is the father" (13, 16). Day's *The History of Little Jack* (1788) more amusingly literalizes the masculine invocation and displacement of maternal nurture with a lame old man and a goat. The success of the orphan "thus left to nature" validates the daddy-soldier's literacy and mammy Nan's fostering.[105] It takes a man to mentor a mind, but any teat will do.

Edgeworth's revision rebukes the Amazonian equation of female learning and sexual license, the idea that the woman who knows anything is also sexually knowing, as well as the contemporary masculine fondness for mammy Nans and Sophies, Sabrinas and Virginias: "It is not, I hope, your opinion, that ignorance is the best security for female virtue"—a fallacy (or phallacy) multiply satirized in *Belinda* (1993, 21). Like Wollstonecraft's, Edgeworth's revised argument focalizes female reason; women must learn to think for themselves and to generalize their ideas. Like Wollstonecraft, too, her father figure repudiates men's notions of female essentialism: "unless I could trace the history of female education, it is vain for me to follow what you call the history of female nature" (1993, 32–33). What woman's subjectivity is depends on how she has been educated, what habits of mind she has acquired. There is no necessary connection between "extraordinary strength of mind" and the Amazon or the pedant, nor between bodily and mental strength. But a cultivated understanding both makes a woman's "felicity in some degree independent of matrimony" and furthers the contemporary domestic revolution in maternal care and emancipatory childhood education (1993, 17–18, 29). Social historians have long since familiarized us with structural and affective changes in the eighteenth-century family, but feminist theory and educational history have not always addressed emergent enlightened domesticity as a mixed set of multiply gendered discursive practices, available for divergent uses and interpretations.[106] Maternal pedagogy has more often been read as coercive (for both mother and child) than liberatory.

Yet, again like Wollstonecraft, Edgeworth's second gentleman aligns the progress of female intellect and maternal teaching: "Ladies have become ambitious to superintend the education of their children, and hence they have been induced to instruct themselves, that they may be able to direct and inform their pupils. The mother, who now aspires to be the esteemed and beloved instructress of her children, must have a considerable portion of knowledge" (1993, 20). Freed from "all the melancholy apparatus of learning," the classical drudgery that is the gentleman's gender-marked fate, women excel in vernacular writing and reading: "in domestic life they have leisure to be wise" (1993, 27). The ambiguities in this period's gender constructions left implicit in the 1795 father's reply are foregrounded by the revised 1799 argument as well as the new epigraph favoring wit: the frank recognition that there is no essential female nature, that woman just like man is a "bundle of habits," that "social virtue" is a matter of everybody's happiness (the Edgeworths never muddy the waters with God or duty), yet that the current "larger interests of society" are, for now, connected with the "utility of forms apparently trifling" (1993, 22).[107] The boys' version of this conflict between individual development and cultural demand is their subjection to classical education: hard to justify rationally because it cramps their intellects (and sometimes their morals), wastes their time, and ruins their writing skills, but a necessity for living in this society. It is noteworthy that the second gentleman is made to voice the parallel accommodations to society as currently constituted for both boys and girls, as well as the progressive nature of "public opinion" and cultural demand—what is pragmatically requisite now may be different in the future, for the second gentleman's is emphatically a progressive society continually being reshaped by print culture (1993, 19).

Neither literary participation nor literary property remains an entailed inheritance. It is "absolutely out of [men's] power to drive the fair sex back to their former state of darkness"; because the "art of printing has totally changed their situation," the second gentleman understands that it is no longer "our option to retard or to accelerate the intellectual progress of the sex." Like the first gentleman, the father recognizes that women's implication in cultural transmission and the literary marketplace poses dangers as well as opportunities. A daughter must therefore develop the "strength of mind which enables people to govern themselves by their reason" if she is to avoid imbibing "preposterous notions of love, of happiness, from the furtive perusal of vulgar novels." The 1799 father's new emphasis on the "choice of books" and occupations (botany, chemistry, arithmetic) that give girls a "taste for truth and utility" foregrounds women who reason, read, and write socially constructive female literature and who thus elude Day's, Polwhele's, and perhaps also literary history's binary opposition of the public Amazon and the domestic woman (1993, 24–25, 34).[108] Edgeworth's own career, of course, goes the rational father one step better by shaping the fiction he warns women against into women's most socially functional (and always implicitly political) form: what Maria Edgeworth's insistence on calling her work "moral tales" signifies is not prudery but purposeful intervention in the public sphere. If texts are acts, one way to rethink "didactic" authors is to read them as writers who really believe that the world might be changed through the writing of texts.[109] Richard Lovell Edgeworth learned from the daughter he had once forbidden to read *Cecilia,* but Day died "despis[ing] the writings of women," especially fiction—ironically fated not only to be scripted into a retrograde plot easily refuted, but to be remembered best for his juvenile stories, his own case demonstrating that fiction may be better politics than state politics (1993, 25).

The two notions of literary woman about which Edgeworth's two gentlemen contend simultaneously express strikingly different ideas of reasoned opinion and of the public good. In Edgeworth's fictional letters as in his life, "Day" figures reason as Rousseauian and authoritarian as opposed to the consensual rationality evolved through sociable discussion that the father and the daughter would endorse. If Day, Rousseau, and the fictional *Forester* seek to recover the model of an ancient polis, the woman writer's publication of two gentlemen's private converse miniaturizes something new: the nascent public sphere as a potentially inclusive community of discourse, an associative "public of private people making use of their reason."[110] As a female author writing as two men arguing about literary women, as a private person shaping a personal wound into a public rationale for a literary career, as an artist deploying the spatially ambiguous intimate letter that is also a public forum and political statement, Maria Edgeworth thoroughly scrambles reductive equations of men with a magisterial public sphere of high politics versus a feminized domestic private sphere. Her use of the letter genre helps her escape such binary thinking, for its reciprocity formally embodies the new communal ideal of productive interaction between the sexes, between the family and larger worlds, that it advocates. Like many other women, Edgeworth goes public through letters, constituting female authorship as epistolary and dialogic. But Edgeworth the epistolarian (like Edgeworth the novelist) queries clichés about letters as a feminized discursive space, a gendered container for subjective interiority. Junius, Burke, and Burke's opponents were not sentimental heroines.

Edgeworth reminds us that letters (like women) simultaneously belong to overlapping spheres, that they (like her novels) are hybrid forms, alluding to multiple planes of experience, employing diverse forms of representation, and enacting a continuum of communicative acts from face-to-face conversation to private epistles to public dissemination: all the discursive strategies that make up the new Republic of Letters.[111] However idealized Jürgen Habermas's authentic public sphere may be, whether normative ideal or actual entity, his notion of a historically specific, distinctively modern formation arising out of the private sphere for rational discussion of matters relevant to the civil polity does seem to correspond to what enlightened writers, including women like Edgeworth, felt themselves to be doing. It is worth recalling that Habermas's public sphere takes shape within the *private* realm of civil society, that it is preeminently a literary space where public opinion takes shape, and that these usages of "public" and "private" are incommensurate with the simplistic opposition of private and public spheres—domestic ideology versus state politics—still endemic in feminist literary studies.[112] When Edgeworth transmutes Mandeville's *Private Vices, Publick Benefits* to "private *virtues* are public benefits," when she reverses Erasmus Darwin's enlistment of "Imagination under the banner of Science" to "Science has of late *'been enlisted under the banners of imagination,'*" she is testifying to the permeable boundaries between the culturally "feminine" and the culturally "masculine," between the domestic happiness she values and the public good she writes for.[113] Not bad for an apprentice work.

5 | Jane Austen and the Culture of Circulating Libraries: The Construction of Female Literacy

Barbara M. Benedict

It is a cliché blazoned recently on film that Jane Austen depicts money, love, and the fulfillment from their conjunction.[1] Most readers, however, acknowledge that her scrutiny of the struggle between duty and desire anatomizes the social oppression of women. Many see Austen's criticism of oppression as a longing for a lost or future world in which commercialism does not taint feelings, perceptions, or relationships. This view, however, ignores the way, as a reader and writer, in both her novels and her letters, Austen represents morality through materiality.[2] Increasingly in her modernizing economy, domestic commodities, especially literary objects, are the site where values reside and thus the avenue of social and self-expression. Rather than opposing commercialization, Jane Austen dramatizes commercial culture as the arena for moral choice. Her work shows especially the way literary commodification shaped middle-class female identity at the beginning of the nineteenth century.[3]

Austen presents choices as the path to happiness.[4] Like her readers, her heroines desire personal fulfillment, and Austen shows that this goal, although hedged by social restrictions, can be achieved through relationships that permit the flowering of character, defined as discrimination, or the power of choosing on just principles. While character is Austen's fundamental criterion of personal virtue, she portrays this choice as extending to every aspect of existence, not merely to the traditional categories of spouse and friends. Heroines exhibit their "accomplishments"—be these the traditional achievements of musical training, knowledge of modern languages, and dancing, or the new, moral accomplishments of wit, judgment, and taste—in their choice of language, literature, clothes, objects, and entertainments. As opportunities for both self-display and social exchange, these goods represent good taste. They permit the display of sensitivity to beauty, aesthetic receptiveness—a quality that promises potential spouses that their wives will be able to move up in society. Thus, the anxiety revealed in Austen's letters about the correct consumption of language, letters, and books, as well as clothes and food, and about the way that consumption represents one's self is transformed in her novels into an exegesis of the way such choices define identity. As Joanne Finkelstein has explained, "In a culture where the possession and control of goods and services are highly valued, transforming the body into a commodity which can be used for the display of coveted items becomes a social goal in itself."[5] In Austen's society, where the identities of women and men, the roles of servants, merchants, and every social class, and the nature of sociability were all changing, subjectivity itself was conditioned by fashionable consumption.[6] The arenas of privacy seeped into areas of public display, even while increasingly rigid gender roles apparently asserted their separation.[7] Austen's novels attempt to regulate the usurpation of identity threatened by such interpenetration. They return some power back to the consumer-reader by serving as guides through a cluttered cultural marketplace.

In this essay I will explore the way Austen portrays the female middle-class identity as cultural consumer. First I analyze the culture of circulating libraries as a site of literary consumption in the context of women's self-representation through fashion and in newspaper advertisement, while in the second I examine the representation within Austen's work of reading and books as consumer items. I suggest as a whole that the conditions of literary production and reception shape Austen's work and that her representation of the marketing of identity through literature reveals a new female identity. In Austen's fiction, the eighteenth-century dialectic of alternately attacking and advocating female consumption transforms into the feminization of discriminating choice. Middle-class femininity is regulated consumption, discreet display, the social performance of private taste.[8]

Early Library Culture

Prominent among the commodities represented as inducing unmonitored consumption, social masquerade, and vanity were clothes. Like printed culture, they offered the opportunity to lift women out of their rank. Clothes have long carried moral associations, particularly for women, as emblems of deceit and display, sexuality and consumption: "Unhappy Cause! Thus from the Fall of Man / Garment[s] invented were, and Dress began."[9] Aileen Ribeiro notes the elision between eighteenth-century "character" dress, in which the masquerader acted in the role dictated by the costume, and "fancy" dress, which simply allowed a small adjustment of fashionable clothes.[10] Isaac Watts adjured women, "Nor, while you are dressing, should you forget that you are sinners, and therefore should put on shamefacedness; for all our ornaments and clothing are but a memorial of our first sin and shame, and when we take a pride in our garments, it looks as if we had forgotten the original of them, the loss of our innocency."[11] Both Austen's own letters, threaded through with anxiety about the right clothes, and commercial printed culture often addressed clothes as a means of social mobility. "One of the purposes behind the eighteenth-century women's magazines was to teach the correct way to dress, through advice columns ('Always dress rather above your time of life than below it,' said the *Lady's Magazine* of 1783) and novelettes, where the heroine was always dressed in the best of taste."[12] In *Sense and Sensibility*, Austen pinpoints the ambition of the needle-eyed Steeles by their knowledge of "the price of every part of Marianne's dress," and "the number of her gowns."[13] Clothes allow social masquerade.

This function paradoxically allows self-expression since dress displays the self for purchase, as Mary Wollstonecraft knew when she asserted that "an air of fashion is but a badge of slavery."[14] In *Northanger Abbey*, Austen's narrator mocks Mrs. Allen and Catherine for their interest in clothes by saying that dress is "at all times a frivolous distinction," but her real point is that women believe they dress for men when in fact they dress for themselves (73).[15] This self-display, intensified by the recent importation of cheap muslin, galvanizes moral (and male) attacks on women's consumption.[16] Early sumptuary laws were based on the belief that clothes lead to sins of pride and envy, and thus needed regulation, a view reiterated by John Wesley. In his sermon "On Dress," a sequel to "The Danger of Riches," Wesley opposes apparel and intellect by arguing that finery engenders pride, breeds vanity, begets anger, and inflames lust: "Nothing is more natural than to think ourselves better because we are dressed in better clothes . . . the wearing [of] costly array is directly opposite to being 'adorned with good works.' "[17] Parallel to this moral concern ran a social one. As Aileen Ribeiro explains, "Throughout the eighteenth and nineteenth centuries moralists worried about the class struggle, as expressed in the desire of the lower classes to imitate the manners and costumes of their betters, and about the amount of money spent on sartorial display and emulation."[18] Yet during the early modern period, cultural critics like Sir Richard Steele argued that by buying fabrics plentifully, women supported the native textile industry and thus the national economy. Dress could even display humility or love: "Dress should reveal not just a humble state of mind, but show by its simplicity that the wearer spends little time on the adornment of the body, and is thus free to devote more—time and money— to the poor." Moreover, it should display conformity: "Early Christian teachings stress the link between the outward appearance and the state of the soul, and a dislike of individualism in dress which draws attention to the self."[19] These contrary forces play out in Austen's morality of consumption—individual display—as the metaphor for women's power.

Delicate distinctions in dress and appearance are characterized in conduct literature as distinguishing not merely class and wealth, but morality and even identity. In *The Mirror of the Graces,* for example, published in London in 1811, the author remarks, "Fine taste in apparel I have ever seen the companion of pure morals, while a licentious style of dress is, as certainly, the token of the like laxity in manners and conduct."[20] Such high-minded interpretations moralize earlier, more pragmatic assertions of the importance of dress: "Dress is a foolish thing; and yet it is a very foolish thing for a man not to be well dressed, according to his rank and way of life. . . . Dress, insignificant as some people may think it, is an object worthy of some attention; for we cannot help forming some opinion of a man's sense and character from his dress. All affectation in dress, implies a flaw in the understanding: men of sense carefully avoid any particular character in their dress."[21] Throughout the early modern period, conspicuous consumption signifies social rank transmuted into character, particularly gendered character. Clothes, indeed, constitute a chief topic in a tradition of satire against particularly female sensuality, spendthriftiness, superficiality, consumption, display, vanity, pride, and envy: all symptoms of social power.[22] "Throw modesty out from your manners and face, / A la-mode de françois, you['re] a bit for his Grace," sneers one early satire.[23] Many eighteenth-century poems blame women's love of dress for spoiling their social relations, while novels and plays frequently use the deceptiveness of dress to signify the mutability of moral character and social rank: Richardson's *Pamela,* Farquhar's *Beaux' Stratagem,* Sheridan's *Rivals,* and Fielding's *Tom Jones,* where Molly Seagrim's finery draws village envy, all use masquerade to question the basis of social distinctions. Such traditional attacks gathered force as clothes became an aspect of commodified fashion and "female self-expression" at the turn of the century.[24] This is exemplified by a satirical celebration of dress as prosperity, signed "Beau Nash." Arguing that sartorial simplicity allows women to be broached more easily, and induces love and lust where finery repels, the epistle collapses commercial and moral arguments:

Fashions of the Season. May [1799]

At no time, for these five years, have we had so gay, or so full a season in the metropolis, as at the present. Fashion has not only resumed all its splendour, but it has, from the interval of rest and economy, acquired new taste for the capricious and expensive. Fancy is now racked for novelties of decoration, and dress is daily flying from Greek simplicity into Eastern magnificence.

This does not arise, I hope, Mr. Editor, from the mere natural versatility of fashion, but is the result of a wise and profound policy in the administration of the mode. It has been a subject of deep regret, that plainness of dress in public assemblies not only countenances the malignant principle of equality, by confounding distinctions, but cherished [*sic*] the sentiment in the mind, reconciles the taste to simplicity and corrects all the notions of dignity and distance which the costume of courts so properly inculcates. Plainness begets familiarity. . . .

But this is not the only argument for the change which has been recently introduced. What an illustration of the resources of England is the superb style of the present year? Our fêtes, our balls, our assemblies, are not only more numerous than ever, but our dress is more brilliant; and, thus if the state demands sacrifices from the people, the higher orders, with the magnificence which reconciles the heart to their distinction, liberally spread among the arts their wealth, and like the sun, restore to the mass of society the vivifying riches which they originally draw from their toil.[25]

Dress becomes an emblem of female fashion and power in the marketplace, and in this text even carries political connotations as a symbol of rank—or rancid—social hierarchy.[26] As this text reveals, dress elided with periodicals, novels, and other fashionable books as a commodity both exhibiting and expressing femininity.

In her fiction, Austen explores the uses of a variety of purchases to advertise the self, including not only books and clothes, but also accomplishments—skills or arts that displayed the woman for purchase through marriage, such as singing, speaking in languages, drawing, dancing, and playing music. Parents bought these skills either through such schools as Frederica Vernon, Lady Susan's daughter, attends, or via such private governesses as Jane Fairfax in *Emma* will become. Lady Susan cynically polishes Frederica for sale in the marriage market; Mrs. Elton similarly attempts to sell Jane to raise the cultural prestige of her acquaintances and, through the exchange, herself. These women are used by the consumer culture around them, yet Jane, at least, has also improved herself enough to become the wife of Frank Churchill, heir to a fortune, and even Frederica attracts Sir Reginald. It is the correct consumption of these commodities— be they skills or objects—that concerns Austen, a consumption that respects their social value and power to illustrate the self, yet preserves personal integrity. When Harriet Smith in *Emma* is distracted by all the different colored ribbons while looking for a hat, she is overcome by shopping and loses her sense of purpose to commercialism. Similarly, Lydia Bennet in *Pride and Prejudice,* entranced by shops, buys a hat she dislikes and must "pull it to pieces" to make it wearable (219). Emma sneers at Harriet's indecision as a sign of mental weakness, but it is equally a sign of social ambiguity. Harriet does not know where she belongs, and therefore what to consume; she does not know who she is, and therefore what to wear. She cannot purchase the elegant thing. Lydia will take anything—or anyone, as her choice of elopement and Wickham proves. Similarly, Mary Bennet performs on the piano to "exhibit" herself, as her father remarks, whereas Anne Elliot in *Persuasion* plays to conceal herself, wholly for the amusement of others (*Pride and Prejudice,* 100). Elizabeth Bennet, who does not "perform to strangers" represents the golden mean (176).

Food also obviously provides an opportunity to dramatize the politics of consumption for Austen. The acquisition of various goods, but notably of food as well as clothing, forms the chief topic of Austen's letters, as well as one of the central motifs in her fiction. In her correspondence, however, she omits any moral framework to contextualize the significance of these goods because both the consumption of food outside the money economy, and the presentation of the body in appropriate dress were the ways in which she and her family retained their (declining) class status: their significance was self-evident to her correspondents. But if such issues as "the torments of rice puddings and apple dumplings," and "the exorbitant price of fish," like the declining fashion for "gores" in dress "tails," preoccupies Austen in her letters, in her novels she shows the way the acquisition and use of goods in an exchange reveals personality.[27] Mrs. Norris in *Mansfield Park,* for example, demonstrates both her social identity as parasite and her moral character as selfish by winkling a cream-cheese from the housekeeper at Sotherton without giving anything for it. Her pleasure at acquiring something free for her own consumption contrasts with her companions' suffering under a variety of balked, social desires. She embodies one of the wrong ways to consume; the torpid Lady Bertram, purchased for her looks and docility, another.[28] In contrast, Fanny Price, whose services are priceless, purchased for a different but related set of social purposes, herself consumes and displays virtually nothing but a few bookish views, and thus her virtues remain undiscovered until forced by the crass Crawfords from London into play.

Throughout the eighteenth century, cultural critics complained about female consumption in general, often linking moralistic objections to female appetite with attacks on women's reading, especially of circulating library fiction. George Colman's *Polly Honeycombe* bluntly identifies literary with other commodities. In recounting Polly's illicit love for the novelist Scribble instead of the approved Ledger, who reads only *The Daily Advertiser* and Lloyd's list, the play roundly attacks women's literature for violating neoclassical dicta. In his preface, Colman ironically cites his mother's criticism that "the *Catastrophe* (that was really her word) is directly contrary to all known rules" and sarcastically lists female principles of good drama as valuing romantic love, "reconciliation," and moral "reformation" above satire.[29] As illustration, the play contains an "Extract" from an imaginary circulating library catalogue that subtitles Fielding's *Amelia* "The Distressed Wife" to highlight its appeal to victimized women. Moreover, Colman portrays this corrupt feminine taste as shaping the entire consumer culture of London. When Polly is confined for refusing Ledger, she recalls that Clarissa Harlowe had drawers made to conceal her writing supplies, but, "Indeed now they make standishes, and tea-chests, and dressing-boxes, in all sorts of shapes and figures—But mine are of my own invention.—Here I have got an excellent ink-horn in my pin-cushion—And a case of pens, and some paper, in my fan" (17). She hides letters in her hat box with her new cap and ruffles. Colman portrays both material and metaphorical reality etiolated by women's secret spaces and desires.

Colman attacks circulating library literature for nourishing women's self-pity, secrecy, and self-importance. He also associates these with women's other appetites. As the play opens, Polly reads a passage from the novel that compares the dawn with "iced cream crimsoned with raspberries" (1). While burlesquing Fielding's own mock-heroic diction in *Tom Jones,* this analogy both derides romances' derivative style and satirizes the frothiness of feminine taste. Furthermore, the supposedly licensed public fantasizing of circulating library fiction is depicted as stimulating women's self-display. The stage directions describe Polly as "acting it as she reads" and as "reading and acting" as she imagines accepting a marriage proposal (2). She is performing what should be private feelings to an imagined audience—as well as to the audience in the theater. According to Colman, romantic values breed artifice and exhibitionism. As Polly's father exclaims, "a man might as well turn his Daughter loose in Covent-garden, as trust the cultivation of her mind to A CIRCULATING LIBRARY" (31). He depicts female reading as a public display of the self that makes gender, class, and morality dangerously unreadable.

This distrust of staged female identity is a response to contemporary changes in the avenues and languages of self-representation, especially of female self-representation. Markedly, as the population of London grew and traditional social bonds loosened, city dwellers began to advertise their desires in newspapers. Typically, early advertising plagiarized literary texts, leveled traditional distinctions of value and provenance, and translated satire into enthusiasm in order to tout novelty; these techniques affected not only the style of popular novels but people's self-presentation in print.[30] The depiction of women and men as marriage commodities was commonplace in eighteenth- and early nineteenth-century printed culture, in which advertisements characteristically jumble the pecuniary and the moral. In 1785, *The Public Advertiser* rather hypocritically mocks the homogeneity advertising confers on commodities:

> The Advertising Age.
> "This is the *Advertising Age*," said a friend to me t'other day, as we were remarking the great number of advertisements in the news-papers.
> This is the *Age of Advertising*. If you want to buy an estate—
> > To sell an estate.
> > To get a place at Court.
> > To shew a comedy.
> > To shew a pig.
> > To make known your writings.
> > To teach turkeys to dance.
> > To procure charity.
> > To hire a house.
> > To marry a wife.
> > To keep a mistress.
> > To buy dogs.
> > To let horses.
> > To nurse children.
> > To vamp pamphlets.
> > To go up in a balloon.
> > To teach dancing.
> > Or
> > To sell hair-powder.
> In all these and many other cases, you will experience the good effects of *advertising*. . . . When we consider the language and artful manner of these advertisements, the lures they throw out, and the success they have, we may say, *lead us not into temptation*. (*Public Advertiser*, April 13, 1785)

Advertising equalizes things and services that traditionally occupy very different planes in a moral hierarchy.

The power of advertising to level traditional distinctions of value produces a conservative rhetoric of resistance, even while it shapes self-presentation in print. One man very like Sir Walter Elliot deplores his declassé "recourse to advertisement" in the newspapers, yet clearly requires it, since he reissues his 1790 plea for a wife or companion in 1791.[31] Another declares himself as a good bargain in a long advertisement that echoes Mr. Collins's sycophantic bullying:

> No character in this kingdom can be more respectable than that of a clergyman; and yet how many worthy men are there of that profession whose incomes, barely sufficient for the present maintenance, afford them not the means of making the smallest provision for their children.—There are undoubtedly at this very instant several young ladies under this description, who, though accomplished both in mind and person, have no better prospect than the necessity of submitting to stations unworthy their birth and education.
>
> To the parents or near relations of any lady thus accomplished, the advertiser now addresses himself. He is a gentleman of easy fortune, and can provide for a wife in case of death. He presumes to say, that the offer of his hand in marriage would be both honourable and advantageous to a lady of little or no fortune; nor could she miss of happiness if her temper and inclinations dispose her to search for it within the circle of domestic enjoyments. Nevertheless he had not the vanity to suppose that a handsome and accomplished lady would make him the object of her choice—That his good temper, indulgence, and attention to her would secure her esteem he had not the least doubt. But he is at the time same [*sic*] conscious, that her consent to receive his addresses must take its rise from an honest pride wishing for independence, and from a laudable ambition which she feels to move in a station for which both nature and education seem to have intended her.
>
> Charles Winterton, Esq. (*Whitehall Evening,* 1771)

Accomplished women with "a laudable ambition" like Charlotte Lucas, conventionally trained in religious principles, whose poverty and plainness situate them below companionate marriage, have the opportunity of selling themselves to Mr. Winterton, and hoping to feel "esteem" from his "indulgence." Women did indeed so sell themselves, and marriage was not their only venue, albeit the only one Austen openly acknowledges:

> A Young Gentlewoman, by birth unexceptionable of good character, solicits the friendship of a Gentleman who answers the following delineation: Free from every incumbrance, in the enjoyment of a good fortune, independent, possessed of sense, sentiment, delicacy, and humanity, in short, she wishes him to possess the endowments of the heart to an eminent degree, those permanent, and would sufficiently compensate for age, or the want of per-

sonal qualifications; let him have stability too, and be divested of hypocrisy. Letters to be left at a snuff shop. . . . High Holborn, for R.S.T. (1771)

The language of such advertisements elides marriage and prostitution.

One publication, specifically directed to subscribers, illustrates the terms in which people were advertised to prospective purchasers. This "Matrimonial Plan," entitled *The Imprejudicate Nuptial Society; or, Grand Matrimonial Intercourse Institution,* separates its entries by class: the first class holds "all parties, male and female, whose expectations exceed £5,000," the second contains those possessing between £5,000 and £500, and the third "or lowest Class comprehends all expectations from a Guinea up to £500."[32] This rhetoric leaves no room for moral claims: class is money. In the fictional examples, financial and aesthetic language mingles to objectify the commodity: "I am 19 years of age, heiress to a freehold estate, in Kent, of the value of £500 per annum, besides £15,000 in the Public Funds; I have lately lost my father, and am under a guardian; I am of the middle size, my eyes dark, my person agreeable, my temper and dis-position gay, my religion of the Church of England, Etc." (2). Like the opening sentences of *Mansfield Park* and *Emma,* this passage both sketches and links the physical appearance, the social identity, and the possible destiny of a young woman. In the papers, advertisers sell their own com-modities by rhetorical packaging; if that commodity is themselves, they must present themselves in the conventional language of advertisement. Similarly, in Austen's novels, the narrator initially advertises the heroine, but she must also advertise herself.

Despite objective physical descriptions, the primary trait for marriage is money; this alone permits choice. Although the classes remain distinct, the wealthy may indulge love: "The First Class has a right to the List of the other Two, and the second to the List of the Third, which leaves an opening to the opulent, who have fortune enough themselves to make happy the objects of their choice; though in an inferior rank, or of an inferior fortune, where either the agreeable charms of a lovely person, or the engaging manners, may fascinate the heart; while at the same time, expectation may be indulged, that the lower may be favored with the correspondence of the higher Class (4)." This (possibly parodic) projector further recommends his plan because it promotes sincerity, since, "in the common way men first fall in love, and then disgracefully retreat, if there is not money enough; but here the circumstances are first known, and [so there is] nothing to prevent sincere love afterwards. It is easy to conceive, that love may be formed in the heart by this mode, even before the actual interview (4)." Austen describes this very process in Willoughby's betrayal of Marianne for money and Mr. Elton's rapid marriage to a rich woman for it. In the opening of *Emma*, she quantifies her heroine's strengths in similar language: "Emma Woodhouse, [was] handsome, clever, and rich, with a comfortable home and a happy disposition," although Emma fails to fall in love with Frank Churchill despite her prejudice in favor of doing so (*Emma*, 5). This objectification of people leaves moral qualities undescribed—and those are the subject of Austen's narrative. Similarly, *Mansfield Park* describes Miss Maria Ward's "good luck" in capturing Sir Thomas Bertram, since "her uncle, the lawyer, himself allowed her to be at least three hundred pounds short of any equitable claim to it" (3). Austen deliberately contrasts these commercial values with the moral ones her novels explore. Nonetheless, even moral qualities require advertisement in this commercialized world, and correct consumption—particularly of literature—forms one of the chief ways of doing so.

Austen's emphasis on reading reflects the changes in the production, marketing, and reception of books during Austen's lifetime. Literature served several functions in Austen's world, including entertainment, company, socialization, and information, and as the nineteenth century waxed, these increasingly separated into moralized categories. As a source of entertainment, literature substituted for society when none was available, or furnished conversation when it palled. As Patricia Howell Michaelson has pointed out, principles of elocution, derived partly from the works of Vicesimus Knox and Blair, influenced Austen's style and subject, since public reading formed part of the family ethos and education.[33] As Austen records in a letter to her sister, literature ranked second to intimate conversation: "You distress me cruelly by your request about Books; I cannot think of any to bring with me, nor have I any idea of our wanting them. I come to you to be talked to, not to read or hear reading. I can do *that* at home; & indeed I am now laying in a stock of intelligence to pour out on you as *my* share of Conversation" (letter 26, Wednesday, 12 November 1800, 89). Reading aloud could demonstrate the intimacy of a community, as it does in Mr. Martin's home in *Emma*, or the new value, exemplified by Henry Crawford in *Mansfield Park*, of personal display.

At the same time, both in *Pride and Prejudice* and elsewhere, Austen examines the claim that literature could expand the mind by encompassing a broad spectrum of knowledge. Literature was seen to function as a tool for social intercourse, not only talking to the reader but teaching the reader how to talk to others. Even this function, however, was commodified. In her letter to her sister, Austen continues: "I am reading Henry's History of

England, which I will repeat to you in any manner you prefer, either in a loose, disultary [*sic*], unconnected strain, or dividing my recital as the Historian divides it himself into seven parts. The Civil & Military—Religion—Constitution—Learning & Learned Men—Arts & Sciences—Commerce Coins & Shipping—& Manners;—so that for every evening of the week there will be a different subject" (89). Austen mocks several of the ways literature is used: as an intermediary between friends, as a status symbol demonstrating the speaker's intelligence, and as an artificial substitute for sincerity, spontaneity, or originality. By specifically ridiculing the form of this *History of England,* furthermore, Austen demonstrates her understanding of the way these literary functions were exploited by booksellers. This text parcels information into conversation pieces that can be recombined at the user's will. Its information thus stands equal with other practical conversational gambits, as Austen reveals by concluding, "With such a provision on my part, if you will do your's by repeating the French Grammar, & M^{rs}. Stent will now and then ejaculate some wonder about the Cocks & Hens, what can we want?" (89). Teasing her sister for fearing silence by reciting the conventional uses of reading, Austen ridicules the function of literature as a social lubricant. In matching a segment of text to an evening of the week, moreover, she satirizes the fragmentation of knowledge and of social intercourse into units that can be recombined randomly. The source of her joke is not the irreverent use of the text, but the necessity of turning to a written text when the social dynamic fails. The mechanical arrangement of the information, moreover, further questions the tenet that reading improves a woman's social graces.

This questioning of the uses of reading sprang from the changes in the production and dissemination of literature at the end of the eighteenth century. Increasingly, publishers and booksellers issued books in forms that allowed dip-and-skip reading suitable for those without great leisure and that selected for them the texts and topics deemed respectable by the new professional critics: Johnson, Goldsmith, Griffiths, and other poets and journalists hired by booksellers. These books promote a new way of reading that encourages the "extensive" apprehension of a broad range of texts that Darcy recommends, albeit such an ideal of reading, as Austen observes, tends to value the quantity of literary consumption over depth of understanding.[34] Both critics and the popular texts booksellers issued particularly appealed to urban women who could now afford domestic labor and had the time and education to read, as well as a public tradition of female reading extending back for over fifty years. Moreover, the gentlemanly ideal of the contemplative life of cultivated leisure that entailed

The four columns of verse beneath the engraving read:

When Fools fall out, for ev'ry Flaw,
They run horn mad to go to Law,
A Hedge awry, a wrong plac'd Gate,
Will serve to spend a whole Estate;
Your Case the Lawyer says is good,
And Justice cannot be withstood:
By tedious Process from above,
From Office they to Office move;

Then Pleas Demurrs — the Devl & all
At length they bring it to the Hall,
The Dreadfull Hall by Rufus rais'd,
For lofty Gothick Arches prais'd:
The First of TERM, the fatal day,
Doth envious Images convey;
First from ye Courts ye clam'rous bawl
The Cryer, their Attorneys call;

One of ye Gown, discreet and wise,
By Proper means his Wishes tries;
From Wreathocks fixing-nod Right to Law,
Il assures his trembling Clients Cause;
This finam's his Handkerchief whilst that
Gives the kind galena: Nymph his Hat,
Here one in love with Choiristers
Minds Singing more than Law Affairs.

A Serviant limping on behind —
Shews Justice lame, as well as Blind;
To gain new Clients some dispute,
Other protract an Antient Suit,
Jargon and Noise alone prevail
While Sense and Reason sure to fail;
At Babel thus Law Terms begun,
And now at Westm—er go on.

Plate 1. "The First Day of Term." Gravelot Del. C. Mosley Invt. Et Sculp. London: printed for John Ryall at Hogarth's Head in Fleet Street. Engr. 10⁷/₁₆ × 12¹/₂ in. 1755(?). Courtesy of the Print Collection of the Lewis Walpole Library, Yale University. This engraving shows Westminster Hall, the site of religion and government, converted to stalls selling books and prints. The satirical subtext collapses printed, legal, and social culture into litigious "Jargon" and "Noise."

both reading and writing had become available—or at least imaginable—to socially ambitious members of the lower and middle classes, as well as to women.[35] Since both the choice to spend leisure time reading and the choice of what to read exhibited social status, literary knowledge retained its éclat as a class sign while it became commercial. The students of self-improvement who bought these texts demonstrated their (fashionable) morality with their money. These social shifts both reassured and worried social commentators. Some believed that reading encouraged a kind of sociability and consumption that provided a safe alternative to dangerous assembly, particularly the "tippling" or coffee-drinking in private clubs or public houses that supposedly brought rebellious feelings to the fore; for others, however, women assembling publicly or perusing privately threatened social order.[36] This tension between reading as social ambition and reading as social control was crystallized by the debate over what to read: novels with heroines that licensed desire, or poetry by men that depicted its pains. Booksellers and printers exploited this debate over cultural literacy. Partly because of the easing of copyright restrictions on reprinting eighteenth-century literature that resulted from the decision in the *Becket v. Donaldson* trial of 1774, they began to issue fiction and verse in inexpensive forms, including a wide variety of anthologies, and series of novels and poetry.[37] Ranging from monthly issues of two or three poems, such as Roach's sixpenny *Beauties of Literature* (1796–98?) or *The Literary Miscellany* (1798–1805?), to mini-libraries like Bell's *British Poets,* these publishing ventures commercialized literary culture for many different kinds of readers who had many uses for reading.[38]

In offering specifically elite literature to untraditional readers, however, these inexpensive editions disseminated an ideal of cultural consumption as the display of choice. Culture—an education in the arts and sciences that brought moral improvement and aesthetic refinement—became something individual readers could buy; correspondingly, so did the social and moral values implied in these texts, and endorsed by contemporary writers.[39] Politeness was packaged in cheap copies of Chesterfield's *Advice to His Son;* oracular style sold through Blair; sensibility, benevolence, and generosity generated in shilling sheafs of Sterne, Mackenzie, and Goldsmith; the picturesque and refinement of taste parceled in books of "Beauties" boasting Pope, Fielding, and Beattie; virtue vended via Horne and Halifax. As popular texts, furthermore, could shape—sometimes, indeed, coopt—subjectivity, so the public expression of knowledge of them could exhibit that subjectivity to purchasers. Austen in her correspondence, as well as her novels, herself demonstrates her awareness of the power of texts to define and display the self. Completing a long letter to Cassandra, she exclaims, "I am now alone in the Library, Mistress of all I survey—at least I may say so & repeat the whole poem if I like it, without offence to anybody" (letter 84; Thursday, 23 September 1813, 335). After writing and reading aloud alone a text of sentimental independence, she enjoys the power of cultural display in the private space of her father's library. Her humorous self-consciousness indicates her ability simultaneously to indulge and to reject being shaped by her reading. While she internalizes, ironizes, and feminizes Cowper's imperial gaze, however, such characters as Marianne Dashwood are not so powerful.

Female literacy, the ability to read, write, and discuss literature, allowed women to demonstrate their capacity for moral improvement, social mobility, intelligent companionship with men, and affordably quiescent appetites. Women could also reveal these qualities through their physical appearance and behavior. Although Austen favors the social skill of entertaining conversation over the traditional accomplishments of playing music and singing, for example, she places strong emphasis on useful arts that combine private pleasure with public artistry, such as Elinor Dashwood's screen-painting and Fanny Price's sewing. But the spending of money, especially on clothes and food, similarly exhibits either the traditional vices of profligacy and vanity, or the virtues of providence and modesty.[40] As Sheila Kaye-Smith notes, both food and clothes were changing as urban, trade-oriented habits infected the gentry's manners: now four meals replaced two or three.[41] Moral writers often directly associated different categories of commodities that permitted the fashionable display of the mind and body. In *Liberal Education: or, A Practical Treatise on the Methods of Acquiring Useful and Polite Learning,* the popular anthologist, cleric, and educational philosopher Vicesimus Knox defends the social compatibility of both kinds of accomplishments: "There are many prejudices entertained against the character of a learned lady; and perhaps, if all ladies were profoundly learned, some inconveniences might arise from it; but I must own it does not appear to me, that a woman will be rendered less acceptable in the world, or worse qualified to perform any part of her duty in it, by having employed the time from six to sixteen, in the cultivation of her mind. Time enough will remain, after a few hours every day spent in reading, for the improvement of the person, and the acquisition of the usual accomplishments."[42] In accordance with the new ideals of female education, women in Austen's world were expected not merely to inform themselves of modern literature but to exhibit that information through genteel conversation, well-bred manners, and a stylish appearance.

For Austen, books serve most importantly to distinguish servile from powerful femininity through the opportunities they present for self-shaping and self-display. Printed culture offered plenty of opportunities for exhibiting identity. In Austen's society, both books and different kinds of libraries offering them to different kinds of readers abounded, directed to men as well as women. Studies show that in public libraries fiction, history, biography, and memoirs overshadowed other categories, as novels became the most plentiful form of literature, but drama, travelogs, romances, miscellanies of poetry, and cheap editions of the classics were also in rich supply.[43] Moreover, as T. Wilson's pamphlet *The Use of Circulating Libraries Considered* recommended, libraries profited if they held twice as many novels and romances as all the other holdings put together.[44] Just as the ideology of much of this fiction advertised commercial items, so these novels themselves could be acquired alongside other fashionable luxuries.[45] The commercialism of libraries was blatant and hardly new. As they had done since the early eighteenth century, libraries and bookshops sold various fashionable goods. Harrod's *Catalogue* for 1790 omits the titles of "upwards of Three Hundred Plays" as "too tedious to mention" but cites a long list of medicines, stationary, "Dewdney's Powder for leaning Leather Breeches," "Terra Cotta Inkstands," and "Riley's coloured Pencils for drawing upon Silk," among other items.[46] N. L. Pannier's Circulating Library *Catalogue* in 1812 advertises "Tooth Power" as an "elegant Dentrifice" prominently on its first page (2s. 6d. or 4s. 6d. a box).[47] Ebers further advertises tickets for the Opera.[48] Even William Lane's Minerva Press followed this trend by selling its books as complements to other goods: "In its heyday the Minerva Library had a stock of nearly seventeen thousand books and circulated thousands of volumes throughout Britain, both to individual subscribers and in collections loaned to shopkeepers in provincial and seaside towns. In 1791 Lane was advertising complete circulating libraries of one hundred to ten thousand volumes for sale to shopkeepers interested in a sideline to their business."[49] Thus, books were only one—if one of the most important—of the items for urban consumption, and they were linked with items for the display of accomplishments such as drawing, music, writing, and riding. They did, however, supply reasons to linger and show off one's consumer skills by being seen selecting something "elegant" in a public venue.

Different kinds of libraries in particular reflect the gendered differences between apparently unmonitored, public uses of literature, and restricted or trained, educated uses.[50] Although the public renting of books had been a feature of London and provincial society, notably Bath, for at least a hundred years, in the Regency it became a central issue for cultural critics and authors, whose profit could only be guaranteed if they wrote the kind of literature sold at circulating libraries.[51] Subscription libraries, particularly popular in the provinces, were a fresh form of an eighteenth-century practice that endowed subscribers with a power close to that once held by aristo-

Plate 2. *"Messrs. Lackington Allen and Co. Temple of the Muses,"* 17 *Finsbury Square. No. 4 of* Ackermann's Repository of the Arts, *Publ. 1 April 1809, 101 Strand, London. Aqua. col. 4⁶/₁₆ × 7³/₄ in. Courtesy of the Print Collection of the Lewis Walpole Library, Yale University. This depiction of Lackington's elegant but cut-rate bookshop, which catered to a huge clientele in the early nineteenth century, appears in a periodical devoted to publicizing the latest fashionable commodities. The spectacular architecture of the square placed between St. Luke's Hospital and Bedlam daunted Frances Burney, but Johnson replied that "a very moral use may be made of these new buildings": to sober the imagination. Apparently, Finsbury Square was the first public place lit by gas lamps. (Peter Cunningham,* London: Past and Present, *vol. 2 [London: John Murray, 1891], 44–45.) My thanks to Joan Sussler.*

cratic patrons.[52] These libraries, like subscription volumes such as Pope's *Iliad* that were financed by a group of friends or special customers, tended to present themselves as selecting sophisticated, expensive, and elite or morally unexceptionable texts. Austen herself acted as a literary patron when she requested to be "put down as a subscriber to Mr. Jefferson's works," partly as a charitable measure (letter 53, Sunday, 26 June 1808, 199–200). The vast majority of books, however, were produced in a commercial system in which authors were paid by professional printers or booksellers. This professionalization of literary culture meant that authors wrote to please middle-class publishers, who were themselves imagining the tastes of anonymous readers in what was rapidly becoming a mass market.

Whereas subscription libraries were in a sense owned by the subscribers who appointed officials to run the library, circulating libraries were commercial enterprises run for profit in a world of mobile readers with no necessary connection to one another or to the proprietors of the library. If subscribers devised their own literary education as part of a small group, customers of circulating libraries in contrast were obliged to choose from among the selection of the library's entrepreneurs. These merchants comprised a new class of literary monitors trained in business not elite culture and engaged in profiting from, not improving, taste. Nonetheless, they represented themselves as servants to a public who possessed the most refined yet encyclopedic tastes. One announcement by "the Proprietors of Circulating Libraries" advertises its stock for "Utility, Extensiveness, and Amusement."[53] From the 1790s to the 1820s, moreover, the circulating library enjoyed an unprecedented heyday. These crucial years saw the social consequences of the increase in eighteenth-century literacy and urbanization in the form of these burgeoning commercial enterprises with their unprecedentedly open access to literature both for any writer who could publish her works, and any reader who could pay the small fee. By 1801 "there were at least one thousand circulating libraries in England of various sizes," and these included establishments that lent a spectrum of the products of print culture: books, pamphlets, newspapers, and music. Their customers could buy annual or quarterly memberships, or even borrow material at the rate of a penny for the day, if they left collateral. By 1821, according to the *Monthly Magazine,* there were at least fifteen hundred.[54] Servants, artisans, shopkeepers, professionals, gentry, and even royalty belonged: reading, as the consumption of a luxury rapidly turning into a mass commodity, became a main avenue for social interaction. Indeed, since the subsequent downturn in the economy diminished the number of such libraries, it was during Austen's career that the availability of books, and the anxiety about what circulating libraries were doing to the country peaked.

This commercial culture was identified with female desire. Circulating libraries had long attracted criticism for their promotion of romances about love unlicenced by parental authority.[55] Despite the fact that less than 30 percent of novel readers were women in the eighteenth century, the circulating library was culturally understood as feminine.[56] George Colman's mock prologue to *Polly Honeycombe* invokes "Romance" as the "dread" muse of circulating library culture, a muse that sings women's rebellious power. Polly herself lucidly expresses conventional critical objections to circulating library literature:

My poor Papa's in woeful agitation—
While I, the cause, feel here, [striking her bosom,] no palpitation—
We Girls of Reading, and superior notions,
Who from the fountain-head drink love's sweet potions,
Pity our parents, when such passion blinds 'em,
One hears the good folks rave—One never minds 'em.
Till these dear books in fus'd their soft ingredients,
Asham'd and fearful, I was all Obedience.
Then my good father did not storm in vain,
I blush'd and cry'd—I'll ne'er do so again:
But now no bugbears can my spirit tame,
I've conquer'd Fear—And almost conquer'd Shame:
So much these Dear Instructors change and win us,
Without their light we ne'er should know what's in us . . .
Not only Sentiments refine the soul,
But hence we learn to be the Smart and Drole;
Each awkward circumstance for laughter serves,
From Nurse's nonsense to my Mother's NERVES.

Not only does this literature breed rebellion, but it also reformulates manners so that modesty mutates into wit, and women abandon maidenly silence for public speech. This self-assertion replaces domestic industry:

'Tho' Parents tell us, that our genius lies
In mending linnen and in making pies,
I set such formal precepts at defiance
That preach up prudence, neatness, and compliance;
Leap these old bounds, and boldly set the pattern,
To be a Wit, Philosopher, and Slattern—
O! did all maids and wives my spirit feel,
We'd make this topsy-turvy world to reel:
Let us to arms!—Our fathers, Husbands, dare!
NOVELS will teach us all the Art of War:
Our Tongues will serve for Trumpet and for Drum;
I'll be your Leader—General HONEYCOMBE!
Too long has human nature gone astray,
Daughters should govern, Parents should obey;
Man shou'd submit, the moment that he weds,
And hearts of oak shou'd yield to wiser heads:
I see you smile, bold Britons!—But 'tis true—
Beat You the French;—But let your Wives beat You.
(32–33: ll. 1–14, 17–38)

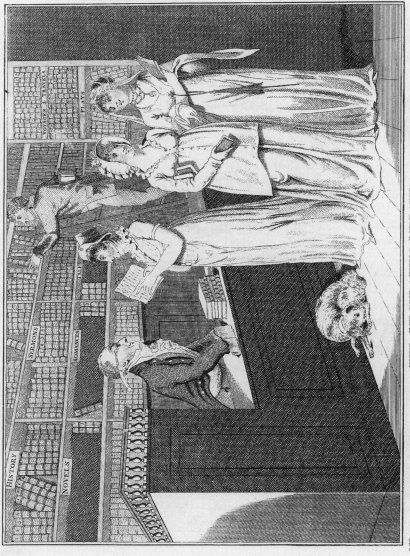

THE CIRCULATING LIBRARY.

Pray, my dear Mr Page," cried a pretty lisper, looking over a Catalogue "will you let me have that dear Man of Feeling. I have so long waited for—Well, this will do for one. N° 689. Cruel Disappointment, for another. Reuben, or Suicide, high N° 1546. I suppose he killed himself for love. Seduction, yes, I want that more than any thing. Unguarded Moments, ah we all have our unguarded moments. True Delicacy, N° 3 that must be a silly thing by the title. School of Virtue, heaven knows I want no more than enough of that. Test of Filial Duty, at any rate she puts me to that test pretty often. Mental Pleasures, worse & worse! I'll look no longer. Oh! stay a moment. Mutual Attachment, Vexation, Frederick or the Libertine, just add those Mr Page, & I shall not have to come again, until the day after to-morrow".*

Published as the Act directs, by LAURIE & WHITTLE, 53, Fleet Street, London.

Colman suggests that circulating novels militarize domesticity and sexuality; the private home becomes a public field of competition. As Nancy Armstrong and Margaret A. Doody have argued, novels themselves can be seen as a female genre promoting women's choice, power, and significance. In their emphasis on novels, especially, circulating libraries appealed to women, although, as James Lackington observed, they also provided means for more conventional education.[57] Still, circulating libraries were generally used for leisure reading, not for learning. Indeed, it seems likely that they earned gendered criticism not merely because of the kind of literature they promoted, but because of the kind of reading: reading that existed outside traditional institutions of learning, and that supposedly aroused sentimental responses.[58]

These attacks reflect contemporary fears about the democratizing power of cheap reading. Novel prices generally increased from 2s. 6d. a volume in 1780 to as much as 7s. in 1810, but readers relied on ways of borrowing and renting books that diminished the importance of such increases.[59] Libraries accommodated different social ranks and incomes, typically offering three "classes" of membership.[60] In Ebers's Circulating Library, for example, the first class were "entitled to the newest and most expensive Works," and the second class for half the cost could peruse "the New Publications in the Octavo and Duodecimo sizes," while the third class were "not entitled to the immediate perusal of New Works" (1–2). Similarly, readers were categorized into "classes," based on their wealth. Like other libraries, the Minerva Library, for example, featured levels of subscription, including a costly 5 guineas that permitted subscribers to borrow "twenty-four volumes at a time while in London, and thirty-six if residing in the country."[61] Users thus demonstrated their class by the number and novelty of their readings. Most importantly, however, these libraries offered books censored elsewhere—notably the recent novels that Mr. Collins deplores. Circulating libraries acquired books at the whim of the proprietor—generally a bookseller or bookselling publisher who gambled on what would be popular or acquired as many new books as he could afford: his concerns were profit not prestige. For example, "Lownds' Circulating Library," featuring more than ten thousand books, promises that

Plate 3 (opposite): *"The Circulating Library," number 369 in a series. Publ. Laurie and Whittle, 1 October 1804. Courtesy of the Print Collection of the Lewis Walpole Library, Yale University. This plate satirizes women's taste by showing the shelves holding novels and romances stripped bare, while those holding voyages, history, and particularly sermons remain full.*

"All New BOOKS on every Subject are purchased, as soon as possible, for the Use of Subscribers."[62] This practice ostensibly opposes that of book clubs and private subscription libraries, which often required the consent of all members to purchase a new book, and thus touted the discrimination of their selection. They purportedly favored "serious" reading—histories, poetry, sermons, and philosophy—in imitation of the private libraries of gentlemen and collectors.[63] Circulating libraries, however, openly valued the sort of texts that women were represented as favoring, as both readers and writers. Thus, not only did these libraries provide a social space for women, but they modified conventional literary hierarchies by valuing most highly what was written last, not what was written to last.

Circulating libraries facilitated and reflected changes in the social makeup of the country, in the production of literature, and in culture itself. *The Gentleman's Magazine* of 1805, for example, opines that "the circulating-libraries and reading-rooms in every market-town degrade us by the impertinence and abuse of curiosity. They poison our leisure hours without improving them."[64] This discourse characterizes the reading of circulating library literature as an incitement to illicit desire, a rebelliousness identified with women, and unrestrained passion; similarly, the vaunted accessibility of literature suggested that readers uncommitted to cultural improvement might be reading in licentious, unordered, or at least unrestricted ways. As Sir Anthony Absolute in Sheridan's *The Rivals* puts it, "A circulating library in a town is as an evergreen tree of diabolical knowledge" that incites sexual immorality and idleness. In that play, Lydia Languish and her maid hide within religious tomes their intoxicating sentimental novels, all borrowed from the circulating libraries of Bath; if the maid knows the titles, she may also have read the contents. Sheridan's typical characterization of circulating fiction as a vehicle for a female gender identification that even blurs class boundaries indicates that the social and mental area of library reading was designed not merely for gentry, but as much for the middle and urban working classes when they were not working.[65] Furthermore, the printed catalogues and rules of the library promoted a novelty and volume that invited a wide range of readers. In 1767, the "Proprietors of Circulating Libraries" advertised on the flyleaf of the second edition of Eliza Haywood's novel *The Fruitless Enquiry* that, "finding it impossible to continue the Business of Lending Books to Read on the *late low Terms of Subscription* . . . as we did at a Time when neither so great a Number of *New Books* were published, nor the Demand for them so great as now," they have raised the cost of membership to 1s. a quarter, or 1s.6d. annually, but they acknowledge the existence of rival, lower-cost libraries with putatively older novels to lend (v). Libraries seemed to promote novelty, the promiscuous use of literature, and unregulated cultural exchange.

Contemporary attacks thus reveal another aspect of the changing society: these social spaces were seen as providing a female alternative to the male social space of the library, with its tradition of masculine literary choice, inherited property, and privilege. Paul Kauffman observes that booksellers' shops and libraries were replacing coffee houses as social centers allowing class mixing.[66] Obviously, they also permitted women to socialize and discuss literature with one another, a practice common in elite French society but only gradually taking hold in England. Since libraries lent a volume at a time and novels generally ran to three volumes, however, several clients could read the same novel simultaneously, a practice that might invite speedy rather than considered perusal. Similarly, the dramatic formula of novels might encourage a private reading that would sustain the plot's mystery, or discussions that focused on female topics, rather than the evaluation of aesthetic merit and moral content traditionally associated with leisure reading in eighteenth-century male society. Such possibilities underscored the differences between the kind of reading encouraged by these new venues and what was seen as the traditional reading of private libraries. Whereas drinking clubs and book clubs were social spaces for exclusive companions, circulating libraries were places of cultural display for women, the social and economic arena for female literacy.

This new role for the reader partly results from the form of the circulating library novel, a form determined by the conditions of publication at the time. Austen's struggle with the conventions of female literacy indicate that it was not only readers who were shaped by the choices of the proprietors of circulating libraries. Authors, too, were dependent on this venue to disseminate their work, for it was by selling novels to circulating libraries that authors earned their money: the format for their work was established by that market more than by any other. If this were true of all fiction writers, it was especially true of women, whose work found a uniquely profitable market in the circulating library. Frances Burney ironically repudiates the suggestion that she change the ending of *Cecilia* by claiming that if she did, "the last page in any novel in Mr. Noble's circulating library may serve for the last page of mine, since a marriage, a reconciliation, and some hidden expedient for great riches concludes them all alike."[67] The formula that these circulating novels promoted was the three-volume novel, the genre bridging eighteenth-century periodical fiction and the Victorian serial. Early periodical fiction, such as Addison and Steele's

Spectator (1711–12, 1714), by establishing a consistent persona or group of characters who commented in every issue on current cultural phenomena and told tales of their families, recent encounters, or impressions, not only established a fictional intimacy with the reading public, but constructed a novelistic world of social detail, moral commentary, and heroic or individual experience.[68] As competitors for the audience in leisure reading, three-volume novels shared some of these characteristics, although as an author Austen differs from many of her contemporaries by mingling political and literary satire with fashionable topicality. This kind of fiction, however—directed to a faceless audience, structured by an impersonal formula, and geared to the distribution and reading practices of circulating libraries—lacks the flexible interaction of author and audience characteristic of the eighteenth-century periodical, with its small, vocal, and contributing audience, and of Victorian serialized fiction, which, expanded over a period as long as two years, permitted authors to incorporate the criticisms and reactions of its audience.[69] In three-volume novels, the story is the thing: the narrator takes a back seat to events, acting merely as an interpretative authority elucidating the apparent moral for the reader. This narrator, unlike the personae of eighteenth-century serialized fictions, reports as an objective and uncharacterized functionary, not either as a participant or a character, in either sense of the term. Since the formula for these fictions remained relatively inflexible, and since they were designed to be lent to an audience of mixed classes for one-time reading, a volume at a time, the author's identity became increasingly impersonal. Trained on genteel notions of literary culture, yet identifying and writing for the new market, Austen mediated between this modern, mechanical, authorial identity, and the traditional notion of the author as cultural critic. These conflicting ideas of authorship and of the moral prestige of writing meant that her authorial authority was both guaranteed and compromised by her venue.

As well as redefining the role of the author as something between a writer-for-pay and the disembodied voice of social morality, the format of the three-volume novel designed or directed its own consumption in a particular way. Victorian serials recount a developing story that allows readers to consume it in small portions between and within the other activities of life.[70] Eighteenth-century periodicals remain episodic, permitting audiences to ingest reading matter rapidly, perhaps rather than profoundly. Austen satirizes this kind of reading through her depiction of the superficiality of Catherine's understanding of her clipped cultural fragments in *Northanger Abbey,* a superficiality promoted by their publishing format. As Gary Kelly argues, *Northanger Abbey* advocates "social reading" modeled on proper novel reading.[71] Episodic plots, repeated points of plot, and passages of non-narrative pleasure were also features in many of the eighteenth-century novels Austen had read by Fielding, Richardson, and Radcliffe.[72] These features helped contemporary readers remember and follow stories that took hundreds of pages to conclude, but novels that were read at the rate of a volume a day had little need of such devices. New novels by women, especially Burney's *Cecilia,* were paying more attention to developmental, sequential plotting, requiring readers to give concentrated attention to plot, character and language.[73] Designed for lending a volume at a time, three-deckers, however, demanded a plot that climaxed at the end of each volume, yet preserved a continuing, mounting excitement to propel the reader through the third tome. This was reading geared to induce excitement, but also reading that presupposed some exercise of memory on the part of readers, and enough time at a stretch to finish a volume. Such a format became more than later readers could afford: in 1833, the editor Leitch Ritchie reports already that "It has been suggested to the proprietors by the Circulating Libraries, that the volumes of the Library of Romance are inconveniently long, and should be rendered capable of being divided into two, so as to enable them to supply their subscribers with the usual quantum of reading at a time."[74] Austen's publisher John Murray anticipates this move by printing her final novels, *Northanger Abbey* and *Persuasion,* in a four-volume compact to make a set that could be borrowed for four days—a format highly profitable to a circulating library.

The social power of reading and books, enacted by the social mixing circulating libraries fostered, becomes an important theme in Austen's novels. Despite endorsing fiction as instruction as well as delight, Austen nonetheless represents the dangers of books—both novels and poetry— that are improperly read and written, or turned into fetishized objects (mis)representing sentiment. They serve for Austen, like the manners and clothing adopted for self-performance, to demonstrate the misshaping of self in society. *Northanger Abbey* most obviously indicts the promiscuous consumption of fiction, not only by condemning Catherine Morland's manner of reading Radcliffe, but by characterizing Isabella Thorpe, the source of these mysteries, as the very model of affectation and self-serving insincerity, who hunts hats, young men, and money without distinction (43). In *Pride and Prejudice,* Lydia hints to her indulgent mother that the place to flirt with officers is "standing in Clarke's library" (30). In portraying this promiscuous circulation as social, not literary, Austen alludes to the contemporary protest that the novels in circulating libraries stimulated female passions. Whereas Lydia uses these libraries to show her body off, however, they can offer more sophisticated means of showing off. In an ironic parallel, Darcy suggests to Elizabeth that they talk of "books" at the ball at Netherfield as a way of becoming acquainted (93). He invites Elizabeth to show her mind off while her body dances—which she does, but not by discussing literature. Both Bennet sisters' uses of literary space—literal or figurative—document the female occupation of what was once a privileged male culture for female purposes, but Austen does not accord them equal approval.

Private libraries, in contrast to circulating libraries, signified gentility, for they presupposed the leisure, education, inheritance, and engagement in high culture of the privileged. It is by his occupation in the library that Mr. Bennet retains the stamp of the gentleman. Austen, however, problematizes this gentility by depicting the failure of such libraries to educate their owners in social behavior. Bingley uses his library to display his idleness: "I wish my collection [of books] were larger for your benefit and my own credit; but I am an idle fellow, and though I have not many, I have more than I ever look into," he boasts (38). While implying that his sociability keeps him too busy to read, Bingley insinuates that he possesses the aristocratic accouterment of an extensive library. Caroline Bingley springs to identify herself as one of these cultured gentry by deploring her father's "small collection of books" and admiring that at Pemberley (38). Darcy himself confirms this equation of books with class by declaring that he supplements his father's collection because he "cannot comprehend the neglect of a family library in such days as these" (38). Presumably, these days offer plenty of fine literature; by purchasing it, Darcy asserts his patronage of high culture.

Darcy views his library as an extension of his identity, but Elizabeth represents an opposite ideal that expresses Austen's resistance to the use of literature to commodify the self. Aware of the insult of being rejected as a conversationalist in favor of a book in the scene above, Miss Bingley declares, "Miss Eliza Bennet . . . despises cards. She is a great reader and has no pleasure in anything else" (37). Elizabeth's reply articulates the book's ideal of literacy as only one of many ways to learn about the self and others. '"I deserve neither such praise nor such censure,' cried Elizabeth; 'I am *not* a great reader, and I have pleasure in many things'" (37). In rejecting the identity of "a great reader," Elizabeth distinguishes herself from her pedantic sister Mary and from bluestockings, women defined by their reading and attacked for sexual license and unsociability.[75] For Elizabeth, reading is an activity not an identity. She defines reading as a "thing" of "pleasure"—something she uses, not something that establishes her social role.

The negotiation of elite literacy is a fundamental concern in Austen's use of letters.[76] Historically, writing was commercially twinned with reading. Indeed, stationery shops had from the Restoration become booksellers or libraries, and libraries always sold writing materials. As the expressive aspect of literacy, writing—including letters—in Austen's world both represents the self and functions as a social activity. Austen praises a letter of Cassandra's as an "exquisite piece of Workmanship," the "cheif" [*sic*] of which she read to a visiting acquaintance (letter 84, Thursday, 23 September 1813, 329, 332). When she is dying, Austen asserts to her sister, "Beleive [*sic*] me, I was interested in all you wrote, though with all the Egotism of an Invalid I write only of myself" (letter 145, Thursday, 22 May 1817, 495). Bingley asseverates his natural gentility in claiming that he writes "carelessly" and "rapidly," as if the gentlemanly skill were innate (48).[77] Indeed, when he calls Darcy's bluff by teasing him for affectation in writing—"He studies too much for words of four syllables"—Bingley pinpoints Darcy's self-consciousness about his own status (48). By ironically comparing the nouveau-riche Bingleys, who care to have books not to read but to own, with Darcy, who both owns and reads them, Austen exposes the contemporary anxiety about the competing definitions of class as birth or manners. She also exposes the hypocrisy of a culture that proclaims the value of mental self-possession through reading, but rewards the acquisition of material possessions.

The slippery power of written words to define and deconstruct selves and subjects also interested Austen, especially as an aspect of epistolarity. Inheriting from eighteenth-century literary models a skeptical respect for the physical facts of life, she remained fully aware of the materiality of her own writing.[78] She jokes to Cassandra on the material uses of literature, punning about Owenson's *Ida of Athens:* "If the warmth of her Language could affect the Body it might be worth reading in this weather" (letter 64, Tuesday, 17 January 1809, 251). Her manuscripts employ the eighteenth-century device of emphatic capitalization, often adding double-entendres lost in the regularized punctuation of the printed novels. Her letters particularly, reveal her consciousness of the connection between the representation of ideas in writing and those ideas themselves. In writing to Cassandra, Austen most often represents her own letters similarly with food and clothes as objects of consumption about the correctness and cost of which she (and presumably the whole family) continually worry. Prominent among these worries is that of topics. "I can recollect nothing more to say at present;—perhaps Breakfast may assist my ideas," she writes, employing in the fashion of sentimental fictions by Sterne and Mackenzie a dash to illustrate her hope for a quick association of ideas. "I was deceived—my breakfast supplied only two ideas, that the rolls were good, & the butter bad" (letter 22, Wednesday, 19 June 1799, 21–22). Repeatedly, she writes that she has nothing to write, bemoaning that the conventions of exchange dominate her labor and that letters are not only transmissions of information but also things. Occasionally, she plays with the physicality of words on the page—writing one letter to Cassandra backwards in mirror prose, and repeatedly deploring her own "scrawl" in comparison to Cassandra's apparently neat script (letter 52, Monday, 20 June 1808, 196–97). In her poem "On reading in the Newspaper, the Marriage of 'Mr. Gell of Eastbourne to Miss Gill,'" Austen undercuts Platonic cliché by punning on the vowels distinguishing Gell from Gill:

> Of Eastbourne Mr. Gell
> From being perfectly well
> Became dreadfully ill
> For the love of Miss Gill.
>
> So he said with some sighs
> "I'm the slave of your eyes,
> Oh! restore if you please
> By accepting my ease."[79]

This early rhyme is a charade on "i.e." as well as a pun on the couple's names, and on the letters the reader encounters, "i" and "e." In fusing the meanings of the letter '"e's" and the word "ease," Austen plays with the written appearance as well as the sounds and meanings of language. This pleasure in dialect and pronunciation appears most clearly in her juvenilia. For example, in "The first Act of a Comedy," she spells "will" when spoken by the cook "wull," and stresses the forced rhyme and weak syllable in her parodic eclogue: "I shall be married to Streephon, / And that to me will be fun" (*Minor Works*, 172–73). Her work persistently jokes with the physical artificiality of literature, as well as its conventions, to reassert the difference between authoring and being authored by printed culture.

Frequently, indeed, Austen worries about her management of writing, specifically her inability to tailor her script to her subject. "I will keep this celebrated Birthday by writing to you, & as my pen seems inclined to write large I will put my lines very close together," she announces to Cassandra (letter 90, Wednesday, 3 November 1813, 364).[80] At another point, her complaint at the dearth of subject transforms into a dissatisfaction at manner and method: "You are very amiable & very clever to write such long Letters; every page of yours has more lines than this, & every line more words than the average of mine. I am quite ashamed. . . . Mr. Lyford supplies you with a great deal of interesting Matter (Matter Intellectual, not physical)—but I have nothing to say of Mr. Scudamore. And now, that is such a sad stupid attempt at Wit, about Matter, that nobody can smile at it, & I am quite out of heart. I am sick of myself, & my bad pens" (letter 52, Monday, 20 June 1808, 196–97). Wanting matter to discuss, she discusses want of matter; her bad pens produce bad puns. This witty interplay on the physical and the intellectual foregrounds the close relationship they have for her. Often she deplores the limitations of the genre: "You will have had such late accounts from this place as (I hope) to prevent your expecting a Letter from me immediately, as I really do not think I have wherewithal to fabricate one today," she confesses to Cassandra. "I am not at all in a humour for writing; I must write on till I am" (letter 89, Tuesday, 26 October 1813, 359). Throughout her fiction, perhaps most notably in *Emma,* Austen turns her penchant for punning on words to fictional ends by showing how this literary play reduces words to superficial signs, devoid of moral content. This use of literature and language, like Catherine Morland's and Emma's use of Radcliffe's fiction, is wrong because it redefines social reality, be this the meaning of evil or of words, by idiosyncratic desire: it is a decadent, if delightful, enjoyment of language for its own sake. This is one of the dangers of being shaped by literature.

Like the letters of the alphabet, letters between writer and reader also represent material objects in exchange, language in circulation. Notably in Richardson's *Pamela,* letters serve both to indicate the refinement of the "hand-maiden" Pamela, too delicate for outdoor manual labor, and to aid the plot by constituting a precious object—Pamela's soul—which is hidden, stolen, and finally given freely. Austen herself uses letters in her fiction frequently to allow the expression of individual consciousness outside the rigidly ruled exchange system of conversation. *Pride and Prejudice* employs the device of Darcy's private communication, at the heart of the novel, to establish a new medium of exchange with Elizabeth. Austen brings about the denouement of *Persuasion* by means of Captain Wentworth's impassioned epistle, which permits "speech" censored only by internal consciousness. While these examples testify to the heroes' control over their written presentation, for women this assertion can be more dangerous. In *Sense and Sensibility,* Marianne's letters articulate a self plunged into the circulation economy of the marriage market; Willoughby's return of them is, as she rightly read it, a rejection of their intimacy, the self he was then, and her identity. Further, by signing his own name to an epistle written by his wife, he shows his loss of a self; he has signed away his soul. Isabella Thorpe's epistles in *Northanger Abbey,* like Lucy Steele's in *Sense and Sensibility* and Mary Crawford's in *Mansfield Park,* similarly expose the way literary artifice can facilitate avarice, affectation, and jealousy. These examples show the various dangers of literary self-representation.

As a correspondent herself, Austen examines the way writing both molds identity and represents a self that exhibits values to others, whether intimates or strangers. Indeed, the representation of self in letters forms one of her persistent concerns. "I am very much flattered by your commendation of my last letter," she writes jokingly to Cassandra, "for I write only for fame and without any view to pecuniary emolument" (letter 2, Thursday, 14 January 1796, 5). Given the date of this letter, it is probable that Austen alludes to *Northanger Abbey,* then titled *Susan,* as well as to her communication with her sister, forming a double irony. By her grandiose diction, she suggests that the rhetoric of private letters and public fictions coalesce—indeed, that her epistolary self is influenced by another self, shaped by a professional and hypocritical construction of disinterested authorship. She writes as an author, not merely as a correspondent. Moreover, as reader of her sister's letters, she further demonstrates the seepage of roles in literary culture into one another: she reads again not merely as a correspondent, but here as a professional reader, trained in careful reading: "You must read your letters over *five* times in future before you send them, and then, perhaps, you will find them as entertaining as I do. I laughed at several parts of the one which I am now answering" (letter 17, Tuesday, 8 January 1799, 48). In this letter, she also displays her anxiety about using her language to represent specific objects of consumerism. Here, evidently replying to several queries, she balks at detailing a cap: "I am not to wear my white satin cap to-night, after all; I am to wear a mamalone cap instead, which Charles Fowle sent to Mary, and which she lends me. It is all the fashion now; worn at the opera, and by Lady Mildmays at Hackwood balls. I hate describing such things, and I dare say you will be able to guess what it is like" (16–17). After specifying the provenance of the cap, a loan, she differentiates this gown from "the blue one" her sister knows by noting the details of sleeve, wrap, apron, and band. In claiming she "hates" describing "such things," she portrays herself as preferring relationships to objects; likewise, in her novels, objects have significance as items in a social context. In later letters, moreover, Austen either concedes to the wishes of her familial readers, or indicates the increasing problem of finding money by describing clothes in more detail.[81] In 1801, when attempting to describe the fashion of her new gown, she confesses to being "afraid that I am not being particular enough" (letter 35, Tuesday, 5 May 1801, 125). Her anxiety about her topics, handwriting, and descriptive details may echo a discourse of incorrectness that historically is particularly female, yet it is one entirely absent from the finished form of her novels. Certainly, this preoccupation reveals her awareness of the way conversational and writing skills display the self and her increasing consciousness of the role of objects in fashioning identity.

If circulating libraries dictated a format for novels and reading, they also promised a clientele. Not only as a reader did Austen rely on them as an inexpensive source of material, but as an author she was well aware of their power to make literature profitable. In common with many other gentry, she was forced to sell books from her father's private library once Napoleonic taxes and other changes reduced her to increasingly shabby gentility. Although an avid reader of her father's library, in one letter she suggests that James take the 500 volumes that her father must "dispose of . . . at a venture at half a guinea a volume," an unrealistically high price that may reflect her high valuation of the collection (letter 31, Wednesday, 14 January 1801, 111).[82] Later, she records that "Mr. Bent seems *bent* upon being very detestable, for he values the books at only £70. The whole World is in a conspiracy to enrich one part of our family at the expence [*sic*] of another." Evidently, however, it is her father's prose volumes she values so highly, for she observes, "Ten shillings for Dodsley's Poems however please me to the quick & I do not care how often I sell them for as much. When Mrs. Bramston has read them through I will sell them again" (letter 37, Thursday, 21 May 1801, 133). In her role as bookseller, she has learned the trick of circulating libraries to "sell" or lend the same text repeatedly. However, although she has no private space for a library of her own, she also indicates that some books are worth repeated perusal: Austen mentions abandoning *Alphonsine* for a rereading of *The Female Quixote* (letter 48, Wednesday 7 January 1807: 173). Instead of private libraries, however, she turns early on to public ones for this kind of reading: her letter of Tuesday, 18 December 1798, records that she has been invited to subscribe to Mrs. Martin's library with the assurance that it contains "every kind of Literature," not merely "Novels," adding "She might have spared this pretension to *our* family, who are great novel readers, and not ashamed of being so" (38). Austen roundly rejects the correlation of social class and literary genre. Nonetheless, she acknowledges the power of literature to shape—or misshape—identity.

What Books Prove

Since literature and literary culture were essential yet rapidly transforming aspects of Jane Austen's world, both her letters and fictions ubiquitously question their status and function and the significance and manner of literary consumption by both characters in the novels and readers of them. Her work charts the middle-class appropriation of literature as a commodity promising social mobility. She both demonstrates and markets the notion that books, literary language, literary ideas, and the very notion of literacy can be attained and absorbed by anyone with sufficient means—including her own readers—but that this process can deform the personality as easily as it can fashion and display it on the social stage. Austen shows the way literacy itself exhibits the purchaser by permitting customers to display their improvement by using literature publicly: by buying books, reading in public, evoking literary characters, or using literary tropes in conversation. In describing the way consumption reveals vices as much as virtues, raw social ambition as much as refined social advancement, she perforce endorses it as a moral gauge. Her novels portray the social meanings of choosing to read, of what you choose to read, and of how to read or to be seen reading.

Each of her novels has a distinct message about reading. In her first two, *Northanger Abbey* and *Sense and Sensibility,* Austen modifies the late eighteenth-century invective against literary illusions. While she warns that literature tells lies about life, and that readers—especially female readers—must learn to distinguish life from romance, she suggests that they do so by buying better literature than sentimental fictions or romantic poetry: Austen's own novels. In the pair of books written in the middle of her brief career, *Pride and Prejudice* and *Mansfield Park,* Austen examines the differences between male and female reading cultures. Here, she suggests that although reading reveals refinement and mental cultivation, it must be contextualized. In her last two novels, *Emma* and *Persuasion,* Austen largely criticizes categorical literary judgments. She shows that what matters is not merely reading for its own sake, but what books you choose to read, and what you do with what you have read: it is the choice and use of literature that marks the heroic spirit. Despite these distinctions, Austen consistently condemns gendered reading cultures. As a satirist, throughout her work she castigates the abuse of reading by mocking hypocritical, pretentious, or stupid readers, and by demonstrating the social costs of immersion in literature rather than life. At the same time, she parodies the conventional indictment of reading as a dangerous indulgence for women and endorses as the acquisition and demonstration of virtue reading the right things the right way. All her novels recommend the regulation of reading.

Both as a fashionable commodity and as a vehicle for social ideology, literature contains moral ramifications for Austen. Her characters use it in ways that reveal their moral, social, and gendered identities. Very few buy books for their own libraries, like Darcy: such purchases demonstrate both the power to choose, to select the finest from culture, and an investment in this culture for the sake of heirs, and few of Austen's female heroines possess such power. Many characters, however, subscribe to circulating libraries, like Fanny Price and Robert Martin, or borrow books from friends, like Captain Benwick; such uses can demonstrate "laudable" intellectual ambition or a hazardous dependence on others' tastes. Some read in public, either aloud, like John Willoughby in *Sense and Sensibility* and Henry Crawford in *Mansfield Park,* or to themselves like Darcy and the taciturn Mr. Palmer in *Sense and Sensibility;* such a monopoly of public space generally shows selfishness or self-interest (it is not so bad that Edward reads aloud inexpressively). Moreover, the form literature adopts also conveys moral ideas. In her juvenilia, Austen identifies selfishness with literary commodification in the sentimental conventions of late eighteenth-century fiction. In *The Beautiful Cassandra; A Novel in Twelve Chapters,* for example, Austen parodies Mackenzie's *The Man of Feeling* (1771), to which she had already referred in "The Adventures of Mr. Harley." This novel uses the self-conscious device of the discovery of a shredded manuscript to lend the text authenticity and to permit an impressionistic rendering of incomplete incidents from Harley's life that display his sensitivity in his day-to-day affairs.[83] Austen parodies this fragmentation by recounting in one- or two-sentence chapters the quotidian adventures of the heroine as she walks through the city. After such encounters as that in Chapter the Fourth—"She then proceeded to a pastry-cook's, where she devoured six ices, refused to pay for them, knocked down the pastry cook, and walked away"—the narrator exposes the moral retreat implied by this acausal literary convention: "[Cassandra] entered [her father's house] and was pressed to her mother's bosom by that worthy woman. Cassandra smiled and whispered to herself, 'This is a day well spent'" (*Minor Works,* 74, 75). Moral dissociation echoes narrative dissociation; this literary consumption parallels the eating of sweets without paying for them.

Austen repeatedly attacks standardized literary fare that presents sentiments in the forms of atemporal fantasies and packaged, bite-sized pieces.

In *Northanger Abbey,* her most outspoken attack on bad books and bad reading, Austen also publishes her most outright defense of the genre of the novel. She thus contrasts the literature she is supplying with that already in the marketplace: Gothic fictions and recycled eighteenth-century periodicals. Rather than merely reviling the feminine taste for fiction, however, she supplies the very commodity readers want, further improved by updating. Her belated "Advertisement," added when the novel was finally published, emphasizes its topicality by apologizing for the "considerable changes" in the thirteen years since its acceptance in "places, manners, books, and opinions" (12). This claim echoes that of eighteenth-century novels, whose novelty in fact constituted their appeal.[84] At the same time, in other contexts Austen derides the market-driven production of books. In a letter to her sister, she sneers that Owenson's *Ida of Athens* "must be very clever, because it was written as the Authoress says, in three months" (letter 64, Tuesday, 17 January 1809, 251). Like Bingley's boasted epistolary rapidity, this scramble to print rates performance above product.

Austen's contempt for the literature produced as cheap self-display extends to the literature packaged for similar purposes. When she describes Catherine Morland's fashionable literacy, she uses conventional printing techniques to mimic the format of books of literary "beauties." Newly inventing herself as a heroine, Catherine begins to read, but not for knowledge. Excerpts from Pope, Gray, Thompson, and Shakespeare, neatly excerpted in Austen's own text as they are in commercial anthologies, teach Catherine the additude of sentimental indulgence: to respect "woe" rather than to laugh at it, to encourage youthful expression, "the young idea," rather than to repress it, and to regard "trifles" as significant rather than to look for proof. Like Sterne's Uncle Toby, she learns to sympathize with insects, and like Viola in Shakespeare's *Twelfth Night,* she studies self-pity. This printing format of selecting short passages from their original texts, and listing them under categories for quick reference redesigns literature as sentimental snippets for the culturally illiterate, particularly women and children. Although Catherine *can* "read poetry, and plays, and things of that sort," and does not "dislike travels," it is significant that she prefers novels, although the narrator attributes to poetry the female posture of sentimental reception by which Catherine learns to feel like a heroine. Her decontextualization of General Tilney as a Gothic murderer rather than a domestic tyrant demonstrates the flaws in this literary culture and in this use of it, as do the lies of the boorish John Thorpe, who is educated like Catherine only by reading—so thoughtlessly that he forgets the author's name—Mrs. Radcliffe's novels (38–39).[85]

Catherine's preference for fiction exposes the gender bias of a literary culture that packages male sentiments for female consumption. Famously in this novel, Austen indicts a marketplace that segregates praise from popularity by rewarding male literature and denigrating novels and heroines. *Northanger Abbey* openly discusses the politics of the literary marketplace in terms of both gender and genre. Defending contemporary literature, the author in her own voice avers that women writers belong to a "literary corporation" and need to promote their own products both within and beyond the text; only this will combat the "pride, ignorance, [and] fashion" of male "Reviewers," who prefer the works of "the nine-hundredth abridger of *The History of England*," Addison and Steele's *Spectator*, Milton, and Prior, and collections of eighteenth-century texts to Frances Burney's novels (37). Since works by these male authors were plentifully republished in the late eighteenth and nineteenth centuries, notably in anthologies, they exemplify the contents of such libraries as Austen's father's.[86] In attacking this narrow yet commercial literary taste, Austen argues for new books pleasing to a current and a female audience: novels with style, realism, and morality.

Austen's fictional values advocate female self-reliance. Whereas fashionable texts popularize female self-destruction, Austen's novels redefine fine feeling and style as rational judgment.[87] Especially in *Sense and Sensibility*, Austen lambasts a commercialization of literary values that injures women. In this novel about the romantic Marianne and the self-disciplined Elinor, popular poetry corrupts personality. More refined and talented than Catherine Morland, both sisters like literature, but whereas Elinor balances reading with social duties, Marianne fashions herself on late eighteenth-century verse. She vets her romantic suitor Willoughby only by determining that he loves music, dancing, Cowper, and Scott while "admiring Pope no more than is proper" (47). So ignorant is she of the common motivations of flattery, desire, and duplicity that she never questions that he cherishes exactly "the same passages" and poetic "beauties" as she does (47). To please her, however, Willoughby easily mimics a taste conditioned by commercially packaged culture. Indeed, Marianne herself, like Catherine Morland, is educated by editorial formulae that fragment poetry into specific passages and "beauties"; in according Pope, the representative of a prior generation, "proper" admiration, she even proportions her "instinctive" taste by convention. As Edward Ferrars jokes, were Marianne rich, "she would buy" Thomson, Cowper, and Scott "over and over again," indeed "buy up every copy . . . to prevent their falling into unworthy hands; and she would [buy] every book that tells her how to admire an old twisted tree" (92). Her identity as a woman of rare taste is shaped by the hackneyed judgments of editors and critics.[88]

Not only does Marianne's fashionable reading tell her how to feel, but it desocializes her. It keeps her ignorant of such vices as Willoughby's mercenary weakness and confirms her prejudice against good manners: whenever she enters a house, she seeks the library "however it might be avoided by the family in general," instead of civilly joining her hosts (304). She even interprets others' social demeanors according to current theories about how to display taste. When she pities her sister for the "spiritless" and "tame" way in which Edward reads Cowper aloud, she assumes that she can gauge his capacity for love from his manner of poetic delivery (17). By confusing art with the heart, Marianne misreads the very cribs on oratory on which she bases her taste. In the typical *Hints for Improvement in the Art of Reading,* for example, the schoolteacher J. Walker underscores the artistry of reading aloud and the way, properly manipulated, rhetorical delivery can advertise the speaker: "as a skilful [*sic*] painter covers, but does not totally hide the muscles of the body, so a perfect speaker, even in the most careless and rapid pronunciation, gives a certain delicate hint to the existence of the letters, which infallibly shows he is acquainted with the orthography of his language."[89] Walker suggests that this skill demonstrates the speaker's education. Furthermore, by arguing that "those readers are the best, who can act the part of the author or speaker most naturally," he advocates reading in a manner that transforms the reader into a surrogate for the writer (3). He endorses fashioning the self according to the text: "The art of reading with justness, energy and ease, consists chiefly in adopting as much as possible, the words of an author for our own, and pronouncing them as if they were conceived expressly for the present purpose" (1). This is precisely what Henry Crawford, the creature of London fashion, does in *Mansfield Park,* when he mutates his public self by reading Shakespeare to enchant Fanny Price.[90] Marianne innocently adheres to Walker's theory by interpreting Edward's "impenetrable calmness" and "dreadful indifference" in reading as a sign of his imperviousness to love (18). Ironically, she deplores in him the very integrity she is seeking. While "it was impossible for her to say what she did not feel," she conforms entirely to literary models, whereas Edward's subjectivity rejects fashionable shaping (122). For Marianne, reading realizes the self rather than connecting that self with a moral world.[91] Similarly in *Sanditon,* Sir Edward Denham, awash in Scott, Burns, and "all the usual Phrases" praising their "Sublimity," constructs an identity as a romantic rake, which he verifies by "the number of his Quotations," and received, poetic opinions that "bewilder" his meaning (396). Like him, Marianne is a victim of the commercialization of reading.

In *Sense and Sensibility,* commercial culture commodifies feeling and usurps identity. Marianne's wish to "buy up every copy" of the verse she loves "to prevent it from falling into unworthy hands" betrays her naive transference of the values of rarity and refinement to print culture. She fetishizes print, ignoring these books' commercial conditions of production and reproduction and instead sentimentalizing and personalizing them as expressions of her individuality.[92] Her passion for the piano similarly indicates her adoption of fashionable skills to display romantic identity. Significantly, circulating libraries rented music as well as books, so the same source feeds her musical as her literary taste. This definition of the self as consumer reappears in the motif of purchasing in the novel. For example, Marianne and Elinor Dashwood are exchanging "a few old-fashioned jewels of [their] mother" at Gray's in Sackville Street, a jeweler's shop that flourished around 1800. The shop is busy:

> and they were obliged to wait. All that could be done was, to sit down at that end of the counter which seemed to promise the quickest succession; one gentleman only was standing there, and it is probable that Elinor was not without hope of exciting his politeness to a quicker dispatch. But the correctness of his eye, and the delicacy of his taste, proved to be beyond his politeness. He was giving orders for a toothpick-case for himself, and till its size, shape, and ornaments were determined, all of which, after examining and debating for a quarter of an hour over every toothpick-case in the shop, were finally arranged by his own inventive fancy, he had not leisure to bestow any other attention on the two ladies, than what was comprised in three or four very broad stares . . .
>
> Marianne was spared from the troublesome feelings of contempt and resentment, on this impertinent examination of their features, and on the puppyism of his manner in deciding on all the different horrors of the different toothpick-cases presented to his inspection, by remaining unconscious of it all; for she was as well able to collect her thoughts within herself, and be as ignorant of what was passing around her, in Mr. Gray's shop, as in her own bed-room.
>
> At last the affair was decided. The ivory, the gold, and the pearls all received their appointment and the gentleman having named the last day on which his existence could be continued without the possession of the toothpick-case, drew on his gloves with leisurely care, and bestowing another glance on the Miss Dashwoods, but such a one as seemed rather to demand than express admiration, walked off with an happy air of real conceit and affected indifference. (220–21)

Mr. Robert Ferrars, arrogant, empty-headed fop and brother to Elinor's love Edward, dallies self-pleasingly over his choice in a vulgar display of pseudo-aristocratic sensitivity. He glances at the waiting women, his audience, to make sure that they see and admire him, and to evaluate their suitability as items to be bought: he examines their features as he does his toothpick-cases. But in commodifying them as cases for his implement, he commodifies himself. He performs discrimination, as his brother Edward so obstinately refuses to do when to Marianne's despair he admires Elinor's painting "as a lover, not as a connoisseur" (17). Robert's performance of discrimination is designed to display his wealth, fine taste, and high standing in the sexual or marriage market, but it makes him a thing. Ironically, by remaining locked in her own sorrow and blind and deaf to all around her, Marianne escapes the irritation Elinor feels, but she exemplifies romantic self-display: her subjectivity is molded by bought culture. Marianne is engaged in a sentimental performance; her poetic consumption almost consumes her to death.

Consumer items such as this ivory, gold, and pearl box, and especially jewelry, exemplify the commodification of the self, and it is no coincidence that the two most important symbolic uses of jewelry occur in the novels that comment most openly on sentimentalism.[93] Austen treats jewelry as the display of relationships. In *Mansfield Park*, Fanny Price combines the gold chains given to her by Edmund and Henry with her brother's amber cross to fashion herself as loved by and related to the high society of Mansfield at her coming out ball. In *Sense and Sensibility*, the faithless Willoughby cuts a lock of Marianne's hair as a keepsake, an act interpreted as proof of their engagement; and Edward wears a hair ring, which Elinor falsely believes to be her own hair, but which actually belongs to Lucy Steele, and symbolizes their engagement. This motif of hair rings, at once unique and replicable, reprises Marianne's confusion of commodity and feeling. Rings traditionally represent romantic commitment, and hair jewelry, albeit all the rage in the Regency, was not a new fad.[94] Hair rings and lockets were popular throughout the eighteenth century. When the Baron rapes Belinda's lock in Pope's poem, a court-lady laments:

> Gods! shall the Ravisher display your Hair,
> While the Fops envy, and the Ladies stare! . . .
> And shall this Prize, th'inestimable Prize,
> Ezpos'd thro' Crystal to the gazing Eyes,
> And heighten'd by the Diamond's circling Rays,
> On that Rapacious Hand for ever blaze? (IV, 103–4, 113–16)

While jewelry made from the body of the beloved seems to proclaim sexual or marital possession, its display as a trophy connotes the public proclamation of sexual unity, as Pope explicates when Belinda, the epitome of vanity and show, laments to the Baron: "Oh hadst thou, cruel! been content to seize / Hairs less in sight, or any hairs but these!" (IV, 175–76). This rape is particularly noxious because of its publicity: it is the public usurpation of the woman's will. When Elinor misreads Edward's ring as her own hair, she assumes a public proclamation of a private feeling, just as Marianne believes Willoughby will marry her. Willoughby, however, conceals Marianne's hair whereas Edward displays Lucy's: this symbolizes Willoughby's desire to possess Marianne privately, and Edward's public admission of belonging to Lucy. If objects do not carry feeling with them, they nonetheless represent it in public. These tensions between feeling and form, display and concealment, literary and social values are the focus of the book.[95]

Pride and Prejudice juxtaposes two uses of reading: as self-exhibition or self-concealment, both versions of selfishness, and as a means for the socialization of the self. This latter, social use is exemplified by Colonel Fitzwilliam, whose excellent "manners" include talking entertainingly of "new books and music" to Elizabeth Bennet at Rosings (172). In contrast, Caroline Bingley reads to advertise her pliancy as a marriage partner to Darcy. After dinner at Netherfield,

> Darcy took up a book; Miss Bingley did the same; and Mrs. Hurst principally occupied in playing with her bracelets and rings, joined now and then in her brother's conversation with Miss Bennet.
>
> Miss Bingley's attention was quite as much engaged in watching Mr. Darcy's progress though *his* book, as in reading her own; and she was perpetually either making some inquiry, or looking at his page. She could not win him, however, to any conversation; he merely answered her question, and read on. At length, quite exhausted by the attempt to be amused with her own book, which she had only chosen because it was the second volume of his, she gave a great yawn, and said, "How pleasant it is to spend an evening in this way! I declare after all there is no enjoyment like reading! How much sooner one tires of any thing than of a book!—When I have a house of my own, I shall be miserable if I have not an excellent library."
>
> No one made any reply. She then yawned again, threw aside her book, and cast her eyes round the room in quest of some amusement. (54–55)

Austen compares Caroline's reading to her sister Mrs. Hurst's playing with her jewelry: both activities draw attention to their "improvement." For women whose status depends on their husbands, books and jewelry become commodities announcing refinement.

Austen equates silent reading in public with other forms of inadequate entertainment like cards—a symbol of disunity in *Sense and Sensibility* and *Emma*—that work to veil yet preserve rifts between characters, instead of joining them in rational sociability. Although innocent of Caroline's publicizing of her "good taste" in ostentatiously reading, Darcy himself is similarly guilty of using books for tainted purposes—not to win a spouse but to escape one. Elizabeth demonstrates the right uses of reading by abandoning her book as soon as she is asked. By asking Elizabeth to walk about the room, Caroline intends to display a charm in which she wisely has more confidence than her mind: her figure. Her display leads Darcy, hoping for a parallel display of Elizabeth's mind, to "unconsciously [close] his book," initiating his symbolic movement from self-absorption to socialization (56). But it is Mr. Bennet who exemplifies the misuse of reading. He retreats regularly to his library, his "sanctuary," to escape his wife and his responsibilities in bringing up his five daughters. "In his library he had been always sure of leisure and tranquillity; and though prepared, as he told Elizabeth, to meet with folly and conceit in every other room in the house, he was used to be free from them there" (71). The result of this retreat is disastrous. It brings on Darcy's contempt for the family, the temporary division of Jane and Bingley, and the elopement of his youngest daughter Lydia with the penniless liar Wickham. Mr. Bennet and Darcy exhibit the social distortion promoted by the dangerously isolating fascination of the male, private library.

Just as Mr. Bennet has abandoned his paternal role and will lose his estate and name, however, so his gentlemanly ideal of intellectual converse is retreating before the new values, embodied in the sociable Mr. Collins. "Much better fitted for a walker than a reader," yet posturing as a man of learning, Collins, "nominally engaged with one of the largest folios in the collection, but really talking to Mr. Bennet," penetrates Mr. Bennet's male sanctuary to gossip (71). To assert his weightiness, he chooses a book that symbolizes elite culture by style and format, "one of the largest folios in the collection." For him, as for Caroline Bingley, books are props. Although he lingers about Mr. Bennet's library, he does no more there than in his own, where he perpetually looks out of the window in search of Lady Catherine De Bourgh. Nonetheless, he advocates reading as moral improvement for women. Protesting in horror that "he never read novels," he remarks: '"I have often observed how little young ladies are interested by books of a serious stamp; though written solely for their benefit. It amazes me, I confess;—for certainly, there can be nothing so advantageous to them as instruction'" (69). Darcy repeats this sanctimonious opinion when he proclaims reading the most essential element of (female) education. In describing women's ideal accomplishments, he concurs with Caroline Bingley in listing music, singing, drawing, dancing, modern languages, elegance, gentle manners, but adds as most "substantial" "the improvement of her mind by extensive reading" (39). Austen satirizes this masculine prescription by showing the way it turns reading into an exhibition of marriageability. The pedantic Mary Bennet, satirically described as "a young lady of deep reflection" who reads "a great many books, and make[s] extracts," performs reading as she does playing the piano: to show off (7). Unlike Marianne Dashwood, she is aware of it—but this scarcely excuses her in Austen's eyes. On the contrary, her performance reveals a cynical conformity to male standards.

Austen's next novel may partly reflect a new-found evangelicalism by representing solitary reading as a sign of moral purity, but it also ridicules unsocialized reading.[96] *Mansfield Park* recounts the story of the timid Fanny Price, who selflessly watches the seduction of her cousins Edmund, Maria, and Julia Bertram by the sophisticated Mary and Henry Crawford from London. The Crawfords, her moral opposites, are well-read but in an outmoded tradition that spurs their moral depravity. This is exemplified by Mary's witty parody of Isaac Hawkins Browne's "Address to Tobacco," itself a parody of poetic styles:

> "Do you remember Hawkins Browne's 'Address to Tobacco,' in imitation of Pope?—
>> 'Blest leaf! whose aromatic gales dispense
>> To Templars modesty, to Parsons sense.'
> I will parody them:
>> Blest Knight! whose dictatorial looks dispense
>> To Children affluence, to Rushworth sense." (161)

This clever impertinence mocking the authority of Sir Thomas Bertram, the head of the household, links Mary's moral corruption to literary decadence: she is parodying a parody, showing herself to be shaped by an exhausted culture. Indeed, as actors in their own play mimicking Kotzebue's sexual melodrama, *Lover's Vows,* both Mary and Henry perform the sentimental dictum of seeking the fulfillment of personal desire, albeit this paradoxically is a desire that encompasses "affluence" and "sense."

Likewise, Fanny's reading educates her inadequately. Admittedly, works by Cowper, Thomson, and Crabbe, and travelogues such as Lord Macartney's *Embassy of China* have taught her the names of the stars, love of nature, and reverence for history. However, this education is outdated.

When she learns of Mr. Rushworth's desire to modernize or "improve" his estate by cutting down an avenue of trees, she quotes Cowper sadly, "Ye fallen avenues, once more I mourn your fate unmerited" (56). When she visits his chapel, she deplores the absence of grandeur by quoting from Sir Walter Scott's *Lay of the Last Minstrel* (86).[97] When she applies sentimental poetry to life, she shows a naive bookishness like Marianne Dashwood's. When she visits her sister in Portsmouth and learns that a silver knife causes dissension between her sisters, she presumes that the rivalry arises from jealous sentiment, because the knife is the relic of a dead sibling. On buying Susan a replacement with her modest £10, however, she discovers how wrong she is, for Susan is delighted: "its newness giving it every advantage over the other" because it is a "full possession of her own" (397). The siblings' rivalry is focused on possession, not affection. Whereas the sentimental poetry Fanny reads teaches a false sanctification of the symbolically laden object, public libraries offer a more powerfully enfranchising form of possession by translating reading into social authority and personal control. Missing the "potent and stimulative" force of reading, symbol of the refinement of Mansfield Park,

> Fanny found it impossible not to try for books again. There were none in her father's house; but wealth is luxurious and daring—and some of hers found its way to a circulating library. She became a subscriber—amazed at being any thing *in propria persona*, amazed at her own doings in every way; to be a renter, a chuser of books! And to be having any one's improvement in view in her choice! But so it was. Susan had read nothing, and Fanny longed to give her a share in her own first pleasures, and inspire a taste for the biography and poetry which she delighted in herself. (398)

In a circulating library Fanny exercises almost masculine power in her own person—Austen emphasizes the significance of this role by using the Latin legal term—as discriminating cultural consumer, educator of a family, model for an heir, and patron of authors.

Reading in gender-neutral or female spaces distinguishes moral from mercenary values. Austen dramatizes this point briefly in *The Watsons* by depicting books as Emma Watson's escape both from her society's "hard-hearted prosperity, low-minded conceit, and wrong-headed folly," and from her own dissatisfaction. Her father, "being a Man of Sense and Education" is "a welcome companion," but if he is too ill for "converse," in his bed chamber at least she has "leisure" to "read & think." Literature also distracts the mind from brooding: "when Thought had been freely indulged, in contrasting the past & the present, the employment of the

Plate 4: "The Library" by Elias Martin, 1771(?). Courtesy of the Print Collection of the Lewis Walpole Library, Yale University. This watercolor depicts an elegant, solitary young lady reading a folio that rests on a globe, and holding her forehead pensively in a library adorned with bookshelves and a classical bust. While the setting symbolizes the temporal and spatial scope of knowledge afforded by the library, the figure's elaborate costume, headdress, and jewelry identify reading as a fashionable feminine pursuit.

mind, the dissipation of unpleasant ideas which only reading could produce, made her thankfully turn to a book" (*Minor Works,* 361). Like Fanny Price, Emma Watson uses reading for mental discipline, escape, and education. Literature here offers spiritual improvement in contrast to the displays of wealth, class, and the body through the clothes and the consumption of food that engrosses the rest of the characters.

Emma explores an opposition between frankness and duplicity that reprises perceived changes in the industrializing world, where village relations and intimate connections were being severed, and Austen works out this theme in the uses of literacy in the book. Cultural tensions between openness and concealment are manifested in the negotiation of traditional and new conditions of both reading and authorship for Austen and her audience. Reading is the mark of gentility for Emma Woodhouse. Snobbishly, she resists the fact that the farmer Mr. Martin (surely partly named after the Mrs. Martin to whose library the Austen family subscribed) reads for entertainment, "information," and moral improvement, not only supposing that he "does not read," but, when corrected, arguing that he should not (29, 34). Her resistance betrays Emma's belief that such tastes indicate a social mobility threatening to Emma's romantic economy of social status. By maintaining that those engaged in the "market" should not read, Emma attempts to separate the realm of imagination, gentility, and elegant culture from the commercial world. Ironically, Emma intends to usurp Mr. Martin's role as reader to Harriet by educating Harriet herself: Mrs. Weston asserts that Emma and Harriet "will read together. She means it, I know" (36). Mr. Knightley retorts that "Emma has been meaning to read more ever since she was twelve years old," and recites her various principles of organizing literature, imitating those of anthologizers like Vicesimus Knox, whose texts are cited in the novel (37).[98] Emma, however, uses her education for self-display, not self-discipline. Whereas Mr. Woodhouse utters childish rhymes, and Emma initiates Harriet in Gothic fictions, Mr. Martin, by reading the *Elegant Extracts* aloud, exhibits social responsibility—just as Mr. Knightley does when he corrects Emma. In forgetting her request for Radcliffe's *Romance of the Forest* when pressed about business, Mr. Martin also exhibits a masculine regard for money over mystery, which Emma reads as a class sign (32). As an example of a contented, self-made man, moreover, Mr. Martin portrays the ideal that Pierre Bourdieu has observed of peaceful peasants reading in groups, an image which, after the French Revolution, symbolized harmonious class relations.[99] Mr. Knightley reinforces this value when he responds aloud to Frank's self-exculpatory, explanatory letter by condemning his effeteness (436–48). Emma, herself undisciplined, genders as feminine reading for self-indulgence, while reading for profit remains masculine.[100]

Elegance is the most contentious value in *Emma*. Reiterated throughout the novel, it is the cherished criterion both of Emma and of Mrs. Elton, for both women see it as the boundary demarcating classes: gentlemen like Mr. Knightley possess it, whereas upstarts like Mr. Elton, as Emma recognizes, ape it.[101] Emma detects it in what she terms "manner": gesture, attitude, conversation, self-presentation (32). She applauds her father's "gentleness" as truly gentlemanlike in contrast to Mr. Martin's "unmodulated" voice, yet she labels Mr. Knightley's abruptness exemplary (32–33). In seeing the sign "gentleman . . . so plainly written" on his face, she confuses the superficial and the behavioral. Indeed, she herself is guilty of vulgarity, as Austen's satiric narrator shows by glossing "elegance" as a commercial code for exploiting the socially ambitious, a show of fineness in direct opposition to "real" values (33). The narrator sneers, for example, at the advertisement of fashionable schools that promise in "long sentences of refined nonsense, to combine liberal acquirements with elegant morality upon new principles and new systems—and where young ladies for enormous pay might be screwed out of health and into vanity," preferring such establishments as Mrs. Goddard's "real, honest, old-fashioned Boarding-School" (21). Again, she contrasts superficial and moral evaluation by means of Frank Churchill's first letter: "For a few days every morning visit in Highbury included some mention of the handsome letter Mrs. Weston had received. 'I suppose you have heard of the handsome letter Mr. Frank Churchill had written to Mrs. Weston? I understand it was a very handsome letter, indeed. Mr. Woodhouse told me of it. Mr. Woodhouse saw the letter, and he says he never saw such a handsome letter in his life' " (18). Vetted by the elite Mr. Woodhouse, the letter's superficial elegance supposedly guarantees its moral worth. In fact, it foreshadows Frank's less than frank manipulation of appearances to conceal his selfish desires. Nonetheless, for Highbury the letter stands for the man (as D. for Dixon, and M.A. for perfection). The letter serves socially to represent his handsome self. In contrast, Austen compels Emma herself to acknowledge the superior style of Mr. Martin's epistle to Harriet: "The style of his letter was much above her expectation. There were not merely no grammatical errors, but as a composition it would not have disgraced a gentleman; the language, though plain, was strong and unaffected, and the sentiments it conveyed very much to the credit of the writer. It was short, but expressed good sense, warm attachment, liberality, propriety, even delicacy of feeling" (51). Reluctant to grant a farmer such female delicacy, Emma suggests that "one of his sisters must have helped him," yet she detects gender in his style: "and yet it is not the style of a woman; no, certainly, it is too strong and concise; not diffuse enough for a woman. No doubt he is a sensible man, and I suppose may have a natural talent for—thinks strongly and clearly—and when he takes a pen in hand, his thoughts naturally find proper words" (51). Emma naturalizes education in a confused attempt to maintain class distinctions. Refusing to grant him education, she attributes his skill to his gender, and as a result reluctantly accords him innate gentlemanliness, like Mr. Knightley. Writing style and the interpretation of literary codes exhibit character. Similarly, other tasteful skills offer the opportunity to display an aesthetic receptiveness that can promise potential spouses that their wives will be able to advance in society. Emma's use of her skills, however, show her social indifference, or imperviousness. Her drawing should demonstrate pliability, talent, and taste, but in fact it exhibits her middle-class tendency to quantify value. When she exclaims, "What an exquisite possession a good picture of [Harriet] would be! I would give any money for it," she reveals her confusion of art and life, seeing both the friend and the portrait as possessed commodities (43). Emma's performance, however, makes her the object to be bought by Mr. Elton's flattery, not Harriet.

The equivalence of books and values exposes a network of social assumptions and practices based on gender and class prejudices, but Austen seeks not so much a rejection as a correction of materialization of value. Nowhere is this clearer than in *Persuasion*. The novel opens with a blunt satire on the vanity fostered by aristocratic, male literary culture.

> Sir Walter Elliot, of Kellynch-hall, in Somersetshire, was a man who, for his own amusement, never took up any book but the Baronetage; there he found occupation for an idle hour, and consolation in a distressed one; there his faculties were roused into admiration and respect, by contemplating the limited remnant of the earliest patents; there any unwelcome sensations, arising from domestic affairs, changed naturally into pity and contempt, as he turned over the almost endless creations of the last century—and there, if every other leaf were powerless, he could read his own history with an interest which never failed. (3)

Sir Walter avoids domestic feeling and responsibility by reading his own public identity. Indeed, the printed record replaces the current reality, since his extravagance drives him to rent his own estate, and thus sell his identity as a landed baronet. Male, print culture, however, protects him: it "naturally detaches" him from the immediate by contextualizing him in history,

as he recontextualizes the women related to him by printing "most accurately" the dates of his wife's death, his three daughters' birthdays, and the
marriage of his youngest child. Similarly, contemporary poetry shapes the
identities of the mobile classes. The recently bereaved Captain Benwick,
like *Sanditon's* Sir Edward Denham, advertises his capacity for love to
Anne by displaying that he is "intimately acquainted with all the tenderest
songs of [Scott], and all the impassioned descriptions of hopeless agony of
[Byron]" (100). The repetition of "all" slyly insinuates that Sir Edward
quantifies this poetry as much as the booksellers and printers who reproduce it in volume. Anne, however, rejects this self-display. When "he
repeated, with such tremulous feeling, the various lines which imaged a
broken heart, or a mind destroyed by wretchedness . . . that she ventured to
hope he did not always read only poetry," she suggests "such works of our
best moralists, such collections of the finest letters, such memoirs of characters of worth and suffering, as [are] calculated to rouse and fortify the
mind by the highest precepts, and the strongest examples of moral and
religious endurances [*sic*]" (100–101). Whereas Anne uses literature to
educate the heart, Benwick uses it to display it.

This difference between the uses of literature as self-affirmation and as
information reappears at the end of the novel when Anne disputes Captain
Harville's claim that men have more loyalty than women. Harville grounds
his argument in literary tradition, whereas Anne refutes both. He says:

> "we shall never agree upon this point. No man and woman would, probably.
> But let me observe that all histories are against you, all stories, prose and
> verse. If I had such a memory as Benwick, I would bring you fifty quotations
> in a moment on my side [of] the argument, and I do not think I ever opened
> a book in my life which had not something to say upon woman's inconstancy.
> Songs and proverbs, all talk of woman's fickleness. But perhaps you will say,
> these were all written by men."
>
> "Perhaps I shall.—Yes, yes, if you please, no reference to examples in
> books. Men have had every advantage of us in telling their own story. Educa-
> tion has been theirs in so much higher a degree; the pen has been in their
> hands. I will not allow books to prove any thing." (234)

Austen underscores the difference between her own novel and the literature absorbed by such men as Harville and Benwick. Whereas this male
literary culture indicts women, women now have the opportunity to write
and read the other side of the story. By this intratextuality, Austen inscribes
herself into history, usurping Sir Walter Elliot's social and literary lineage
with a new print culture of female fiction.

Austen's final work, written well into the nineteenth century, *Sanditon,* most openly derides the reduction of literary culture to a commodity for acquisition and self-advertisement. Sanditon symbolizes the commercialization of social relations, culture, and identity. In describing the efforts of an entrepreneur and his hypochondriacal sisters to establish a new seaside resort, the story addresses the effect of commercialization and self-promotion. Since it embodies Mr. Parker's dreams of profit and prominence, he scrutinizes every aspect of it as a sign of class. The subscription library, notably, represents Sanditon's promise of an eminence ostensibly intellectual but actually social: as did circulating libraries throughout the period, it provides a space that facilitates the mingling of the elite with other classes.[102] Early in the novel, after dinner Mr. Parker takes the heroine Charlotte Heywood there to find companionship, since "The Shops were deserted—the Straw Hats and pendant Lace seemed left to their fate both within the House & without" (*Minor Works,* 389). Mr. Parker equates the library as a site of consumption and display with shops, particularly dress shops, seeing both as offering commodities that exhibit a refined self. He uses commodities to find company, in the fashion that Michael Schudson theorizes:

> a consumer culture is . . . a society in which human values have been grotesquely distorted so that commodities become more important than people, or, in an alternative formulation, commodities become not ends in themselves but over-valued means for acquiring acceptable ends like love and friendship. The criticism [of this culture] is either that people sacrifice themselves to the pursuit of goods in order to accumulate wealth or that they sacrifice themselves to the pursuit of goods in order to accumulate people.[103]

In his pursuit of people to inhabit Sanditon, and of Sanditon to contain people, Mr. Parker mirrors the new values of the nineteenth century. Indeed, by the end of the previous century, advertisements were endemic, and display, notably of women's fashions, an art, especially in London. Sophie von la Roche notes in 1786,

> the fine shops jut out at both sides of the front doors like big, broad oriels, having fine large window-panes, behind which wares were displayed, so that these shops look far more elegant than those in Paris. . . . Every article is made more attractive to the eye. . . . We especially noted a cunning device for showing women's materials. Whether they are silks, chintzes or muslins, they hang down in folds behind the fine high windows so that the effect of that material, as it would be in the ordinary folds of a woman's dress, can be studied.[104]

Plate 5: "Beauty in search of Knowledge," 30 Dec. 1782. Courtesy of the Print Collection of the Lewis Walpole Library, Yale University. This print portrays a woman dressed in the height of fashion, carrying an elegant parasol and sporting a modish hat, pausing in front of the windows of a circulating library where equivalently fashionable books and prints are displayed.

Indeed, as Christopher Breward has observed, "Display became an increasingly important element of the shopkeeper's repertoire, alongside the promotional panache of advertising, in a bid to convince buyers that they too were engaging in a world of refined fashionability."[105] Sophie von la Roche reveals the way such displays mold appetite: "Behind great glass windows absolutely everything one can think of is neatly, attractively displayed, and in such abundance of choice as almost to make one greedy" (87). *Persuasion* also anatomizes the new value of display. At the center of the novel is Louisa Musgrove's exhibitionism, indicted through a significant fall that injures her mind and her marriageability. The still more vain Sir Walter also embodies the values of cheap display by rating passing women on their faces and boasting of his own good looks, even while he prides himself on his lineage. By advertising his face yet refusing to advertise his house, he exhibits the contemporary hypocrisy of snobbish distinctions. Similarly, in *Sanditon*, Mr. Parker desires not to read books, but to con "the Library Subscription book," which, like Sir Walter Elliot's *Baronetage*, locates him in society. He finds this list "but commonplace"—a punning play on the reciprocal mediocrity of social and literary contexts—since it contains few titled subscribers. It is "not only without Distinction, but less numerous than he had hoped" (389). Far from an intellectual resource, the library is a social gauge used to show the self in a culture of display. This library exemplifies the coopting of literary culture, and by extension moral values and social roles, by commercialism.

This commercial literacy offered opportunities and dangers particularly to women, newly enfranchised as readers and writers in a fluid society. If in their role as writers women like Burney and Austen herself can use this culture, in their role as consumers their integrity can be threatened. Like Austen herself, Charlotte subscribes in *Sanditon*, yet this very act—which allows her to choose texts and thus to influence the taste of the town—simultaneously makes her, as a tourist, a commodity the town can sell.[106] The narrator reports, "Charlotte having added her name to the List as the first offering to the success of the Season, was busy in some immediate purchases for the further good of Every body, as soon as Miss Whitby could be hurried down from her Toilette, with all her glossy Curls & smart Trinkets to wait on her" (390). Charlotte is the "offering" for the "further good of Every body," as is Marianne in *Sense and Sensibility* through her marriage to Colonel Brandon. Moreover, although the books she examines include women's literature, the social and financial freedom they represent for women is threatened by the promotion of a role for women as consumers. The library's proprietor, significantly, is a woman who acts as seller. In observing that "Mrs. Whitby at the Library was sitting in her inner room, reading one of her own Novels, for want of Employment," Austen attacks a literary culture dedicated to marketing commodities rather than promoting reflection or self-control: Mrs. Whitby's novels—those she possesses—are those she vends, not those she has written or read. Whereas this spend-mad culture encourages female profligacy, women's texts like *Sanditon* and Burney's *Camilla* urge thrift, charity, modesty, and balance for moral as well as fiscal reasons.

> The Library of course, afforded every thing; all the useless things in the World that c^d not be done without, & among so many pretty Temptations, & with so much good will for M^r P[arker] to encourage Expenditure, Charlotte began to feel that she must check herself—or rather she reflected that at two & Twenty there c^d be no excuse for her doing otherwise—& that it w^d not do for her to be spending all her Money the very first Evening. She took up a Book; it happened to be a vol: of *Camilla*. She had not *Camilla*'s Youth, & had no intention of having her Distress,—so, she turned from the Drawers of rings & Broches [*sic*] repressed farther solicitation & paid for what she bought. (390)

In contrast to Mrs. Whitby's pecuniary practice and in spite of the consumerism of the libraries in which it appears, Burney's text teaches restraint. Indeed, *Cecilia* offers the model of charity to counter self-pleasuring expenditure, but such a moral lesson violates Mr. Parker's aims and the culture of purchase and self-promotion in *Sanditon*.[107]

Libraries represent one form of the commercialization of value in the book, one particularly threatening to women, but the class ambiguity of money forms a central theme in *Sanditon*. Lady Denham is especially anxious for Sanditon to fill quickly with the rich and bluntly identifies people who promise to settle there as sources of wealth.

> Miss Diana Parker's two large Families were not forgotten. "Very good, very good, said her Ladyship.—A West Indy Family & a school. That sounds well, That will bring Money."—"No people spend more freely, I believe [*sic*], than W. Indians." observed Mr Parker.—"Aye—so I have heard—and because they have full Purses, fancy themselves equal, may be, to your old Country Families. But then, they who scatter their Money so freely, never think of whether they may not be doing mischeif [*sic*] by raising the price of Things—And I have heard that's very much the case with your West-injines—and if they come among us to raise the price of our necessaries of Life, we shall not much thenk [*sic*] them Mr Parker." (392)

Austen's language underscores the reduction of people to possessions: her locution suggests that the two "Families" belong to Diana Parker as capi-

tal, an innuendo emphasizing their marginal status as colonials or colo-
nized people. Lady Denham's snobbery emphasizes the hypocrisy of the
class system that feeds off colonial wealth but refuses social equality to
colonials, a system based on envy and denial. Moreover, by the contradictions in this argument that promotes spending yet blames inflation on
those who do spend, Austen accentuates the moral confusion symptomatic
of a society unable to distinguish "necessaries" (uncapitalized) from
"Things." Such class attitudes threaten women's integrity and autonomy,
as Charlotte's poverty and dependence exemplify. *Sanditon* anatomizes the
new role of women as middle-class consumers. Even while pointing out its
dangers, at the same time Austen suggests that commercialized culture can
offer virtuous models for women—through women's literary spaces, texts,
and sociability.

Conclusion

Deeply concerned in the debate about how, what, and why to read, Austen
endorses reading as the avenue to moral maturity, but she erodes the
various boundaries between kinds of literature. Herself writing in the
format of the popular novels she read, she illustrates the tensions between
women as literary creators through writing, and as literary subjects commodified by writing, and the parallel tensions between women as cultured
trophies, exhibited by men, and as cultural consumers, exhibiting for them.
As literary consumer and producer, she promotes a feminine ideal of correct consumption that entails the public use of things to symbolize relationships. Her books depict how, in a world where rural exchange is reced-
ing before a strengthening urban ethic, reading—especially reading her
own novels—and writing allow women to define and display themselves in
society. Thus, she reveals that both genre and literary hierarchy are mu-
table, since the writer's and reader's practices, themselves significantly
shaped by commercial venues and values, make texts meaningful.

Austen wrote in a genre oriented toward rapid reading and purveyed
primarily in a social and commercial space conceived as feminine: the
public library. This genre values development over repetition, periodical
climaxes over reflective passages, attention to fashion rather than to political topicality, and narrative guidance over epistolary self-revelation. This
formula was thematically geared for women's consumption, and organized
for a library borrowing system that demanded long but easily read narratives that were designed for sequential reading over a short time. Even
while conforming to these restrictions, however, Austen challenged the

division between male and female literacy. Her novels redefine women's literature as a method of socialization that claims moral equality for female readers and that transfers the private space of the father's library into a mental library of intertextual and intratextual allusions for women.[108] While Austen's novels move between echoing and mocking the conventional indictment of reading as a dangerous indulgence for women and between applauding and satirizing reading as the acquisition and demonstration of virtue, they all credit reading with the power to express self in a commercial culture. Austen claims for women self-determinacy in the space of literacy.

Notes

Preface

1. Annette Kolodny, "Dancing through the Minefield," in *The New Feminist Criticism,* ed. Elaine Showalter (New York: Pantheon, 1985), 154–55.

2. Toni Bowers, "Sex, Lies, and Invisibility," in *The Columbia History of the English Novel,* ed. John Richetti et al. (New York: Columbia University Press, 1994), 71.

3. Examples are Christine Blouch, "Eliza Haywood and the Romance of Obscurity," *SEL* 31 (1991): 535–52; Jane Jones, "New Light on the Background and Early Life of Aphra Behn," *Aphra Behn Studies* (Cambridge: Cambridge University Press, 1996), 310–20; and Carol Shiner Wilson, "Introduction," *The Galesia Trilogy and Selected Manuscript Poems of Jane Barker* (Oxford: Oxford University Press, 1997), xv–xliii.

4. Like Patrick Brantlinger and others who contributed to the MLA *Forum,* we find cultural studies, diverse as it is, to be a coherent discipline with well defined focii; see especially Brantlinger and Lutz P. Koepnick's contributions in *PMLA* 112 (1997): 266–67.

5. For example, both Everett Zimmerman's *The Boundaries of Fiction: History and the Eighteenth-Century British Novel* (Ithaca: Cornell University Press, 1996) and Homer O. Brown's *Institutions of the English Novel* (Philadelphia: University of Pennsylvania Press, 1997) give only passing attention to women writers.

6. Jane Miller, *Women Writing about Men* (London: Virago, 1986), 262.

Chapter 1: The Novel's Gendered Space

1. William B. Warner, "The Elevation of the Novel in England: Hegemony and Literary History," *ELH* 59 (1992): 577.

2. Paula Backscheider and John J. Richetti, eds., *Popular Fiction by Women, 1660–1730: An Anthology* (Oxford: Clarendon Press, 1996), ix–x.

3. Homer Brown summarizes the treatment of Defoe's texts and the prob-

lems novel theorists consistently raise in "The Institution of the English Novel: Defoe's Contribution," *Novel* 29 (1996): 299–313.

4. I am assuming, as numerous recent studies have documented, that the concept of an English literary canon postdates the period under discussion and must always be historicized.

5. See, for instance, Janet Wolff, "Texts and Institutions," in *Feminine Sentences* (Berkeley: University of California Press, 1990), 103–19, especially 108–11.

6. Throughout this chapter, I shall use "prose fiction" as a somewhat broader, more encompassing term than "novel." Operative definitions of "novel" are William Congreve's Preface to *Incognita,* Tobias Smollett's dedication to *Ferdinand Count Fathom,* and Clara Reeve's *Progress of Romance;* the pertinent sections are excerpted in *British Novelists, 1660–1800,* ed. Martin C. Battestin, *Dictionary of Literary Biography* (Detroit: Gale, 1985), 39:2, Appendix.

7. For Defoe and the old canonical writers, conceptions of the prose fiction context have not undergone much revision since the publication of books by Percy Adams, Maximillian Novak, Michael McKeon, and my own *Daniel Defoe: Ambition and Innovation.* It could be argued persuasively that evidence of an increasingly gendered history and criticism of the English novel is characteristic of the present time. "Thick description" is Gilbert Ryle's term, but it has been elaborated and made familiar by Clifford Geertz; see *The Interpretation of Cultures* (New York: Basic Books, 1973), 6–9. Thick description requires the recognition and unpacking of the "stratified hierarchy of meaningful structures" in terms of which gestures, utterances, and the like are "produced, perceived, and interpreted" (p. 7).

8. Michael McKeon raises the issue of "the origins of [the novel's] consciousness as a distinct category" in *The Origins of the English Novel* (Baltimore: Johns Hopkins University Press, 1987); for a summary of his conclusions, see pp. 265–67 and 410–11.

9. This is Julia Kristeva's definition, "Word, Dialogue, and Novel," *The Kristeva Reader,* ed. Toril Moi (New York: Columbia University Press, 1986), 36.

10. I would include representations and resolutions dictated by the conventions of genres and literary modes under "ideological" and largely agree with Terry Eagleton, *Criticism and Ideology: A Study in Marxist Literary Theory* (London: New Left Books, 1976), chap. 2; W. J. T. Mitchell finds the laws of gender to be the most fundamental ideological basis for laws of genre in George Lessing and others, *Iconology: Image, Text, Ideology* (Chicago: University of Chicago Press, 1986), 109.

11. In 1713, Defoe published *Memoirs of Count Tariff* and followed it with a series of political narratives that included such texts as *The Secret History of the White Staff,* and he published his last novel, *Roxana,* in 1725. For a brief discussion of the pre–*Robinson Crusoe* fictions, see my *Daniel Defoe: His Life*

(Baltimore: Johns Hopkins University Press, 1989), 342–44, 406–11, 417–23, and 442–47. See also Geoffrey Sill, *Defoe and the Idea of Fiction, 1713–1719* (Newark: University of Delaware Press, 1983), 96–118 et passim. I am aware of Furbank and Owens's desire to revise the Defoe canon, most recently in *Defoe De-attributions: A Critique of J. P. Moore's Checklist* (London: Hambledon Press, 1994); although I disagree with some of their opinions, I have been conservative in what I attribute to Defoe here.

I am not suggesting that Defoe was feminist or proto-feminist. As I have argued elsewhere and will assert briefly here, he reinscribes the patriarchy on his women characters; see " 'The Woman's Part': Richardson, Defoe, and the Horrors of Marriage," *The Past as Prologue,* ed. Carla Hay and Syndy Conger (New York: AMS Press, 1995), 205–31.

12. This figure has to be regarded cautiously; Michael Crump used the ESTC holdings in the British Library only, counted texts that used "novel" in the title (635 in the eighteenth century) and did not correct his figures for tales (957) or romances (195), Michael Crump, "Stranger than Fiction: The Eighteenth-Century True Story," *Searching the Eighteenth Century,* ed. Michael Crump and Michael Harris (London: British Library, 1983), 59–73. On the other hand, assuming that the libraries in the ESTC have a representative sample of everything printed in England, running statistical confidence intervals allows us to set the figure for novels at between 0.13 percent and 0.17 percent; the point estimate would be the same 0.15 percent. Laeticia Barbauld summarizes accurately: "But till the middle of the [eighteenth century], theatrical productions and poetry made a far greater part of polite reading than novels," "On the Origin and Progress of Novel-Writing," *The British Novelists* (London, 1810), 1:37.

13. See J. Paul Hunter, *Before Novels: The Cultural Contexts of Eighteenth-Century Fiction* (New York: W. W. Norton, 1990), for an overview of what was available to the reading public.

14. Representative titles are *The Northern Atalantis* by "Captain Bland," *The Court of Atalantis,* and, in 1715, *The German Atalantis,* "Written by a Lady." There was even *The New Atalantis, for the year 1713,* which included Barker's *Love Intrigues* and other fictions such as *The History of the Yorkshire Gentry; particularly the amours of Melissa.*

15. In *Farther Adventures,* for example, Crusoe is forced off the ship by a mutinous crew, just as Vendchurch had been. Jonathan Swift, a shrewd reader and unsympathetic critic of the early novel, selects this plot motivator for inclusion in *Gulliver's Travels* (part 4). Many of these books included pious passages in which travelers search for God's will; Paul Hunter catalogues in impressive detail the strain of "guide" books with their wealth of stories, *Before Novels,* 259–60 and 391–94.

16. Even very good recent books have neglected many of these writers and texts. Ros Ballaster does not consider Mary Hearne at all and has two pages on

Mary Davys, three on Penelope Aubin, and three on Jane Barker, *Seductive Forms* (Oxford: Oxford University Press, 1992). Catherine Gallagher does not mention Hearne, Davys, or Barker, has but two mentions of Haywood, and the only reference to Aubin is in a note, *Nobody's Story* (Berkeley: University of California Press, 1994). Janet Todd has one page on Hearne and calls her a "scandal writer"; she has four pages on Aubin and five on Davys, *The Sign of Angellica* (New York: Columbia University Press, 1989). Jane Spencer has a single page on Hearne, *The Rise of the Woman Novelist* (Oxford: Basil Blackwell, 1986). On the "stories" of the history of the novel and the handling of women writers, see William B. Warner, "The Elevation of the Novel in England: Hegemony and Literary History," *ELH* 59 (1992): 577–96; Cheryl Turner, *Living by the Pen* (London: Routledge, 1992), 1–4, 13–16; and Paula Backscheider and John J. Richetti, "Introduction," *Popular Fiction by Women, 1660–1730: An Anthology* (Oxford: Clarendon Press, 1996). Warner calls them "another earlier cultural terrain" but gives them considerable importance as "intertextual support" for the great novels of Richardson and Fielding (p. 584). In "Licensing Pleasure," he implies that the new attention to the earlier novels depends "upon a contemporary reinterpretation of what is happening in the novels" and topics with contemporary "critical currency," *The Columbia History of the British Novel*, ed. John Richetti et al. (New York: Columbia University Press, 1994), 18. Jerry C. Beasley has consistently noted that the later male novelists were "keenly aware of their female predecessors" and displayed "dependency upon" them; cf. "Politics and Moral Idealism: The Achievement of Some Early Women Novelists," *Fetter'd or Free?* ed. Mary Anne Schofield and Cecilia Macheski (Athens: Ohio University Press, 1986), 216–36, especially 221, 232–34. Catherine Gallagher remarks that as early as Sir Walter Scott the story of the novel is seen as progress away from women writers, *Nobody's Story*, 2.

17. In this short, early period, eight is a significant number, Judith Stanton, "Statistical Profile of Women Writing in English from 1660 to 1800," *Eighteenth-Century Women and the Arts*, ed. Frederick Keener and Susan Lorsch (New York: Greenwood, 1988), 251. Cheryl Turner lists fewer, but she counts book-length prose fiction only; her graphs are consistent with my reading of the significance of the 1720s, see *Living by the Pen*, 35–37, 212.

18. I have not counted three captains, Alexander Smith, Charles Walker, and Charles Johnson, who primarily collected "lives" of robbers, highwaymen, and interesting women. Except for Defoe, none of the men were primarily writers of fiction, and attributions to some of them remain uncertain. For example, William Pittis may not be the author of *The Jamaica Lady* and Arthur Blackamore is not always identified as the author of *Luck at Last* (1723). Pittis was primarily a poet, and Blackamore's only other fiction was *The Perfidious Brethren*, something of an imitation of *Tale of a Tub. Luck at Last* was based on Behn's

Wandering Beauty, William H. McBurney, *Four before Richardson* (Lincoln: University of Nebraska Press, 1963), xvi and 5.

19. Even in discussions of Thomas Southerne's adaptation of *Oroonoko,* Gildon subordinates discussion of the play to praise of Behn, *The Lives and Characters of the English Dramatick Poets* (London, 1699), 136. Janet Todd makes a circumstantial argument that Gildon wrote three other lives, *The Works of Aphra Behn,* ed. Janet Todd (Columbus: Ohio State University Press, 1992), 1:ix–x. Robert Adams Day demonstrates that little in the first biography was not already in print, "Aphra Behn's First Biography," *SB* 22 (1969): 227–40. For a brief biography of Gildon, see my introduction to *The Plays of Charles Gildon* (New York: Garland, 1979).

20. Lawrence Klein, "Gender, Conversation, and the Public Sphere in Early Eighteenth-Century England," *Textuality and Sexuality,* ed. Judith Still and Michael Worton (Manchester: Manchester University Press, 1993), 103 and 112.

21. See my discussion of public/private sphere issues in *The Intersections of the Public and Private Spheres in Early Modern England,* ed. Paula R. Backscheider and Timothy Dykstal (London: Frank Cass, 1996), 1–21.

22. My sources are ESTC searches and William McBurney, *A Checklist of English Prose Fiction, 1700–1739* (Cambridge: Harvard University Press, 1960), 33–35.

23. For some insight into the popularity of pirate and island narratives, see Percy Adams, *Travel Literature and the Evolution of the Novel* (Lexington: University Press of Kentucky, 1983), 123–31. Novels set in or partially in Turkey have been almost completely ignored.

24. This text is sometimes attributed to Charles Gildon, and some people have even questioned Butler's existence. Among her other publications are *Irish Tales* (1716).

25. For a related discussion of this novel's form and its influence, see my *Spectacular Politics* (Baltimore: Johns Hopkins University Press, 1993), 112–15. The form, of which the works of Madeleine de Scudéry are representative, has been receiving increased attention; see also Joan DeJean, *Tender Geographies: Women and the Origins of the Novel in France* (New York: Columbia University Press, 1991), and Ballaster, *Seductive Forms,* 42–66. The novels of the earlier period are permeated with now-lost allusions; for instance, Barker's heroine in *Exilius* is Clelia, and she shares many of the characteristics of de Scudéry's Clélie.

26. Many of the stories in collections by English authors are not original. For instance, Behn's "Lover's Watch" and "The Lady's Looking-Glass" in *The Histories and Novels of the Late Ingenious Mrs. Behn* (1696) are from Balthasar Bonnecorse's *La Montre,* Todd, *The Works of Aphra Behn,* 4:278; five of the fictions in Manley's collection *The Power of Love* are adapted from William

Painter's *Palace of Pleasure* (1566); Paul Chamberlen admits in the dedication to *Love in its Empire* that he wrote only the first "novel."

27. Michael Crump, "Stranger than Fiction," 16. Alvin Kernan brings together evidence that points to a sharp rise in the number of books published and then a slump; he notes that Alexander Pope's *Dunciad* (1728) "came at the end of a period of great expansion in printing activity," *Printing Technology, Letters and Samuel Johnson* (Princeton: Princeton University Press, 1987), 60–62. The percentage of novels published was not that great until the 1780s, Crump, "Stranger than Fiction," 17.

28. The poem can be read as intriguing commentary on Hearne's heroine; it advertises Matthew Prior as author and had commercial value for Curll. Katherine was the second daughter of Henry Hyde, earl of Clarendon and Rochester, and granddaughter of King Charles's Lord Chancellor and the author of *The History of the Rebellion*. In 1720, she married Charles Douglas, duke of Queensberry, and, later, in her support for John Gay would be banished from court. A woman of confidence, spirit, and independent mind, she wrote bantering notes to Jonathan Swift. Edmund Curll had published the poem as "The Female Phaeton"; it appears as "Upon Lady Katherine H-de's first appearing at the Play-House in Drury Lane" (London: Chetwood 1718) in *The Literary Works of Matthew Prior*, ed. H. Bunker Wright and Monroe K. Spears, 2 vols. (2d ed.; Oxford: Clarendon Press, 1971), 2:787–88, but they question Prior's authorship and note that it is also attributed to Simon Harcourt. Hearne may be responsible for the initial identification of the poem with Prior.

29. Woman, thus, became infinitely various—"splendid and sordid; infinitely beautiful and hideous in the extreme," Virginia Woolf, *A Room of One's Own* (New York: Harcourt Brace Jovanovich, 1957), 45. Society rarely agrees with Goethe about woman as trope for positive change: "Woman is the only remaining vase into which we can pour our ideality," quoted by Claudine Herrmann, *The Tongue Snatchers*, trans. Nancy Kline (Lincoln: University of Nebraska Press, 1989), 49. Jonathan Culler writes that French theorists see "*le feminin* as any force that disrupts the symbolic structures of Western thought," *On Deconstruction* (Ithaca: Cornell University Press, 1982), 49. Cora Kaplan argues that women as sites of anarchy and unreason are common and that "female sexuality, became the displaced and condensed site for the general anxiety about individual behavior," "Pandora's Box: Subjectivity, Class and Sexuality in Socialist Feminist Criticism," *Making a Difference: Feminist Literary Criticism*, ed. Gayle Greene and Coppélia Kahn (New York: Methuen, 1986), 172 and 165, respectively.

30. These descriptions are from Laura Brown, *Ends of Empire* (Ithaca: Cornell University Press, 1993), 16–17, 147, 150, 155–56, and Sandra Sherman, "Lady Credit No Lady; or, The Case of Defoe's 'Coy Mistress,' Truly Stat'd," *TSLL* 37 (1995): 186, 189, 202.

31. As Toni Bowers remarks, this fact is widely acknowledged; she cites

"critics as different as [Michael] McKeon and [Nancy] Armstrong," "Sex, Lies, and Invisibility," in Richetti et al., *Columbia History of the British Novel*, 58.

32. Quoted in Joan DeJean, *Tender Geographies*, 92.

33. Xavière Gauthier, from "Existe-t-il une écriture de femme?" in *New French Feminisms*, ed. Elaine Marks and Isabelle de Courtivron (New York: Schocken Books, 1981), 163.

34. Julia Kristeva, from "Oscillation du 'pouvoir' au 'refus,'" in *New French Feminisms*, 165–67.

35. Hélène Cixous, "Sorties," in *The Newly Born Woman*, trans. Betsy Wing (Minneapolis: University of Minnesota Press, 1986), 83.

36. Luce Irigaray, *The Sex Which Is Not One*, trans. Catherine Porter (Ithaca: Cornell University Press, 1985), 30–32.

37. Delarivière Manley, *The Adventures of Rivella* (1714; New York: Garland, 1972), 115.

38. Manley's *Rivella* is attracting new, sophisticated attention and is now recognized as "a brisk riposte to masculine appropriations of the female 'form,' physical and textual," an argument related to my own here, Ballaster, *Seductive Forms*, 150.

39. Ros Ballaster notes that "the interpretative conflict between the genders . . . is the structuring feature" of amatory plots by women writers, *Seductive Forms*, 29. Unlike my chapter, her fine book is concerned specifically with early women writers and women readers and the construction of gender ideology.

40. See Kristeva, "Word, Dialogue, and Novel," 43–44; this section has been influenced by her essay, especially 43–54.

41. Quoted in Joan DeJean, who, significantly, is writing of the absences in *La Princesse de Clèves*, "Lafayette's Ellipses: The Privileges of Anonymity," *PMLA* 99 (1984): 891.

42. Michael McKeon uses "improvement" and "application" to illustrate the "unstable strategies of Protestant casuistry" in Crusoe's discourse, *Origins of the English Novel*, 119.

43. There is growing evidence that by the end of the century, women had developed extremely sophisticated ways of overlaying sign systems; see Mitzi Myers's work on Maria Edgeworth's *Ennui;* she points out how Edgeworth "reimagines" cultural narratives to create "an allusive archaeology" of Revolution that is literalized in a "nested narrative . . . , a story about the stories that make up who we are—the genealogies and affiliations through which identities are shaped . . . and renovated," "Completing the Union," *Prose Studies* 18 (1995): 41–77. Davys's *Merry Wanderer* is in *The Works of Mrs. Davys: Consisting of Plays, Novels, Poems, and Familiar Letters* (London, 1725).

44. Julia Kristeva, "Word, Dialogue, and Novel," 55.

45. I have argued this position at some length regarding Aphra Behn in *Spectacular Politics*, 101–24.

46. Pierre Macherey explains literary discourse, especially fiction, "as a con-

testation of language" and elaborates that fiction "is the substitute for, if not the equivalent of, knowledge" and "knowledge is not interpretation but explication," *A Theory of Literary Production* (London: Routledge & Kegan Paul, 1986), 61–65. Mikhail Bakhtin calls the baroque novel (identified with Honoré de'Urfé and Scudéry) "the most significant, historically influential, and unalloyed subcategory of the novel of ordeal" because it "best reveals the organizational possibilities of the idea of testing," "The *Bildungsroman* and Its Significance," in *Speech Genres and Other Late Essays,* trans. Vern McGee (Austin: University of Texas Press, 1986), 13. Bakhtin lists this test of the hero's discourse as one of the defining characteristics of the novel, *The Dialogic Imagination,* trans. Caryl Emerson and Michael Holquist (Austin: University of Texas Press, 1981), 388.

47. We can often see the outcome of the judgments, as phrases such as "monstrous regimen of women" came into play and writers such as Behn and Haywood became author functions categorized as "scandalous" and "loose."

48. Homi K. Bhabha argues persuasively that within the "nation-space" the Other "emerges forcefully, within cultural discourse" and reveals itself as "never outside or beyond us"; in this same essay, he suggests that in this space, we may see "cultural authority . . . in the act of 'composing' its powerful image," *Nation and Narration* (London: Routledge, 1993), 4 and 3, respectively.

49. Defoe was a toddler at the time of the St. Bartholomew's Day, 1662, "silencing." Rowe's parents met in the prison where her father was incarcerated for preaching, and the persecution of ministers and teachers may have played a part in Defoe's decision not to pursue the ministry, his first vocational goal.

50. This is one of Bakhtin's formulations; see *The Dialogic Imagination,* 11, 31–32, 39. This paragraph has benefited from the stimulating ideas of my colleague Donald Wehrs.

51. Although some might disagree, I believe that the common denominator of their sex gives Royalist and "Revolution" women much the same perspective on a large number of novelistic topics.

52. Jane Barker, *Love Intrigues; or, The History of the Amours of Bosvil and Galesia* (London, 1713), 12.

53. At one point her parents order her to stop wearing plain dress, because it will affect her chances of marriage, "prove a Hindrance to my Fortune," p. 25.

54. The explanation is DeJean's, "Lafayette's Ellipses," 890.

55. *Love Intrigues,* 2. When King George I came to the throne in 1714, England experienced two years of serious unrest and a number of dangerous Jacobite rebellions; the Tory party, which had been in power during the last years of Anne's reign, were turned out.

56. The Galesia novels are *Love Intrigues, A Patch-Work Screen for the Ladies* (1723), and *The Lining of the Patch-Work Screen* (1726), now available in *The Galesia Trilogy and Selected Manuscript Poems of Jane Barker,* ed. Carol Shiner Wilson (New York: Oxford University Press, 1997).

57. This role deserves systematic study. It was respected in some women and considered an important kind of knowledge for women to have; William Ellis, for instance, includes furnishing "their Closet with such Remedies as may relieve the necessitous poor people" in *The Country Housewife's Family Companion* (1750), quoted in Bridget Hill with other examples, *Women, Work, and Sexual Politics in Eighteenth-Century England* (New York: Basil Blackwell, 1989), 162–63. But the role was also ridiculed, as it is with George Farquhar's Lady Bountiful (*Beaux' Stratagem*, 1707).

58. For a description of the duties and responsibilities of women skilled at household management, see Hill, *Women, Work, and Sexual Politics*, 28–32. She includes hiring, training, and overseeing servants, including gardeners; taking responsibility for pigs, poultry, dairy, orchard, and vegetable garden; and, in many cases, keeping the accounts.

59. Facts about her life are from Fern Farnham, *Madame Dacier: Scholar and Humanist* (Monterey, Calif.: Angel Press, 1976). The biography is somewhat too apologetic and laudatory.

60. The print of this painting and a brief description of it are in Joan DeJean, *Tender Geographies*, 33–35 and 67.

61. Mazarine's death and the publicity surrounding it and especially *The Duke and Dutchess of Mazarin's Case* with its many references and quotations from her *Memoires of the Dutchess Mazarine* inspired Mary Astell's *Some Reflections upon Marriage*. All three of these texts give details, with varying degrees of reliability, and evidence of Mazarine's intelligence. *The Duke and Dutchess of Mazarin's Case* is in *The Arguments of Monsieur Herard, for Monsieur the Duke of Mazarin* (London, 1699); the first edition of *The Memoires of the Dutchess of Mazarin* was licensed 22 February 16$\frac{76}{77}$, earned a second edition that year, and was published as "The third impression with additions," that is, a letter "containing a true character of her person and conversation" in 1690. The title of the 1700 edition of Astell's publication was *Some Reflections upon Marriage, Occasion'd by the Duke & Dutchess of Mazarine's Case.*

62. A prefiguring of this argument is in Harris's *A Passion for Government: The Life of Sarah, Duchess of Marlborough* (Oxford: Oxford University Press, 1991). She notes, for instance, that "participation in government was a birthright" for the duchess's social class and that Sarah consistently saw her job to be devoting "colossal administrative labours to consolidate the fortunes of her family," 1–2 et passim.

63. Manley, *Rivella*, 68–70; Harris, *A Passion for Government*, 3, 141–43, 158–64. In an astute move, both Manley and Haywood make characters invisible and increase their power and access to knowledge by this means (Astrea in Manley's *New Atalantis* and the narrator in Haywood's *Invisible Spy*).

64. Bakhtin points out that the author "in all his [sic] various masks and faces, [moves] freely onto the field of his represented world," *The Dialogic*

Imagination, 27. See also his extended development of this idea in "The Problem of the Text," *Speech Genres and Other Late Essays.*

65. I have made a similar argument for other women's texts, especially plays, in *Spectacular Politics.* In a different, broader context Paula McDowell argues that women's and other oppressed groups' access to publication generated "new collective identities" and helped them realize their "particular instances" were part of a general condition, *The Women of Grub Street* (Oxford: Clarendon Press, 1998). MacDowell's study makes a major contribution to our ongoing documentation of the ways women got access to publication and of the social relations and institutions in which writing is produced.

66. Nancy K. Miller, *Subject to Change* (New York: Columbia University Press, 1988), 84. Pierre Macherey uses Defoe to illustrate similar theories, *A Theory of Literary Production,* 240–48.

67. Jon Stratton argues that fiction creates the illusion that production and reproduction are the same thing, *The Virgin Text* (Brighton, Sussex: Harvester, 1987), 201–2. Both are in the private sphere but are often gendered into binaries.

68. John Richetti astutely calls Moll's seduction "a rite of passage into the world of sexual and social exploitation," *Defoe's Narratives* (Oxford: Clarendon Press, 1975), 102.

69. Daniel Defoe, *The Fortunes and Misfortunes of the Famous Moll Flanders,* ed. G. A. Starr (Oxford: Oxford University Press, 1981), 32–41.

70. Relational identity is the concept of selfhood dependent upon, in fact inseparable from, the community to which a person belongs and defines oneself as a member of.

71. Peregrine purchases a poor girl from her mother, cleans her up, teaches her fashionable conversation, and presents her in society. When she confronts a cheater at cards and begins to swear, her origins are revealed. John Richetti notes that Smollett "actually affirms [class differences] treating her dialect and its accompanying carnivalesque gestures of defiance as her irrepressible class signature . . . what cannot be suppressed," "Class Struggle without Class," *ECTI* 32 (1991): 204. By Smollett's time, class seems to be a more pressing issue, and Smollett's novels show considerable anxiety about it, which he contains, as other novelists do, by presenting it as essentialist.

72. David Oakleaf, "Marks, Stamps, and Representations: Character in Eighteenth-Century Fiction," *Studies in the Novel* 23 (1991): 304.

73. The concept of socially symbolic act is Fredric Jameson's; see *The Political Unconscious* (Ithaca: Cornell University Press, 1981), 74–102, 236–38. "The symbolic act . . . begins by generating and producing its own context in the same moment of emergence in which it steps back from it, taking its measure with a view toward its own projects of transformation," 81.

74. Note that this is also different from the way classic realist fiction "interpellates" the reader, "addresses itself to him or her directly, offering the reader as

the position from which the text is most 'obviously' intelligible, the position of the *subject in (and of) ideology*"; this definition is from Catherine Belsey, "Constructing the Subject, Deconstructing the Text," *Feminist Criticism and Social Change*, ed. Judith Newton and Deborah Rosenfelt (New York: Methuen, 1980), 45.

75. Eliza Haywood, *The City Jilt; or, The Alderman Turn'd Beau* (London: J. Roberts, 1726), 10.

76. Joan DeJean describes the discussion of *La Princesse de Clèves* orchestrated by *La Mercure galant* and points out that the letters were collective, representative of several people's views, *Tender Geographies*, 116–24.

77. Bakhtin, *The Dialogic Imagination*, 388.

78. Aphra Behn, *Love Letters between a Nobleman and His Sister* (Hammondsworth, England: Penguin, 1987), 89; Part I also refers to the trial of Lord Grey for stealing an heiress, accounts of which were published in newspapers (*Loyal Protestant, London Mercury, London Gazette*, and others) and periodicals and pamphlets (*Monthly Review* and *Whoredom, Fornication and Adultery*) throughout September, October, and November. See also Cecil Price, *Cold Caleb* (London: Melrose, 1956) and my *Spectacular Politics*, 108–18.

79. Critics have argued that the harsh judgments characters make encourage the reader to apply situational ethics and be less condemning.

80. Defoe, *The Fortunes and Misfortunes of the Famous Moll Flanders*, 89, 288. All page numbers are from this edition (Oxford, 1981).

81. The full-length portrait of Clarissa is lost; the scene of Clarissa with her family is the only known, surviving illustration. Richardson mentions seeing a third *Clarissa* illustration by Highmore, *Correspondence of Samuel Richardson*, ed. A. L. Barbauld (1804; New York: AMS Press, 1966), 4:255–56. See also Charles R. Beard, "Highmore's Scrap-book," *The Connoisseur* 93 (1934): 292. I am grateful to Hope Cotton for her research into the "series."

82. Bakhtin, *The Dialogic Imagination*, 300, and *Speech Genres*, 3–7, 125–27, in which he argues that the reader is "a constitutive aspect" of the text.

83. *Oroonoko* was written twenty-four years before England received the Asiento as part of the treaty that ended the War of Spanish Succession.

84. Robert Jordan and Harold Love, eds., *The Works of Thomas Southerne* (Oxford: Clarendon Press, 1988), 2:96. These editors also comment on the later introduction of anti-slavery interpretations, 2:95. By 1778, a prohibition noted that *Oroonoko* too closely mirrored the characters and conduct of Liverpool merchants engaged in slave trading, R. J. Broadbent, *Annals of the Liverpool Stage* (New York: Benjamin Blom, 1969), 72. John Ferriar's 1788 adaptation is an overtly anti-slavery document.

85. Catherine Clément, "The Guilty One," in *The Newly Born Woman*, 7.

86. Quoted in Kristeva, "Women's Time," *The Kristeva Reader*, 211 n. 3.

87. See Macherey, *A Theory of Literary Production*, 79–81, 87. Jon Stratton has argued that an "abyss" exists in the novel form that "replicates the abyss

between text and reader, forcing the reader . . . to produce the 'meaning' of the text," *The Virgin Text,* 204; this is one of the major arguments in his book. Stratton sees the abyss created by the bourgeois world's simultaneous suppression of and obsession with sex and a mirroring of realist and gothic trajectories in the novel form; he tellingly uses the epistolary novel and *Wide Sargasso Sea* to illustrate his points. I would argue that interpretation is sometimes impossible because there are as yet no culturally negotiated solutions or no strategies for bringing text, author, and reader into harmonious interplay; consider the lasting disagreements over Elizabeth Inchbald's text.

88. Carl Lovitt has said that the "transition to the segment devoted to Moll's criminal exploits poses the most serious challenge to any argument about the novel's internal coherence," "Defoe's 'Almost Invisible Hand': Narrative Logic as a Structuring Principle in *Moll Flanders,*" *ECF* 6 (1993): 21.

89. Lincoln Faller notes this element in criminal biographies, an important paradigm for many earlier novels, *Crime and Defoe: A New Kind of Writing* (Cambridge: Cambridge University Press, 1993), 33 et passim. Carol Kay points out that in some novels "an implicit rivalry between novel and court" is set up, *Political Constructions: Defoe, Richardson, and Sterne in Relation to Hobbes, Hume, and Burke* (Ithaca: Cornell University Press, 1988), 117–18.

90. The novel exhibits emancipatory potential as social and political commentary and as it represents scenarios for change; therefore it works against traditional patriarchal exchange and acquires the possibility of use value even as it retains its exchange value. Compare Donna Landry and Gerald MacLean's discussion of feminism as commodity, *Materialist Feminisms* (New York: Blackwell, 1993), 50–59.

91. What Martin Price said of Defoe could be said of most of them: people "aware of the frequent conflict between the demands of commercial gain and those of spiritual salvation," *To the Palace of Wisdom* (New York: Doubleday, 1964), 263. Habermas notes the "specifically bourgeois dialectic of inwardness and publicness" and its "capture" of the literary world in "Further Reflections on the Public Sphere," *Habermas and the Public Sphere,* ed. Craig Calhoun (Cambridge: MIT Press, 1992), 426.

92. For a good discussion of the complex matrix of literacy, access to publication, and genre, see John Guillory, *Cultural Capital: The Problem of Literary Canon Formation* (Chicago: University of Chicago Press, 1993), especially 55–82. He reminds us that "class determines whether and how individuals gain access to the means of literary production, and the system regulating such access is a much more efficient mechanism of social exclusion than acts of judgment" (ix), and "literacy is not a simple matter of knowing how to read or write, but refers to the entire system by which reading and writing are regulated as social practices in a given society" (77). Alvin Kernan reminds us that these decades were early in the transition from an oral to a print culture and that the novel, unlike other literary genres, was print genre only, *Printing Technology,* 48, 68.

93. As my discussion makes clear, this is not Victor Turner's term, but see Turner, *Dramas, Fields, and Metaphors: Symbolic Action in Human Society* (Ithaca: Cornell University Press, 1974), 15, 256, and see also 232 and 252. Among the most pertinent observations Turner makes about liminal spaces is that they "do not lend themselves to being reduced to the terms of practitioners of a single discipline or subdiscipline" and may make it possible to examine more fruitfully "art, religion, literature, philosophy, and even many aspects of law, politics, and economic behavior" (257, 270). I have been influenced by John Bender's use of "liminal," *Imagining the Penitentiary* (Chicago: University of Chicago Press, 1987), especially 26–40. Similar ideas may be derived from Bakhtin, *Dialogic Imagination,* 4, 15 et passim. Some initial discussion of "liminal" is in the special edition of *Prose Studies* that Timothy Dykstal and I edited, 18 (1995): 13–18.

94. Jameson, *The Political Unconscious,* 84, and "Religion and Ideology," in *1642: Literature and Power in the Seventeenth Century,* ed. Frances Barker et al., Proceedings of the Essex Conference on the Sociology of Literature (Colchester: University of Essex, 1981), 317–18.

95. "The institutional core of the public sphere comprises communicative networks amplified by a cultural complex, a press and, later, mass media; they make it possible for . . . a public of citizens of the state to participate in the social integration mediated by public opinion," Jürgen Habermas, *The Theory of Communicative Action,* trans. Thomas McCarthy (Boston: Beacon Press, 1987), 2:319. Lawrence Klein usefully defines "an associative public sphere, a sphere of social, discursive and cultural production," "Gender and the Public/Private Distinction in the Eighteenth Century," *ECS* 29 (1995): 104.

96. Jürgen Habermas, *The Structural Transformation of the Public Sphere,* trans. Thomas Burger (Cambridge: MIT Press, 1991), 55.

97. Dena Goodman, "Public Sphere and Private Life," *History and Theory* 31 (1992): 20. Similar terms have been applied to the early novel ("volatile, undecidable ground," William Warner in "The Elevation of the Novel," 583) and continue to be used in discussions of the novel form's resistance to concrete definition (the novel is "like a 'woman,' an unstable fetish," Stratton, *The Virgin Text,* xiv; "pivots within an unstable vortex," Warner, 593).

98. Habermas has called himself "the last Marxist," and he is using the private in its classic formulation.

99. Elaine Hobby remarks that "more and more women refused to stay silent on the great religio-political questions of the day," *Virtue of Necessity* (Ann Arbor: University of Michigan Press, 1989), 27 and see 26–75. In *The Women of Grub Street,* Paula McDowell points out that religious controversies were "a summoning to public political activity" (124) and documents the importance of women in the book trade. This description, of course, fits Defoe.

100. Behn, Barker, Manley, and Aubin all belonged to families who suffered directly or were personally affected; in her somewhat autobiographical *Love*

Intrigues, for instance, Barker has Galesia say, "My Father, with the rest, lost a very honourable and profitable Place at Court," *Love Intrigues,* 3.

101. John Richetti's categorization of her remains the only opinion of her work, *Popular Fiction before Richardson* (1969; Oxford: Clarendon Press, 1992).

102. I am grateful to L. Randall Smith for this insight; he has also identified examples of her Nonconformist hostility to the Restoration and nobility.

103. Widespread recognition that new forms of delivering didactic messages were necessary contributed to the growth of fiction writing. Although often identified with the rising quantity and respectability of women's writing and dated to Richardson, this function of literature, including the novel, has been discussed more comprehensively by others, see McKeon, *Origins of the English Novel,* 268–70 et passim.

104. Jürgen Habermas, *Philosophical Discourse of Modernity* (Cambridge: MIT Press, 1987), 36.

105. Faller, *Crime and Defoe,* 60–61.

106. See Richetti, who reinforces this opinion in the second edition of *Popular Fiction before Richardson,* xvii, xxv, and 8, 9. Some women writers recognized this element; cf. *The Adventures of Rivella,* ed. Patricia Köster (Gainesville, Fla.: Scholars' Facsimiles & Reprints, 1970), 2:740.

107. DeJean, *Tender Geographies,* 115. See Jürgen Habermas's discussion of Heidegger and Derrida, *Philosophical Discourse of Modernity,* 160. Ellen Donkin, "Mrs. Siddons Looks Back in Anger," *Critical Theory and Performance,* ed. Janelle Reinelt and Joseph R. Roach (Ann Arbor: University of Michigan Press, 1992), 278.

108. Faller, *Crime and Defoe,* 69.

109. Stratton, *The Virgin Text,* 201; Kristeva, "Word, Dialogue, and Novel," 43.

110. David Saunders and Ian Hunter, "Lessons from the 'Literary': How to Historicize Authorship," *Critical Inquiry* 17 (1991): 504. In general, the work of Pierre Bourdieu has allowed us to link the details of mundane life to sophisticated analyses of social power.

111. In the theatre, disguise is likely to reveal a stable character, even to reveal personality in the Lockean sense.

112. Eliza Haywood, *Fantomina; or, Love in a Maze* (London, 1725), 259.

113. John Richetti quotes this passage from *Roxana* and reads it thematically in "The Family, Sex, and Marriage in Defoe's *Moll Flanders* and *Roxana,*" *Studies in the Literary Imagination* 15 (1982): 34–35.

114. Carol Kay points out the implications of the Mint in *Political Constructions;* this section has been influenced by her book, 93–117.

115. Faller, *Crime and Defoe,* 70; Michael Boardman remarks that Defoe's narratives "leave the reader . . . pondering," *Narrative Innovation and Incoherence* (Durham: Duke University Press, 1992), 24.

116. *Roxana* is the novel he wrote with women's fiction most clearly in mind,

see my *Daniel Defoe: Ambition and Innovation* (Lexington: University Press of Kentucky, 1986), 182–214. It is in Roxana that the will to power and domination present in some of Haywood's fictions is most obvious.

117. These criticisms are commonplace; see Richetti, *Defoe's Narratives;* Lovitt cites the "incredible incidents" in *Moll Flanders* and makes other criticisms; "Defoe's 'Almost Invisible Hand,'" 5, 27–28.

118. Bhabha, *Nation and Narration,* 3.

119. Typical responses are Ian Watt's in the classic *Rise of the Novel* (Berkeley: University of California Press, 1957) and Richetti's, *Defoe's Narratives,* 144.

120. Defoe allows Moll this power, but he assures that she will not have it often and will establish a relationship with her victim (the man she robs in the coach). Haywood leaves this power intact. This is but one example of Defoe's masculine neutralization of female power. Beasley's description of women characters such as Pamela inadvertently documents this appropriation, "Politics and Moral Idealism," see especially 217–19.

121. Bakhtin, *Speech Genres,* 40, and 23, 25, 53. See also "Forms of Time and the Chronotope in the Novel," *The Dialogic Imagination,* 84–258.

122. Several critics remark on the "instability" of Defoe's texts. Michael McKeon fears it will be "mistaken" for Defoe's "central narrative energy," and Michael Boardman identifies it as a major source of Defoe's innovation, *Origins of the English Novel,* 337, and *Narrative Innovation and Incoherence,* 22, respectively.

123. Bakhtin, *Speech Genres,* 23, 25.

124. In later novels by Haywood and in mid-century novels by women as moralistic as Frances Brooke, such women and their houses would take on a surreal quality more similar to Moll's underworld.

125. In a stimulating essay, Malinda Snow argues this position with *Roxana,* "Arguments to the Self in Defoe's *Roxana*," *SEL* 34 (1994): 525–28.

126. Seyla Benhabib, *Situating the Self: Gender, Community, and Postmodernism in Contemporary Ethics* (New York: Routledge, 1992), 110.

127. Julia Kristeva, "Women's Time," *Feminisms,* ed. Robyn Warhol and Diane Herndl (New Brunswick: Rutgers University Press, 1991), 456.

128. Boardman, *Narrative Innovation and Incoherence,* 31.

129. Benhabib, *Situating the Self,* 105.

130. I am using "literary" as Habermas does and referring to the whole range of printed texts; I am indebted to Benhabib's *Situating the Self* in this section.

131. Guillory, *Cultural Capital,* 77.

132. Benhabib, *Situating the Self,* 104–7.

133. Joanna Russ defines lyric structure as "setting various images, events, scenes, or memories to circling round an unspoken, invisible center. The invisible center is what the novel . . . is about; it is also unsayable in available dramatic or narrative terms." The result is often a lack of "plot," "repetitiousness, the gathering up of the novels into moments of epiphany [initiation], . . .

indirection," "What Can a Heroine Do?" in *Images of Women in Fiction,* ed. Susan Koppelman Cornillon (Bowling Green: Bowling Green University Press, 1972), 13. This insight has been enhanced by Faller, *Crime and Defoe,* 33, 60–61.

134. Kristeva, "Word, Dialogue and Novel," 39–43.

135. Saunders and Hunter, "Lessons from the 'Literarory': How to Historicise Authorship," 502.

Chapter 2: The Rise of Gender as Political Category

1. Penelope Aubin, for instance, remarks on the novel's moral possibilities in the preface to *The Strange Adventures of the Count de Vinevil* (London, 1720). See John Richetti, *Popular Fiction before Richardson* (Oxford: Clarendon Press, 1969), 226–29, 260–61, and Leopold Damrosch, *God's Plots and Man's Stories* (Chicago: University of Chicago Press, 1985), 220–21. Mikhail Bakhtin quotes Gustav Shpet's assertion that the novel became "the contemporary form of moral propaganda," *The Dialogic Imagination,* trans. Caryl Emerson and Michael Holquist (Austin: University of Texas Press, 1981), 267–68.

2. Tassie Gwilliam, *Samuel Richardson's Fictions of Gender* (Stanford: Stanford University Press, 1993), 53-59; quotation from 53.

3. Terry Eagleton, *The Rape of Clarissa* (Minneapolis: University of Minnesota Press, 1982), 1-4. He writes that Richardson's novels are "instruments which help to constitute social interests," 4. See also Rita Goldberg, *Sex and Enlightenment: Women in Richardson and Diderot* (Cambridge: Cambridge University Press, 1984), who disputes the view that Clarissa is an ideal of female passivity; Jean Hagstrum writes, "Clarissa is a champion of the downtrodden woman of her day and all days," *Sex and Sensibility* (Chicago: University of Chicago Press, 1980), 206.

4. Richardson printed through sig M, exclusive of the preface, William Sale, *Samuel Richardson: Master Printer* (Ithaca: Cornell University Press, 1950), 162-66. Between the first edition of *Religious Courtship* and Richardson's printing a significant number of novels took as their central subject conflicts between parents and children (usually daughters) over marriage partners; in most of the texts duty and personal preference were issues; 1725 seems to have been a year in which these stories were especially numerous. Margaret Anne Doody points out some of the similarities between *Clarissa* and one of them, Mary Davys's *The Lady's Tale* (1725) in *A Natural Passion* (Oxford: Clarendon Press, 1974), 132–35.

5. "Achsah" is Hebrew for "bangle," "ankle ornament," and she was given to the man who conquered a piece of property; once married he asked her to go to Caleb and secure additional property, specifically water rights. Thus, this text subtly underscores woman's status and also associates her with the transfer of property among men.

6. See, for instance, Defoe's *Conjugal Lewdness* (London, 1727), 101–6.

7. In one passage, which may be coincidental, Lovelace tells Belford, "Then for improving a hint, thou wert always a true Englishman. I never started a roguery that did not come out of *thy* forge in a manner ready anvilled and hammered for execution, when I have sometimes been at a loss to make anything of it myself" (8:149); all quotations are from the third edition (London, 1751) in the AMS Press edition (New York, 1990). In works such as *A General History of Discoveries and Improvements* (London, 1725–26), iii, 78–79, and 232–38; and *A Plan for the English Commerce* (London, 1728), 299ff., Defoe insisted that the English might not have been great inventors or explorers but their genius for improving was unmatched. In another place, Richardson quotes one of Defoe's favorite lines from a sermon by Samuel Annesley: "We have nothing to do but to choose what is right" (1:128).

8. The conduct book aspects of Richardson's novel have been discussed in Katherine Hornbeak, "Richardson's 'Familiar Letters' and the Domestic Conduct Books," *Smith College Studies in Modern Languages* 19 (1938): 1–29; Nancy Armstrong, *Desire and Domestic Fiction* (Oxford: Oxford University Press, 1987), 109ff.; Carol Houlihan Flynn, *Samuel Richardson: A Man of Letters* (Princeton: Princeton University Press, 1982), 50–98; and Rita Goldberg, *Sex and Enlightenment,* 29–65.

9. "Defoe and Richardson—Novelists of the City" in *Dryden to Johnson,* ed. Roger Lonsdale (London: Barrie & Jenkins, 1971), 229, 248–50.

10. This quotation is from the Rev. Samuel Wright's prefatory letter to the first edition; see the Scholar's Facsimile Edition (Delmar, N.Y., 1989) for the collected statements Defoe makes on his method; in addition to those in the second edition, those in the first are appended to the text. Compare Richardson's Postscript, in which he explains that he represents "real Life" and that he knows women as virtuous as Clarissa, 8:297–98. In *A New Family Instructor* (London, 1727), Defoe writes, " 'Tis enough that such Families have been, and, we may be encourag'd to believe, such may be again," 2.

11. In *Licensing Entertainment: The Elevation of Novel Reading in Britain, 1684–1750* (Berkeley: University of California Press, 1998), 180–85, William Warner draws connections between Penelope Aubin's texts and Richardson's.

12. Defoe mentions the subject of *Religious Courtship* in Notes on the First Dialogue in *The Family Instructor,* first edition, Appendix, 324: "Religious Parents ought to be more especially very careful in the matching those Children." On the letters in Defoe's fictions, see John Robert Moore, "Daniel Defoe: Precursor of Samuel Richardson," in *Restoration and Eighteenth-Century Literature: Essays in Honor of Alan Dugald McKillop,* ed. Carroll Camden (Chicago: University of Chicago Press for Rice University, 1963), 365–69; Moore also quotes the *Biographia Britannia* entry, 353–54. As Margaret Anne Doody says, "It has entertained critics to see in the *Familiar Letters* the future

Richardsonian characters in embryo," *A Natural Passion,* 29; many of the themes and opinions are, of course, similar as well.

13. Belford has received relatively little attention. Among those who have carefully figured him into their arguments are Doody, *A Natural Passion,* especially 100, 132–35, and 183, and William B. Warner, *Reading "Clarissa": The Struggles of Interpretation* (New Haven: Yale University Press, 1979), especially 42–45 and 151, and David Robinson, who gives careful attention to Belford's character within the context of his friendship with Lovelace, " 'Unravelling the cord which ties good men to good men': Male Friendship in Richardson's Novels," in *Samuel Richardson: Tercentenary Essays,* ed. Margaret Doody and Peter Sabor (Cambridge: Cambridge University Press, 1989), 167–87. Gordon Fulton compares Belford's and Lovelace's descriptions of Clarissa, "Why Look at Clarissa?" *ECL* 20 (1996): 21–52.

14. Rita Goldberg, *Sex and Enlightenment,* 101.

15. See, for instance, 6:76–77 when Lovelace asks him to go to Clarissa with his promise to "bind my soul to her for my honour."

16. Thomas Beebee and others have pointed out that the conception of *Clarissa*'s readership, both in English and in translations, shifted from largely male to largely female, *Clarissa on the Continent* (University Park: Pennsylvania State University Press, 1990), 186. A count of the letters, with a recognition of the detailed attention to Belford's states of mind and personal changes, shows the serious and increasing attention Richardson gives Belford.

17. See Doody for a somewhat detailed discussion, *A Natural Passion,* 153–63, 182–85, 213–14; as she says, the devotional literature "provides part of the texture of the novel from beginning to end," 213. The explication of the importance of the deathbed scenes is especially strong. The "uses" of religion in Penelope Aubin's novels contrast markedly to Richardson's; there is no evidence that he read Aubin.

18. "Of Saving Faith" and "Of Repentance unto Life" in the Westminster Confession of Faith (1646); see also "A Sermon of the Salvation of Mankind" in *Creeds of the Churches,* ed. John H. Leith (Garden City: Doubleday, 1963), 239–51. For one of Belford's confessions, see 6:301–2; Wyerley also comes to replicate a similar pattern to Defoe's hero; see 7:236–39.

19. *Clarissa,* 4:130. The concluding letter reinforces this idea, for it says, "such awakening calls are *hardly ever afforded to men of his cast,*" 8:274.

20. Cf. "What, therefore, upon the whole, do we get by treading in these crooked paths, but danger, disgrace, and a too late repentance?" 4:136; see also 6:98, 255; 7:164, 314, 354, et passim.

21. Cf. 6:394–95 and 7:161–62. Richardson adds intertextual density with allusions to familiar books of piety, cf. 7:167–69.

22. "Puritan" is something of a vexed term, especially when applied to an Anglican writing about one hundred years after the Puritan Interregnum; N. H. Keebler points out that the term was used in the seventeenth and eighteenth

centuries for "any serious Christian witness" and that it became "a disparaging sobriquet," *The Literature of Nonconformity* (Athens: University of Georgia Press, 1987), 3. It is often applied to residual structures of feeling, especially as associated with the primacy of individual conscience and expressed in tensions felt between the soul or inner self and the world, or the structures, mores, and institutions of society. See Leopold Damrosch, *God's Plot and Man's Stories,* 214–62, for a recent exploration of how the term might be applied productively to *Clarissa.*

23. Among the critics who represent the process in the novel as her "sanctification" is John Dussinger, "Conscience and the Pattern of Christian Perfection in *Clarissa,*" *PMLA* 81 (1966): 236–45.

24. "A very considerable length of time is required before we can forget the sordid scenes through which Clarissa has passed and remember only the final radiance," Watt, *The Rise of the Novel* (Berkeley: University of California Press, 1957), 218. In a somewhat overwrought introduction, Harold Bloom praises "the transformation of the gorgeously dying Clarissa," *Modern Critical Views: Samuel Richardson,* ed. Harold Bloom (New York: Chelsea House Publishers, 1987), 2. Dorothy Van Ghent and others have ridiculed the way Clarissa's clothing remains "beyond imagination white" in the most improbable circumstances, *The English Novel: Form and Function* (New York: Rinehart, 1953), 47–51.

25. See Barker's *Love Intrigues* (1713), *A Patch-Work Screen for the Ladies* (1723), and *The Lining of the Patch-Work Screen* (1726). In her fine discussion of Barker, Jane Spencer calls Galesia's "failure to marry" "a tale of success," *The Rise of the Woman Novelist* (New York: Blackwell, 1986), 62–70. See p. 38 of *Patch-Work Screen* for the motive for the robbery.

26. *The Cousins* in *The Works of Mrs. Davys: Consisting of Plays, Novels, Poems and Familiar Letters,* 2 vols. (London, 1725), 2:226.

27. *The History of Miss Betsy Thoughtless* (London: Pandora, 1986), 64.

28. Claudine Herrmann, *The Tongue Snatchers,* trans. Nancy Kline (Lincoln: University of Nebraska Press, 1989), 23 and 32–39.

29. *Clarissa,* 6:275. He even denies that tears are "unmanly" and endorses them as signs of a "humane nature," 7:160.

30. Doody, *Frances Burney* (New Brunswick, N.J.: Rutgers University Press, 1988), 127, 133, et passim.

31. Susan Staves speculates that some laws restricting women's property rights were designed to keep women grateful as well as dependent, *Married Women's Separate Property in England, 1660–1833* (Cambridge: Harvard University Press, 1990).

32. See, for instance, Eagleton, *The Rape of Clarissa,* 94–97, and Armstrong, *Desire and Domestic Fiction,* 97. James G. Turner, "Lovelace and the Paradoxes of Libertinism," *Samuel Richardson: Tercentenary Essays,* 83–87, and Tassie Gwilliam, *Samuel Richardson's Fictions,* 109 et passim.

33. I use "feminist" here as Nancy Miller describes feminist writing in *Subject to Change* (New York: Columbia University Press, 1988), 8, 17, 39–40, especially as the texts exhibit "self-consciousness about woman's identity," awareness of the "difficulty of [the relation of] woman in fiction to Woman," and as they resist traditional plots and dominant ideologies.

34. A common interpretation is that Clarissa's sins are her presumption and her reliance on her own strength. Eagleton summarizes the faults critics have found in her, *The Rape of Clarissa*, 71. Cf. Ira Konigsberg, *Samuel Richardson and the Dramatic Novel* (Lexington: University of Kentucky Press, 1968), 84; Howard Anderson, "Answers to the Author of *Clarissa*," *PQ* 51 (1972): 859–73.

35. See Letter 12 and compare the Postscript on love, 8:290–91. One of Richardson's most revealing passages on love is in *Pamela* 4:322–23. Susan Staves identifies the characteristics, including "trustfulness and affectionateness," that made young women vulnerable to seduction in "British Seduced Maidens," *ECS* 14 (1980–81): 115–16, 118–19.

36. Richardson knew Mme de Lafayette's text; in *Sir Charles Grandison* there is explicit discussion and criticism of it, 3:395–401. See T. C. Duncan Eaves and Ben D. Kimpel, *Samuel Richardson: A Biography* (Oxford: Clarendon Press, 1971), 583–84. All quotations from *La Princesse de Clèves* are from the Penguin Classics edition, trans. Nancy Mitford (Harmondsworth, 1978).

37. Quoted in Jocelyn Harris, *Samuel Richardson* (Cambridge: Cambridge University Press, 1987), 97.

38. Terry Eagleton argues that Richardson "cunningly pressed the Christian ideology of his audience to its intolerable limits" and banters those who want Clarissa to live, *The Rape of Clarissa*, 75-77. He writes that "Clarissa exposes the rift between bourgeois pieties and bourgeois practice . . . those pieties themselves, once submitted to the pressures of fictional form, begin to crack open," and quotes Christopher Hill's statement that Richardson's "respect for Clarissa's integrity led him to push the Puritan code forward to the point at which its flaw was completely revealed, at which it broke down as a standard for conduct in this world," 77.

39. "I am only telling you to behave as I would myself, I said, because personally I value sincerity so much that though I should be miserable if my mistress, or even my wife, were to come and say frankly that she was attracted by another it would not make me bitter. I would then cast off the role of husband or lover in order to advise and sympathize with her as best I could.

"At these words, which seemed to have a bearing upon her own state of mind, Madame de Clèves blushed deeply," 76–77.

40. The quotation is from *A Plan for the Conduct of Female Education in Boarding Schools* (1797), in which Darwin states that he has relied on the judgments of "very ingenious" women in compiling his list of acceptable novels and quotes Madame de Genlis's recommendation of Richardson, 36. Herr-

mann calls this the capacity a woman has to "act against her feelings," *Tongue Snatchers,* 19–20.

41. Sources of power have been identified as reward, coercive, legitimate (from such things as social structure, position, and negotiation), referent, and expert in such classic studies as John R. P. French, Jr., and Bertram Raven, "The Bases of Social Power," *Studies in Social Power,* ed. Dorwin Cartwright (Ann Arbor: Research Center for Group Dynamics, Institute for Social Research, University of Michigan, 1959), 150–65.

42. In addition to Barker's novels, Haywood published several, including *The British Recluse,* that show women retiring together in prosperity and contentment. Various explanations have been given for this literary theme; for two, see Janet Todd, *The Sign of Angellica* (New York: Columbia University Press, 1989), 29–30, 42, and Ruth Perry, "The Veil of Chastity," *Sexuality in Eighteenth-Century Britain,* ed. Paul-Gabriel Boucé (Totowa, N.J.: Barnes & Noble, 1982), 141–58. Doody speculates that the stated preference for a single life was already a convention, *A Natural Passion,* 134.

43. See letters 19, 32 and 40, vol. 1.

44. 8:178; Anna Howe suggests that her parents argued violently and were not very happy (see 2:241, 3:269), and her mother clearly prefers the single, independent life; her Aunt Hervey was not happy; Belton's sister is "indigent" "owing to a vile husband," 7:246; both Clarissa's siblings have miserable marriages.

45. Nancy Miller usefully summarizes the charges of implausibility associated with *La Princesse de Clèves* in *Subject to Change,* 38–39 and 41.

46. Quoted in Doody, *Natural Passion,* 87.

47. *The Life of Charlotta Du Pont* (London, 1723), 99–100 and 233; Richetti in *Popular Fiction before Richardson* features Aubin in his chap. 6, "The Novel as Pious Polemic," 211–61.

48. *The Body in Swift and Defoe* (Cambridge: Cambridge University Press, 1990), 64, and see the entire chapter, "Consuming Desires: Defoe's Sexual Systems," 61–87.

49. James Turner argues that even for Lovelace "sex is empty and disgusting," "Lovelace and the Paradoxes of Libertinism," 70–88; the quotation is from p. 70. Michael F. Suarez points out that Clarissa is infantilized, "Asserting the Negative: 'Child' Clarissa and the Problem of the 'Determined Girl,'" *New Essays on Samuel Richardson,* ed. Albert J. Rivero (New York: St. Martin's Press, 1996), 69–84. See also Fulton, "Why Look at Clarissa?" 26–29.

50. For examples, see Belford's witticism on dress, 6:391, and on Mowbray's conduct, 7:292.

51. Robinson also comments on Belford's physical appearance as a part of the men's competitiveness, "'Unravelling the cord,'" 172–73.

52. Mowbray describes Belford "taking minnutes [sic] of examinations, ac-

cusations, and confessions, with the significant air of a Middlesex justice," 6:87. Later he will manage the "concerns" of Mowbray and Tourville, 8:257.

53. Jocelyn Harris points out that Grandison is "a new kind of gentleman" and, among other characteristics, finds him "womanlike and Christlike rather than man-like in the old pagan, heroic and patriarchal ways," *Samuel Richardson*, 138; she also points out that Grandison can seem "stiff, awkward, and almost unable to move" (133)—thus, different from the domesticated man that women writers were creating; see also 142 and 164. Michael McKeon writes similarly of "founding a new family," *The Origins of the English Novel* (Baltimore: Johns Hopkins University Press, 1987), 220–21.

54. This marriage conforms to the ideological pattern Flynn finds in Defoe's conduct books: "containment appears 'necessary,' the logical response to the dangers the unaccommodated woman represented. Yet the containment also needed to be considered 'natural,' a voluntary submission to the good," "Defoe's Idea of Conduct: Ideological Fictions and Fictional Reality," in *The Ideology of Conduct*, ed. Nancy Armstrong and Leonard Tennenhouse (New York: Methuen, 1987), 74.

55. This is not to say that Richardson did not know "ardent love." Margaret Anne Doody quotes one of his letters in which he mentions a woman "whom his soul loved," *A Natural Passion*, 8; and see her illuminating discussion of Richardson and love, 7–12. William B. Warner describes Belford as "Clarissa's epigone," *Reading "Clarissa,"* 42, a term that reduces him to a parallel to Anna's messenger.

56. Flynn, "Defoe's Idea of Conduct," 73–95.

57. Rather than suggesting that he was more pleased by the marriage than she, this rhetoric may be an indication of a male writer's tendency to identify with males more strongly than with females.

58. Armstrong and others have noted the need to invent a language to express these changes, see *Desire and Domestic Fiction*, 37, 57.

59. Alexander Pettit, "Wit, Satire, and Comedy: *Clarissa* and the Problem of Literary Precedent," *Studies in the Literary Imagination* 28 (1995): 35–53.

60. *Sir Charles Grandison* (London: Oxford University Press, 1972), 3:399. All quotations are from this edition, edited by Jocelyn Harris.

61. Herrmann writes, "Everyone knows that woman's desire exists, but to see it appear without dissimulation instantly makes a bizarre impression that shares in the very essence of the fantastic," *Tongue Snatchers*, 72. Fictions by Behn, Haywood, and Manley especially have suffered from this phenomenon.

62. In Miller, *Subject to Change*, 213. This definition leads to the confining conclusion that Miller shares with Linda S. Kauffman and Sylvère Lotringer that the princess acts to preserve her passion, Kauffman, *Discourses of Desire: Gender, Genre, and Epistolary Fictions* (Ithaca: Cornell University Press, 1986) and Lotringer, "La Structuration romanesque," *Critique* 26 (1970): 498–599.

63. *Clarissa*, 8:104; note what is added to the third edition. See also 8:32, in

which Clarissa urges Anna to marry in order to "supply to herself the friend she will have lost in her."

64. The fullest discussion of this topic is in Gerald McLean, "What Is a Restoration Poem? Editing a Discourse, Not an Author?" *Text: Transactions of the Society for Textual Scholarship,* ed. D. C. Greetham and W. Speed Hill (New York: AMS Press, 1987), 331–34 and 342 n. 9, although it is present in almost all modern studies of Philips. He and Harriette Andreadis argue that Philips's contemporaries and near contemporaries allude to "qualities that we call lesbian." See Harriette Andreadis, "The Sapphic-Platonics of Katherine Philips, 1632–1664," *Signs* 15 (1989): 36–40, 53–59. Lillian Faderman defines "romantic friends" as those who wanted "to share their lives, to confide and trust and depend upon each other, to be there always for each other," *Surpassing the Love of Men* (New York: William Morrow, 1981), 142; see especially 15–18, 27–29, 45–46, 68–72, 115–18, and 411–12.

John Dussinger refers to "a lesbian contempt for men" in Clarissa, *The Discourse of the Mind in Eighteenth-Century Fiction* (The Hague: Mouton, 1974), 104. Robinson remarks mildly that the women's intimate friendship "encourages women's independence of and separation from men," but he, too, labels it "a threat to the established sexual order," " 'Unravelling the cord,' " 167.

65. Michael McKeon links demographics to "strategies of patriline repair" and also draws telling comparisons between women and younger brothers, *The Origins of the English Novel,* 153–54 and 255–65.

66. Staves, "British Seduced Maidens," 110, 120, 121–22, 134.

67. *Clarissa,* 4:248. Here, as in many other places, Lovelace extends common opinions to their outrageous implications, but, in doing so, undoubtedly evokes residual cultural longings.

68. See Harris's chapter, aptly named "King Lovelace" in *Samuel Richardson,* 66–85. She points out that Lovelace is "a tyrannical Filmer," 63. Numerous critics whose focus in on the class struggle encoded in *Clarissa* have commented on the political metaphors and analogies that permeate the book; see Eagleton, *The Rape of Clarissa,* and Rita Goldberg, *Sex and Enlightenment.*

69. Nancy Armstrong, *Desire and Domestic Fiction,* 38, and Gwilliam, *Samuel Richardson's Fictions,* 76–81.

70. In one startling line, Richardson writes, "all female words, though we are not sure of their derivation, have very significant meanings," 7:408–9 (Belford to Lovelace). Other critics have seen, in Terry Eagleton's words, that "Richardson converted the still indeterminate status of the novel to effective ideological use," that "warring discourses" make the novel the great social and literary text it is, and made different arguments about the female sign; see Eagleton, *The Rape of Clarissa,* 17.

71. Anna Letitia Barbauld, *The Correspondence of Richardson* (1804; New York: AMS Press, 1966), 6:130. Tassie Gwilliam finds Richardson depicting "the consolidation of masculine power over women" and *Clarissa* dependent

upon and fascinated with "the part played by male cruelty in the creation of its heroine's exemplarity," *Samuel Richardson's Fictions,* 14 and 162, respectively.

72. Backscheider, *Spectacular Politics* (Baltimore: Johns Hopkins University Press, 1993), 125–48. It is significant that Nancy K. Miller locates "the textual politics of closure" in eighteenth-century France and England, *Subject to Change,* 125–27; see also Elizabeth J. MacArthur's useful book on closure and openness (which she calls "metaphor" and "metonymy"), *Extravagant Narratives* (Princeton: Princeton University Press, 1990).

73. The quotations are from Eagleton, *The Rape of Clarissa,* 74, and Gwilliam, *Samuel Richardson's Fictions,* 76.

74. Fulton, "Why Look at Clarissa?" 30.

75. Although I agree with the optimism expressed in books such as Katherine Sobba Green's *The Courtship Novel, 1740–1820: A Feminized Genre* (Lexington: University Press of Kentucky, 1991) and Janet Todd's *The Sign of Angellica,* I am asking for an examination of the resistances. See especially Green's chapter, "The Blazon and the Marriage Act," 69–79.

Chapter 3: Renegotiating the Gothic

1. For Collier's essay, see Betty Rizzo, *Companions without Vows: Relationships among Eighteenth-Century British Women* (Athens: University of Georgia Press, 1994), 45–50 et passim. For Richardson's and Harris's putative contribution to the essay, see 46, 337, n. 10.

2. *The Standard Edition of the Complete Psychological Works of Sigmund Freud,* trans. James Strachey, 22 vols. (London: Hogarth Press, 1964), 7:236; Shari Benstock, ed., *The Private Self: Theory and Practice of Women's Autobiographical Writings* (Chapel Hill: University of North Carolina Press, 1988), 12.

3. Paula Backscheider, *Spectacular Politics: Theatrical Power and Mass Culture in Early Modern England* (Baltimore: Johns Hopkins University Press, 1993), 156–57.

4. Ellen Moers, *Literary Women* (Garden City: Doubleday & Co., 1976), 126.

5. Eve Kosofsky Sedgwick, *The Coherence of Gothic Convention* (New York: Methuen, 1986), 12, notes that the gothic victim is blocked off from something to which it should have access—as family secrets, air, love, life itself.

6. See, for instance, Patricia Myer Spacks, *Imagining a Self: Autobiography and the Novel in Eighteenth-Century England* (Cambridge, Mass.: Harvard University Press, 1976), 65, where Spacks points out that in writing romance women at the very least showed themselves dimly aware of their social victimization; Margaret Anne Doody, "Deserts, Ruins and Troubled Waters: Female Dreams in Fiction and the Development of the Gothic Novel," *Genre* 10 (Winter 1977): 560: "It is in the Gothic novel that women writers could first accuse

the 'real world' of falsehood and deep disorder"; see also Doody, *Frances Burney: The Life in the Works* (New Brunswick: Rutgers University Press, 1988), 182: "By the last two decades of the century, the tropes and metaphors of 'Gothic' literature provided the codes in which sexual and social misery might be powerfully but unofficially conveyed"; Sandra Gilbert and Susan Gubar, *The Madwoman in the Attic* (New Haven: Yale University Press, 1979), 33, where they point out the correlation between women's entrapment at home and symbolic entrapment in gothic literature; Jane Spencer, *The Rise of the Woman Novelist* (Oxford: Basil Blackwell, 1986), 209: "In Lee's and Radcliffe's fictions, Gothic horrors act implicitly as imaginative parallels for women's condition."

7. Mary Astell, *Some Reflections upon Marriage*, quoted by Ruth Perry, *The Celebrated Mary Astell, an Early English Feminist* (Chicago: University of Chicago Press, 1986), 158.

8. Janet Todd, *Sensibility: An Introduction* (London: Methuen, 1986), 17–19; Alice Browne, *The Eighteenth-Century Feminist Mind* (Detroit: Wayne State University Press, 1987), 111; Elizabeth Bergen Brophy, *Women's Lives and the Eighteenth-Century Novel* (Tampa: University of South Florida Press, 1991). "Natural imbecillity" is ascribed to women in a conduct book by Richard Allestree, *The Ladies Calling* (1673), discussed earlier by Brophy (9). For excellent discussions of the imputed incapacity in women for abstract thought, see Brophy, chap. 1, "Made He a Woman" and Browne, chap. 5, "Women's Education and Women's Rationality."

9. For the court tales, see *Lady Mary Wortley Montagu: Romance Writings*, ed. Isobel Grundy (Oxford: Clarendon, 1996), and Grundy's introduction, xvi–xix.

10. For the distinction between the plot-driven novel and the consensus of community novel and an excellent discussion of Millenium Hall, see Betty E. Schellenberg, *The Conversational Circle* (Lexington: University Press of Kentucky, 1997).

11. Tess Cosslett, *Woman to Woman: Female Friendship in Victorian Literature* (Atlantic Highlands, N.J.: Humanities Press International, 1988), 13.

12. Isobel Grundy, *Lady Mary Wortley Montagu: Romance Writings*, xix. For the "Italian Memoir," see 81–105. Grundy discusses the "Memoir" at length in "Mary Wortley Montagu's 'Italian Memoir,'" *The Age of Johnson*, ed. Paul Korshin (New York: AMS Press, 1994), 6:321–46.

13. Isobel Grundy, "Mary Wortley Montagu's 'Italian Memoir,'" 332.

14. Mary Delany, *The Autobiography and Correspondence of Mary Granville, Mrs. Delany*, ed. Lady Llanover, 6 vols. (London: Richard Bentley, 1861–62), 1:31.

15. Autobiography of Elizabeth Chudleigh in Henrietta Louise Von Waldner, Baronne d'Oberkirch, *Memoirs of the Baroness of Oberkirch, Written by Herself*, ed. Count de Montbrison, 3 vols. (London: Colbourn & Co., 1851), 1:225–26. The autobiography is in 1:219–42.

16. Horace Walpole, *The Yale Edition of Horace Walpole's Correspondence,* ed. W. S. Lewis, 48 vols. (New Haven: Yale University Press, 1937–83), 24:141.

17. Dorothy Margaret Stuart, *Dearest Bess* (London: Methuen, 1955), 27.

18. Steele certainly supplied the information for the biography, but it was apparently written by the polemicist William Jackson; see Rizzo, *Companions without Vows,* 363–64, n. 1.

19. Elizabeth Steele, *The Memoirs of Mrs. Sophia Baddeley, Late of Drury Lane Theatre,* 6 vols. (Clerkenwell: For the Author at the Literary Press, 1787), 5:114–20.

20. Sarah Scott, *The History of Sir George Ellison,* ed. Betty Rizzo (Lexington: University Press of Kentucky, 1996), 40. Lamont's conversion is figured in his marriage to Mrs. Blackburn, a widow specifically described as "considerably passed the bloom of life" (206).

21. Ann Radcliffe, "On the Supernatural in Poetry," *New Monthly Magazine* 7 (1826).

22. Frances Burney, *Cecilia: or Memoirs of an Heiress,* ed. Peter Sabor and Margaret Anne Doody (Oxford: Oxford University Press, 1988), 72–73.

23. Frances Burney, *Camilla; or, A Picture of Youth,* ed. Edward A. Bloom and Lillian D. Bloom (Oxford: Oxford University Press, 1983), 356–61.

24. For the plays and commentary, see *The Complete Plays of Frances Burney,* ed. Peter Sabor and Stewart J. Cooke, 2 vols. (Montreal: McGill-Queen's University Press, 1995). Margaret Doody has provided an excellent analysis of Burney's tragedies in *Frances Burney: The Life in the Works,* 150–98.

25. Margaret Doody, *Frances Burney: The Life in the Works,* 191–92. Doody notes that "the plot was evidently to be designed to show Elberta's progressive breakdown into madness under the pain of privation." Stewart J. Cooke, who has virtually reconstructed the play, considers she plays a more peripheral role: see *The Complete Plays of Frances Burney,* vol. 2.

26. Edward A. Bloom and Lillian D. Bloom, eds., "Introduction" to Frances Burney, *Camilla,* x, quoted from Burney's notes for the novel now in the Berg Collection, New York Public Library.

27. Frances Burney, *The Wanderer; or, Female Difficulties* (London: Pandora Press, 1988), 836. These are the last words of the novel.

28. Charlotte Smith, *The Old Manor House* (London: Pandora Press, 1987), 457.

29. Claudia L. Johnson, *Equivocal Beings: Politics, Gender, and Sentimentality in the 1790s* (Chicago: University of Chicago Press, 1995), 11–12. Another problem here is that Johnson appears to assume that males acquired sensibility incrementally as the eighteenth century wore on. In fact many, of whom I am one, note that the vogue for male sensibility peaked by the 1770s and thereafter, sensibility having been discerned as a rather inconvenient demand for altruism, was increasingly (and conveniently) left to women to shoulder.

30. See Elizabeth A. Bohls, *Women Travel Writers and the Language of Aesthetics, 1716–1818* (Cambridge: Cambridge University Press, 1995), 3.

31. Ann Radcliffe, *The Italian: or, The Confessional of the Black Penitents, a Romance,* ed. Frederick Garber (Oxford: Oxford University Press, 1992), 9.

32. Janet Todd, *Women's Friendship in Literature* (New York: Columbia University Press, 1980), 209–26. Todd notes that Maria learns what Jemima has known all along, "that reason and self-preservation are a woman's first duty," and Jemima learns through Maria "that self-esteem—and the affection and emotion it allows—are her second," 225.

Chapter 4: My Art Belongs to Daddy?

1. Because my take on this explanatory paradigm (together with comprehensive documentation) is detailed elsewhere, the full argument and references are not repeated here: see my " 'Completing the Union': Critical *Ennui,* the Politics of Narrative, and the Reformation of Irish Cultural Identity," *The Intersections of the Public and Private Spheres,* ed. Paula R. Backscheider and Timothy Dykstal, *Prose Studies: History, Theory, Criticism* 18.3 (December 1995): 41–77; and " 'Like the Pictures in a Magic Lantern': Gender, History, and Edgeworth's Rebellion Narratives," *Special Issue: Writing Women/Writing Power, Nineteenth-Century Contexts* 19.4 (1996): 373–412. Recent overviews warning against narrow readings of "public" and "private" spheres also support the cultural importance this essay assigns to women's literary production: especially important are John Brewer, "This, That, and the Other: Public, Social, and Private in the Seventeenth and Eighteenth Centuries," *Shifting the Boundaries: Transformation of the Languages of Public and Private in the Eighteenth Century,* ed. Dario Castiglione and Lesley Sharpe (Exeter, U.K.: University of Exeter Press, 1995), 1–21; Lawrence E. Klein, "Gender and the Public/Private Distinction in the Eighteenth Century: Some Questions about Evidence and Analytic Procedure," *The Public and the Nation, Eighteenth-Century Studies* 29.1 (Fall 1995): 97–109; Anthony J. La Volpa, "Conceiving a Public: Ideas and Society in Eighteenth-Century Europe," *Journal of Modern History* 64.1 (March 1992): 79–116; Bruce Robbins, "Introduction: The Public as Phantom," *The Phantom Public Sphere,* ed. Bruce Robbins, Cultural Politics 5 (Minneapolis: University of Minnesota Press, 1993), vii–xxvi; and, most thoroughly, Jeff Weintraub, "The Theory and Politics of the Public/Private Distinction," *Public and Private: Perspectives on a Grand Dichotomy,* ed. Jeff Weintraub and Krishan Kumar, Morality and Society (Chicago: University of Chicago Press, 1997), 1–42. It is worth noting that scholars in American studies, the field where "domestic ideology" began its modern career two decades ago, are now embracing more inclusive views of women's roles in social life than are most students of French and British history; see, for example, Karen V. Hansen, "Making the Social

Central: An Introduction," *A Very Social Time: Crafting Community in Antebellum New England* (Berkeley: University of California Press, 1994), 1–28; and her "Rediscovering the Social: Visiting Practices in Antebellum New England and the Limits of the Public/Private Dichotomy," *Public and Private*, ed. Weintraub and Kumar, 268–302; and Sandra F. VanBurkleo, "Little Monarchies," review of *Founding Mothers and Fathers: Gendered Power and the Forming of American Society*, by Mary Beth Norton, *Women's Review of Books* 13.12 (September 1996): 23–24. Essential studies include Craig Calhoun, ed., *Habermas and the Public Sphere* (Cambridge, Mass.: MIT Press, 1992); Oskar Negt and Alexander Kluge, *Public Sphere and Experience: Toward an Analysis of the Bourgeois and Proletarian Public Sphere*, trans. Peter Labanyi, et al., Theory and History of Literature 85 (1972; Minneapolis: University of Minnesota Press, 1993); and Johanna Meehan, ed., *Feminists Read Habermas: Gendering the Subject of Discourse* (New York: Routledge, 1995).

2. Elizabeth Kowaleski-Wallace's "Home Economics: Domestic Ideology in Maria Edgeworth's *Belinda*," *The Eighteenth Century: Theory and Interpretation* 29.3 (Fall 1988): 242–62; and *Their Fathers' Daughters: Hannah More, Maria Edgeworth, and Patriarchal Complicity* (New York and Oxford: Oxford University Press, 1991) are typical, but most Edgeworth criticism could be cited as well.

3. Originally published by John Stockdale, *The History of Sandford and Merton* is most readily available in the modern facsimile, with an introduction by Isaac Kramnick, Classics of Children's Literature, 1621–1932 (New York: Garland, 1977). Subsequent references are incorporated in the text.

4. One of the most loved and widely circulated children's books in the western world for well over a century, Day's *Sandford and Merton* was originally planned as a short insert for the series Maria's father and first stepmother projected in the late 1770s, when Maria Edgeworth herself was still a child. After Honora Sneyd Edgeworth's death in 1780, the Edgeworths tabled their project until Maria grew up and reanimated it years later. Published in three volumes over six years, Day's tale grew by accretions: a lot was lifted from classics and travel books, and the foundational contrast between good Harry Sandford (benevolent, hardworking, and egalitarian) and Tommy Merton (spoiled, useless, and snobbish) demonstrably borrows from Henry Brooke's *The Fool of Quality; or, The History of Henry Earl of Moreland* (1766–70), even down to the name of Harry, the sturdy critic of worthless fine gentlemen. Anna Letitia Barbauld dryly notices that Day barely skirts plagiarism, not having "made *quite* sufficient acknowledgement in his preface," "On the Origin and Progress of Novel-Writing," *The British Novelists; with an Essay, and Prefaces Biographical and Critical* (1810; London: Rivington, et al., 1820), 1:40. It is Day, however, who makes the bad lad Jamaican. Curiously predictive of the writer's deadly fall from an insufficiently educated horse a few years later, Day's first volume ends with the proper "education" of a colt (1:208–10), as well as

with Tommy's temporary reformation. Tommy falls and "reforms" several times in subsequent volumes. The Brooke family were Irish neighbors of the Edge-worths; Henry's daughter Charlotte, in later years a Longford resident, was another early female shaper of Irish cultural identity. Caroline Robbins, *The Eighteenth-Century Commonwealthman* (Cambridge, Mass: Harvard University Press, 1959), notices the similar "Commonwealth" politics in Henry Brooke's novel and Day's work for children.

5. *Forester,* in *Moral Tales for Young People,* 5 vols. (London: J. Johnson, 1801), is currently most readily available in the three-volume 1802 reprint in The Feminist Controversy in England, 1788–1810 series (New York: Garland, 1974), 1:1–194. The forthcoming Pickering and Chatto annotated critical edition includes *Forester* and *Angelina* from Edgeworth's pioneering stories for the adolescent market; as with other genres, she initiated themes and character types still visible under the modern dress of what is marketed as "YAL" (Young Adult Literature).

6. "The Master's Tools Will Never Dismantle the Master's House," *This Bridge Called My Back: Writings by Radical Women of Color,* ed. Cherríe Moraga and Gloria Anzaldúa, 2d ed. (New York: Kitchen Table; Women of Color Press, 1983), 98–101.

7. *A Room of One's Own* (1929, Harbinger Books; New York: Harcourt, Brace, & World, 1957), 68.

8. The now classic descriptions of women's purported authorship problem derive from Sandra M. Gilbert and Susan Gubar, *The Madwoman in the Attic: The Woman Writer and the Nineteenth-Century Literary Imagination* (New Haven: Yale University Press, 1979).

9. Richard Lovell Edgeworth and Maria Edgeworth, *Memoirs of Richard Lovell Edgeworth, Esq. Begun by Himself and Concluded by His Daughter, Maria Edgeworth,* 2 vols. (London: R. Hunter & Baldwin, Cradock, & Joy, 1820), 2: 173–74. At twenty-one, Maria Edgeworth was little more than four feet, seven; the Darwin men were well over six feet, and several weighed close to 350 pounds. The father wrote the first volume of the *Memoirs* and the daughter the second, printing many family letters, as here; subsequent references to this work are incorporated in the text. I use "Edgeworth" for both father and daughter when the context is clear, and first names for each when confusion might result.

10. The least personally vain of women, Edgeworth nevertheless habitually fudges on how old she was when her father's attention to her really began, making herself much more of a child than she had been, as well as on how much of her early education she actually received from him. She was fourteen when the family settled in Ireland for good, and she had been sent away to boarding school at seven.

11. The "Original Sketch of Belinda. *Abroad and at Home.* May 10, 1800," first privately printed as an Appendix to the family memoir of Edgeworth, differs radically from both the first edition and the major revisions for later

editions: see *A Memoir of Maria Edgeworth, with a Selection from Her Letters by the Late Mrs. [Frances] Edgeworth,* ed. by Her Children, 3 vols. (London: privately printed by Joseph Masters & Son, 1867), 3:269–76. That the father insisted that Lady Delacour should live—and thus "ruined" the book—is one of the most persistent myths about Edgeworth's work, although there is no evidence whatever that he made that decision. This fable derives from a late Victorian popular biography. In fact, the last Irish Parliament before the Union was still in session in Dublin at this time, and Richard Lovell Edgeworth was a member. As for the Virginia plot, it is not an interpolation but integral to the book, as is Lady Delacour's "reform," although neither is in the sketch. Whatever a critic may make of the "Day" subplot, Edgeworth's father objected, properly Aristotelian, because it was too outré for verisimilitude and hence unavailable for "prudential reasoning," as Maria details at some length in her continuation of the *Memoirs of Richard Lovell Edgeworth* (2:350). The sketch is reprinted in the Everyman edition, which takes the unrevised first edition of 1801 as copy text; *Belinda,* intro. Eiléan Ní Chuilleanáin (London: J. M. Dent, 1993). I discuss Edgeworth's revisions and allusions in detail in the forthcoming Pickering and Chatto annotated critical edition and in other work.

12. *Belinda*'s maternal indebtedness to Frances Burney's *Evelina; or, The History of A Young Lady's Entrance into the World* (1778), an Edgeworth favorite, is obvious from this summary, but the tale has other equally important mothers both literary and historical, only some of whom are cited in the Advertisement, as well as more fathers than are considered here (for example, Jean François Marmontel and Dr. John Moore).

13. Virginia only attains literacy after she is nubile, so she might be reading Bernardin Saint-Pierre's idyllic romance of star-crossed child lovers in Helen Maria Williams's 1796 illustrated version, interspersed with the translator's own poetry: *Paul and Virginia, with Original Sonnets,* trans. Helen Maria Williams (London: Vernor & Hood, 1796). Rousseau's disciple borrows and develops Sophy's recognition of her sexuality with his Virginia's "*mal*" and "*pudeur,*" which Edgeworth mockingly elaborates as a comedy of errors rather than a tragedy of innate female modesty. (Clutching a picture of Paul, Saint-Pierre's heroine sinks in a shipwreck because she will not disrobe.) The tale, astonishingly popular in its day, was later seen as an apolitical story for children despite the sexual and colonialism themes that Edgeworth exploits. It long served as a dirty book for young readers, as susceptible Emma Bovary and disapproving Hester Thrale attest: "He gives them Ideas they never could have had," according to *Thraliana: The Diary of Mrs. Hester Lynch Thrale (Later Mrs. Piozzi) 1776–1809,* ed. Katharine C. Balderston, 2 vols. paged as one (Oxford: Clarendon Press, 1942), 982. Williams's own preface, "written at Paris, amidst the horrors of Robespierre's tyranny," suggests the political subtext of utopian fiction (iii). Fluent in French herself, Edgeworth used (and abused) other works of Saint-Pierre's too.

14. *Belinda,* intro. Eva Figes, rev. ed. (London: Pandora Press, 1986), 424. Subsequent page references in the text refer to this edition.

15. The Arabian Nights and fairy tale references are the author's, and they are everywhere, not just limited to Lady Delacour. Virtually every page in *Belinda* is rife with allusions to an extraordinary range of fictions and facts that determine how the tale should be read.

16. Harriet Edgeworth Butler to Michael Pakenham Edgeworth, 3 January 1838, partially quoted in Marilyn Butler, *Maria Edgeworth: A Literary Biography* (Oxford: Clarendon Press, 1972), 46; the daughter's romantic remembrance, described by Maria's much younger half-sister to her brother (both children of the fourth marriage) is recorded almost sixty-five years after the fact. Maria Edgeworth's head might agree with Adam Smith that "this force of blood . . . exists no-where but in tragedies and romances," but her heart acts otherwise: see "Of the Character of Virtue" (6.2.1.10), *The Theory of Moral Sentiments,* ed. D. D. Raphael and A. L. Macfie (Glasgow ed., 1976; Indianapolis: Liberty Classics, 1982), 222 in this edition. Edgeworth uses what literary critics call the "cri du sang" in later fictions as well, and its compelling force seems almost as applicable to Lady Delacour's Helena as to Virginia. "That blood speaks" is, as Ernest Renan observes, especially a Celtic notion, an aspect of the family affection that Edgeworth values as "Irish," *The Poetry of the Celtic Races and Other Studies,* trans. William G. Hutchinson (London: Walter Scott, [1896]), 6. For the cultural significance of this literary trope, see Clifton Cherpack, *The Call of Blood in French Classical Tragedy* (Baltimore: Johns Hopkins University Press, 1958); and Ruth Perry's fine study of eighteenth-century novels, "De-Familiarizing the Family; or, Writing Family History from Literary Sources," *Modern Language Quarterly* 55.4 (December 1994): 415–27.

17. Well-read in maternal educational theory, Gaskell digresses from her melodrama of the Patrick Brontë household's deprivations to recount the Day-inspired Stoic upbringing of a relative, concluding (as do the Edgeworths) that rearing a child in the ideal savage's isolation is hardly the best preparation for life in society; *The Life of Charlotte Brontë,* 1857, ed. Alan Shelston (Harmondsworth, U.K.: Penguin, 1975), 87–88. Burney knew and highly valued the hard-working Sabrina, whose eccentric youth subsided into many decades of service in two generations of the Burney men's schools as a matron or housemother. She must also have known that Day had unequivocally and unromantically dumped his two pupils. Nevertheless, in Burney's self-consciously literary French Exercise Book II of 1804, the story of Day's selection of two beautiful "jeunes filles" from the Foundling Hospital becomes a highly sentimentalized fantasy in which Day is given to pages of poetic ruminations on his role as benevolent rescuer; yet both girls end up running away to wed somebody else, their happiness marred only by thoughts of poor sad Day; entries for 27 November 1804 and 4 December 1804, French Exercise Book II (unpaginated), Berg Collection, New York Public Library. Whatever effect Burney

may have intended in this fictionalization for an adoring husband's eyes, the pathos is ludicrous next to what facts we have. I thank Betty Rizzo for directing me to the correct exercise book; it is miscited in Roger Lonsdale, "Dr. Burney, 'Joel Collier,' and Sabrina," *Evidence in Literary Scholarship: Essays in Memory of James Marshall Osborn,* ed. René Wellek and Alvaro Ribeiro (Oxford: Clarendon Press, 1979), n. 59; and in Burney, *The Journals and Letters of Fanny Burney (Madame D'Arblay),* ed. Joyce Hemlow, et al., vol. 5 (Oxford: Clarendon Press, 1975) (5:6, n. 2 to Letter 426). Day's wife-fashioning was still inspiring literary recreations in this century: writing in 1911, Charlotte Milligan Fox records a recent dramatization in a successful play called "Mice and Men," *Annals of the Irish Harpers* (London: John Murray, 1911), 178 n.

18. Friend of Mary Wollstonecraft, Mary Hays, and William Godwin, and sometime nurse of the Wollstonecraft-Godwin daughters (Fanny Imlay and baby Mary), Eliza Fenwick prudently published her tale of the noble female unbound by custom as by "A Woman." Fenwick actually has two heroines who interrogate Rousseau's gendered education; like Wollstonecraft, who cites Day's own fictionalization of the girl Selene brought up hardy and free in his children's series, Fenwick stresses female strength, but her reformist tale is more tragic than utopian. Reprinted in Garland's facsimile series The Feminist Controversy in England, 1788–1810, in 1974, *Secresy; or, The Ruin on the Rock* (1795) has recently been edited and introduced by Isobel Grundy in the Broadview Literary Texts (Ontario, Canada: Broadview Press, 1994). Schimmelpenninck, writing years later as a religious woman, officially deplores the pride and naughtiness expressed by her emulation of Spartan virtue in Day's *Sandford and Merton,* but the empowerment that comes from telling off fashionable grown-ups comes through delightfully anyway. She thrilled in hearing of the heroic tests Day's pupil had had to undergo, and when she faced a trial herself (a huge snake in the living room during a Lunar Society meeting), she calmly caught it and disposed of it, just like Harry Sandford rescuing terrified Tommy—a physical feat even her religious self can relish. Little Mary Anne's delight in and emulation of a thoroughly male-oriented book demonstrates once again that girls have no problem identifying with boy heroes: see esp. 7–31 in *The Life of Mary Anne Schimmelpenninck,* ed. Christiana C. Hankin, 2d ed. (London: Longman, Brown, Green, Longmans, & Roberts, 1858).

19. John Blackman, *A Memoir of the Life and Writings of Thomas Day* (London: John Bedford Leno, 1862), 10.

20. "Thomas Day and the Politics of Sentiment," *Special Issue: Perspectives on Imperialism and Decolonization, Journal of Commonwealth and Imperial History,* 12.2 (January 1984): 58, 69. Interestingly, "real, solemn" historians often stumble over Day's politics by other means. The standard biography, George Warren Gignilliat, Jr., *The Author of "Sandford and Merton": A Life of Thomas Day, Esq.* (New York: Columbia University Press, 1932), subsumes *Belinda*'s fictionalization unproblematically within the "factual" account. Langford's helpful chro-

nology of Day's political involvement is not reliable on Day's juvenile work or on his "bizarre experiment": the children's books do not demonstrate innate goodness, and the wife plan was Day's idea alone, 56. Langford also much underestimates the significance of Day's *Dying Negro;* Day's place in antislavery literature is typically misrepresented, even by those who notice the poem's crucial recital in *Belinda.* But that's the Day for another essay.

21. See *Reveries of the Solitary Walker,* trans. Peter France (Harmondsworth, U.K.: Penguin, 1979).

22. Reform through parliamentary participation is envisioned for the wastrel Clarence Hervey in the sketch for *Belinda,* although it plays no part in the book; Edgeworth perhaps had Day's abortive career in mind. Certainly Charles James Fox's mix of idling gambler and brilliant politician is a parallel; Fox's speeches had been republished along with Day's by the SCI. Young Forester, like the younger Day, is associated with debating clubs, a semiradical political press, and national reform through the medium of "private" essays and letters publicly printed. For the reformist political context of Day's writings and SCI membership, see Eugene Charlton Black, *The Association: British Extraparliamentary Political Organization, 1769–1793,* Harvard Historical Monographs 54 (Cambridge, Mass: Harvard University Press, 1963); Colin Bonwick, *English Radicals and the American Revolution* (Chapel Hill: University of North Carolina Press, 1977); Albert Goodwin, *The Friends of Liberty: The English Democratic Movement in the Age of the French Revolution* (Cambridge, Mass.: Harvard University Press, 1979); Robbins, *The Eighteenth-Century Commonwealthman;* and George Stead Veitch, *The Genesis of Parliamentary Reform,* 1913, intro. Ian R. Christie (London: Constable, 1965). Through his friendship with the American Laurens family, Day was also involved with peace negotiations closing the American Revolution. I am grateful to C. James Taylor of The Papers of Henry Laurens Project, University of South Carolina, for providing photocopies of unpublished Day-Laurens correspondence.

23. "Mr. Barlow," in *The Uncommercial Traveller* (no. 34), *The Works of Charles Dickens,* Cleartype ed. (New York: Books, Inc., n.d.), 16:307.

24. Like Edgeworth's, Anna Letitia Barbauld's and her brother John Aikin's, and Sarah Trimmer's, Day's juvenile publications were almost incredibly popular in many countries and languages for over a century. The very important Continental children's author Arnaud Berquin (a major influence on Edgeworth) was his French translator. Day's oeuvre is emphatically male-oriented, but that did not deter eager girl readers, as noticed above. Victorian memoirs and novels abound in loving references to Day; for example, Georgy Osborne's doting mother sells Dobbin's rich Indian shawl to buy Day and Edgeworth so her spoiled brat's Christmas longing will be satisfied in *Vanity Fair,* 1848, chap. 46. The most moving tribute, however, is Leigh Hunt's lengthy reminiscence of Day's *Sandford and Merton* as a harbinger of reformist change: "The pool of mercenary and time-serving ethics was first blown over by the fresh country

breeze of Mr. Day's *Sandford and Merton*—a production that I well remember, and shall ever be grateful to," *The Autobiography of Leigh Hunt*, ed. J. E. Morpurgo (London: Cresset Press, 1949), 50. Even though Day had a hand in an insulting parody of his musical works, Dr. Charles Burney still presented his daughter with *Sandford and Merton* for her son, complete with presentation verses (the volumes still exist at Yale); those Victorians who disliked Day's fictional tutor as an "instructive monomaniac" nevertheless pay tribute to his incredible force, as in Dickens's comic charge that omnipresent "Mr. Barlow" has ruined his life, *Uncommercial Traveller* no. 34, 306–12.

25. *The Rise of English Nationalism: A Cultural History, 1740–1830* (New York: St. Martin's Press, 1987), 101, 107. Valuable as Newman's perspective is in recognizing Day as far more than a paranoid eccentric with a grudge against the beau monde, his nationalistic model has no room for Rousseau's influence or questions of gender, nor does he notice Day's important precursor Henry Brooke, from whom Day frankly borrowed the contrast motif of corrupt rich versus the virtuous Volk. Conversely, G. J. Barker-Benfield's summary of Day's work decontextualizes and depoliticizes *Sandford and Merton's* radicalism into the question of whether real men cry, *The Culture of Sensibility: Sex and Society in Eighteenth-Century Britain* (Chicago: University of Chicago Press, 1992), chap. 3 on "The Question of Effeminacy." Day's animus against French politesse is an animus against French politics: the fine gentleman whose "first qualification" is "never to do any thing useful" is the sycophant of court and female salon tyrants, not a free citizen (*Sandford and Merton*, 3:83).

26. Ruth Salvaggio's *Enlightened Absence: Neoclassical Configurations of the Feminine* (Urbana and Chicago: University of Illinois Press, 1988) exemplifies the pervasive argument that Enlightenment intellectual structures depend on woman's exclusion and suppression; she is the dark, the chaos, the Other that must be suppressed to maintain the system's integrity. Salvaggio's analysis draws on French poststructuralism, but the cultural displacement she depicts has been much theorized from other perspectives as well.

27. Benedict Nicholson notes that unlike many of Wright's portraits, Day's is idealized rather than realistic: the abstracted intellectual whose commitment to principles will not let human frailties stop him, even if he occasions misery to others. There were two versions of Day by Wright and also engravings. The book and writing on the classical column have been variously politicized, but are not really decipherable, *Joseph Wright of Derby: Painter of Light*, 2 vols. (London: Paul Mellon Foundation for British Art, 1968), 1:96, 101–3.

28. James Keir, *An Account of the Life and Writings of Thomas Day, Esq.* (London: John Stockdale, 1791), 12–15. Subsequent references to Keir are given in the text.

29. See, respectively, Sir Michael Sadler, *Thomas Day: An English Disciple of Rousseau*, Rede Lecture 1928 (Cambridge: Cambridge University Press, 1928); Muriel Jaeger, *Adventures in Living from Cato to George Sand* (New York:

William Morrow, 1932); Sir S. H. Scott, *The Exemplary Mr. Day 1748–1789 . . . A Philosopher in Search of the Life of Virtue and of a Paragon among Women* (London: Faber & Faber, 1935); and V. S. Pritchett, *The Living Novel and Later Appreciations* (New York: Vintage; Random House, 1967).

30. The poem's versions differ substantially in length and content, and some readers (including Olaudah Equiano) knew them all. The first is [Thomas Day and John Bicknell], *The Dying Negro, A Poetical Epistle, Supposed to be Written by A Black, Who Lately Shot Himself on Board A Vessel in the River Thames; to His Intended Wife* (London: W. Flexney, 1773). The 1784 *Fragment of An Original Letter on the Slavery of the Negroes; Written in the Year 1776* is bound together and reissued with other pamphlets in *Four Tracts* (London: John Stockdale, 1785).

31. *A Vindication of the Rights of Woman*, 1792, ed. Carol H. Poston, 2d ed., Norton Critical Edition (New York: W. W. Norton, 1988), 40.

32. In the interests of consistency, I use Foxley's spelling in her translation, rather than Rousseau's original "Sophie."

33. The whole miscellany and key pieces are routinely misattributed to Mrs. Barbauld, as in the two versions of Isaac Kramnick's analysis. "Most of the book is Barbauld's," Kramnick claims, but the pieces he discusses as hers are her brother's, "Children's Literature and Bourgeois Ideology: Observations on Culture and Industrial Capitalism in the Later Eighteenth Century," in *Culture and Politics from Puritanism to the Enlightenment*, ed. Perez Zagorin (Berkeley: University of California Press, 1980), 239 n. 49; a briefer version of this essay is reprinted without correction in *Republicanism and Bourgeois Radicalism: Political Ideology in Late Eighteenth-Century England and America* (Ithaca: Cornell University Press, 1990). Barbauld actually wrote only 15 out of 101 entries, though she appeared as her brother's coauthor. The writers of individual selections in *Evenings at Home* are identified by Lucy Aikin in the fifteenth edition, which rearranges the pieces according to the age of the presumed reader; Aikin's "Presence of Mind," which includes maternal domestic heroism about bloodletting as well as bulls, is reprinted in John Aikin and Anna Letitia Barbauld, *Evenings at Home; or, The Juvenile Budget Opened*, 15th ed. rev., ed. Arthur Aikin and Lucy Aikin (London: Baldwin & Cradock, et al., 1836), 239–46. John Aikin would have known the story from Keir's 1791 biography; the raging bull deflected by "presence of mind" also turns up in Day's own *Sandford and Merton*, Harry first saving Tommy and then being saved himself by a noble black (2:298–305).

34. Day argues that "universal morality" equals the method "by which the whole human species may attain the greatest possible degree of happiness." Because slavery is the "absolute dependence of one man upon another," it is incompatible with both civil justice and natural rights: "a crime so monstrous . . . that all those who practise it deserve to be extirpated from the earth," *Fragment of an Original Letter* in *Four Tracts*, 17–18, 24; [Thomas Day and

John Bicknell], *The Dying Negro, A Poem, To Which Is Added, A Fragment of a Letter on the Slavery of the Negroes,* by Thomas Day (London: John Stockdale, 1793), 62–63, 67–68. The conflict between Day's eloquent defense of black rights and his attitudes toward women exemplifies wider tensions in masculine Enlightenment thought.

35. Bernard Burke's incongruous inclusion of Day's love life in his scandalous compendium, *Anecdotes of the Aristocracy, and Episodes in Ancestral Story,* 2d ed. (London: Henry Colburn, 1849), 2:390–400, exemplifies this point. Had she still been living, Seward, who had attacked even her friend Dr. Erasmus Darwin for plagiarism, would certainly have sued.

36. A 1790 letter replying to Dr. Darwin captures the struggle between Keir's propriety and his recognition that Day's educational experiment is revealingly "characteristic." Darwin had evidently suggested that Keir lie; but "what you propose is too well known *not to be the accurate state;* and it could be easily contradicted." Instead, deflecting attention to Rousseau's seductive "ignis fatuus of the fancy," Keir simply obfuscates all details. See [J. Keir Moilliet, ed.], *Sketch of the Life of James Keir, Esq., F.R.S., With a Selection from His Correspondence* (London: Privately printed Robert Edmund Taylor, [1868?]), 108–9; and Keir, 26. Seward's public account, *Memoirs of the Life of Dr. Darwin, Chiefly During His Residence at Lichfield, with Anecdotes of His Friends, and Criticisms of His Writings* (London: J. Johnson, 1804), is supplemented by her correspondence, *Letters of Anna Seward,* 6 vols. (Edinburgh: Archibald Constable, et al., 1811); page references to both are cited hereafter in the text.

37. *Call Back Yesterday: A Book of Old Letters Chosen from Her Collection with Some Memories of Her Own,* 2d ed. (London: Eyre & Spottiswoode, 1938), 101.

38. Indeed, like previous raconteurs of Day's life, Edgeworth's descendants were unaware of this composition; I thank Dr. Frances Harris of the British Library, whose searches failed to locate the manuscript there, either.

39. Historians sometimes write as if the Edgeworths' educational work derived from Rousseau, when it is in part a reaction against Richard Lovell's initial experiment. Maria was not included in this scheme, nor was she brought up in the precepts of *Practical Education* (the family manual for parents of 1798) like the children of the last two marriages, although her account of home education in the continuation of her father's autobiography suggests otherwise. She was sent to boarding school very young and stayed there till the family's final removal to Ireland in 1782. For Dick's education and consequent "invincible dislike to control," see *Memoirs of Richard Lovell Edgeworth* 1:177–79, 257–59, 273–79, 353. Although the *Memoirs* do not say so, Edgeworth formally disinherited his unruly eldest son in 1787; see Edgar E. MacDonald, *The American Edgeworths: A Biographical Sketch of Richard Edgeworth (1764–1796)* (Richmond, Va.: n.p., July 1970).

40. *Maria Edgeworth: Letters from England, 1813–1844,* ed. Christina Col-

vin (Oxford: Clarendon Press, 1971), 99. Subsequent references to this collection are given in the text.

41. Useful overviews of the period's changing constructions of masculinity include Anthony Fletcher, *Gender, Sex, and Subordination in England, 1500–1800* (New Haven: Yale University Press, 1995); and Michèle Cohen, *Fashioning Masculinity: National Identity and Language in the Eighteenth Century* (London: Routledge, 1996).

42. Maria is never named and never mentioned again in the portion of the *Memoirs* her father completed.

43. *Émile*, 1762, trans. Barbara Foxley, Everyman's Library, 1911 (London: Dent; New York: Dutton, 1966), 321. The most recent entry in the large literature on Rousseau and gender, Mary Seidman Trouille's valuable overview, *Sexual Politics in the Enlightenment: Women Writers Read Rousseau*, The Margins of Literature (Albany: State University of New York Press, 1997), focuses almost exclusively on French writers, with only a few pages on Wollstonecraft. Curiously, Trouille takes Rousseau as seriously as he took himself and does not consider how many women (including Wollstonecraft as well as Edgeworth) sport with his ideas.

44. During the Edgeworths' 1802–3 visit to France, Richard Lovell described Suard and her salon, noting that she "aims at singularity and independence of sentiment. Would you believe it, Mr. Day paid his court to her thirty years ago?" *Maria Edgeworth in France and Switzerland: Selections from the Edgeworth Family Letters*, ed. Christina Colvin (Oxford: Clarendon Press, 1979), 32. Day urged Seward to burn a 1772 letter about his failed affairs because he was now "under the Tuition, of fair French Philosophers," quoted in Mary Alden Hopkins, *Dr. Johnson's Lichfield* (New York: Hastings House, 1952), 158.

45. See Hopkins, *Dr. Johnson's Lichfield*, 157. Ironically, Margaret named the daughter who became Maria's most influential critic of her own generation "Sophy"; with their appreciation of women's talk and ways, Margaret and Sophy Ruxton exerted a significant feminine influence on Maria Edgeworth's work. Mrs. Ruxton had such "grace and charm of manner" that the family *Memoir* of Maria records a gentleman's insisting he would address her as "Madam" even if she were concealed in beggar's rags, *A Memoir of Maria Edgeworth*, 1:18.

46. M. Lockwood, "Thomas Day," *Nineteenth Century* 42 (July 1897): 79; R. H. Nichols and F. A. Wray, *The History of the London Foundling Hospital* (London: Oxford University Press, 1935), 4, 382. Day was following Rousseau au pied de la lettre: "I meant to train a helpmeet for Émile, from the very first, and to educate them for each other and with each other"; a wise father would marry his son to "the woman . . . adapted to him, were she born in a bad home, were she even the hangman's daughter" (*Émile*, 368–69). In 1769 the London

Foundling Hospital apprenticed 1430 children rather than the eighteen or so per year of a decade before because Parliament had backed wider admissions; there were no resources for sufficient inquiry into children's placement. Sabrina and Lucretia were lucky; for horrific accounts of rape, abuse, and murder, see Ruth K. McClure, *Coram's Children: The London Foundling Hospital in the Eighteenth Century* (New Haven: Yale University Press, 1981), 132–35.

47. The art term for fictitious or historical dress in portraiture here also suggests that Virginia is Hervey's fancy or kept woman, meanings that the text itself puts in play (132, 215). His exhibition of his supposed mistress at Somerset House less than halfway through the novel epitomizes the illegible behavior that forces Belinda to keep her feelings for him in check. Only at the tale's conclusion is his act revealed as a desperate ploy to find Virginia's real father, so that he can hand over his quondam pupil and thus free himself to love Belinda openly.

48. For the French version of this new domesticity, what Yvonne Knibiehler calls "L'Exaltation de l'Amour Maternel," see part 2 of Knibiehler and Catherine Fouquet, *L'Histoire des Mères du Moyen-Age à Nos Jours* (Paris: Montalba, 1980), but the new domesticity was inflected in different ways depending on country, gender, class, and so on.

49. This important preface is usually said to have been added to the third edition, but UCLA owns what may be a unique copy of the second with the Rousseau material, *The Dying Negro, A Poetical Epistle, From A Black, Who Shot Himself on Board A Vessel in the River Thames; to His Intended Wife*, 2d rev. ed. (London: W. Flexney, 1774), vi. The content and even the title change from edition to edition, some including drawings depicting stabbing instead of shooting.

50. "An Ambler" writing on his "Sandford and Merton" run in "The Gentle Art of Cycling" captures the enormous popularity Day's book enjoyed for a century. All little boys got the Bible as their first book, then *Sandford and Merton*: "It is an awful thing to reflect upon now, that some of us had a hazy notion that the two books were by the same writer," *Macmillan's* 27 (January 1898): 205. In 1862, John Blackman similarly recalled his first discovery of the book as "one of the sunniest reminiscences of my early life," *A Memoir*, 9. Leigh Hunt's already cited tribute emphasizes Day's inauguration of a higher morality for children's literature than Newbery's coarse material rewards—the thinking boy's book. For the book's enormous long-term readership, see Gignilliat, *The Author of "Sandford and Merton,"* 337–48. F. C. Burnand's late-nineteenth-century parody, *The New History of Sandford and Merton* (London: Bradbury, Evans, 1872), relies on its audience's total familiarity with Day, so closely does it follow Day's incidents.

51. Marilyn Butler, "Edgeworth's Stern Father: Escaping Thomas Day, 1795–1801," in *Tradition in Transition: Women Writers, Marginal Texts, and the*

Eighteenth-Century Canon, ed. Alvaro Ribeiro and James G. Basker (Oxford: Clarendon Press, 1996), 75–93, argues for Day's influence on Edgeworth's children's tales, but the parallels she cites are also to be found in the French tales of Berquin and Genlis, to which Maria Edgeworth so often refers, as well as in English writers like Mrs. Barbauld and her brother. It is Day's masculine tone and ideology that are so striking, for almost all of the stories that make up the book's bulk are borrowed; even the strongest incidents in the Harry-Tommy frame are lifted from Henry Brooke. So notorious is Day for inserted chunks of other writers that his parodist Burnand hilariously focalizes these digressions. Ghostwriting *Professional Education* for her father, Maria Edgeworth herself calls attention to Day's book "as likely to inspire manly feelings, and to form the character to fortitude, courage, truth, and all the virtues of a patriot and a soldier," *Essays on Professional Education* (London: J. Johnson, 1809), 124.

52. "A Spartan mother had five sons with the army. A Helot arrived; trembling she asked his news. 'Your five sons are slain.' 'Vile slave, was that what I asked thee?' 'We have won the victory.' She hastened to the temple to render thanks to the gods. That was a citizen" (*Émile,* 8 in Foxley's translation). Paul Thomas, "Jean-Jacques Rousseau, Sexist?" *Feminist Studies* 17.2 (Summer 1991): 195–217, and Joan B. Landes, chap. 3, "Rousseau's Reply to Public Women," in *Women and the Public Sphere in the Age of the French Revolution* (Ithaca: Cornell University Press, 1988), demonstrate especially clearly the debt Rousseau's construction of the independent male citizen owes to domestic woman.

53. Day's opinion of pre-Revolutionary France had not improved by 1771; on another fruitless trip to turn himself into an elegant gentleman, he complained to Anna Seward that "Politics, in this blessed Country of passive Obedience, are as scarce as honest women—And Love is still an emptier name" (ALS 18 December 1771, Lichfield Joint Record Office AS 4).

54. Not surprisingly, Day and Richard Lovell Edgeworth star in Henri Roddier's list of eighteenth-century disciples of Rousseau, *J.-J. Rousseau en Angleterre au XVIII Siècle: L'Oeuvre et L'Homme* (Paris: Boivin, 1950), 166–75, but like many others, Roddier fails to distinguish between the French tradition of "experimental" education and that more properly associated with the Birmingham Lunar Society with which both men were affiliated. Most English contemporaries (especially the later Edgeworths) found the tutor's continual duping and trickery of the pupil repellent: even Sophy is a "plant," set up for Émile to find. For the Lunar background of experimentation, see Robert E. Schofield, *The Lunar Society of Birmingham: A Social History of Provincial Science and Industry in Eighteenth-Century England* (Oxford: Clarendon Press, 1963).

55. As editor of her father's life, Maria Edgeworth included this and a number of other letters between Day and Richard Lovell that throw odd lights

on their early educational schemes. Despite Day's failure, for example, Richard Lovell, by then bringing up his third family, later proposed adopting a lower-class child to rear; Day was eloquently dissuasive (*Memoirs of RLE*, 2:95–101).

56. The Reverend George Robinson, Chancellor's Vicar at Lichfield Cathedral, likewise records in an unpublished manuscript of 27 October 1812 that "What Miss Seward says respecting Sabrina's not bearing pain heroically is not true. I have seen her drop melted sealing wax voluntarily on her arm, and bear it heroically without flinching," cited in Hopkins, *Dr. Johnson's Lichfield*, 148. Schimmelpenninck was the daughter of Samuel Galton, a member of the famous Birmingham Lunar Society that attracted so many scientists, inventors, and entrepreneurs, including Erasmus Darwin, Richard Lovell Edgeworth, James Watt, and Joseph Priestley. She was brought up on *Sandford and Merton* herself, thinking a fine lady "a Mayday dancer who could afford to have better tinsel" and catching snakes barehanded like little Harry (Schimmelpenninck, *Life*, 8–10, 27–31). The Galtons' source, Miss De Luc, reader to Queen Charlotte and acquaintance of Frances Burney, boarded at the same house with Sabrina Sidney after Day dismissed her.

57. Seward is another of this period's neglected major woman writers, mostly relegated to denigrating footnotes in Johnson-Boswell and Edgeworth scholarship and just beginning to count with Romanticists and queer theorists. Outspoken, unabashed, a loyal lover and a good hater, she is usually laughed at for her style's floridity. But she can be an impressive poet, as in her sonnets to Honora Sneyd, and she had an extraordinary capacity for friendship with both men and women, as her letters testify. Older works like Margaret Ashmun, *The Singing Swan: An Account of Anna Seward and Her Acquaintance with Dr. Johnson, Boswell, and Others of Their Time* (1931; New York: Greenwood Press, 1968), and Hesketh Pearson, *The Swan of Lichfield* (London: Hamish Hamilton, 1936), based on printed sources, are character studies of an engaging eccentric. Lillian Faderman, *Surpassing the Love of Men: Romantic Friendship and Love between Women from the Renaissance to the Present* (New York: William Morrow, 1981), 132–38, and Emma Donoghue, *Passions between Women: British Lesbian Culture, 1668–1801* (1993; New York: Harper Perennial, 1996), 120–21, glance at Seward and Honora Sneyd. Hopkins, *Dr. Johnson's Lichfield*, uses a few manuscript letters and considers sympathetically Seward's personality and her many friendships, including the scandal over John Saville, who left his wife to maintain an apparently platonic relationship with Seward. Material included in the standard correspondence of 1811 was often abridged and misdated in publication, as James L. Clifford, "The Authenticity of Anna Seward's Published Correspondence," *Modern Philology* 39.2 (November 1941): 113–22, demonstrates. But these six volumes (only part of Seward's voluminous production) and the many letters in the *Journals and Correspondence of Thomas Sedgewick Whalley, D.D.*, ed. Hill Wickham, 2 vols. (London: Richard Bentley, 1863), remain the best sources for Seward. Even though both begin in midlife,

they are full of references to her earlier years, Honora (many more than the indices record), the Sabrina-Day story, and her relationships with the Edge-worths. If Day partially shapes *Belinda*'s hero, the coolly enigmatic Honora Sneyd, so passionately loved by so many women and men, colors the titular heroine.

58. Acting Adjutant-General of the British Army in New York when he was implicated in the Benedict Arnold affair, André had been favored by Seward as Honora's suitor, and she published poems and private letters glamorizing the relationship that the Edgeworths deeply resented. Perenially susceptible to romantic fictionalizing, Seward's material resurfaces yet again in Anthony Bailey, *Major André: A Novel* (New York: Farrar, Straus, & Giroux, 1987).

59. Writing to Mary Powys (a mutual connection of Anna's and Honora's and a long-time friend of the Edgeworths), Seward describes the 1770–71 visits of "a whole cluster of Beaux, one of them no *common Beau,* the lively, the sentimental, the accomplish'd, the scientific, the gallant, the learned, the cele-brated, Mr. Edgeworth"; "Our rambles up on the Terrace have been *very* ani-mated these last evenings, Mr. Edgeworth enlivening us by a wit, extensive as the light of the Sun & active as its heat. . . . Mr. Day *improving* our minds while he delights our imaginations," quoted in Hopkins, *Dr. Johnson's Lichfield,* 112.

60. Day's flirtation with fancy clothes (including wig and decorative bag) and fashionable accomplishments was very brief and marked with self-loathing. This whole letter to Anna Seward fiercely satirizes the French "Gentleman" (ALS 18 December 1771, Lichfield Joint Record Office AS 4).

61. Increasingly unmaneageable, young Dick spurred his adoring little sister on to mischief too; both were packed off to boarding school young when even the efficient Honora failed to tame them. Dick went to sea early, disgracefully jumped ship in the East, and wound up a struggling American colonist with— to the Edgeworths' dismay—a Methodist wife. He died early after a last visit home in the mid 1790s, much regretted by the sister who immortalized his teasing and sauciness in the brother of her autobiographical child heroine, Rosamond. The unreformed Lady Delacour's Methodistical readings just be-fore her breast surgery signal her irrationality.

62. After their deaths, Mrs. Day's nephew published her juvenile efforts and uncollected work by Day in Thomas Lowndes, ed., *Select Miscellaneous Produc-tions, of Mrs. Day, and Thomas Day, Esq. in Verse and Prose* (London: Cadell & Davis, 1805). "A Description of A Learned Lady" is typical in its contrast of the pretentious Classica with the idealized self-portrait of Sophronia, who "unites true learning and manly strength of understanding, to feminine purity and delicacy of manners," Lowndes, 163. Like Day, she was a talker so their retired life was one long debate, apparently to the taste of both. Ironically, he found the wife who matched his contradictory expectations among the fine ladies he theoretically despised. But Sophron and Sophronia had no children. The *Sand-ford and Merton* character who is one of Day's imagined selves conflates the

classical Sophron of Syracuse; Johnson's Sophron, the practical philosopher in *Rambler* 57, ed. W. J. Bate and Albrecht B. Strauss (New Haven: Yale University Press, 1969), 3:305–9, in *The Yale Edition of the Works of Samuel Johnson;* and Thomas Percival's traveler in one of Day's sources, *A Father's Instructions,* in *The Works, Literary, Moral, and Philosophical, of Thomas Percival, M.D.,* 2 vols. (London: J. Johnson, 1807), 1:1–377 (3 pts., 1775, 1777, 1800). Sophron's story takes up most of Day's third volume. Mrs. Day's similar autobiographical appropriation unwittingly demonstrates the gendering of enlightened discourse, for Johnson has a Sophronia as well as a Sophron, a parsimonious scold as opposed to a domestic philosopher, *Rambler* 113, 4:239–40. Butler's misreading of "Strephon" for "Sophron" decontextualizes Day's allusive alter ego into a pastoral convention, "Edgeworth's Stern Father," 90.

63. The *Gentleman's Magazine* obituary section for June 1792 records the death of Thomas Day's "relict": "This lady . . . fell a victim to conjugal affection, never having had a day's health since the death of her husband" (62, pt. 1, 581). Mrs. Day's reclusive behavior and willed death turn up in several Joe Miller compilations: a living pun, she ventured forth only at night and never saw the light of Day after her husband died.

64. Quoted in Gignilliat, *The Author of "Sandford and Merton,"* 243.

65. Nancy Senior, *"Les Solitaires* as a Test for Emile and Sophie," *French Review* 49.4 (March 1976): 528–35; and Susan Moller Okin's chapter "The Fate of Rousseau's Heroines" analyze Sophy's adulterous fall, illicit pregnancy, and abandonment, *Women in Western Political Thought* (Princeton: Princeton University Press, 1979), 167–94. *Les Solitaires,* Rousseau's uncompleted sequel to *Émile,* shows that the natural man cannot survive in society either, but Émile's training preserves him as Sophy's dependence on love cannot. He flees; Sophy—left like Sabrina with children to support—dies. Written about 1763, first published in 1780, and included in the 1793 *Oeuvres Complètes de J. J. Rousseau* (Paris: Bélin, Caille, Grégoire, Volland, 1793), 10:161–254, *Émile et Sophie, ou Les Solitaires* is most recently reprinted in *Oeuvres Complètes,* ed. Bernard Gagnebin and Marcel Raymond (Paris: Gallimard, 1969), 4:881–924.

66. Day repeatedly eulogized Laurens; Lowndes prints two of the poems, *Select Miscellaneous Productions,* 10–13. Sabrina Bicknell's letter (16 May 1787) thanking Charles Burney, Jr., for the educational opportunities offered her sons is in the James Marshall and Marie-Louise Osborn Collection at Yale University; I am grateful to Stephen Parks, Curator of the Collection, for his assistance. Mrs. Bicknell is often mentioned in Frances Burney's letters and journals; Frances was "extremely pleased" with her "gentle & obliging . . . good & amiable" nature and worried for her when she outworked her strength, *The Journals and Letters of Fanny Burney (Madame D'Arblay),* ed. Joyce Hemlow, et al. (Oxford: Clarendon Press, 1972), 1:70; and *The Journals and Letters,* ed. Joyce Hemlow (Oxford: Clarendon Press, 1973), 4:373. The French Exercise Book cited above idealizes Sabrina's working relationship with Charles as a

"liaison" characterized by "douceur" as well as "utilité," for her brother treats his "amie fidelle . . . . comme son egal." (Burney also tactfully changes Day's "Lucretia" for the second girl to "Juliana.") For a different view of the Bicknell-Burney liaison, see *The Piozzi Letters: Correspondence of Hester Lynch Piozzi, 1784–1821 (Formerly Mrs. Thrale)*, ed. Edward A. Bloom and Lillian D. Bloom, vol. 4: 1805–1810 (Newark, N.J.: University of Delaware Press, 1996), 296, 298 n. 7. In a letter of 27 July 1810, Piozzi claims that Dr. Charles Burney, erroneously thought responsible for attacks on her in the press, was "a man well known to be a habitual Drunkard . . . living all but openly with a Woman in his own *house.*" After Burney had acquired several livings, Sabrina lived in his rectory at Deptford.

67. Roger Lonsdale discusses "Joel Collier"'s *Musical Travels*, a parody of Burney's *Tours* directed against the musician's involvement with the Foundling Hospital, noting that a Bodleian Library copy of *Sandford and Merton* attributes the book to Day as well as Bicknell, *Dr. Charles Burney: A Literary Biography* (Oxford: Clarendon Press, 1965), 153–57. In a subsequent essay, "Dr. Burney, 'Joel Collier,' and Sabrina," Lonsdale conjectures that later additions to Bicknell's ribald satire equating castration and music are by Day. Had he compared the moralistic Appendix added to the expanded third and fourth editions more closely with Day's pieces in Lowndes's *Select Miscellaneous Productions*, his published and unpublished letters, and the Edgeworths' portrayals of him, he would have had convincing proof in Day's incessant linkage of degenerate female education and authorship with foreign effeminacy and English men's emasculation: see "Joel Collier" [John Bicknell and Thomas Day], *Musical Travels Through England by the Late Joel Collier, Licentiate in Music*, 4th ed. (London: G. Kearsly, 1776). The Appendix (28 pages in the 4th edition) is clearly Day's: the concerns and phrases repeatedly echo his. Day's and Bicknell's satire emblematizes the emergent ideologies of English national culture contextualized by Gerald Newman, *The Rise of English Nationalism*, and Richard Leppert, *Music and Image: Domesticity, Ideology, and Socio-cultural Formation in Eighteenth-Century England* (Cambridge: Cambridge University Press, 1988). Leppert's attention to gender in this sociocultural formation also illuminates the symbolic centrality of dancing and music in Maria Edgeworth's satire of Day in *Forester,* as well as in Day's own *Sandford and Merton.*

68. In 1788 Seward brought the situation of the "sweet unfortunate" who had "married rather from discretion than from choice" to the attention of George Hardinge, Solicitor-General to the Queen, renowned for his philanthropic fund-raising. She thought Bicknell's brothers unfeeling to let their sister-in-law "work in a situation scarce above that of a common servant, and much more harrassing," but she was angrier with Day, "whose still more bounden duty it is to consider her as his child, so far at least as to shield her from the miseries of apprehended want, and from fatigues to which her tender degree of strength is incompetent. This *one* gives away two-thirds of a large income"

while "amidst an ostentatious display of moral exertions, wondrous prone to neglect and defy the claims of obvious duties." Hardinge informed her of Bicknell's "bachelor voluptuousness" in the course of his "nobly generous exertions in favour of sweet Mrs. B——, whose story is so extraordinary, and so interesting; whose conduct has been so amiable; whose fate so hard," *Letters of AS*, 2: 176, 195–96, 250, 234.

69. Seward wrote Thomas Whalley that "his foolish pride is stung by the publicity of circumstances concerning his mother's singular story, which cast no shade of reflection upon her in any respect, viz. her being originally a foundling child, and having been left in straitened circumstances, and a subscription having been raised for her. Surely she appears in a very amiable light from my representation, and for that glowing testimony to her merit, this is my reward," Whalley, *Journals and Correspondence*, 2:263.

70. Feeling that she owed her happiness to Sabrina's failure, Mrs. Day continued (and increased) the widow's annuity until her death in 1792, "from the belief that she once really loved the ever lamented Object of my fondness & veneration"; Richard Lovell continued remittances to Sabrina for many years: see the manuscript letters printed in Gignilliat, *The Author of "Sandford and Merton,"* 318; and Lady [Dorothea] Charnwood, "A Habitation's Memories," *Cornhill Magazine* 63.377–78 n.s. (November–December 1927): 535–47, 664–77, at 676. Maria includes Sabrina's gratitude to Richard Lovell in the *Memoirs*—"You have not said enough—you *cannot* say enough of your father's kindness to me"—but the former pupil's outburst was for private letters only. She also slightly obscured Sabrina's foundling (and presumably illegitimate) origin out of deference to her feelings, *Memoirs of RLE*, 2:114. Keir's 1791 biography obliterates the active search for likely subjects to train and wed; in his account the charitable Day simply "received into his guardianship two female children"; 27.

71. Gignilliat, *The Author of "Sandford and Merton,"* 350.

72. *A Memoir of Maria Edgeworth*, 1:11–12.

73. *The Madwoman in the Attic*, 151, 148.

74. As a reductio ad absurdum of stereotypical feminine irrationality, *An Essay on the Noble Science of Self-Justification*, the third of the *Letters for Literary Ladies*, calls into question essentialist clichés about woman, reason, and argument. The same *Critical* reviewer who thought the volume the work of Dr. John Aikin rates the burlesque's "vein of ironical humour, not inferior to Swift" and its style worthy of Addison: see the review of *Letters for Literary Ladies*, *Critical Review*, 2d ser. 19 (January 1797): 170–74, at 174. Because it brilliantly reproduces the faulty female rhetoric it would erase, the work is peculiarly liable to a literalism that mistakes its prowoman satire for baby-eating: see Gilbert and Gubar, *The Madwoman in the Attic*, 148. Edgeworth's politics of quotation signals her tongue in cheek with an opening epigraph from a notoriously misogynist poem by Thomas Parnell. For Edgeworth as accomplished parodist, see

my "Goring John Bull: Maria Edgeworth's Hibernian High Jinks Versus the Imperialist Imaginary," in *Cutting Edges: Postmodern Critical Essays on Eighteenth-Century Satire*, ed. James E. Gill (Knoxville: University of Tennessee Press, 1996), 367–94.

75. *ME in France and Switzerland*, 7.

76. See, for example, the subtle analysis in Anne Freadman, "Of Cats, and Companions, and the Name of George Sand," in *Grafts: Feminist Cultural Criticism*, ed. Susan Sheridan (London: Verso, 1988), 125–56. Current fashion magazines play with this dual vision of women's crossdressing all the time: for every male turned off by the mannish woman in pants and tie, another finds the female in boys' attire twice as sexy and "feminine." The breeches part, as recent queer theorists imply, is not necessarily the signifier of an incipiently lesbian text.

77. *Letters for Literary Ladies*, 170.

78. Diane Dugaw, *Warrior Women and Popular Balladry, 1650–1850*, Cambridge Studies in Eighteenth-Century English Literature and Thought 4 (Cambridge: Cambridge University Press, 1989), 158–59, 160.

79. See, for example, Lisa Moore, "'Something More Tender Still Than Friendship': Romantic Friendship in Early-Nineteenth-Century England," *Feminist Studies* 18.3 (Fall 1992): 499–520; Susan C. Greenfield, "'Abroad and at Home': Sexual Ambiguity, Miscegenation, and Colonial Boundaries in Edgeworth's *Belinda*," *PMLA* 112.2 (March 1997): 214–28; Donoghue, *Passions between Women*, 100–103; Anne K. Mellor, "A Novel of Their Own: Romantic Women's Fiction, 1790–1830," in *The Columbia History of the British Novel*, ed. John Richetti, et al. (New York: Columbia University Press, 1994), 327–51; Patricia Juliana Smith, *Lesbian Panic: Homoeroticism in Modern British Women's Fiction*, Between Men–Between Women: Lesbian and Gay Studies (New York: Columbia University Press, 1997), 8–11. Crediting the phrase "lesbian panic" to her former student Smith, Mellor herself identifies *Belinda*'s "'macho' Harriet [sic] Freke as a 'freak' or 'caprice' of nature," although, as both the tale and the OED indicate, that was not the contemporary meaning of the character's name (332–33). There was, as I discuss elsewhere, a real Mrs. Freke. *The Columbia History of the British Novel*'s positioning and title for Mellor's chapter foreground complex issues of literary history: the writers grouped as "Romantic" follow novelists of the 1790s, the Gothic, Austen, and Scott—their contemporaries and in many cases their successors—and situate them next to the Brontës.

80. Tania Modleski, *Feminism without Women: Culture and Criticism in a "Postfeminist" Age* (New York and London: Routledge, 1991), documents numerous recent examples of masculine cooptations of the feminine that simultaneously devalue or erase woman, a postmodern recuperation of the fin de siècle "postfeminism" of the 1790s.

81. Lowndes, *Select Miscellaneous Productions*, 80–82.

82. Sarah Maza, "The Diamond Necklace Affair Revisited (1785–1786): The Case of the Missing Queen," in *Eroticism and the Body Politic*, ed. Lynn Hunt, Parallax Re-visions of Culture and Society (Baltimore: Johns Hopkins University Press, 1991), 68.

83. Day's reading in Rousseau obviously extended much beyond *Émile*. For example, the antitheatrical *Letter to M. D'Alembert* shows parallels with Day's worries over women in public, women's art (or deficiencies therein), and influence: "Everywhere that women dominate, their taste must also dominate; and this is what determines the taste of our age," *Politics and the Arts: Letter to M. D'Alembert on the Theatre*, 1758, trans. Allan Bloom (Ithaca: Cornell University Press, 1977), 103 n. Dena Goodman's work, much of it now collected in *The Republic of Letters: A Cultural History of the Enlightenment* (Ithaca: Cornell University Press, 1994), exemplifies feminist rereadings of woman-led French salon culture and its political implications, but major women historians also continue to reproduce the male-dominated exclusionary model of the French public sphere that Joan Landes pioneered. Biancamaria Fontana's hostile review of Joan Wallach Scott's *Only Paradoxes to Offer: French Feminists and the Rights of Man*, *TLS* 4900 (28 February 1997): 31, demonstrates the ongoing argument over French women's position and power. Fine critiques of Landes's formulation of Habermas's public sphere that also offer alternative woman-friendly models include Goodman, "Public Sphere and Private Life: Toward a Synthesis of Current Historiographical Approaches to the Old Regime," *History and Theory* 31.1 (1992): 1–20, and Keith Michael Baker, "Defining the Public Sphere in Eighteenth-Century France: Variations on a Theme by Habermas," in *Habermas and the Public Sphere*, ed. Craig Calhoun, 181–211. Baker is especially helpful because much of his discussion of Wollstonecraft applies to Edgeworth too.

84. Keir, *An Account of the Life and Writings of Thomas Day*, 42–44, is reprinted in Lowndes, *Select Miscellaneous Productions*, 5–7.

85. Lowndes, *Select Miscellaneous Productions*, 73–90.

86. Overwriting one style of condescension with another, Mrs. Day's nephew frames the writings he selects as "peculiarly characteristic" of Day's mind with a dedication to the "Fair Females of the British Isles": the Days' work shows that the inequality of male and female understanding is less than some imagine, that owing to their "quicker flow of animal spirits," ladies are "naturally eloquent" though their minds are too often "unfurnished fair mansions," Lowndes, *Select Miscellaneous Productions*, vii–ix. Ironically, in 1820, Edgeworth, who had been unable to find the correspondence among her father's papers, was presented Lowndes's collection of the Days, "which Mr. TL published it seems some years ago and which nobody ever heard of." The giver, she thought before she read it, "could hardly have chosen a more judicious or acceptable present for me," *ME: Letters from England*, 227–28.

87. *The Unsex'd Females: A Poem*, ed. Gina Luria, The Feminist Controversy

in England, 1788–1810 (New York: Garland, 1974), Polwhele pays brief tribute to women writers he considers properly religious (though they do not include the politically activist Unitarian Anna Letitia Barbauld), but he cannot get sex off his mind or separate it from enlightened philosophy. The bosoms of women botanists heave as they dissect a plant prostitute's "organ of unhallow'd lust," and Wollstonecraft, "whom no decorum checks," is accused of "Instructions in Priapism" (8–9, 13, 21 n), lessons which the Reverend Polwhele evidently did not need. Further illustrating the period's gender confusions, however, Polwhele (unlike many conservatives) surprisingly values Erasmus Darwin's highly sexualized poetry on the love life of plants. Conversely, Polwhele's (and Darwin's) naughty vegetable world was much recommended by many educators as especially suited to female students, as Ann B. Shteir, *Cultivating Women, Cultivating Science: Flora's Daughters and Botany in England, 1760–1860* (Baltimore: Johns Hopkins University Press, 1996), demonstrates.

88. Lowndes, *Select Miscellaneous Productions,* 116–17.

89. For the crisis-thinking of these decades, see James Raven, *Judging New Wealth: Popular Publishing and Responses to Commerce in England, 1750–1800* (Oxford: Clarendon Press, 1992), chaps. 7–9; Paul Langford, *A Polite and Commercial People: England, 1727–1783* (Oxford: Clarendon Press, 1989), chaps. 3, 7, 10, and 12; Diana Donald, *The Age of Caricature: Satirical Prints in the Reign of George III* (New Haven: Paul Mellon Centre for Studies in British Art/Yale University Press, 1996), chaps. 3–4; Linda Colley, *Britons: Forging the Nation, 1707–1837* (New Haven: Yale University Press); Newman, *The Rise of English Nationalism;* and Leppert, *Music and Image.* This period's caricatures of Francophile "macaroni manners"—fops, viragos, and fine ladies—strikingly illustrate the national and gender crossdressing that fret Day. John Sekora's standard study, *Luxury: The Concept in Western Thought, Eden to Smollett* (Baltimore: Johns Hopkins University Press, 1977), stops too early to be helpful. One sentence (Sekora 107–8) refers to Day as a Quaker, which he was not, apparently because his antislavery work is mentioned by David Brion Davis, *The Problem of Slavery in the Age of Revolution, 1770–1823* (Ithaca: Cornell University Press, 1975), in the context of Quaker thought, 230.

90. Lowndes, *Select Miscellaneous Productions,* 111–18.

91. Because Smith was so renowned a wit, the praise for Edgeworth that his daughter records is especially noteworthy, Lady Holland [Saba Smith Holland], *A Memoir of the Reverend Sydney Smith: With a Selection from His Letters (ed. Mrs. Austin),* vol. 1 of 2 vols., 2d ed. (London: Longman, Brown, Green, & Longmans, 1855), 1:396.

92. Oddly, it is the anonymous and less effective first edition that is included in the Garland facsimile series as Edgeworth's "first appearance in print under her own name," *Letters for Literary Ladies* (London: J. Johnson, 1795), The Feminist Controversy in England, 1788–1810 (New York: Garland, 1974), 6. The changes made in 1798 for the revised and expanded edition, *Letters for*

Literary Ladies, 2d ed. (London: J. Johnson, 1799), leave the first gentleman's letter mostly untouched, so that the 1795 and 1799 editions are differentiated in the text only for the second gentleman's response. The 1795 quotations refer to the 1974 Garland facsimile of *LLL;* because the Everyman reprint of the revised edition, *Letters for Literary Ladies, to Which Is Added an Essay on the Noble Science of Self-Justification,* intro. Claire Connally, Everyman Library (London: J. M. Dent, 1993), is the most accessible, it is used for references to the 1799 revision, even though this edition's apparatus is not always helpful because quotations and contexts are not fully identified. For example, the important epigraph on wit from Lyttelton's "Monody" for his dead wife, another stanza from which supplies the epigraph for *Belinda,* is missing. See *The Works of George Lord Lyttelton,* ed. George Edward Ayscough (London: J. Williams, 1775), 476. The Everyman text itself is misdated as 1798; changes and additions are not noted, for example, the new note to Marmontel (1993: 66, 91). Such omissions are noteworthy because Edgeworth was reworking these pieces shortly before she began *Belinda;* the Marmontel story citation added is also used in that novel, and much of the rewritten argument of the second gentleman, even down to specific phrases, turns up in Mr. Percival's and Belinda's responses to Harriot Freke's asserting her version of the "Rights of Woman" in the chapter so entitled. This edition's notes also include some ironically apt howlers concerning crossdressing: the Reverend Vicesimus Knox is conflated with a female persona in an essay wherein "she" complains about the dangers of overly advanced women's education (1993: 10, 81). More humorously yet, "Hercules-Spinster" is identified as "probably an eighteenth-century strong man" (1993: 11, 82). Even the unclassically trained eighteenth-century female reader would know that the joke refers to Heracles or Hercules and Omphale's exchange of garments and occupations so that the great hero took to spinning and weaving. It is a frequent allusion in letters and essays of this period, and, as Mary Sheriff observes, the role switch was the "subject of many eighteenth-century representations," often eroticized, "Fragonard's Erotic Mothers and the Politics of Reproduction," in *Eroticism and the Body Politic,* ed. Lynn Hunt, 30. It is also in any standard modern encyclopedia. Scholars should check the original 1795 and 1799 Johnson imprints. Subsequent references to the two gentlemen's letters appear in the text.

93. *Unsex'd Females,* 6 n.

94. It is worth noting that Keir, Day's official biographer, closes his 1791 portrait with a ringing denunciation of Burke as a malignant magician, "reviving exploded prejudices": "But the Revolution of France is the sole *triumph of Reason,*" 135–37.

95. *Fragment of An Original Letter on the Slavery of the Negroes,* in *Four Tracts,* 35, 38. 95.

96. Henry Cockburn, whose *Memorials of His Time,* ed. Karl F. C. Miller (Chicago: University of Chicago Press, 1974), fills in the charged Revolution-

ary background of *Forester*'s Scottish schooling, records an even odder instance of natural education: a girl whose parents agreed to teach her nothing at all. She "made herself a good carpenter and a good smith" but did not learn to read and write till grown. She turned out to be fearlessly independent, an incessant reader who dressed like a man and was much beloved and respected by all, 55–56.

97. The speech from Richard Brinsley Sheridan, *The Rivals,* 1775, ed. Elizabeth Duthie, New Mermaids Series (London: A. & C. Black; New York: W. W. Norton, 1994), that Edgeworth quotes occurs in the famous circulating library scene, 1.2.231–35, p. 26. Day is like Absolute in both his arbitrary and tyrannical guardianship and in his precise speech—the Edgeworths often notice that Day (like his own Mr. Barlow in *Sandford and Merton*) talked just like a book.

98. In the Advertisement (dated 1 September 1798), Edgeworth points out that the title for the three pieces is the publisher's. Since *Letters for Literary Ladies* is cited as the Edgeworth position paper on the "literary education of the female sex" in *Practical Education* (1798), the pro-woman argument needed to be as strong as possible. Then, too, Edgeworth's work on girls' education for the family guide to parents had convinced her still more fully that "women should have their understandings cultivated and enlarged as much as possible," *Practical Education,* 2 vols. paged as 1 (London: J. Johnson, 1798), 549–50. Another reason is surely the proliferating polemic of the late 1790s, with conservative tirades like Polwhele's jostling reasoned feminist arguments like Mary Robinson's *Thoughts on the Condition of Women, and on the Injustice of Mental Subordination,* 2d ed. (London: Longman & Rees, 1799). Edgeworth's allusions in *Belinda* and elsewhere show that she had read Godwin's posthumous edition of Wollstonecraft's collected works, the publication that stimulated so much antifeminist fury, as well as Wollstonecraft's earlier children's book and the *Rights of Woman.*

99. Edgeworth, like most people, misidentifies the epigraph source as the "Monody on his Wife" and misspells the poet's name: as part of a set of works commemorating the dead Lucy Fortescue, it is actually headed "A Monody: A.D. 1747." She uses this same passage again in later works, and the epigraph to *Belinda* about prudence occurs just a few lines further down the page, *The Works of George Lord Lyttelton,* 476. Lyttelton's second matrimonial venture seems to have been as unhappy as the first was idyllic.

100. "Lord Lyttelton (1709–1773)," *Lives of the Poets (Congreve to Gray),* vol. 1 of 2 vols., Dolphin Books (Garden City, N.Y.: Doubleday, n.d.), 1:425.

101. *Works of George Lord Lyttelton,* 458.

102. *Works of George Lord Lyttelton,* 458; *Memoirs of RLE,* 2:342.

103. *Works of George Lord Lyttelton,* 476; *Belinda* title page.

104. Anna Seward's father had published a poem called "The Female Right to Literature" in 1748, a phrase that Maria Edgeworth echoes in introducing

the second edition of *LLL*. Using, as the Edgeworths did, the broad eighteenth-century meaning of "literature," he urges Britannia to grant intellectual
liberty and advanced education to daughters as well as sons, [Thomas Seward],
"The Female Right to Literature, in a Letter to a Young Lady from Florence,"
in *A Collection of Poems in Six Volumes by Several Hands* (London: J. Dodsley,
1775; St. Claire Shores, Mich.: Scholarly Press, 1972), 2: 294–300. For a brief
discussion of Seward's ideas, see Sylvia Harcstark Myers, *The Bluestocking Circle: Women, Friendship, and the Life of the Mind in Eighteenth-Century England*
(Oxford: Clarendon Press, 1990), 126–28. What happened in Lichfield was
more problematic. Anna was introduced to Milton at three, but when her
teenage verses showed signs of surpassing her father's, he ceased encouraging
her; see Ashmun, *The Singing Swan*, 8–14. Like Seward, Lyttelton is included
in Dodsley's famous *Collection*, often used by Edgeworth; see R. W. Chapman,
"Dodsley's Collection of Poems by Several Hands," *Oxford Bibliographical Proceedings and Papers*, 3, pt. 3 (Oxford: 1933; Nendeln, Liechtenstein: Kraus
Reprint, 1969), for identification of authors.

105. *The History of Little Jack*, intro. Isaac Kramnick, Classics of Children's
Literature, 1621–1932 (London: John Stockdale, 1788; New York: Garland,
1977), 17. Little Jack's story appeared almost simultaneously in two slightly
different versions of a *Children's Miscellany* as well as a separate publication:
[Thomas Day, et al.], *The Children's Miscellany* (includes the first appearance of
The History of Little Jack) (London: John Stockdale, 1788); and *The Children's
Miscellany* (*The History of Little Jack* with slightly different contents, including
material by Isaac Watts and Sarah Trimmer) (Dublin: J. Moore, 1789). Shortly
before Day's death, the Edgeworths wrote to praise the tale and tease the author
about his unorthodox mother: "We admire Little Jack very much—I see you
were resolved to introduce Nurse Goat somewhere or other," Gignilliat, *The
Author of "Sandford and Merton,"* 306–7. The story also literalizes Day's idée
fixe that fashion makes monkeys of men when Little Jack bagwigs one to
ridicule a foppish youth, enacts Day's and Rousseau's favorite Crusoe story, and
finally rewards Jack by making him a rich manufacturer "in order to prove that it
is of very little consequence how a man comes into the world," *History*, 113. In
"Romanticism and the Colonization of the Feminine," Alan Richardson notes
that in moving from an Age of Reason to an Age of Feeling, male writers used
memories and fantasies of identification with the mother "to colonize the conventionally feminine domain of sensibility" in their adult poetry: see *Romanticism and Feminism*, ed. Anne K. Mellor (Bloomington and Indianapolis: Indiana University Press, 1988), 13–25. Similar erasure and exploitation underlie
much thinking about maternal education and juvenile literature. Mary Jacobus's
chapter on Wordsworth's usurpation of the mother's educative role, " 'Behold
the Parent Hen': Romantic Pedagogy and Sexual Difference," in *Romanticism,
Writing, and Sexual Difference: Essays on "The Prelude"* (Oxford: Clarendon
Press, 1989), represents a much needed start at relating the representation of

childhood in the masculine literary canon to the contemporary pedagogic issues with which it is intertwined. The Romantic child as fantasized through male identification with the maternal situates the pragmatic teaching mother as repressive Other when it does not erase her altogether. For similar patterns in *Émile*, see Patricia Parker, chap. 9, "Coming Second: Woman's Place," in *Literary Fat Ladies: Rhetoric, Gender, Property* (London: Methuen, 1987). In "Rousseau's *Émile ou de l'éducation:* A Resistance to Reading," Janie Vanpée provocatively argues that the book's pedagogical mission has been misread, because it is not a method for fathers or mothers, in *Reading the Archive: On Texts and Institutions, Yale French Studies* 77 (1990): 156–76.

106. Day and Rousseau and mentorias like Wollstonecraft and Edgeworth obviously do not speak with one voice, nor is one woman writer just like another. For example, Wollstonecraft, like Rousseau and much of the medical profession, waxes enthusiastic over maternal breastfeeding, but Edgeworth— and she is not alone—never does (one reason why Lady Delacour's wounded breast is often misread). Similarly, the maternal teachers that some modern commentators dismiss as "angels in the house"—as does Isaac Kramnick, in "Children's Literature and Bourgeois Ideology"—can be more generously construed as inhabitants and creators of a Habermasian public space.

107. As *Practical Education*'s chapter on "Female Accomplishments" even more frankly acknowledges, the young woman's "knowledge must be various, and her powers of reasoning unawed by authority; yet she must *habitually* feel that nice sense of propriety" which guards "feminine virtue" (550).

108. Edgeworth as the second gentleman especially warns against the seductive representation of feminine subjectivity epitomized in Rousseau's work. Like Wollstonecraft and other women educators, the father figure observes that women's historical power has derived not from their brains but their bodies and similarly stresses the "infinite danger" in permitting refined coquettes "to obtain power without having acquired habits of reasoning. Rousseau admires these sirens; but the system of Rousseau . . . would make every woman a Cleopatra, and every man an Antony" (1993, 33).

109. For discussion of these points, see Dena Goodman, *Criticism in Action: Enlightenment Experiments in Political Writing* (Ithaca: Cornell University Press, 1989), Introduction; and Roger Chartier, *The Cultural Origins of the French Revolution,* trans. Lydia G. Cochrane, Bicentennial Reflections on the French Revolution (Durham: Duke University Press, 1991), especially chap. 4, "Do Books Make Revolutions?"

110. Jürgen Habermas, *The Structural Transformation of the Public Sphere: An Inquiry into a Category of Bourgeois Society,* 1962, trans. Thomas Burger and Frederick Lawrence (Cambridge: MIT Press, 1992), 51.

111. Dena Goodman observes that "A republic of letters . . . is a community of discourse and in discourse"; her work on Enlightenment salons and that of Daniel Gordon stress the importance of communal conversation in evolving a

new literature and a new politics: see Goodman, "Enlightenment Salons: The Convergence of Female and Philosophic Ambitions," *The French Revolution in Culture, Eighteenth-Century Studies* 22.3 (Spring 1989): 329; and, in the same issue, Gordon, " 'Public Opinion' and the Civilizing Process in France: The Example of Morellet," 315. Relevant recent work on ambiguities in the letter genre includes Janet Altman, "Women's Letters in the Public Sphere," in *Going Public: Women and Publishing in Early Modern France,* ed. Elizabeth C. Gold-smith and Dena Goodman, Reading Women Writing (Ithaca: Cornell University Press, 1995), 99–115; Brewer, "This, That, and the Other"; Amanda Gilroy and W. M. Verhoeven, ed., *Correspondences: A Special Issue on Letters, Prose Studies: History, Theory, Criticism* 19.2 (August 1996); and Goodman, "Epistolary Property: Michel de Servan and the Plight of Letters on the Eve of the French Revolution," in *Early Modern Conceptions of Property,* ed. John Brewer and Susan Staves (London: Routledge, 1996), 339–64.

112. See, especially, Habermas, *The Structural Transformation of the Public Sphere,* 14–56; there is now an enormous body of discussion as to whether this sphere is just a pipe dream and whether it applies to women. From an eighteenth-century perspective, good analyses include Baker, "Defining the Public Sphere in Eighteenth-Century France," and Goodman, "Public Sphere and Private Life." Whatever is argued about such political privileges as voting, it must be recalled that most men did not possess these either and that the associative public sphere, as Habermas himself stresses, is rooted in the literary. Interestingly, in his "Further Reflections on the Public Sphere," Habermas underlines the formative influence of readers and writers and pays special attention to the problematics of gender, in *Habermas and the Public Sphere,* ed. Craig Calhoun, 421–61.

113. The Everyman editor typically notes that "Edgeworth here introduces the domestic woman into the allegory, and thus shifts the emphasis from vice to virtue" (1993, 37, 89 n. 54), but as Bernard Mandeville's editor reminds us, *The Fable of the Bees* endorses "vice" or self-interest because Mandeville follows a rigorist definition of true virtue as so unselfish and dispassionate as to be nonexistent: *The Fable of the Bees; or, Private Vices, Publick Benefits,* ed. F. B. Kaye, 2 vols. (Oxford: Clarendon Press, 1924), 1:xlviii. Erasmus Darwin, Advertisement for *The Botanic Garden, A Poem: In Two Parts,* 1789–91, 4th ed., 2 vols. (London: J. Johnson, 1799), claims that "The general design of the following sheets is to inlist Imagination under the banner of Science" (1:iii), which Edgeworth rewrites as "Science has of late '*been enlisted under the banners of imagination*' " (1993, 20–21).

Chapter 5: Jane Austen and the Culture of Circulating Libraries

1. Critics have been divided over Austen's view of this equation. Pointing to her satire of the urban marriage market, the gentry, and fashionable material-

ism, some have acclaimed Austen for exposing modern hypocrisy whereas others have argued that she supplies the bourgeois moral justification for a capitalistic society. Compare, for example, Alistair M. Duckworth's account of Austen's moralization of the improvement mentality in *The Improvement of the Estate: Study of the Novels of Jane Austen* (Baltimore: Johns Hopkins University Press, 1994), Marilyn Butler's analysis of Austen's evangelical resistance to the commercial world in *Jane Austen and the War of Ideas* (Oxford: Clarendon Press, 1975), and Claudia L. Johnson's analysis of Austen's exposure of bourgeois male dominance in *Jane Austen: Women, Politics, and the Novel* (Chicago: University of Chicago Press, 1988). Recent work concentrates on her use of female, feminist, and anti-feminist traditions: see Alison Sulloway's *Jane Austen and the Province of Womanhood* (Philadelphia: University of Pennsylvania Press, 1989), Deborah Kaplan's *Jane Austen among Women* (Baltimore: Johns Hopkins University Press, 1992), and Margaret Kirkham's *Jane Austen: Feminism and Fiction* (Totowa, N.J.: Barnes & Noble, 1983). For a lucid explanation of the different conceptions of Austen's feminism, see Devoney Looser, ed., *Jane Austen and the Discourses of Feminism* (New York: St. Martin's Press, 1995). Looser differentiates between five feminist arguments: those addressing Austen's publishing limitations, her historical situation, her subtle antipatriarchal messages, her political conservatism, and her strong female characterizations.

2. A few critics have explored Austen's use of material details to express ideology, most recently Tony Tanner's masterful *Jane Austen,* to which I am indebted (Cambridge, Mass.: Harvard University Press, 1986), and the early but valuable Sheila Kaye-Smith and G. B. Stern, *Talking of Jane Austen* (London: Cassell & Co., 1943). See also James Thompson, *Between Self and World: The Novels of Jane Austen* (University Park: Pennsylvania University Press, 1988). In *Consuming Subjects: Women, Shopping, and Business in the Eighteenth Century* (New York: Columbia University Press, 1997), Elizabeth Kowaleski-Wallace examines the evolving construction in the early-modern period of the female as consumer.

3. For examinations of Austen's reworking of the role of the writing woman, see especially Mary Poovey, *The Proper Lady and the Woman Writer: Ideology and Style in the Works of Mary Wollstonecraft, Mary Shelley, and Jane Austen* (Chicago: University of Chicago Press, 1984); Claudia L. Johnson, *Jane Austen;* and Jan Fergus, *A Literary Life* (New York: St. Martin's Press, 1991). Whereas Poovey and Johnson focus on Austen's response to contemporary prejudices against women authors, Fergus analyzes the conditions of literary production and the "idea of authorship" during Austen's period; nonetheless, she does not examine the representations of or cultural attitudes toward reading. Alvin B. Kernan explains the interdependence of materiality and literary culture in *The Imaginary Library: An Essay on Literature and Society* (Princeton: Princeton University Press, 1982), especially 12–13. I am indebted to these books.

4. For an analysis of the relationship between consumption and choice, see

Max Horkheimer and Theodor W. Adorno, "The Culture Industry: Enlightenment as Mass Deception," in *Dialectic of Enlightenment,* trans. John W. Cumming (New York: Continuum, 1972), 120–67.

5. Joanne Finkelstein, *The Fashioned Self* (Philadelphia: Temple University Press, 1991), 5. For seminal discussions of the way social changes mold subjectivity, see Stephen Greenblatt, *Renaissance Self-Fashioning: From More to Shakespeare* (Chicago: University of Chicago Press, 1980) and Richard Sennet, *The Fall of Public Man* (New York: Knopf, 1977).

6. Richard Handler and Daniel Segal analyze the elisions of status in Austen's society in *Jane Austen and the Fiction of Culture* (Tucson: University of Arizona Press, 1990).

7. In *The Intersections of the Public and Private Spheres in Early Modern England,* Paula R. Backscheider collapses the theoretical distinction between public and private, a view that Austen's relocation of literacy upholds: see *Prose Studies: History, Theory, Criticism,* ed. Paula R. Backscheider and Timothy Dykstal, 18, 3 (December 1995), 13. See Jürgen Habermas, *Structural Transformation of the Public Sphere: An Inquiry into a Category of Bourgeois Society,* trans. Thomas Burger with the assistance of Frederick Lawrence (Cambridge: MIT Press, 1991).

8. Many critics discuss Austen's educative function: see especially Jan Fergus, *Jane Austen and the Didactic Novel: "Northanger Abbey," "Sense and Sensibility," and "Pride and Prejudice"* (Totowa, N.J.: Barnes & Noble, 1983); Laura G. Mooneyham, *Romance, Language, and Education in Jane Austen's Novels* (Basingstoke and London: Macmillan Press, 1988); also D. D. Devlin, *Jane Austen and Education* (New York: Barnes & Noble, 1975).

9. *"The Original of Apparel:* Or, the Ornaments of Dress. Presented to Mr. Vernum, Taylor" (London, 1732), 2, ll. 15–16.

10. Aileen Ribeiro, *The Dress Worn at Masquerades in England, 1730–1790, and Its Relation to Fancy Dress in Portraiture* (New York: Garland Publishing, 1984), 275, 278. For general discussions of the cultural significance of clothing, see also Daniel Roche, *The Culture of Clothing: Dress and Fashion in the "Ancien Regime"* (Cambridge: Cambridge University Press, 1994), and Iris Brooke, *Dress and Undress: The Restoration and the Eighteenth Century* (Westport, Conn.: Greenwood Press, 1958).

11. Aileen Ribeiro, *Dress and Morality* (New York: Holmes & Meier Publishers, 1986), 101–2; quoted from Watts' *Works* (1753; 2d ed., London, 1801), 244.

12. Aileen Ribeiro, *Dress in Eighteenth-Century Europe, 1715–1789* (New York: Holmes & Meier Publishers, 1984), 118.

13. Jane Austen, *Sense and Sensibility,* ed. R. W. Chapman (Oxford: Oxford University Press, 1978), 249. All citations to Austen's novels and juvenilia refer to this six-volume edition, in which *Northanger Abbey* and *Persuasion* are printed in one volume, but separately paginated. References to Austen's juvenile

and minor works derived from volume six, *Minor Works,* are cited with that title in the text.

14. *Vindication of the Rights of Women* (London, 1792), 26–27, 200; quoted in Ribeiro, *Dress and Morality,* 117. This air of fashion may also allude to gestural changes and anxieties about gender and identity that were perhaps hidden targets in the attack on women for affectation: Christopher Breward, glossing Rudolph Trumbach, argues: "Extreme bodily gestures, affected mannerisms in speech and contrived magnificence in costume had come to indicate sexual preference. It was against these standards that mainstream masculinity evolved a system of restrained etiquette, handshakes and bows on greeting rather than kissing, and unobtrusive clothing, the sexual and patriotic associations of which remained beyond question." See Christopher Breward, *The Culture of Fashion: A New History of Fashionable Dress,* (Manchester: Manchester University Press, 1995), 139; also Randolph Trumbach, "Sex, Gender, and Sexual Identity in Modern Culture: Male Sodomy and Female Prostitution in Enlightenment London," *Journal of the History of Sexuality* 2 (October, 1991): 186–203.

15. The conviction that women's delight in dress, if reprehensible, ought at least to be for the sake of men appears in a tradition of satire from the early eighteenth century. See Edward Moore's fable "The Spider and the Bee," common in ladies libraries, asserting that "The maid, who modestly conceals / Her beauties, while she hides, reveals" (ll. 19–20).

16. Sheila Kaye-Smith and G. B. Stern, *More Talk of Jane Austen* (London: Cassell & Co, 1950), 37. Kaye-Smith claims that Austen criticizes Lydia in *Pride and Prejudice* for neglecting clothes, but I maintain that Austen reproves her for a more subtle misuse of dress through extravagance and lack of integrity (39).

17. John Wesley, *The Bicentennial Edition of the Works of John Wesley,* ed. Frank Baker, vol. 3, ed. Albert C. Outler (Nashville: Abingdon Press, 1986), no. 88: 251, 254.

18. Ribeiro, *Dress and Morality,* 113.

19. Ibid., 113–14. See Jonas Clarke, "*The Best Art of Dress: Or, Early Piety most amiable and ornamental. A Sermon*" (Boston: D. & J. Kneeland, 1762); also James Laver, *Modesty in Dress: An Inquiry into the Fundamentals of Fashion* (Boston: Houghton Mifflin, 1969), esp. 128–33.

20. Quoted in Ribeiro, *Dress and Morality,* 119. This reiterates the Earl of Chesterfield's remarks, widely circulated in *The Beauties of Chesterfield* and other cheap editions, that female dress reveals the self, and should embody noble simplicity, common sense, and "decent and modest conformity to the fashion" for women under thirty (4th American ed.; Exeter: A. R. Brown, 1831), 129–37.

21. James Stewart, "*Plocacosmos:* or the Whole Art of Hair Dressing; wherein

is contained Ample Rules for the Young Artizan, more particularly for Ladies, Women, Valets, Etc. etc." (London, 1782), 76–77.

22. Marilyn J. Horn notes the multiple functions of clothing in *The Second Skin: An Interdisciplinary Study of Clothing* (Boston: Houghton Mifflin Co., 1968); see also Ruth Barnes and Joanne B. Eicher, *Dress and Gender: Making and Meaning* (Providence and Oxford: Berg, 1993).

23. *The Beau's Receipt for a Lady's Dress* (London, 1748), st. 5, ll. 21–22 (B.L. Rox. III [465]).

24. G. J. Barker-Benfield, *The Culture of Sensibility: Sex and Society in Eighteenth-Century Britain* (Chicago: University of Chicago Press, 1992), especially 173–75.

25. Quoted in Brooke, *Dress and Undress: The Restoration and Eighteenth Century,* 141–43.

26. Anne Buck identifies the social attention to dress with commercialized literacy: "The end of the century saw the beginning of the journalism of fashion. The small pocket or memorandum books which were issued yearly from the middle of the century usually contained one or two small plates, showing examples of dress for the year. . . . Notes on current fashions appeared from time to time in such journals as *The Gentleman's Magazine* and *The London Magazine,* but usually as a subject for comment. . . . At the end of the 1790s there were other journals published particularly for women; *The Lady's Monthly Museum* issued one or two colored plates with fashion notes based on them each month. A series of plates, with descriptive notes, *The Fashions of London and Paris,* was also published from 1798; the notes in *The Lady's Magazine* often relate to these. . . . It was not until the early years of the nineteenth century that fashion for its own sake became a subject for journalism and the business of spreading fashion by the printed word began." See Ribeiro, *Dress in Eighteenth-Century England,* 208.

27. Letter 48, Wednesday, 7 January 1807, and letter 35 for Tuesday, 5 May 1801, in *Jane Austen's Letters to Her Sister Cassandra and Others,* collected and ed. R. W. Chapman (1932; Oxford: Oxford University Press, 1979), 171, 124–25. All references to Austen's letters are to this edition and will be cited by number, date, and page reference in the text.

28. For an exhaustive account of Austen's references to food, see Maggie Lane's *Jane Austen and Food* (London and Rio Grande, Ohio: Hambledon Press, 1995). As Lane also observes, Dr. Grant openly manifests undisciplined appetite in *Mansfield Park.*

29. George Colman, "*Polly Honeycombe,* A Dramatic Novel in One Act" (Edinburgh: A. Kincaid & J. Bell, 1741 [misprinted for 1761]), iv. This epilogue was by Garrick. Subsequent citations in the text refer to this edition.

30. See Francis Doherty, *A Study in Eighteenth-Century Advertising Methods: The Anodyne Necklace* (Lewiston: Edwin Mellen Press, 1992); also Peter M. Briggs, "'News from the Little World': A Critical Glance at Eighteenth-

Century British Advertising," *Studies in Eighteenth-Century Culture* 23 (1994): 29–45.

31. *The Daily Advertiser* 1790, 1791, in *Matrimonial Advertisements, 1746–1862* (B.L. Cup 407 ff 43). Unless otherwise noted, all advertisements cited in the text here can be found in this collection.

32. *Matrimonial Advertisements, 1746–1862* (B.L. Cup 407 ff 43), 1.

33. Michaelson, "Reading *Pride and Prejudice,*" *Eighteenth-Century Fiction* 3 (October 1990): 65–76.

34. Robert DeMaria, Jr. "Samuel Johnson and the Reading Revolution," *Eighteenth-Century Life* n.s. 16 (November 1992): 86–102; also DeMaria, *Samuel Johnson and the Life of Reading* (Baltimore: Johns Hopkins University Press, 1996).

35. Recent work documenting the explosion of printed culture of the eighteenth-century is extremely rich. See, for example, John Brewer's "Reconstructing the Reader: Prescriptions, Texts, and Strategies in Anna Larpent's Reading" in *The Practice and Representation of Reading in England,* eds. James Raven, Helen Small, and Naomi Tadmor (Cambridge: Cambridge University Press, 1996), 226–45; Neil McKendrick, John Brewer, J. H. Plumb, *The Birth of a Consumer Society: The Commercialization of Eighteenth-Century England* (Bloomington: Indiana University Press, 1982); John Brewer and Roy Porter, eds., *Consumption and the World of Goods* (London: Routledge, 1993); Ann Bermingham and John Brewer, eds. *The Consumption of Culture: Image, Object, Text* (London: Routledge, 1995), esp. Terry Lovell, "Subjective Powers? Consumption, the Reading Public, and Domestic Woman in Early Eighteenth-Century England," 23–41; Richard D. Altick, *The English Common Reader: A Social History of the Mass Reading Public* (Chicago: Chicago University Press, 1957); Moira Ferguson, *First Feminists: British Women Writers, 1578–1799* (Bloomington: Indiana University Press, 1985); Dale Spender, *Mothers of the Novel: 100 Good Women Writers Before Jane Austen* (London: Pandora, 1986); Janet Todd, *The Sign of Angellica: Women, Writing, and Fiction, 1660–1800* (New York: Columbia University Press, 1989); Cheryl Turner, *Living by the Pen: Women Writers in the Eighteenth Century* (London: Routledge, 1992); and Margaret Ezell, *Writing Women's Literary History* (Baltimore: John Hopkins University Press, 1993).

36. See *Bromley House, 1752–1991: Four Essays celebrating the 175th Anniversary of the Foundation of The Nottingham Subscription Library,* ed. Rosalys T. Coope and Jane Y. Corbett (Nottingham: Nottingham Subscription Library, 1991), 8–11. James Millar recommends his plan as social control in *Funding System . . . also, A Plan for Forming Reading Societies* (Stirling: Printed for the Author, by J. Fraser, 1818), 57.

37. For an account of the trial and its consequences on publishing history, see John Feather, *A History of British Publishing* (London: Routledge, 1988); for an analysis of the readership for these newly produced, inexpensive editions of

literature, see Jon P. Klancher, *The Making of British Reading Audiences, 1790–1832* (Madison: University of Wisconsin Press, 1987).

38. Barbara M. Benedict, "The 'Beauties' of Literature: Tasteful Prose and Fine Rhyme for Private Consumption," *1650–1850: Ideas, Aesthetics, and Inquiries in the Early Modern Era* 1 (June, 1994): 317–46; Thomas Bonnell, "Bookselling and Canon Making: The Trade Rivalry over the English Poets, 1776–1783," *Studies in Eighteenth-Century Culture* 19 (1989): 53–69.

39. See James Raven, *Judging New Wealth: Popular Publishing and Responses to Commerce in England, 1750–1800* (Oxford: Clarendon Press, 1992).

40. For an examination of the literary construction of the female role of modesty, see Ruth Bernard Yeazell's enlightening *The Fictions of Modesty: Women and Courtship in the English Novel* (Chicago: University of Chicago Press, 1984).

41. *More Talk of Jane Austen* (London: Cassell & Co., 1950), 43, 69.

42. Vicesimus Knox, *Liberal Education: or, A Practical Treatise on the Methods of Acquiring Useful and Polite Learning*, 5th ed. (London, 1783), 256.

43. Charlotte A. Stewart-Murphy, *A History of British Circulating Libraries: The Books Labels and Ephemera of the Papantonio Collection* (Newtown, Pa.: Bird & Bull Press, 1992), 19–20; my thanks to Charlotte Stewart-Murphy. Richard D. Altick notes the same predominance of fiction in *The English Common Reader*, 379, as does Paul Kauffman, *Libraries and Their Users* (London: Library Association, 1969), 139.

44. T. Wilson, *The Use of Circulating Libraries Considered* (London, Kent, 1797); quoted in Stewart-Murphy, *A History of British Circulating Libraries*, 22.

45. See Barbara M. Benedict, "The Curious Genre: Female Inquiry in Amatory Fiction," *Studies in the Novel* 30 (Summer 1998): 194–209.

46. *"A Catalogue of Harrod's Circulating Library* Comprising 700 Novels, Etc. and 300 Plays" (Stamford, 1790).

47. *Catalogue of N. L. Pannier's Foreign and English Circulating Library* (London: R. Juigné, 1812).

48. *Catalogue of Ebers's British and Foreign Circulating Library . . . of the Most Approved Authors* (London: Whittingham & Rowland, 1816).

49. Dorothy Blakey, *The Minerva Press, 1790–1820* (London: For the Bibliographical Society at the University Press, Oxford, 1939), 3.

50. In "From Promotion to Proscription: Arrangements for Reading and Eighteenth-Century Libraries," which examines the conflict between commercial and cultural attitudes toward reading, James Raven points out that the overlaps between private and public libraries fostered the contemporary anxieties about correct reading and reading performance; *The Practice and Representation of Reading in England*, eds. James Raven, Helen Small, and Naomi Tadmor (Cambridge: Cambridge University Press, 1996), 174–201. While Raven rightly emphasizes the lack of real differences between the material read,

the cultural significance of the different venues remained powerful, both socially and symbolically.

51. Stewart-Murphy, *A History of British Circulating Libraries*, 12–14; H. R. Plomer, *A Dictionary of the Printers and Booksellers Who Were at Work in England, Scotland, and Ireland from 1726 to 1775* (London: The Bibliographical Society, 1968), 431. In "The Community Library: A Chapter in English Social History," Paul Kauffman records the plea for "serious" literature in place of novels in the squib "The Poetical Petition of the Books of a Circulating Library in Bath," published in the *Bath Chronicle*, 25 January 1781; see *Transactions of the American Philosophical Society*, n.s. 57 (Philadelphia: The American Philosophical Society, 1967), 6.

52. For examinations of the different forms of eighteenth-century book production, see Lucien Febvre, *The Coming of the Book* (London: Verso, 1976); Harold Love, *Scribal Publication in Seventeenth-Century England* (Oxford: Clarendon Press, 1993); Alvin B. Kernan, *Printing Technology, Letters, and Samuel Johnson* (Princeton: Princeton University Press, 1987); Roger Chartier, *The Culture of Print: Power and the Uses of Print in Early Modern Europe*, trans. Lydia G. Cochrane (Princeton: Princeton University Press, 1989).

53. Proprietors of Circulating Libraries, *Advertisement*, in Eliza Haywood's *The Fruitless Inquiry. Being a Collection of several entertaining Histories and Occurrences, which fell under the Observation of A Lady in her search after Happiness* (London, 1767), v.

54. Stewart-Murphy, *A History of British Circulating Libraries*, 11; see *Monthly Magazine*, April 1801, cited in Kauffman, *Libraries and Their Users*, 192. Information about the standard fees for subscribers are advertised in every circulating library catalog and often appear on the flyleafs of late eighteenth-century editions of novels; see also Stewart-Murphy, *A History of British Circulating Libraries*, 16, 24, 48.

55. Margaret A. Doody argues that romance—the search for love—is indeed the essential element of prose fiction in *The True Story of the Novel* (New Brunswick, N.J.: Routledge, 1996).

56. Paul Kauffman, *Libraries and Their Users*, 224.

57. A. S. Collins, *The Profession of Letters* (Clifton, N.J.: Augustus M. Kelley, 1973), 67; Stewart-Murphy, *A History of British Circulating Libraries*, 48.

58. Robert Darnton explores the difference between sentimental and earlier forms of reading in "Readers Respond to Rousseau: The Fabrication of Romantic Sensitivity," in *The Great Cat Massacre and Other Episodes in French Cultural History* (New York: Vintage, 1985), 215–56.

59. Guinevere L. Griest, *Mudie's Circulating Library and the Victorian Novel* (Bloomington: Indiana University Press, 1970), 11.

60. N. L. Pannier's library asked two guineas annually to borrow ten volumes in town and fifteen in the country, £1 11s. 6d. for six in town and nine in the

country, and £1 4s. for four in town and six in the country; see *Catalogue of N. L. Pannier's Foreign and English Circulating Library*.

61. Stewart-Murphy, *A History of British Circulating Libraries*, 32; Altick, *The English Common Reader*, 27; Griest, *Mudie's Circulating Library*, 10.

62. *A New Catalogue of Lownds's Circulating Library* (London: Thomas Lownd[e]s, [1761]).

63. This was largely only a perceived distinction. See, for example, A. N. L. Munby, ed., *Sale Catalogues of Libraries of Eminent Persons* (London: Mansell Sotheby Parke-Bernet Publication, Great Britain Scholar Press, 1971), twelve volumes containing every kind of literary material.

64. Stewart-Murphy, *A History of British Circulating Libraries*, 52; quoted in Devendra P. Varma, *The Evergreen Tree of Diabolical Knowledge* (Washington, D.C.: Consortium Press, 1972), 6.

65. David Kaser, *A Book for Sixpence: The Circulating Library in America* (Pittsburgh, Pa.: Beta Phi Mu, 1980), 14. Stewart-Murphy, *A History of British Circulating Libraries*, 34.

66. Paul Kauffman, "The Community Library: A Chapter in English Social History," 25.

67. Stewart-Murphy, *A History of British Circulating Libraries*, 53; letter to Dr. Crisp, April 6, 1782, quoted in Hilda M. Hamlyn, "Eighteenth-century Circulating Libraries in England," *Library* 5, 1 (1946–47): 204.

68. See Kathryn Shevelow's anatomy of the early construction of female identity in print in *Women and Print Culture: The Construction of Femininity in the Early Periodical* (London: Routledge, 1989).

69. Bill Bell, "Fiction in the Marketplace: Towards a Study of the Victorian Serial," in *Serials and Their Readers, 1620–1914*, ed. Robin Myers and Michael Harris (New Castle, Del.: Oak Knoll Press, 1993), 126–27.

70. Linda K. Hughes and Michael Lund, *The Victorian Serial* (Charlottesville: University Press of Virginia, 1991), 1–14.

71. Gary Kelly, "Jane Austen, Romantic Feminism, and Civil Society," in *Jane Austen and the Discourses of Feminism*, ed. Devoney Looser (New York: St. Martin's Press, 1995), 30–31. See also Kelly's "Jane Austen's Real Business: The Novel, Literature and Cultural Capital," in *Jane Austen's Business: Her World and Her Profession*, ed. Juliet McMaster and Bruce Stovel (Hampshire: Macmillan Press, 1996): 154–67.

72. Jocelyn Harris notes Austen's indebtedness to male models in "Jane Austen and the Burden of the (Male) Past: The Case Reexamined," in *Jane Austen and the Discourses of Feminism*, ed. Looser, 87–100.

73. In *Narrative Innovation and Incoherence: Ideology in Defoe, Goldsmith, Austen, Eliot, and Hemingway* (Durham: Duke University Press, 1992), Michael M. Boardman argues that *Persuasion* contains an innovative "disrupting motive" that embodies Austen's "desire to tell a new kind of story" about

uncertain causality (76–99). I think rather that Austen continues her negotiation of the genre of the circulating novel, with its contradictory demands for sequentiality and surprise, and thus constructs a new kind of realism; see Benedict, "The Tensions of Realism: Oppositions of Perception in Some Novels of Fielding and Austen" (Ph.D. diss., University of California at Berkeley, 1985).

74. Griest, *Mudie's Circulating Library,* 12; quoted from James Milne, "The Diamond Jubilee of a Great Library," *Strand* 58 (August 1919): 141.

75. In *Jane Austen: Feminism and Fiction* (Totowa, N.J.: Barnes & Noble, 1983), Margaret Kirkham notes the repressive effect of "the Wollstonecraft Scandal" on Austen's feminism (69).

76. Sheila Kaye-Smith and G. B. Stern suggest that the volume of her correspondence indicates the significance of letters to Austen; see *Talking of Jane Austen,* 113–20.

77. Robert Markley notes that sentimental performance indicates a naturalized aristocracy in sentimental fictions; see "Sentimentality as Performance: Shaftesbury, Sterne, and the Theatrics of Virtue," in *The New Eighteenth Century: Theory, Politics, English Literature* (London: Methuen, 1987), 210–30.

78. John Sitter in *Arguments of Augustan Wit* (Cambridge: Cambridge University Press, 1991) points out that the poets of the early eighteenth-century lambast airy pretension with references to the body and the physicality of culture.

79. "Two Poems by Jane Austen," B.L. Cup. 21.g.7 (15), n.d., but accompanied by another poem dated 27 October 1811. In this printed script, a manuscript hand has pointed out the puns, and substituted "At" for the printed "Of."

80. The volume of her correspondence persistently worries Austen; as just one more example from this period in her life, she mentions that she will not "count the lines" of a letter from Martha out of shame at their number (letter 74.1, Sunday, 29 November 1812, 499).

81. Marilyn Butler comments on Austen's increasing poverty and the problem of keeping up appearances in her introduction to *Jane Austen: Selected Letters, 1796–1817,* ed. R. W. Chapman (Oxford: Oxford University Press, 1985), xvi.

82. See Margaret A. Doody, "Jane Austen's Reading" in *The Jane Austen Companion,* ed. J. David Grey, A. Walton Litz, and Brian Southam (New York: Macmillan, 1986), 347–63.

83. Janet Todd, *Sensibility: An Introduction* (New York: Methuen, 1986), 5–6.

84. See J. Paul Hunter, *Before Novels: The Cultural Contexts of Eighteenth Century Fiction* (New York: W. W. Norton, 1990).

85. Regardless of whether one interprets Catherine as totally deluded by the fantasies of fiction, or metaphorically quite right in reading the General as a

murderer, or whether one reads Austen as contrasting England and Italy, or comparing them as networks of "voluntary spies," Catherine still confuses her modern context with that of fiction.

86. See Barbara M. Benedict, *Making the Modern Reader: Cultural Mediation in Early Modern Literary Anthologies* (Princeton: Princeton University Press, 1996), 210–21.

87. In "A 'Sweet Face White as Death': Jane Austen and the Politics of Female Sensibility," *Novel: A Forum on Fiction* 22 (1989): 159–74, Claudia L. Johnson points out the social desire that Marianne die in *Sense and Sensibility*.

88. For an early but still enlightening analysis of Austen's parody of bookishness, and especially of Marianne's taste, see Mary Lascelles, *Jane Austen and Her Art* (Oxford: Clarendon Press, 1939).

89. J. Walker, *Hints for Improvement in the Art of Reading* (London, 1783), 5 (B.L.626.h.26 [2]). See also J. Walker's *Exercises for Improvement in Elocution, Being select Extracts from the best Authors, for the Use of those who study the Art of Reading and Speaking in Public,* which contains selections from Akenside's *Pleasures of the Imagination,* Pope's *Essay on Criticism, The Spectator,* and works by Milton, Sterne, Gray, and others (London, 1777).

90. Tony Tanner notes the restless Crawfords' London-tainted acting skill; as an "improver" and "master stylist," Henry has acting in his heart. See *Jane Austen* (Cambridge, Mass: Harvard University Press, 1986), 149–50, 54–60, 169. Laura G. Mooneyham remarks that "Henry, the consummate actor who can imitate all feelings because he lacks them himself, gives an equally fine rendering of each of the characters"; *Romance, Language and Education in Jane Austen's Novels* (Basingstoke: Macmillan Press, 1988), 89.

91. As Mooneyham observes, Marianne's language shows a "failure of integration" with society, but her argument that the novel's ending endorses "muted" happiness underrates Austen's satirical attack on the way fashionable ideals of sensibility usurp integrity; see *Romance, Language, and Education in Jane Austen's Novels,* 32–37, 44.

92. Walter Benjamin, "The Work of Art in the Age of Mechanical Reproduction, in *Illumination: Essays and Reflections,* trans. Harry Zohn, ed. with intro. by Hannah Arendt (New York: Schocken Books, 1969), 217–51.

93. For an analysis of the incorporation of the sentimental values of simplicity, memory, and classicism into jewelry, see Diana Scarisbrick, "Elegance and Romanticism, 1715–1836," in Scarisbrick et al., *Jewellery: Makers, Motifs, History, Techniques* (London: Thames & Hudson, 1989), 67–83.

94. Ernle Bradford remarks that hair jewelry "must be considered one of the more curious by-products of the Romantic revolution and can hardly be considered even in terms of popular jewellery," yet hair lockets and rings appear from at least the Renaissance; see *English Victorian Jewellery* (Middlesex: Spring Books, 1959), 92.

95. In *Sanditon*, Austen notes a similarly tainted translation of feeling into object when Lady Denham boasts to Charlotte of her gift of Sir Harry's "Gold Watch" to his nephew Sir Edward, as if it proved her fine feeling (400).

96. Marilyn Butler argues that a newly converted Austen was espousing evangelical ideals of sincerity and Christian humility in *Mansfield Park;* the principles of evangelical Protestantism also favor reading and reflection as paths to moral improvement; see *Jane Austen and the War of Ideas* (Oxford: Clarendon Press, 1975).

97. Later, she describes homesickness with Cowper's *Tirocinium* (431).

98. Barbara M. Benedict, "A Source for the Names in Austen's *Persuasion*," *Persuasions* 14 (16 December 1992): 68–69.

99. Pierre Bourdieu, *Distinction: A Social Critique of the Judgement of Taste*, trans. Richard Nice (Cambridge, Mass.: Harvard University Press, 1984), 7.

100. Claudia L. Johnson explicates the turn-of-the-century uncertainty about fixing gender categories in *Equivocal Beings: Politics, Gender, and Sentimentality in the 1790s: Wollstonecraft, Radcliffe, Burney, Austen* (Chicago: Chicago University Press, 1995); see particularly her enlightening discussion of masculinity in *Emma* (191–203).

101. In *The Language of Jane Austen: A Study of Some Aspects of Her Vocabulary* (London: Macmillan, 1991), Myra Stokes defines "Elegance" as "basically a word relating to style or manner that shows grace and distinction" in opposition to written vulgarity (85); the *OED* relates it to careful choice, refinement, and grace. See the discussion of Austen's use of anthologized literary "elegance" in Benedict, *Making the Modern Reader*, 217–18.

102. Susan Allen Ford remarks on the centrality of the library to the commercial definition of Sanditon in "The Romance of Business and the Business of Romance: The Circulating Library and Novel-Reading in *Sanditon*" in *Persuasions* 19 (1997): 177–86.

103. Michael Schudson, *Advertising, the Uneasy Persuasion: Its Dubious Impact on American Society* (New York: Basic Books, 1988), 7.

104. Sophie von la Roche, *Sophie in London, 1786: Being the Diary of Sophie v. la Roche*, trans. and intro. Clare Williams, fwd. George Trevelyan (London: Jonathan Cape, 1933), 87; also quoted in Elizabeth Ewing, *Everyday Dress, 1650–1900* (London: B. T. Batsford, 1984), 51.

105. Christopher Breward, *The Culture of Fashion: A New History of Fashionable Dress* (Manchester: Manchester University Press, 1995), 130.

106. For the eighteenth-century tradition of such symbiotic advertisement, see Barbara M. Benedict's "Consumptive Communities: Commodifying Nature in Spa Society," in *The Eighteenth Century: Theory and Interpretation* 36, 3 (Autumn, 1995): 203–19.

107. Libraries also typically sold medicines, a further, subtle joke in this novel about self-dosing and hypochondria.

108. See Jocelyn Harris, *Jane Austen's Art of Memory* (Cambridge: Cambridge University Press, 1989); also Frank W. Bradbrook, *Jane Austen and Her Predecessors* (Cambridge: Cambridge University Press, 1967), and Kenneth L. Moler, *Jane Austen's Art of Allusion* (Lincoln: University of Nebraska, 1968).

Contributors

Paula R. Backscheider is Pepperell Eminent Scholar at Auburn University and formerly Roswell Burrows Professor of English at the University of Rochester. The author of the biography *Daniel Defoe: His Life*, which won the British Council Prize for 1990, and three critical books, *A Being More Intense, Daniel Defoe: Ambition and Innovation*, and *Spectacular Politics: Theatrical Power and Mass Culture in Early Modern England*, she has published articles in *PMLA, Modern Philology, ELH, Modern Language Studies, Theatre Journal*, and many other journals. Her latest book, *Reflections on Biography*, will be published by Oxford University Press in 1999. A former president of the American Society for Eighteenth-Century Studies and Guggenheim Fellow, she is at work on a book on the competition between the novel and drama.

Barbara M. Benedict is Professor of English at Trinity College, Connecticut, and is the author of two books, *Framing Feeling: Sentiment and Style in English Prose Fiction, 1745–1800* (AMS, 1994) and *Making the Modern Reader: Cultural Mediation in Early Modern Literary Anthologies* (Princeton University Press, 1996). She has also published essays on eighteenth-century fiction, poetry, book history, and popular culture. She is currently writing a book on eighteenth-century curiosity, and another on Jane Austen.

Mitzi Myers teaches at the University of California, Los Angeles. She has published extensively on Maria Edgeworth, Mary Wollstonecraft, Hannah More, and literature for the young from the eighteenth century to the present. She has guest-edited several journals, including the *Eighteenth-Century Life* special issue on the Irish Rebellion of 1798. She is co-editor of the Pickering and Chatto Works of Maria Edgeworth, with special responsibility for four volumes, including *Belinda*. She has two books in progress on Edgeworth.

Betty Rizzo is a Professor Emerita of the City College of New York and the Graduate Center where she has taught eighteenth-century English literature, writing, and women's studies. Her publications include writing texts, studies of the poet Christopher Smart, *Companion without Vows: Relationships among Eighteenth-Century British Women,* an edition of Sara Scott's *The History of George Ellison,* and the forthcoming, fourth volume of the *Early Journals and Letters of Fanny Burney.*

Index

DATE DUE

CLL	529393	
D 10/4/01		
OCT 2 9 REC'D		
IL: 2947712		
dd: ~~201FOD~~		
dd: 202020108		

GAYLORD   PRINTED IN U.S.A.